This study of canal construction workers between 1780 and 1860 challenges labour history's focus on skilled craftsmen and the model of working-class culture it generated. Canallers, part of the mass of unskilled labour thrown up by industrial capitalism, had an experience that differed in many ways from artisans. Once on the labour market, they were wholly alienated, more fully exploited, worse off economically, and socially fragmented. Their struggle as members of a class pivoted on material conditions, not on skill and shop-floor control.

Canal construction played a significant role in the rise of industrial capitalism by opening new markets, providing an army of workers, and initiating the state–capital ties so important in later years. The work was undertaken with traditional tools powered by men and animals. Workers laboured twelve hours a day in all kinds of weather, exposed to many dangers and illnesses. Increasingly dominated by Irish immigrants, the workforce lived in shanty towns at the work site or in nearby cities, the setting for much vice and violence. These were not the vibrant working-class communities of later labour history, and the situation deteriorated in the late 1830s as labour surplus caused massive unemployment and depressed wages. Class conflict resulted and the state was increasingly drawn in to enforce industrial production, leaving canallers bent, bloodied and beaten. The history of canal workers traces another strand of the labour story, one where the absence of skill bred powerlessness that made common labour's engagement with capital markedly unequal.

COMMON LABOUR

Common Labour

Workers and the Digging of North American Canals 1780–1860

PETER WAY

School of English and American Studies
University of Sussex

CAMBRIDGE
UNIVERSITY PRESS

Published by the Press Syndicate of the University of Cambridge
The Pitt Building, Trumpington Street, Cambridge CB2 1RP
40 West 20th Street, New York, NY 10011–4211, USA
10 Stamford Road, Oakleigh, Melbourne 3166, Australia

First published 1993

Printed in the United States of America

Library of Congress Cataloging-in-Publication Data
Way, Peter, 1957–
Common labour : workers and the digging of North American canals
1780–1860 / Peter Way.
p. cm.
Includes bibliographical references and index.
ISBN 0-521-44033-5
1. Canal construction workers – North America. 2. Canals – North
America – History. I. Title.
HD8039.C259N78 1993
331.12'92713'097 – dc20 93-22970
CIP

A catalog record for this book is available from the British Library.

ISBN 0-521-44033-5 hardback

To Walter and Phyllis Way

Contents

Tables

Acknowledgements

The research and writing of this book were funded in part by a number of institutions. For their gracious financial support, I would like to thank the Social Sciences and Humanities Research Council of Canada, the Hagley Library and Museum, the American Antiquarian Society, the history departments of the University of Maryland at College Park and Simon Fraser University, and the School of English and American Studies at the University of Sussex. The kind aid by the staffs of a number of libraries and archives has also been invaluable. I would especially like to acknowledge those who lent their assistance at the Manuscript Reading Room of the National Archives in Washington, the Manuscripts Division of the Maryland Historical Society, the Hagley Library and Archives, the American Antiquarian Society, the Baker Library of the Harvard University Graduate School of Business Administration, the Ohio Historical Society and Ohio State Archives, the Manuscripts Department of the University of North Carolina at Chapel Hill's Southern Historical Collection, the Archives Division of the Indiana Commission of Public Records and the Indiana State Library, the Chicago Historical Society, the Research Division of Environment Canada – Parks in Cornwall, Ontario, and, finally, the Public Archives of Canada. Some of the fruit of my endeavours so ably abetted has been published elsewhere: parts of Chapter 7 appeared as "Shovels and Shamrocks: Irish Workers and Labor Violence in the Digging of the Chesapeake and Ohio Canal" in *Labor History* (Fall 1989), and much of Chapter 6 and part of the Introduction appeared as "Evil Humours and Ardent Spirits: The Rough Culture of Canal Construction Laborers" in *The Journal of American History* (March 1993). I am indebted to these journals for permission to reprint this material and to their readers for their helpful comments in preparing the articles for publication.

Inevitably, the greatest debts that one incurs in producing a book are of a personal nature. For reading parts of this study and offering their advice over the years, not to mention lending their friendly support, these colleagues deserve special mention: Elwood Jones, Ira Berlin, Richard Price, John McCusker, Lawrence McDonnell, Milton Cantor, Kerby Miller, Bruce

xi

Boling, Michael Fellman, Vivien Hart, Stephen Fender and Allen Seager. Such an acknowledgement is but a poor measure of their contributions. I would particularly like to thank David Grimsted, whose challenging mind and comforting demeanor helped guide this project from its inception. I am also indebted to Frank Smith of Cambridge University Press and to Herbert A. Gilbert and W. M. Havighurst for their skillful shepherding of the manuscript through the editorial process. Closer to home, I wish to express my gratitude to my mother and late father, to whom this work is dedicated, for performing the rough labour of raising me. And to Rick Mofina, Don Reid, and Murray Camp, whose friendship has meant so much over the years, my fondest thanks. Finally, I owe an incalculable amount to Susan Weinandy-Way, not only for her continuing love, support and intellectual stimulation, so crucial to whatever I have achieved, but also for the work she did in collating data and rigorously scrutinizing the manuscript. I can never adequately repay her.

Chronology of construction for main canals

Canal	Begun	Completed
Potomac Company	1785	1802
James River Company	1786	1789
Schuylkill & Susquehanna	1792	1794
Delaware & Schuylkill	1792	1795
Northern Inland Lock Navigation	1793	1797
Western Inland Lock Navigation	1793	1803
Santee	1793	1800
Dismal Swamp	1793	1814
Middlesex	1794	1803
Chesapeake & Delaware	1804	1805
Schuylkill Navigation	1816	1835
Erie	1817	1825
Ottawa River canals	1819	1834
James River Company	1820	1829
Union	1821	1826
Lachine	1821	1825
Chesapeake & Delaware	1824	1829
Welland	1824	1829
Miami & Erie	1825	1828
Ohio Canal	1825	1832
Delaware & Hudson	1825	1828
Morris	1825	1837
Lehigh Coal & Navigation	1826	1829
Pennsylvania Mainline	1826	1834
Dismal Swamp enlargement	1826	1828
Rideau	1826	1832
Chesapeake & Ohio	1828	1850
Delaware & Raritan	1830	1834
Wabash & Erie	1832	1851
Miami & Erie extension	1833	1845
Cornwall	1834	1843
Lehigh Coal & Navigation extension	1835	1838

James River & Kanawha	1835	1851
Illinois & Michigan	1836	1848
Erie enlargement	1836	1862
Beauharnois	1842	1845
Welland enlargement	1842	1850
Lachine enlargement	1843	1848
Williamsburg canals	1844	1851
Delaware & Hudson enlargement	1845	1853
Union enlargement	1850	1857
Delaware & Raritan enlargement	1851	1853
Lehigh enlargement	1851	1856
St. Mary's	1853	1855

Sources: Christopher Baer, *The Canals and Railroads of the Mid-Atlantic States, 1800–1860* (Wilmington, Del.: Regional Economic History Research Center, Eleutherian Mills-Hagley Foundation, 1981), Appendix table "Canal Companies: Basic Organizational Information"; Robert F. Legget, *Canals of Canada* (Vancouver, B.C.: Douglas, David & Charles, 1976); Ronald E. Shaw, *Canals for a Nation: The Canal Era in the United States 1790–1860* (Lexington: University Press of Kentucky, 1990).

Abbreviations

C&O/LR	Letters Received by the Office of the President and Directors, Chesapeake and Ohio Canal Company Papers, series 190, NA/RG79.
C&O/LS	Letters Sent by the Office of the President and Directors, Chesapeake and Ohio Canal Company Papers, series 194, NA/RG79.
C&O/PRO	Proceedings of the President and Directors, Chesapeake and Ohio Canal Company Papers, series 182, NA/RG79.
IN/II	Internal Improvements Papers, Land Department, Records of the Auditor of State, Indiana Commission on Public Records, Archives Division, Indianapolis.
JRCR	James River Company Records, entry 83, VA/BPW.
MHS	Manuscripts Division, Maryland Historical Society, Baltimore.
NA	National Archives of the United States, Washington, D. C.
NA/RG79	Records of the National Park Service, RG79, NA.
NCA	North Carolina State Archives, Raleigh.
OH/CC	Board of Canal Commissioners Correspondence, Canal Commission and Board of Public Works Papers, Ohio State Archives, Columbus.
PAC	Public Archives of Canada, Ottawa.
PAC/RG8	British Military and Naval Records, series C-I, RG8, PAC.
PAC/RG11	Records of the Department of Public Works, series A-1, RG11, PAC.
PAC/RG43	Records of the Department of Railways and Canals, RG43, series C-VI, PAC.
PA/RG17	Board of Canal Commissioners Records, Canal and Public Works Papers, Part I, Division of Internal Affairs, Bureau of Land

Records, RG17, Pennsylvania Historical and Museum Commission, Harrisburg.

POT/COR   Correspondence and Reports, Potomac Company Papers, series 162, NA/RG79.

POT/PRO   Proceedings, Potomac Company Papers, series 160, NA/RG79.

RG   Record Group.

SHC   Southern Historical Collection, Wilson Library, University of North Carolina at Chapel Hill.

VA/BPW   Virginia Board of Public Works Records, Archives, Virginia State Library, Commonwealth of Virginia, Richmond.

W&E/COR   Wabash and Erie Canal Correspondence, IN/II.

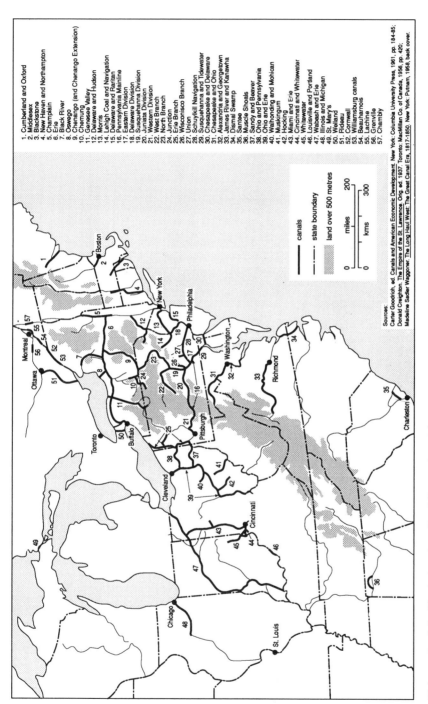

1. Cumberland and Oxford
2. Middlesex
3. Blackstone
4. New Haven and Northampton
5. Champlain
6. Erie
7. Black River
8. Oswego
9. Chenango (and Chenango Extension)
10. Chemung
11. Genesee Valley
12. Delaware and Hudson
13. Morris
14. Lehigh Coal and Navigation
15. Delaware and Raritan
16. Pennsylvania Mainline
17. Eastern Division
18. Delaware Division
19. Susquehanna Division
20. Juniata Division
21. Western Division
22. West Branch
23. North Branch
24. Junction
25. Erie Branch
26. Wiconisco Branch
27. Union
28. Schuylkill Navigation
29. Susquehanna and Tidewater
30. Chesapeake and Delaware
31. Chesapeake and Ohio
32. Alexandria and Georgetown
33. James River and Kanawha
34. Dismal Swamp
35. Santee
36. Muscle Shoals
37. Sandy and Beaver
38. Ohio and Pennsylvania
39. Ohio and Erie
40. Walhonding and Mohican
41. Muskingum
42. Hocking
43. Miami and Erie
44. Cincinnati and Whitewater
45. Whitewater
46. Louisville and Portland
47. Wabash and Erie
48. Illinois and Michigan
49. St. Mary's
50. Welland
51. Rideau
52. Cornwall
53. Williamsburg canals
54. Beauharnois
55. Lachine
56. Grenville
57. Chambly

canals
state boundary
land over 500 metres

miles 0   100   200

kms 0   300

Sources:
Carter Goodrich, ed. Canals and American Economic Development. New York: Columbia University Press, 1961, pp. 184–85;
Donald Creighton. The Empire of the St. Lawrence. Orig. ed. 1937. Toronto: MacMillan Co. of Canada, 1956, pp. 420;
Madeline Sadler Waggoner. The Long Haul West: The Great Canal Era, 1817–1850. New York: Putnam, 1958, back cover.

Main canals of the North American Canal Era, 1780–1860

Introduction

In accordance with the good character you gave the gentleman in Youghal, I expect him, if he undertakes to write the history of that town, not to be prejudiced for or against either the Gael or the Gall, nor to praise or discredit unwarrentedly, nor to take sides against either rich or poor, but to give an account of all – good and bad – as they deserve, so far as he is able to ascertain the facts. Any historian who does not hold to this rule in his writing deserves not the name of historian but that of idle roller, a prating liar who makes a fool of others as well as of himself.[1]

William Fee was a young Irishman indentured to the Potomac Company of Virginia. Disliking the demanding work of lock making and river improvement, or perhaps resenting his bondage, he ran away from the canal in 1786, only to be recaptured. The company shaved off Fee's eyebrows and sheared two streaks in his hair, intersecting to form a cross, as punishment and to mark him as a miscreant. Francis Murray, another absconding servant who lost his eyebrows when apprehended, also had an iron collar forged around his neck, the mark of the incorrigible fugitive. Company policy was that shaving should continue every week "until their behaviour evinces that they are brought to a sense of their duty." Many of the Potomac's servants, bought from European ships in Philadelphia and Baltimore, refused to be complaisant beasts of burden, and absconding was rife on company works, as it was wherever indentured servitude was practiced. Those recaptured were literally stigmatized for their past conduct and as a hedge against future light-footedness. Less brutal than the branding or ear cropping often inflicted on bonded labour, head shaving

1 Pádraig Cúndún to Tomás Stac, 18 Oct. 1851, in *Pádraig Phiarais Cúndún, 1777–1856*, ed. Risteárd Ó Foghludha (Baile Atha Cliath: Oifig Díolta Foillseacháin Rialtais, 1932). I would like to thank Dr. Bruce D. Boling of the University of New Mexico for translating this letter from the Irish, and his courteous permission to allow me to quote from it. Cúndún was an Irishman who emigrated in the 1820s to the United States, where he worked temporarily on the Erie Canal before settling on a farm near Utica, New York. The above-cited letter, written to an acquaintance in Ireland, discusses a third party who was planning to write a history of Youghal, a town near Cúndún's birthplace.

was a scarlet letter meant to shame its wearers into moral conduct. For shaming to be effective, however, the culprit must accept the essential justice of the system. This seemed to elude Fee and Murray, as both absconded again at the earliest opportunity.[2]

Over fifty years later in June 1843, Irish workers on Quebec's Beauharnois Canal mounted a general strike. They were tired of working days that were too long for wages that were too short and resented having to buy provisions at their employers' stores, which left them little cash and sometimes even a debt to show for a month's hard labour. For almost two weeks the workers stood united against contractors who refused their wage and hour demands. Violent demonstrations involving hundreds of strikers affirmed this unity until in the midst of one such protest they were confronted by British troops called out by their employers. The men stood firm, refusing to disperse at the reading of the Riot Act, though offering no real threat of violence. Finally, a harried magistrate gave the order and a volley was fired into the workers' ranks. Five died on the spot, and more were swept away by the river in which they sought refuge from the cavalry. Peace was restored and the strike broken.[3]

Between 1786 and 1843 significant shifts had occurred in the experiences of "canallers."[4] Theirs is a tale of great relevance to the general labour experience. Individuals faced a powerful master on the Potomac in the 1780s, while hundreds of combined workers confronted employers, magistrates and the military on the Beauharnois in 1843. The axis of labour relations had shifted from an individual to a collective level in the intervening years. The Potomac workers were unfree (although they worked alongside free labourers as well as slaves), bonded to whoever owned their indenture, pledged to yield up their labour and obedience. The Beauharnois workers were free, able to sell their labour where and to whom they would. Most canallers in the interim had thus been liberated from any form of servitude, with mixed blessings. Servants ran away on their own or in small groups when they did not like the way they were treated, while workers rioted and went on strike to improve their lot. Protest had shifted from the small to the large scale and from personal to collective concerns and tactics. Capital's response mirrored this change: the Potomac Company

---

2 [Alexandria] *Virginia Gazette*, 22 June, 27 July 1786; [Annapolis] *Maryland Chronicle*, 16 Feb. 1786. See also Cora Bacon-Foster, "Early Chapters in the Development of the Potomac Route to the West," *Proceedings of the Columbia Historical Society*, v. 15 (1911), 162–64; Ulrich B. Phillips, ed., *Plantation and Frontier 1649–1863* (orig. ed. 1910; New York: Burt Franklin, 1969), v. 2, 178.

3 "Report of the Commissioners appointed to inquire into the Disturbances upon the line of the Beauharnois Canal, during the summer of 1843 . . . ," *Journals of the Legislative Assembly of the Province of Canada*, 1843, Appendix T (hereafter "Beauharnois Report").

4 I will be using the term "canallers" to apply to all workers engaged in canal construction, for whom (excluding skilled workers) there was not a specific title at the time except the generic "labourers" or "hands." They were sometimes called canallers (or canalers or "canawlers," a play at Irish brogue), and very infrequently "navvies" (a British term stemming from "navigators" or those who built the navigation works), which I will be using as well for the sake of variety.

punished and shamed individual culprits for their bad conduct, while the state violently repressed the Beauharnois general strike. The status and organization of labour had altered, while capital had grown in scale and strength. What unites the two examples is that in both cases the labourers were relatively powerless, able to resist by flight or strike but unable fundamentally to alter their condition. Still, the stakes of class conflict had become higher. Already a harlequin mask in the late eighteenth century, bald pate and brows disguising the individual beneath, the visage of labour by the 1840s could be somehow rendered grotesque and faceless; a mass unrecognizable to capital as human thus became subject to the most extreme form of discipline. This transformation had been a complex one.

These years encompassed the seminal period in the rise of the industrial-capitalist order and the modern class system in North America. Significant capital and labour accumulation had to occur both before and during this prolonged process, which was international in dimension and entailed the breakdown of a hierarchical agrarian society and the creation of an industrial, market-directed system that ultimately co-opted the state as caretaker. This transformation, the subject of much debate, matured in Britain during the seventeenth and eighteenth centuries. Lands were enclosed and converted to commercial production, factories emerged and the market was extended. In the process people were torn from the land and artisans separated from the small workshop, both ultimately to be pushed into wage labour. Marx called this preliminary stage to capitalism "primitive accumulation."[5] The timing of this transformation in North America (and in fact its very existence) is a matter of much controversy. One group of historians, influenced by the classical economics of Adam Smith, argues for the existence of capitalism from early in the colonial period, if not the beginning, while another, drawing on Marx, maintains the shift to capitalism was delayed and piecemeal, traditional, non-commercial cultural patterns buffering and retarding the impact of the market.[6]

The experience on canals supports the contention that the years spanning

5 Karl Marx, *Capital: A Critique of Political Economy* (orig. ed. 1867; New York: Modern Library, 1906), Part VIII.
6 This debate has been nicely summed up by Allan Kulikoff in "The Transition to Capitalism in Rural America," *William & Mary Quarterly*, v. 44 (Jan. 1989), 120–44. See Winifred B. Rothenberg, "The Emergence of Farm Labor Markets and the Transformation of the Rural Economy, 1750–1855," *Journal of Economic History*, v. 48 (Sept. 1988), 537–66; James A. Henretta, "Families and Farms: *Mentalité* in Pre-Industrial America," *William & Mary Quarterly*, v. 35 (Jan. 1978), 3–32; Christopher Clark, "Household Economy, Market Exchange and the Rise of Capitalism in the Connecticut Valley, 1800–1860, *Journal of Social History*, v. 13 (Winter 1979), 169–90; Marcus Rediker, " 'Good Hands, Stout Heart, and Fast Feet': The History and Culture of Working People in Early America," *Labour/Le Travail*, v. 10 (Autumn 1982), 123–44; Rediker, "Toward a 'real, profane history' of early American society," *Social History*, v. 10 (Oct. 1985), 367–81; Bryan Palmer, "Social Formation and Class Formation in North America, 1800–1900," in *Proletarianization and Family History*, ed. David Levine (Orlando: Academic Press, 1984), 229–309.

the late eighteenth and early nineteenth centuries constituted an era of transition, in which industrial capitalism spread in the form of business organization and labour relations and many traditional social and economic forms persisted. An older world of work was breaking down, characterized by petty agricultural production or a personal relationship between journeyman and master based on an exchange of labour for the provision of worldly needs. A new complex of social and economic relations was being woven by an interrelated process of social change, which incorporated the growth of large-scale enterprise, increasing competition of market-oriented production, and the development of a labour market awash with individuals either uprooted from the soil or with one foot on land and the other wavering over the abyss of wage work. In effect, the modern industrial class system had all but appeared in this short span of time where once traditional forms of production and social relations prevailed.

Canal construction played a significant role in this transformation by opening up new markets, mobilizing an army of workers, creating new consumers, developing business strategies and initiating the state–capital ties so important in later years. As a result of having to mount a massive production process, the industry also charted a new course in labour relations from unfree through free labour; at the same time the canal builders invented innovative forms of industrial discipline, spanning regulation to military repression, which became a blueprint for the future. That canals were but a temporary stage in the technology of transportation and eventually yielded to railroads does not belie the key role they played in sparking change.

Given the industry's vanguard status, the experience of canallers assumes an added importance, providing insight into the leading edge of class formation. Marx called England's railway navvies "the light cavalry of capitalism," skirmishers at the forefront of both economic development and class struggle.[7] In much the same way, canallers were miners and sappers digging the earthworks of North American capitalism, agents of change burying the past and digging the trenches of a future world of industrial production with every spadeful of earth removed.

Most of what has been written on the rise of industrial capitalism in North America comes from one perspective: the breakdown of an artisanal world and the gradual emergence of working-class culture and class politics from the ashes of the craft experience. This history charts the rise of the factory system and the concomitant decline in the fortunes of the skilled worker. Yet this is only one pathway through to the present. There have been others, arguably much rockier, that trace out a variant experience of class formation. The rough labour that dug canals trod such a trail.

7 Marx quoted in Nicholas Faith, *The World the Railways Made* (London: Bodley Head, 1990), 193.

While accepting the severe limitations placed on their subjects by the material realities of industrial capitalism, labour historians have chosen to focus on people's collective control over their experience, with class consciousness and working-class culture being the ultimate expressions of this human agency.[8] The rough synthesis of labour experience that emerges is of the breakdown of an older, more traditional form of production based on the household and the craft shop. Master and journeymen were coproducers who both worked and lived in close personal contact, imbibing an artisanal republicanism that vaunted independence, equality and opportunity. If not an egalitarian era, it was traditional, familiar and more humane. This world began to crumble under pressure from the burgeoning market; masters or the local merchant became manufacturers, while most masters and journeymen made a protracted descent to wage worker status through a process of specialization of task, deskilling and destruction of craft. Throughout this transformation they still held to their republican ideology, but with independence a mixed blessing under capitalism, equality visibly receding and opportunity moving beyond their grasp, republicanism became the basis of a new, emergent class consciousness. The first union movements and strikes of the 1820s–1830s punctuate this development, and by mid-century the class forces were in place. Artisans had become workers, crafting from the fragments of the past a new sense of being that would allow them to wage the class battle. It is a near-linear model of declining status and rising class consciousness.[9]

This is a compelling and convincing portrayal of proletarianization and class conflict. But for all its detail, it is flawed. The model does not embrace the experience of all, nor even a majority of workers, being based primarily on the experiences of only one element of the working class, the skilled and organized, who, for the first part of the nineteenth century at

8 In British labour history, E. P. Thompson's case for working-class culture and the primacy of agency was promptly taken to task and has been a source of heated debate ever since. Thompson, *The Making of the English Working Class* (Harmondsworth, England: Penguin, 1968); Perry Anderson, *Arguments Within English Marxism* (London: Verso, 1980); John Foster, *Class Struggle and the Industrial Revolution: Early Industrial Capitalism in Three English Towns* (London: Weidenfeld & Nicolson, 1974); Patrick Joyce, *Work, Society and Politics: The Culture of the Factory in Later Victorian England* (Brighton: Harvester Press, 1980); Richard Price, *Labour in British Society: An Interpretive History* (London: Croom Helm, 1986), 4–5. This debate has had little impact in North America, where Thompson's message, popularized by Herbert Gutman and elaborated by such historians as Alan Dawley and Sean Wilentz, has been left virtually untouched. David Montgomery breaks with this model by emphasizing struggles for control of the point of production, but his emphasis is still primarily on the trades, the cult of skill and militant political action. Gutman, *Work, Culture, and Society in Industrializing America: Essays in American Working-Class and Social History* (New York: Vintage, 1977); Dawley, *Class and Community: The Industrial Revolution in Lynn* (Cambridge, Mass.: Harvard University Press, 1976); Wilentz, *Chants Democratic: New York City and the Rise of the American Working Class, 1788–1850* (New York: Oxford University Press, 1984); Montgomery, *The Fall of the House of Labor; The Workplace, the State, and American Labor Activism: 1865–1925* (New York: Cambridge University Press, 1987).

9 The unilinearity of this trajectory is captured in the title of Bruce Laurie's labour history text, one of the first syntheses to emerge from the field: *Artisan into Workers: Labor in Nineteenth-Century America* (New York: Noonday Books, 1989).

least, tended to be white native males. This orientation colours the entire picture. Skill imparts power, and the craftsman utilized this to assert both control within the workplace and independence in the community. Labour historians are thus able to paint the past impressionistically as a world where workers combined against and combatted capital, drawing strength from their burgeoning working-class culture. But by crafting an essentially benign view of this culture and empowering workers with control over their world, these scholars have underestimated the destructive effects of the rise of industrial capitalism on the individual and group. Other realms of working-class experience are undervalued. New worker protagonists are needed, and manual workers have yet to find their voice.

Common labourers' experience differed because their struggle as members of a class did not pivot on skill and control of production but on material conditions. During the early nineteenth century developing capitalism moulded an army of wage workers in North America, not out of thin air or solely from a declining artisanate, but by impressing immigrants, redundant agricultural labour, slaves, free blacks, women and children. The labour force, as a result, was divided by lines of skill, gender, race and ethnicity. Theirs was a history of movement from the land into the lower reaches of wage work propelled by forces beyond their control, and, once on the labour market, they were wholly alienated, mere animal power to prepare the ground for industrial production.[10] While sharing many general experiences with skilled workers – a breakdown of paternalistic labour relations, tightening industrial discipline, falling wages and resulting labour conflict – their tale was not one of lost craft and robbed skill filtered through a republican world view. Common labourers were more fully exploited, worse off economically, socially fragmented, and, as a result, with a culture (or, more accurately, cultures) that reflected their alienation as much as a sense of community. Class conflict for them thus did not entail rear-guard actions to strengthen their loosening grasp on the means of production, but uncoordinated efforts to secure and maintain employment, and, less often, to better conditions once they had a job. This meant frequent moving to find work and occasionally fighting, both with bosses and other workers, to keep it. It was a situation that promoted so-called anti-social behaviour such as excessive drinking and interpersonal violence, unsurprising given the raw materials of their lifestyle. Worker culture's rough dimension has received far less attention from historians, but was equally important, being the negative side of class struggle in which class antagonisms were submerged and sublimated by labourers, to be vented on themselves and co-workers. In the process, consciousness was inhibited at

10 Andrea Graziosi suggested that different dynamics pertained to common labourers in the steel mills and machine shops in the late nineteenth century because of their marginal role in the production process. "Common Laborers, Unskilled Workers: 1880–1915," *Labor History*, v. 22 (Fall 1981), 512–44.

the same time as a culture was being built, and material forces were the determining factors. The exploitation inherent in the capitalist wage relationship exacted real costs and engendered long-term harm for labourers.

In many ways then, unskilled workers stand outside the craftsman-to-worker model, providing an alternative view of labour's confrontation with industrial capitalism that is less pleasing but arguably more representative. Their experience remained roughly similar from industry to industry and over time, while there was little in the way of mounting class conflict or increasingly sophisticated worker organization. Instead, it was more of the same, as common labourers were exploited to a higher degree than skilled workers. While similar at its roots − the scraping away of surplus value from their toil − it left less behind and offered fewer options. The social and economic marginality of workers like canallers also meant their cultural adaptation to industrial capitalism was made more difficult, as the goal of a stable community and an institutional base with which to parry the thrust of history proved elusive. Without the power that skill brought, lacking the status of independent craftsmen and bereft of the ideological framework to absorb and resist unwanted change that republicanism seemingly offered artisans, common labourers were more fully exposed to the ravages of the market and less able to posit an alternative world view to that of the emerging industrial-capitalist order. In sum, persisting powerlessness and social dislocation was the lot of common labourers, not ongoing contests of strength with their employers and the development of a vibrant oppositional culture. The experiences of this emerging manual labour force, different yet akin to its artisanal cousins, is crucial to an understanding of industrial development, as the majority of the workforce has always been composed of the unskilled and non-unionized. Canallers provide an example of this alternative labour experience, of this parallel but distinct pathway into the working class.[11]

Canal, lockage and river improvement schemes were first implemented in the 1780s. These ventures were small in scale relative to later projects, yet

---

11 The main studies on canal workers are H. C. Pentland, "The Lachine Strike of 1843," *Canadian Historical Review*, v. 29, no. 3 (1948), 255−77; Richard B. Morris, "Andrew Jackson, Strikebreaker," *American Historical Review*, v. 55 (Oct. 1949), 54−68; W. David Baird, "Violence Along the Chesapeake and Ohio Canal: 1839," *Maryland Historical Magazine*, v. 66 (Summer 1971), 121−34; Ruth Bleasdale, "Class Conflict on the Canals of Upper Canada in the 1840's," in *Pre-Industrial Canada 1760−1849*, ed. Michael S. Cross and Gregory S. Kealey (Toronto: McClelland and Stewart, 1982), 100−38; Bleasdale, "Irish Labourers on the Cornwall, Welland and Williamsburg Canals in the 1840's," M.A. thesis, University of Western Ontario, 1975; Bleasdale, "Unskilled Labourers on the Public Works of Canada, 1840−1880," Ph.D. diss., University of Western Ontario, 1983; Raymond Boily, *Les Irlandais et le canal de Lachine: La grève de 1843* (Ottawa: Lemeac, 1980); William N. T. Wylie, "Poverty, Distress, and Disease: Labour and the Construction of the Rideau Canal, 1826−32," *Labour/Le Travailleur*, v. 11 (Spring 1983), 7−30; and Catherine Teresa Tobin, "The Lowly Muscular Digger: Irish Canal Workers in Nineteenth Century America," Ph.D. diss., Notre Dame University, 1987.

they were still hampered by capital and labour shortages. Consequently, there were only 100 miles of canals in the United States by 1816. A second wave of construction followed in the wake of the Erie Canal (1817–25), with 1,277 miles completed by 1830, more than doubling to 3,326 miles in the ensuing ten years. These figures do not include Canadian public works, such as the first Welland Canal (27 miles) and Rideau (120 miles), which were completed at this time. The panic of 1837 and the ensuing depression took the bloom off canals in the States, as companies and boards of works were forced by lack of funds to scale back or shut down construction. By comparison, the Canadian government committed itself to a comprehensive building program, taking advantage of the now-flooded labour market to push through such projects as the Cornwall and Beauharnois canals, as well as the Lachine and Welland improvements. Still, these only amounted to a few hundred miles, and even when the depression lifted in the mid-1840s, the residual wariness of canal investment and the increasing competition of railroads meant the virtual death-knell of artificial water transportation. Less than 400 miles had been built in the States during the 1840s, and by 1850 abandonment of existing lines exceeded new canal mileage. By 1860, there was a total of 4,254 miles of canals in the United States.[12] The Canal Era had drawn to a close by the end of the fifties. Although there would be later canals, these would be large ship navigation systems strategically placed where they could compete efficiently with railways, such as the New York barge canal and the St. Lawrence Seaway system.

This is the familiar framework for studying canals, marking the peaks and valleys of the industry. Yet behind these bland business realities (and lost in much of the historical literature) lies a more intriguing story of a changing world of work, erected upon innovations in the organization of production and a burgeoning state role in the economy, which pioneered new forms of labour relations and altered forever the lives of canal workers and promoters alike.

The projects of the late eighteenth century, while small relative to what was to come later, were considerable business ventures for their time, requiring thousands of dollars in investment and hundreds of workers. They were carried on by joint-stock companies that always felt a strain in meeting these demands. Canals unsuccessfully turned to the state to bring in capital and utilized whatever labour they could lay their hands on, but still most ventures failed, as both were in short supply. Early canals

---

12 Mileage figures have been drawn from George Rogers Taylor, *The Transportation Revolution, 1815–1860* (New York: Rinehart, 1951), 52–53; Christopher Baer, *The Canals and Railroads of the Mid-Atlantic States, 1800–1860* (Wilmington, Del.: Regional Economic History Research Center, Eleutherian Mills-Hagley Foundation, 1981), Appendix tables "Canals Miles Added 1801–1862" and "Canals Total Miles 1800–1862"; and Ronald E. Shaw, *Canals for a Nation: The Canal Era in the United States, 1790–1860* (Lexington: University of Kentucky Press, 1990), 228.

experienced the demands of industry in an essentially commercial, pre-industrial world. Problems of capital and labour supply persisted throughout the Canal Era, although by the second wave of construction, beginning in 1817 with the Erie, the state played an increasing role in funding and directing what were now termed "public works." This relationship, expressed in government support of private companies or by the creation of public agencies to implement a state policy of internal improvements – canal commissions or boards of works – anticipated the interpenetration of state and capital that would bear great fruits for industry later in the nineteenth century. Canal projects at the same time became swollen bureaucracies, complex management structures of directors, engineers, surveyors, maintenance superintendents and locktenders needed to build transportation networks, which now could measure hundreds of miles in length and require thousands of workers and millions of dollars. A great distance had been travelled with speed from the first small endeavours, just a series of locks or a few miles of canal, to the creation of such leviathans as Indiana's Wabash & Erie, the longest of all canals at almost 400 miles. The age of big industry arrived early in canal construction.

The contractor was a key figure in this development. As the production process grew more distended and companies tired of direct responsibility for the funding, staffing and disciplining of a labour force, they turned to these independent builders. Contractors put up initial capital, mobilized and provided for their workforce, and were contractually bound to complete their "section" of the line to specifications laid down by the engineer. In return, they were paid according to a set scale for types of work done, minus a retained percentage to ensure their good faith to management. The small scale of their job meant that the contractor forged close ties to his hands, often providing food and shelter, while working and living alongside them. A form of paternalism developed, mutual but unequal, and born of the limitations imposed by the undeveloped capitalist marketplace. These ties were always tenuous and were soon severed when a builder proved unable to provide for his men, a situation that became more common over the years. The competitive nature of the bidding process by which contracts were won and the continuing financial problems of the industry meant that these builders walked a tightrope between profit and bankruptcy, a balancing act that became near-impossible as the depression of the late 1830s undercut funds and construction. To survive in the new, financially restrained environment, contractors had to grow, to become businesses in their own right. They also had to cut costs, which meant the paternalistic overtones of the labour relationship would be stripped away and most work carried on strictly according to market forces. Class conflict was the natural consequence. Contracting had been a stratagem to overcome the problems of capital and labour supply. This contractors were never entirely able to do, but they did manage to localize the difficulties and allow construction to continue, failed builders quickly being replaced. It was these individuals in their thousands that were largely responsible for the prosecution of canal building.

As the business organization shifted within the industry in the eighty years under study, so did the social relations in which the workers participated. Broadly, the movement was from an unfree, or dependent, labour relationship to free labour, and from the small-scale and personal to the giant and anonymous. Slaves, indentured servants and wage labourers could work alongside each other in the early years, often sharing the same accommodation, food and clothing provided by the company. Free labour soon came to predominate (outside the South), now with contractors acting as patrons. While labour shortages persisted, free canallers received fairly good wages as well as food and shelter. Still, theirs was a near-subsistence existence, and the depression and ensuing contraction of the industry undercut canallers' tenuous grasp on solvency. Labour surplus drove down wages and freed contractors from providing for their employees, as the labour relationship was completely commercialized. Unemployment, underemployment, misery and want resulted for most navvies and their families. The situation would improve as the depression eased, but the relatively better conditions of earlier years never reappeared. In a continuing process of class formation, most canallers became workers in the modern sense: wholly separated from the control of the means of production, only partially rewarded for their toil and at the whim of the market for the means of their survival.

The work itself was unlike the increasingly mechanized manufactories. It remained largely the same throughout the period, powered by human and beast using traditional tools, shovels, picks, wheelbarrows and carts. Canallers laboured twelve to fifteen hours a day in all kinds of weather. They were exposed to many health-threatening illnesses, including malaria, yellow fever and cholera, as well as work-related injuries. Most lived in all-male barracks or family shanties on the worksite or in nearby towns. Their accommodations were meant to be temporary and were limited in comfort. These shanty towns, the setting for much drinking, criminality and bloody violence, were looked upon by local residents as sinks of iniquity to be avoided. Canallers were set off from society by the type of work they did and where they lived, as well as by their lifestyle, a marginal existence reinforced by their ethnic or racial background. Increasingly, the work became stigmatized as the roughest of rough labour performed by the lowest of the low, Irish immigrants and slaves. These two pariah groups, pushed into the worst kinds of work as the most disadvantaged of labourers, pulled canal construction further down in the estimation of potential workers from the late 1820s. Republican freemen soon lost their appetite for canalling, making it one of the first truly lumpen proletarian professions in North America. In sum, the various "Corktowns" and "Slabtowns" were hardly Lowells, Lynns, or even St. Clairs. They were environments that left little scope for self-determination.

Declining economic well-being, the work's harshness and the fragility of social life bred a significant degree of conflict, but it was turned inward as often as against employers. The segmented nature of the work and the pull of old allegiances prevented the emergence of a broad-based class consciousness. Canal workers fought with each other incessantly over perceived social differences or for the limited number of jobs available. But increasingly they focused their hostilities on the foremen, contractors and canal officials whom they blamed for the assorted ills of shanty life, using terrorist attacks and the waging of strikes to achieve their class ends. These epiphanies were usually short-lived, as the centripetal forces of their existence threw canallers back into their shanties, their squabblings, and their rounds of work and intoxication. Collective action was sufficiently daunting, however, to draw the capitalist class together to discipline workers, while the state was repeatedly drawn in as the enforcer of industrial production, particularly in the form of military or judicial repression of labour protest. The experience of canal construction for the years studied thus provides a paradigm for the emergence of the modern industrial class system in its broad social and economic consequences.

In the late eighteenth century, there had been a world of small projects, limited government involvement, both free and unfree labour, and paternalistic productive relations; by 1860 the world was competitive, market-driven and increasingly dominated by relatively large business organizations fueled by multitudes of unattached workers. Canallers were not paid enough to live in any comfort and had little control over their labour's application or quality, while many were penalized for certain ascribed failings, such as ethnicity, gender and race, not to mention class. To return to the opening examples, the period straddling the flight of Fee and Murray from the Potomac Company and the military repression of the Beauharnois strikers marked the emergence of industrial capitalism and the modern worker. While sharing the general experience with exploitation that this entailed, the different makeup of the workforce and the lower reaches of society to which their occupation consigned them meant the canallers' tale differed materially from that of erstwhile artisans. At the same time, their story was similar to that of many other workers, the unskilled and unorganized, particularly dockers, miners and other public works labourers, as well as the numerous common day labourers who hung on the fringes of urban society looking for any kind of work. Thus they were no less representative than those engaged in manufacturing. In fact, their experience as a casual workforce subject to periodic deprivation was a forewarning of what many could expect from the industrial world.

In the telling of this story a number of decisions inevitably were made about how to present the material. I have operated under the same limitations as earlier historians. Canallers left few first-person accounts, as most were illiterate, and those who could write rarely laid their hand to the type of materials that have been preserved. The nature of the industry strongly influenced this selection process. Most canal construction was carried on by independent contractors, responsible for supplying workers. Company records, reflecting this bifurcation of capital and labour, focus on technical and financial matters. Thus, canallers' marginal position, fragmented into numerous pockets isolated from the bases of power, rendered them histori- cally mute. What remains are scattered references from contractors and canal officials, usually relating to labour problems of one sort or another. To overcome these difficulties I cast my net widely so as to draw in as many stray fish of information as possible. Enough material on workers was discovered in the extensive business records to offset the elitist thrust of their host collections. This was supplemented by newspapers, personal papers and government records, which all tended to give a view from above but often revealed a sympathy with canallers' sufferings that provided many insights. I also visited as many repositories as possible so as to achieve a representative portait of the entire industry from place to place and over time. This not only broadened the evidenciary base but enabled a wide time frame and comparative component that I felt were necessary to an understanding of the industry and its place within broader economic and social development.

My study period, 1780–1860, was chosen because, while inevitably arbitrary, it most closely approximated the so-called Canal Era, from the first furtive efforts at river improvement through the golden age of visionary transportation networks, generous state investment and high employment, to the final feeble stabs at completion. Also, it was a period that has never been fully explored as a whole. In particular, the early pre-Erie years, usually neglected, are crucial to an understanding of the industry's development. This broad framework helps to invest canals with their rightful historical significance.

This is also a study with comparative dimensions, examining, as it does, Canada and the North and South of the United States. As such, it embraces British colony and American republic, not to mention free and slave societies. The one unifying factor from the perspective of the industry was capitalism, which moulded the very different social systems to the same purpose. The result was similarity – of production and technology – amid social diversity. In this, the industry offers an interesting insight into the versatile yet indiscriminate nature of early industrial capitalism. The industry's organization makes incorporation of national or regional distinc- tions academically arbitrary. Canal workers, contractors, engineers and promoters did not find borders a barrier, and moved freely between countries and regions depending on where construction was ongoing and jobs were available. To focus on a single area distorts the flows of labour and capital that shaped the experience of the industry; hence my decision to treat the industry as a whole, as a *North American* phenomenon, while admitting it was primarily an Eastern and Midwestern concern in which much of the South, the Far West, the Canadian North, and Mexico do not figure.

The Canadian–American comparison is something that has been done all too infrequently by historians in general, and canal scholars have resolutely abided by national particularity. I attempt to fill this void, yet it will be clear that this is not a comparative study in the common sense, that is, between two largely distinct entities. I do not pretend to be studying the different cultures of the United States and Canada. There are times when the predominant conservatism of British North America and the American republican tradition influenced events on canals, particularly in the area of state response to social problems and labour violence. Here, Canadian government and canal officials were more likely both to ameliorate conditions and to suppress riots and strikes by force. This was a matter of degree and not substance, however, and cut both ways for workers. More important was the fundamental similarity of objective conditions within the industry. This was rooted firmly in the nature of production; construction was funded in roughly the same way, carried on using identical technology, performed by a similar workforce and organized into carbon-copy labour processes. There was not much scope in this material world for cultural forces to invade, manipulate and differentiate along national lines, and this study broadly suggests how similar and malleable were "national" traditions in response to fundamental economic development.

I also incorporate a North–South comparison in my work. Canal construction in the South has been the subject of fewer studies and these in isolation from the North. Thus, the stereotype of the canal worker as Irish immigrant has not been overly disturbed by the reality of slave labour. While this is hard to establish, it appears that the greater part of work south of Maryland was carried on by slaves, particularly in the early years. Free white labour – both locals and Irish immigrants recruited from the North – was always a factor, but the dominance of the peculiar institution and the growing dislike of wage labour (at least as practiced in the North) meant that unfree African-Americans did much of the digging. This is significant because race and slavery obviously made for a different canalling experience, which has been lost in the resolute Northern focus within most of the literature. Southern slavery resisted the forces of change that exerted pressure on the industry as a whole. There was no shift to free labour in the South (although it was used more in later years than it had been before), whereas indentured servitude and even slavery had been tried elsewhere before wage workers became the norm. As well, most Southern canals remained small affairs requiring less capital investment and fewer workers than those in the North. One reason for this relative underdevelopment was a suspicion of public works projects, partly rooted in an aversion to governmental interference as a potential threat to the institution of slavery. While Southern differences pose problems when synthesizing the historical material, the region accounted for a comparatively small component of the industry and slaves were always a minority of the total workforce. Thus, I will largely write about Canada and the American North, hinging my arguments on the experience of workers there, and bringing in the South and slaves when they depart from the main current of change as a means of comparison to underline these developments.

This study is also primarily about men, partly due to the gender composition of the workforce, overwhelmingly made up of young single males. Women rarely figure in the primary sources that have survived, having been, even more so than male workers, silenced by history. Yet they did play a key subsidiary part that I will attempt to piece together. The lives of canallers' wives and daughters were shaped by the industry whether they dug ditches or not. Women worked on the periphery of canal construction, serving men as cooks, cleaners and laundresses in the shanty camps, usually in the pay of contractors at wages considerably below those of men. They also ran boarding houses in which canallers stayed, and were thus independent but inevitably reliant on the meagre earnings of their tenants. Many women lived off work camps back in some city to which their men would return during the off-season. They were forced into sweated labour as seamstresses to support their families or took up domestic service, both difficult, poorly remunerated jobs. In effect, it can be seen that women were proletarianized along with men. Whether at work on public works sites or in the cities, women contributed to a family income that canal wages alone could not support. Consequently, their subordination helped pay for canal construction. But women's relegation to the more disadvantaged employment was not solely a function of capitalism's need, but also of the male prerogative as breadwinner: their subordination served the psychic needs of men to be the superior sex, provider and protector of the family.

Canal camps were largely societies of men, where hard living, hard working and hard drinking were cherished values. Canallers participated in sport, fighting, boozing and various contests of strength, in the process developing a proletarian sense of virility associated with manual labour and physical prowess. Yet they derived few rewards from society for their gender, other than their limited superiority over women. There was little economic power to be divied up at the bottom of the pile, while women's key but subordinate contributions to the family economy conceivably gave them some leverage in the relationship. Women may have always been situated beneath men in the ideal, but in their mutual deprivation the material gap between them and men was narrow. One could conjecture that this proximity of power and place corroded men's sense of superiority and they compensated by exaggerating their masculinity in dangerous work and prodigious feats of excess. Men may have embraced the harshness of their lives as a badge of distinction, as developing gender roles both absorbed and perpetuated prevailing forms of exploitation. The seeming male domain of canal construction thus reveals upon closer inspection a realm inevitably bifurcated along gender lines, which this study will tentatively attempt to illuminate whenever the records allow.

My approach to the subject is a combination of the chronological and the topical, so as to convey the historical process and at the same time provide a more focused scrutiny on particularly important elements of the story. In Chapter 1 I examine the early canal industry in the years 1780–1812, a time when capital and labour shortages limited the scale of construction and led to the use of both free and unfree labour. Still, the seeds of a bureaucratic management structure and shanty culture were sown in this period, not to mention the labour unrest that would dog later canals. Next, I look at the business end of the industry during the peak of the Canal Era from 1817 to 1840. This chapter deals with organization and finance, the increasing role played by the state, the engineering corps' supervision of construction and the development of a contracting system to take the actual building from management's hands, a move fraught with importance for labour relations. In Chapter 3 the canallers are traced back to their roots on American farms, Southern slave quarters, French-Canadian seigneuries and, most importantly, Irish rural areas. This diversity made for a very heterogeneous workforce, which (excluding slaves) nonetheless shared a roughly similar experience of movement from traditional agricultural subsistence production to wage work within an industrial system. I then outline the payment system on canals, which was not fully monetized until late in the period. Free labourers received a combination of wages and the provision of food and shelter, contractor paternalism linking builder and hands in a reciprocal though unbalanced relationship. Even at the best of times, however, navvies lived at or below the subsistence line.

Chapter 5 focuses on the nature of canal work, essentially hard manual labour with a high degree of physical risk in an environment promoting debilitating and life-threatening diseases. The combination of marginal economic rewards and onerous physical costs made for a social setting that was temporary in nature and erected upon weak foundations. This fragility was reflected in the worker culture of canallers, which is investigated in the next chapter. While revealing important social props, such as the family, church and ethnic affiliations, life amongst the shanties exhibited a degree of social pathology in the form of alcohol dependency, criminality and physical violence that made mere existence a trial, and set work camps at odds with the working-class communities of much labour history. Like other workers, however, canallers periodically united to resist the material constraints imposed upon them. Building upon the Irish tradition of secret societies and terrorist tactics, they waged war with each other, but also turned their sights on their employers, as measured by an increasing number of riots and faction fights in the 1830s, which are the subject of Chapter 7. This wave of labour unrest surged over into the 1840s, becoming more class-oriented as a result of fundamental changes in the system of production, as documented in the last chapter. The depression of the late 1830s caused a shutdown of construction in the United States and a migration of unemployed navvies into Canada where work continued. The resulting flooding of the labour market led to a drop in wages and a stripping away of the customary provision of food and shelter, which, coupled with rising unemployment, made for a very desperate situation. Crystallizing class lines were reflected in an upsurge in strike activity and the repeated use of the military by the state to enforce free market principles. Canallers were approaching the world of the industrial state with all its consequences for labour just as the industry was winding down. The trail they blazed would be tramped by many other fellow workers.

The world of canallers hints at the untapped sources of the labour story. Recent history on the nineteenth-century working class has focused on skilled labourers and the successful achievement of class consciousness within a particular community. Such studies, while providing rich detail on the lives of workers in the past, have produced a somewhat warped perspective. With their bias toward demonstrating solidarity, they tend to exaggerate the militancy and coherence of worker culture. Forces that tended to fragment labour – such as religion, ethnicity, gender, skill, the nature of work under the industrial regime and the efforts of capitalists to disrupt labour organization – are understated or explained away. As a result, the majority of workers are virtually ignored, or assumed to have shared in the republican ideology labour historians believe shaped the world view of America's declining artisanate. But this model can only apply to a minority of the working class. At the same time that the crafts were waning, a proletariat was waxing. Members of this massive army of manual labourers, although subject to the same exploitation inherent in the capitalist wage relationship as their skilled allies, had fundamentally different experiences. Theirs was not a frantic effort to hang onto the shreds of skill's respectability, but a sundering of ties to the land, destruction of household production and submersion in a pool of floating casual labour. This transformation acted out on canals was a paradigm for the broader experience of labour and capital within the rise of industrial capitalism. Realistically, workers had little power to influence this process, had difficulty even grasping what was happening to them, and could only fight a holding action in an attempt to stem the worst effects. While participants in the process, they were very much driven by forces beyond their control. The difference was between merely absorbing and moderating change and actually being able to direct it.

By writing "history from the bottom up" labour historians have sought to empower people, to remake the past in their image, an exercise fraught with danger. Such studies have done a marvellous job in painting a broader picture of an older world by showing how the majority of society once lived. They have given dignity to what has heretofore been disrespected. Yet, by rescuing those at the bottom of society from historical limbo and conferring agency upon them, these historians have abstracted the masses from their essentially powerless position. It is time that a more Malthusian rendering of the past should once again be allowed to creep into our interpretations. This does not mean treating people as victims, but as merely human. They were sentient beings with limited control over their existence who erected class and ethnic structures to shape their lives, but were often subjected to harsh and inhuman treatment nonetheless. The emerging industrial world for which canals laid the infrastructure was a hard place to live for most. To emphasize cohesion and romanticize the rough life of the canallers would be to do them a disservice by minimizing the difficulty of their existence.

CHAPTER I

Early canals, 1780–1812

Here smooth CANALS, across th' extended plain
Stretch their long arms to join the distant *main*.
The Sons of Toil, with many a weary stroke,
Scoop the hard bosom of the solid rock;
Resistless through the stiff, opposing clay,
With steady patience, work their gradual way;
Compel the Genius of th' unwilling flood,
Through the brown horrors of the aged wood;
Cross the lone waste the silver urn they pour,
And cheer the barren heath, or sullen moor. . . .
The ductile streams obey the guiding hand,
And *social Plenty* crowns the HAPPY LAND![1]

"Rivers are ungovernable Things, especially in Hilly Countries: Canals are quiet and very manageable," Benjamin Franklin assured the Mayor of Philadelphia in 1772.[2] Franklin's comment would have been wildly off the mark had he not been writing before there were any canals in North America and referring to finished improvements rather than their construction. The building of the first artificial waterways was anything but easy, being plagued with capital and labour problems that eventually brought most projects to a premature end, evidence of the dangers involved in mounting large-scale industry in an essentially commercial world and a forewarning of what canal construction could expect for years to come.

As some of the earliest ventures in big business, requiring heavy investment, a large workforce and a managerial apparatus to oversee their dispersed construction process, the canals and lockage systems of the late eighteenth century faced numerous problems. For this was an era of merchant not industrial capital. The internal market was underdeveloped, capital tied up in land and the overriding business ethos one of extending

1 Unattributed poem on the title page of [William Smith,] *An Historical Account of the Rise, Progress and Present State of the Canal Navigation in Pennsylvania* . . . (Philadelphia, 1795).
2 Benjamin Franklin to Samuel Rhoads, 22 Aug. 1772, *The Papers of Benjamin Franklin*, ed. William B. Willcox (New Haven: Yale University Press, 1975), v. 19, 279.

existing commercial relations, not undertaking wholly new, perhaps more profitable money-making ventures. These factors acted as a powerful brake on what canal promoters could do, but less so than the problem of labour supply, as an industrial working class was only just beginning to take shape. The vast majority of the population was involved in slave production, petty agriculture or crafts, and there was little discretionary labour for budding entrepreneurs to tap. Thus, bonded, slave and free labour overlapped. Canals utilized all these types, but in their striving for a flexible yet disciplined workforce, companies outside the South showed a preference for wage labour.

While firmly rooted in the past of small commercial endeavours and traditional forms of production, the early years of canal construction and river improvement were a testing ground for later, large-scale, highly capitalized industries. These projects developed a nascent corporate organization with a hierarchical management structure that anticipated later industry, while pointing in the direction of state intervention in the economy. Hundreds of labourers were mobilized, organized into work units, housed and supplied to create the extended production process that was required to tackle such imposing tasks. And companies developed new forms of labour discipline not only to squeeze the maximum amount of work out of canallers for the minimum investment, but also to keep these armies under control. The essence of future canal construction was contained in these first initiatives, albeit in incipient form.

In the projects of the late eighteenth century, thus, we can see old and new worlds overlap. The genteel proprietors pursuing profit, the coexistence of slave, indentured and free labour, the decidedly archaic technology, all pointed to the past. But also here we can intuit the shape of things to come: the increasing emphasis on efficiency and economy, the growing disposition for free labour and the concomitant need for added control over a massive productive process suggest the encroachment of industrial capitalism. By constructing artificial waterways and wrestling with their capital and labour problems, early canal companies were unwittingly building a modern world where production reigned, spurred by investment and powered by human capital. Early canals were thus conduits of change, bridging an earlier, more localistic world with the modern integrated society of later years. Like Franklin (that child of the crafts and father of the capitalist ethic), they were products of their age: neither "quiet" nor "very manageable," both looking back to the past while being predictive of things to come.

North America's first artificial waterways were commercial ventures, seeking to extend the market for agricultural and manufactured goods as well as to tap the rich lands of the interior. Their mercantile potential had been demonstrated in Europe, and was put succinctly by an early British chronicler of canals: "As consumers, by means of canals we are enabled to import more cheaply; as producers, we export with greater facility."[3] This promise appeared more golden in the New World where rich lands lay waiting to be milked, and many promoters had property interests that would be served by opening up the veins of commerce and migration. For instance, the directors of the Schuylkill Navigation Company rejected their engineer's recommendation that the canal should be constructed on one side of the river so that it would pass through their lands on the opposite bank.[4] At the same time, promoters promised national dividends. Canals would unify an infant country and enhance the general wealth. Within the thinking of the time, there was little clash between private and public interest, a reality captured in the person of George Washington, one of the most enthusiastic transportation boosters and head of the Potomac Canal Company before he was elected President of the United States. "Extend the inland navigation of the Eastern waters, communicate them as near as possible (by excellent Roads) with those which run to the westward. Open these to the Ohio, and such others as extend from the Ohio towards Lake Erie," urged Washington, "and we shall not only draw the produce of the western Settlers, but the Fur and peltry trades of the lakes also, to our Ports (Being the nearest, and easiest of transportation) to the amazing encrease of our Exports, while we bind those people to us by a chain which never can be broken."[5] In this light, canals were merely an extension of earlier public works like roads, bridges, fortifications, dams, weirs, dikes, brush cutting and commons clearing.[6] These twinned springs of public and private interests fed early canal promotion.

Regardless of whatever interest they served, canals were speculative in nature, and, whether freeing up coastal river systems or penetrating the mountain fastness, they were meant to make a profit. And they only made money once the work was done, while construction costs came out of capital resources, so there was a built-in incentive to speed the job along as inexpensively as possible. Early waterways thus had necessarily limited objectives. There were few continuous canals of the kind that would dominate later years. Instead, projects were meant merely to improve on nature's existing paths of commerce by clearing out channels in riverbeds, digging a short stretch of canal or building a series of locks around waterfalls or rapids.

3   J. Phillips, A General History of Inland Navigation, Foreign and Domestic . . . (London, 1793), vi.
4   Duc de La Rochefoucault-Liancourt, Travels through the United States of North America . . . in the Years 1795, 1796, and 1797 (London, 1799), 15.
5   George Washington to Jacob Read, 3 Nov. 1784, in The Writings of George Washington from the Original Manuscript Sources, 1745–1799, ed. John C. Fitzpatrick (Washington: Government Printing Office, 1938), v. 27, 489.
6   Richard B. Morris, Government and Labor in Early America (orig. ed. 1946; New York: Harper & Row, 1965), 6–10; Ulrich Bonnell Phillips, A History of Transportation in the Eastern Cotton Belt to 1860 (orig. ed. 1908; New York: Octagon, 1968), 64.

The first locks in North America were built between 1779 and 1783 by a detachment of British Royal Engineers (aided by Loyalist soldiers and Cornish miners) to overcome the rapids above Montreal and facilitate the movement of fur-bearing bateaux. The Susquehanna Canal in Maryland was incorporated in 1783 and eight miles were finally opened to partial traffic in 1803. In 1789 the James River Company completed a four-mile canal to circumnavigate the falls above Richmond, Virginia, and allow passage to tidewater; the upper part of the James was improved so that 220 miles of the river were navigable above Richmond by 1808. The Potomac Company began construction in 1785 on a series of five short canals (amounting to five miles in length) that mastered the falls upriver from Georgetown, including one completed in 1802 that cut through the precipitous rock walls of Great Falls. The Dismal Swamp Canal, originally opened in 1784 as little more than a navigable ditch, was enlarged between 1807 and 1812 to form a nine-mile waterway straddling the Virginia–North Carolina border. Two companies were incorporated in New York in 1792: the Western Inland Lock Navigation Company, which aimed to open navigation from the Hudson River to Lake Ontario by widening the Mohawk River and which built a mile-long canal containing five locks; and the Northern Inland Lock Navigation Company, which sought to connect the Hudson River with Lake Champlain. Two Pennsylvania canals, the Schuylkill & Susquehanna and the Delaware & Schuylkill, finished fifteen miles of work between 1792 and 1794 before grinding to a halt, while the Conewago, a one-mile channel around the Great Falls on the lower Susquehanna, was built between 1793 and 1797. The Spanish dug a four-mile canal between New Orleans and Lake Pontchartrain in the 1790s, and another line was dug from the Mississippi River to Bayou Barataria. And in 1797, Montreal's North West Company built a lock on the Canadian side of the Sault Ste. Marie rapids between Lakes Huron and Superior to facilitate passage of its fur-laden bateaux. But the two largest projects were the Santee and the Middlesex canals. South Carolina's twenty-two-mile-long Santee, connecting the Santee and Cooper rivers and extending Charleston's reach into the interior, was dug mostly by slaves between 1793 and 1800. The Middlesex, twenty-seven miles in length, paralleled the Merrimac River in Massachusetts from Boston to the future site of Lowell, and was built during the years 1794–1803. All these projects reflected the limitations of the capital and labour markets as much as the contemporary mercantile mentality. For the times, though, they were quite ambitious and relatively successful.

Capital and labour

As a rule, artificial waterways of this period were organized as joint-stock companies. Private risk capital was scarce at this time and tended to be invested in proven ways: land schemes, trading ventures and financial institutions, for example. A company structure promised to skim off the excess liquidity from a multitude of sources. Promoters turned to the state for a charter giving permission to market stocks and pursue their particular improvement plan, which amounted to a monopoly. Conditions of construction and operation were laid upon them in return: building specifications, time limits and ceilings on stock circulation, among others.

Capital accumulation remained a problem, as indicated by the involvement of canal companies in state-sponsored gambling. Although public investment was a rarity in this period, governments did try to accommodate the needs of early canals by granting companies charters to run lotteries. The Schuylkill & Susquehanna, for instance, planned to sell 50,000 tickets at $10 each, with cash and company stock as prizes, in a lottery designed to raise $400,000.[7] As a rule, these schemes were not very successful, people being as unwilling to risk hard cash on the remote chance of winning as they were to invest in the almost-as-chancy canal stocks.

Canal-building projects experienced money problems because they were unusually expensive business ventures for the time. Conceived as commercial enterprises meant to extend trade and open up new markets, their lifeblood would be the tolls charged on the commerce funneled through the artificial waterway. Before this goal could be achieved, however, the works had to be constructed. An initial survey had to be made to establish a route, the work to be done charted, and obstructions in the riverbed, rapids and other potential obstacles identified. Then a management cadre of administrators, engineers and overseers were employed. Land through which the works passed had to be bought from often reluctant owners who saw the chance to drive a hard bargain; much litigation resulted. Companies also had to provide a workplace with all its physical plant to carry on construction. The Middlesex Canal, for instance, had two blacksmith shops, two sawmills and two gristmills. In addition, many tools were needed, as well as teams of horses and oxen. Hundreds of workers had to be located, then bought, hired or employed, and then housed, clothed and fed.[8] Such an exercise in primitive accumulation

7 Schuylkill & Susquehanna Canal Navigation Company Conference Committee Minute Book (1795–96), 24 April 1795 and following, box 897, Series 2: Records of Associated and Subsidiary Companies, The Reading Company Archive (Accession 1520), Manuscripts Division, Hagley Museum and Library.
8 See Lewis M. Lawrence, "Middlesex Canal" (Boston, 1942), unpublished transcript in the possession of the American Antiquarian Society, Worcester, Mass., 23; Christopher Roberts, *The Middlesex Canal, 1793–1860* (Cambridge, Mass.: Harvard University Press, 1938), 65–67, 108–09; Contract with James Cochran, May 1804, Committee of Survey Minutes, 7 April 1804, file 2, Chesapeake & Delaware Canal Papers, Historical Society of Delaware, Wilmington; Benjamin Latrobe to Benjamin Horner & Son, 2 Sept. 1804, Benjamin Henry Latrobe Collection, MS. 2009, Manuscripts Division, Maryland Historical Association, Baltimore (hereafter MHS); Latrobe to Joshua Gilpin, 8 Sept. 1804, ibid.

meant that, if anything, canal construction at this time was more problematic than setting up early manufactories.

Financial problems usually occurred soon after the opening of construction. Most companies, confronted with climbing costs and defaulting investors, were forced to reorganize and scale back construction, while many, unable to find fresh sources of investment, died a slow death.[9] For example, the Western Inland Lock Navigation Company was incorporated in 1792 with the promise of a matching grant from the New York state legislature. Construction began with 300 hands the following May, but by September had to close down because of the defalcation of many stockholders. The directors even had to borrow $2,500 on their individual credit so as to be able to pay off the mechanics and labourers. Work reopened in January 1794 but on a smaller scale as investors were still not paying. The company consolidated with the Northern Company in an effort to cut management costs, but construction again dragged to a halt and it was only with a state subscription of stock that it restarted in May 1795, too late for the Northern, which collapsed in 1797. The Western managed to drag operations into the 1800s but never made money.[10]

In an attempt to achieve efficient and inexpensive production, canals developed a management structure – a hierarchy of proprietors, a president and board of directors, engineers and overseers – that supervised all facets of construction, including the worrisome responsibilities of recruiting and supervising labour. The most important figure was the engineer, who surveyed the route and directly oversaw construction, making sure that the work was done to specification and on time. This required a degree of skill that was sadly lacking in the New World, and consequently most companies looked to Europe where canal construction had been under way for some decades. In 1774, John Ballendine moved from Great Britain to Virginia "with a Number of Engineers and Artificers" to remove obstructions to navigation on the Potomac. His efforts were unsuccessful, as skill proved inadequate in the face of reluctant investors. In the mid-1780s the nephew of England's famous canal patron, the Duke of Bridgewater, was working for the Susquehanna Company and Washington hoped to have him inspect the Potomac. The Santee Canal's engineer was Colonel Christian Senf, a

9 Washington wrote repeatedly about the problem of defaulting investors in the Potomac Company and how this threatened a suspension of work. Washington to George Mason and David Stuart, 4 Nov. 1787, to Stuart, 30 Nov. 1787, to Thomas Johnson and Thomas Sim Lee, 9 Dec. 1787, in *Writings of George Washington*, ed. Fitzpatrick (see n. 5 above), v. 29, 300–01, 324, 334–55; Washington to John Fitzgerald and George Gilpin, 22 Aug. 1788, ibid., v. 30, 57–58; Washington to Tobias Lear, 12 Jan. 1795, ibid., v. 34, 85–87.

10 *Albany Gazette*, 9, 26 Jan. 1794; *Report of the Directors of the Western and Northern Inland Lock Navigation Companies in the State of New York* . . . (New York, 1796), 3–4; Roger Evan Carp, "The Erie Canal and the Liberal Challenge to Classical Republicanism," Ph.D. diss., University of North Carolina at Chapel Hill, 1986, 99–101.

Swede who had fought with the Hessian troops of General Burgoyne during the Revolution, only to be captured and put to work as an engineer for the South Carolina militia. He later became state engineer.[11] The best-known of these imported experts, however, were William Weston and Benjamin Henry Latrobe. Weston, who had worked on several of England's principal canals, arrived in 1793 to oversee the Delaware & Schuylkill, and later was employed by the Potomac, Middlesex and Western companies. Latrobe arrived in the United States from England in 1796 after having worked on the Rye Harbour improvement and Basingstoke Canal. In 1801 he worked on the Susquehanna Canal, then moved onto the Chesapeake & Delaware in 1804 as chief engineer before gaining prominence with his work in the nation's capital. These individuals were assisted by indigenous mechanics and practical-minded individuals who had an aptitude for engineering though not experience. Chief among them was Laommi Baldwin, builder of the Middlesex Canal, who had trained as a cabinetmaker and studied mathematics before turning to civil engineering.[12] With this mix of foreign talent and native know-how, the first artificial waterway projects got under way. Given the shortage of professionals and the scale of the ventures, though, it is not surprising it was not a smooth process.

Canal construction required that an entire industrial production system had to be set up, strung out over miles through what was often a wilderness and not within the convenient confines of a central shop or mill. Money had to be continually fed into this machine to keep it working or the enterprise would begin to sputter and come coughing and choking to a stop, as often happened. By the end of the early phase of construction, companies were looking for a means of shifting much of the financial and managerial burden onto the shoulders of someone else, to be shed of production and to concentrate on exchange. Contractors – independent builders who took on sections of the work for set rates and were entirely responsible for construction – were the solution hit upon. Initially during these early years, but more so during the height of the Canal Era, contracting dominated the building process. It was a strategy spawned by problems of production, and was meant to free promoters of direct responsibility for the dirty business of digging canals.

11 *Virginia Gazette*, 1 Sept. 1774, in *Plantation and Frontier*, ed. Phillips (see Introduction, n. 2 above), v. 2, 177–78; Wilbur E. Garrett, "Washington's Potowmack Canal," *National Geographic*, v. 171 (June 1987), 742; Washington to Governor William Moultrie, 25 May 1786, in *Writings of George Washington*, ed. Fitzpatrick (see n. 5 above), v. 28, 439–41; F. A. Porcher, *The History of the Santee Canal* (Charleston: South Carolina Historical Society, 1903), 4; George Svejda, *Irish Immigrant Participation in the Construction of the Erie Canal* (Washington: Division of History, National Park Service, 1969), 4.

12 *Canal Navigation in Pennsylvania* (see n. 1 above), 68; Bacon-Foster, "Potomac Route to the West" (see Introduction, n. 2 above), 180–81; William H. Shank, *Towpaths to Tugboats: A History of American Canal Engineering* (York, Pa.: The American Canal and Transportation Center, 1982), 16–17; Carp, "Erie Canal and the Liberal Challenge to Classical Republicanism" (see n. 10 above), 102; Shaw, *Canals for a Nation* (see Introduction, n. 12 above), 6.

Mobilizing an adequate labour force in what was a noncapitalistic labour market was the second major problem confronting canal construction. The majority of the population was either involved in petty production or subordinated to a master who controlled their labour, either as a journeyman, bonded labourer or slave, and was thus largely kept out of the labour market.[13] This situation was compounded by the fact that mechanization had not made many inroads, and production, as a result, expanded largely by employing more labour. Yet there was a limit to the number of workers available for casual employment, particularly outside urban areas. And the labour requirements of canal construction were unusually high for the time. Work was carried on in a multitude of small settings within the economy as a whole. Outside of the largest plantations and a very few manufactories, most industries only had five to twenty labourers per place of production. By comparison, larger canals required from five hundred to one thousand workers, and a rough estimate could be hazarded of three to four thousand workers engaged in the industry during the peak of the early phase of construction in the mid-1790s.[14] Companies found it difficult to meet this demand, and labour shortages were a recurring problem into the 1830s.

The late eighteenth-century labour market was also a tableau of productive relationships – owner and slave, master and servant, employer and employee – all of them transforming under economic and social pressures. Canal companies naturally utilized all forms of labour. Slaves were hired and purchased, indentured servants were bought off ships in the Atlantic harbours, and wage labourers were contracted with by the year, month and day.

Slavery as a labour system held certain advantages. Workers did not require payment other than rudimentary food and shelter, and a system of codified racial oppression held them in place and subjected them to virtually open-ended discipline. Conversely, like all labour, slaves could be in short supply and expensive. When owned, they had to be provided for when they could not work because of age, illness, infirmity or the weather, and hired slaves often needed to be supported through short periods of inaction. Also, the option vanished for increasing parts of the industry as state after state in the North abolished slavery. Although the institution persisted and flourished in the South, the dominance of the plantation

---

13 One study roughly estimates that by 1820 only 31% of free labourers in the United States were wage earners (42% by 1850). David M. Gordon, Richard Edwards and Michael Reich, *Segmented Work, Divided Workers: The Historical Transformation of Labor in the United States* (Cambridge: Cambridge University Press, 1982), Table 6.1, 230.

14 Morris, *Government and Labor in Early America* (see n. 6 above), 37–44. For canals, see Bacon-Foster, "Potomac Route to the West" (see Introduction, n. 2 above), 170; *Report of the Directors of the Western and Northern Inland Lock Navigation Companies* (see n. 10 above), 3–4; *Canal Navigation in Pennsylvania* (see n. 1 above), 68; Porcher, *Santee Canal* (see n. 11 above), 6.

agricultural system meant there was a dearth of "floating labour" that could be diverted into transportation projects.[15]

Despite these disadvantages, slaves were the typical labourers on Southern internal improvement projects. As a rule, they were hired from their owners for a stipulated period (most often by the year or quarter-year). In December 1786, for example, the Potomac Company advertised for 100 slaves, offering £20 Virginia currency per annum plus clothes and provisions. Still, planters were loath to risk their valuable property in what was dangerous work. "An idea is entertained by the proprietors of them," wrote Washington, "that the nature of the work will expose them to dangers which are not compensated by the terms." The company took pains to calm such fears. "The Owners of Negroes, who wish to hire, may be assured that their Slaves will be well fed and humanely treated." Some companies in the South avoided the problem by buying slaves, like the Dismal Swamp Canal Company, which owned six in 1807.[16] These labourers would always be at hand, but would also have to be cared for even when their labour was not needed. Hiring thus made slavery more economically flexible and more suited to the needs of the industry.

There was always a component of free labour on Southern projects, figuring most significantly in such border states as Maryland and Delaware, and even in Virginia it played an important role in later years. In fact, the presence of wage workers on the Potomac was one consideration in the decision to hire slaves. In 1785, Thomas Johnson (the first governor of the state of Maryland) complained to Washington that "several disorderly fellows" had to be discharged from the works because of their conduct. In light of such disciplinary problems with free labourers, Johnson recommended hiring slaves and buying indentured servants as "their Labour will be more valuable than that of common white Hirelings." But outside the South, slaves were not a factor; even in Maryland the Potomac Company found it difficult getting slaves and had to petition the state legislature for permission to use those of Virginia.[17] As a result, Northern canals turned to two other sources of labour, indentured servants and wage workers.

Like slavery, unfree white labour was developed to overcome the problem of labour supply in colonial economies. Bonded white servitude occupied a halfway point between chattel slavery and free labour. Neither owned in body nor free to ply their labour where they would, indentured servants

15 Phillips, *History of Transportation* (see n. 6 above), 9.
16 *Virginia Journal*, 7 Dec. 1786; Washington to Thomas Johnson, 20 Dec. 1785, in *Writings of George Washington*, ed. Fitzpatrick (see n. 5 above), v. 28, 365; *Virginia Gazette*, 13 Dec. 1792; Alexander Crosby Brown, *The Dismal Swamp Canal* (Chesapeake, Va.: Norfolk County Historical Society, 1970), 46.
17 Thomas Johnson to Washington, 21 Sept. 1785, McPherson-Johnson Papers, MS. 1714, MHS; *Third Annual Report of the Chesapeake and Ohio Canal Company* (Washington, 1829), Appendix, pp. xxxvii–xxxviii.

signed away a stipulated number of years of their labour in return for the costs of passage and provisions during their term of indenture.[18] In some regions, particularly New England, unfree labour was never that significant, whereas in the South and parts of the mid-Atlantic colonies it was much more important. By the end of the eighteenth century, it was dying out everywhere, although isolated cases are reported as late as the 1820s.[19]

Indentured servitude was fading just as the first artificial waterways were getting under way. Still, it was used and for the same reasons that led to its development in the first place. Labour shortage made a guaranteed supply attractive, but, as with slaves, this became a liability when work slowed or came to a halt and servants still needed to be provided for. Of course, in dire times the problem could be obviated by converting human into liquid capital; for example, when the Potomac Company was in financial difficulties in the late 1790s and work had been suspended, money was raised by selling its German servants. Indentured labour also promised masters a labour discipline that should have sped along construction. This was a selling point for Washington after he was disappointed by reluctant slaveowners.[20] But unfree white labour proved fractious by running away, stealing and fighting. This fact, as well as dwindling availability and the high cost of provisions, led canal companies outside the South to turn increasingly to free labour.

Wage labour dated virtually from the time of settlement. Creeping commercialization of agriculture acted to siphon a segment of the population from the land and into the labour market. There was no immediate transformation from petty agricultural producer to landless proletarian. The production system of early manufacturing offered a means of performing cash labour at home, while others left the farm to work in cities and towns to return periodically with cash in pocket. Canal work figured as such a temporary opportunity. At the time of the first waterway projects, much of the available free labour was at this transitional stage, not fully severed from the land but requiring the cash income that the work offered. These people's needs lured them into canal work, but the soil's continuing promise of independence checked a full commitment to wage labour. They thus tended to move back and forth between the two as need arose.

18 Abbot E. Smith, *Colonists in Bondage: White Servitude and Convict Labor in America, 1607–1776* (orig. ed. 1947; Gloucester, Mass.: Peter Smith, 1965), 4–5; David W. Galenson, *White Servitude in Colonial America: An Economic Analysis* (New York: Cambridge University Press, 1982), 10–13, 176–77; Sharon V. Salinger, *"To Serve Well and Faithfully": Labor and Indentured Servants in Pennsylvania, 1682–1800* (New York: Cambridge University Press, 1987).

19 Galenson argued that it declined between the Revolutionary and Napoleonic wars as a result of a shift to slavery, rising costs and declining immigration. *White Servitude in Colonial America* (see n. 18 above), 4, 174–79.

20 Bacon-Foster, "Potomac Route to the West" (see Introduction, n. 2 above), 186; Washington to Johnson, 20 Dec. 1785, in *Writings of George Washington*, ed. Fitzpatrick (see n. 5 above), v. 28, 365.

Wage work offered canal management a flexible and attractive labour source. Hired when needed, discarded when not, free labourers ideally were factors of production that could be manipulated to make the most profitable business equation. But in times of labour shortages like this period, the very mobility that made wage labour so attractive also contained a constant threat that there would not be enough workers to do the job. They had been liberated from the soil and craftshop to serve the interests of capital, but their freedom was problematic for the employer, for they could move where and when they wanted as circumstances allowed.

River improvement companies faced the dual problem of getting and keeping adequate numbers of workers, and were rarely able to gather together as many workers as they would have liked. They were forced to advertise and to send out recruiting agents to secure an adequate force. The Potomac Company put notices in Philadelphia, Baltimore and Alexandria papers offering "liberal wages . . . with provisions and a reasonable Quantity of Spirits," and promising extra benefits for "such as are dextious [sic] in boring and blowing Rocks." George Washington, the company's president, sought to lure miners experienced with "the blowing of Rocks under Water," promising work if they were "not extravagant in their demands." The Middlesex placed ads in papers and sent representatives into the interior looking for men. New York's Western and Northern Lock Navigation companies called for workers in the hundreds, attracting people from as far as Pennsylvania, Vermont, Connecticut and Canada. The Schuylkill & Susquehanna and Delaware & Schuylkill canals sent agents to the "Eastern States" (New England) to recruit over 1,000 hands.[21] Still, complaints about labour shortages were a common refrain in this early era as for decades to come.

Once they gathered together a group of labourers, canal officials then had to try to keep them at work. The various opportunities opened at this time in household production and alternative employment gave workers a degree of choice that proved a drain on supply. An examination of a payroll from the Delaware & Schuylkill Canal for the period May 1794 to July 1795

---

21 Proceedings, Potomac Company (hereafter POT/PRO), 31 May 1785 (Letterbook A, pp. 2–3), Potomac Company Papers, series 160, Records of the National Park Service, Record Group 79, National Archives of the United States, Washington, D.C. (hereafter NA/RG79); Washington to Clement Biddle, 27 July 1785, in *Writings of George Washington*, ed. Fitzpatrick (see n. 5 above), v. 28, 211–12; Baldwin Report, 15 July–15 Aug. 1795, Middlesex Reports, 1794–1799, Mss. 7, Box 2, file 1 (hereafter Middlesex Reports), Baldwin Collection, Baker Library, Harvard University Graduate School of Business Administration, Cambridge, Mass.; *Albany Gazette*, 6 Dec. 1792, 15 June 1795; Ronald E. Shaw, *Erie Water West: A History of the Erie Canal 1792–1854* (Lexington: University of Kentucky Press, 1966), 19; Nathan Miller, "Private Enterprise in Inland Navigation: The Mohawk Route Prior to the Erie Canal," *New York History*, v. 31 (Oct. 1950), 399–400; Minutes of the Proceedings of Conference Committees, 22 Oct., 16, 17 Nov., 14 Dec. 1792, 13, 25 Feb. 1793, The President, Managers and Company of the Delaware and Schuylkill Canal Navigation Minute Book, 1792–93 (v. 1037), Series 2, Reading Archive, Hagley Museum and Library.

points to the company's reliance on temporary local labour.[22] Of the 152 common labourers who worked for the company, 64, or roughly four in ten, were employed for ten or fewer days, 38 (25%) for only eleven to thirty days, and 23 (15%) laboured between thirty-one and sixty days. Eight hands (5%) worked from sixty to a hundred days, and a mere 19 (13%) worked more than a hundred days in what could be considered fairly regular employment (Table 1). Clearly the workforce changed from day to day, with only a small core of hands steadily at work. Fluctuating demand accounted for part of this change, but much of it resulted from farmers and farm labourers who moved in and out of canal employment as slack times and the need for cash dictated. It was the same story on the Middlesex Canal, where the chief engineer, Laommi Baldwin, had a policy of hiring local "yeomen." But Baldwin had problems keeping them on the line during the planting and harvesting seasons when farm wages went up or they were needed at home.[23]

The volatility of this early labour market was an obvious block to efficiency. Labour shortages meant that certain tactics had to be adopted to keep workers in place, such as having hands sign contracts stipulating the period and conditions of labour. In return for a wage of 1.66\frac{2}{3}$ per day, "good, skilful, and honest Workmen" on the Chesapeake & Delaware were expected to spend all their working hours on the canal, obey all orders from the engineer or master mason, and conduct themselves "in a sober, & honest manner consistent with the good character which they have hitherto maintained as citizens and workmen." Further, these men promised not to quit the work without permission until it was finished, and sealed the contract with a promise to pay a $100 penalty if they broke any of its conditions.[24] Written contracts were more common with skilled workers, but measures were also taken to tie down common labourers. While paid by the day or month, regular workers often agreed to work for the "season," usually spring to autumn, and most companies held back wages a fortnight to a month so that hands would lose money if they left work.[25]

The experience on the Delaware & Schuylkill probably typified that of

22 Workmen's Time Book, 1793–94, Delaware and Schuylkill Navigation Canal Company Accounts, 1792–95, in The Sequestered John Nicholson Papers, Group 96, Part IV – Individual Business Accounts, 1787–1800, Pennsylvania Historical and Museum Commission, Division of History, Harrisburg.
23 Report of Baldwin, 1 June to 1 July 1797; Baldwin to William Crosley, 17 July 1798, Middlesex Reports (see n. 21 above). Baldwin complained of Joseph Snow, who worked from late April to late May, then left for farm work before being paid. He returned in July and promised to stay on the job if Baldwin gave him his arrears, which the engineer agreed to do, but was off again in a few days with his back pay in his pocket. Baldwin to President and Directors, 23 July 1798, ibid.
24 Contract between Benjamin Henry Latrobe and Matthew Connory, Robert Dun and John Justin, 5 June 1804, folder 2, Chesapeake & Delaware Canal Papers (see n. 8 above).
25 Baldwin to President and Directors, 23 July 1798, Middlesex Reports (see n. 21 above); Articles of Regulations for the Workmen to be imployed [sic] on the Middlesex Canal for the year 1799, Middlesex Canal – Instructions to Workmen, Mss. 7, Box 3, Baldwin Collection.

free labour on early canals. Few followed canal digging as a profession; there was too little of it about, and the work was not appealing enough to lure people with other options into making more than a short-term commitment. The majority were casual workers propped up by another main source of income, using canal work as an opportunity to get hard money to participate in the increasingly monetized economy. The job probably formed part of a strategy to keep outside the market as much as possible – a temporary immersion in commercial relations so as to stay involved in farming and petty production. Many of the people who were employed by the industry can thus be seen as a form of "not-yet-free labour," caught between the worlds of traditional production and industrial wage work, marking a transitional phase in class formation in the early stages of industrialization. These individuals were not entirely severed from control of their labour and could exert a degree of power over their existence. As other options dried up in the nineteenth century and labourers became more dependent on their earnings from canals, the casualness of canal work would have a more harmful effect.

As can be seen by this overview, the labour situation on early canals and river improvements was a patchwork: slavery in the South, free labour predominantly in the North, and indentured servitude spotted throughout but most evident in the mid-Atlantic region. Combined with prevailing labour shortages, this fragmented labour system posed obstacles to an efficient system of production, particularly in the areas where all three overlapped. Very different ways of organizing labour had to be dealt with, as well as competing and often contradictory claims of owners, workers and society as a whole. For example, on the Potomac where all three forms of labour were used, the company was at one and the same time hirers of slave labour, owners of indentured servants and employers of wage workers. Trying to handle these multiple roles made the company somewhat schizophrenic in its attempts to deal with labour relations. Ultimately, the company opted largely for free labour in an effort to rationalize its operations.

From the perspective of labour, this state of affairs made for a socially heterogeneous workforce. African-Americans obviously accounted for the slave contingent. Indentured servants were drawn from England and Germany, but the main source was Ireland. For example, the duc de La Rochefoucault-Liancourt saw among the free workers for the Western Inland Company at Little Falls, New York, "many . . . Irishmen newly arrived, nay Irish convicts, whose conduct is far from beneficial to the country."[26] Most free labour was drawn from the resident population, but

---

26 La Rochefoucault-Liancourt, *Travels through the United States* (see n. 4 above), 362. Advertisements for runaway servants from the Potomac Company bear out this link; where nationality was indicated, it was invariably Irish, and virtually all names appear to be Irish. *Virginia Gazette*, 13, 27 July 1786; [Alexandria] *Virginia Journal*, 11 Oct. 1787.

Irish immigrants were also used. They worked alongside the yeomen on the Middlesex, and it was these individuals who probably constituted the solid core of regular workers. The Western Company even employed Native Americans in 1796 but they quit within two days, after threatening the other workers.[27] Nor did gender pose a barrier to enlistment. Although the evidence is fragmentary, there is some indication that women were involved in the industry, just as they would be increasingly drawn into wage work during the next few decades. Usually women worked on the edges, cooking, cleaning and caring for men in what was but a commercialization of their traditional roles. Some women were even involved in construction. Benjamin Latrobe, engineer on the Chesapeake & Delaware, mentioned being sent "two Irishwomen in men's cloaths for Quarriers." And slave women worked side by side with men on the Santee.[28] As on farms and as would be the case in industry, children were also drawn into the workforce as waterboys, animal tenders and errand runners.[29]

People from around the world and in starkly different power relationships all flowed into canal construction. This pattern reflected the fragmented nature of the labour market at this time and merchant capital's willingness to use whatever materials were at hand to achieve its purpose of profit. Companies made the choice of which type to use, according to availability, dependability, flexibility and prevailing norms. Already emerging trends were evident, however. Indentured servitude was declining in importance, there was a shift to free labour in the North tied to growing immigration and the movement of the native-born population off the land, and in the South slavery dominated, although wage work was never fully purged from its public works.

The price of labour

The actual work of canal construction was also a hybrid of old and new. Involving outdoor labour to seasonal rhythms or the more whimsical cycles of weather, with timeworn technology powered by man and beast, the job clearly evoked a familiar world of work. At the same time, the numbers involved and sheer size of many projects, the way individuals moved in and out of the job, the organization of full-time workers into virtually all-male enclaves bent on the single purpose of production, all pointed toward an industrial future. Canallers were caught between the old and the new, and the jarring, uncoordinated shifts from the former to the latter exacted their price in social and physical terms.

27 Shaw, *Erie Water West* (see n. 21 above), 19.
28 Regulations of C. Myers, engineer, 1 Sept. 1796, Potomac Company Correspondence and Reports, Potomac Company Papers, series 162, NA/RG79 (hereafter POT/COR); Latrobe to Thomas Vickers Mason, 15 April 1804, Latrobe Collection; Porcher, *Santee Canal* (see n. 11 above), 6.
29 Joseph Watson and James Welsh show up on the Delaware & Schuylkill Workmen's Time Book as "boys," in Aug.–Sept. 1794, though they were paid a man's wage of 5s. 6d.

Canal work did not change substantially during the period under study. The work was done by pick, shovel, auger, wheelbarrow and cart, powered by man, oxen, horses and gunpowder. River and stream beds had to be cleared of all impediments including rocks, sandbars and dead trees, and new channels sometimes had to be cut. More intransigent obstacles like rapids required the digging of a canal along the riverbank. Usually this involved clearing all trees and brush, levelling the land and excavating the bed, all done by shovel and pick and hauled off by barrow and cart. A significant amount of skilled work was involved as well, especially in lock making, which involved stonecutting and masonry.[30] But most canal work was fairly simple and familiar: pulling stumps and roots and shovelling dirt or rock rubble into wheelbarrows and oxcarts to be wheeled away to a tip.

Canallers worked in gangs of tens or even hundreds, assuming a scale not often seen before.[31] A production line of sorts was set up that was powered by numbers of workers and was geared to get as much done as quickly as possible. A sense of industrial time and discipline was developing, as indicated by the implementation of strict workplace supervision and a drive system for labour. Work quotas were also sometimes set. Labourers excavating locks on the Potomac works, for example, were expected to dig six feet a day or face losing their liquor rations.[32] Workers suffered as a result of the nature and pace of the work.

First and foremost, it made for long hard days. The hours of work on the Northern Inland Lock Navigation were fairly standard. "To begin at sun rise, and work until eight o'clock; then to work until twelve o'clock, and be allowed one hour for dinner, and then to work until sun set: except that from the fifteenth of June to the 15th of August they shall be allowed two hours for dinner."[33] In summer this would mean a fourteen-to-fifteen-hour workday with about two hours in breaks; in winter the day tended to last ten to twelve hours with one to two off to eat. And the men toiled in all but the worst conditions. A company official on the Potomac reported in the winter of 1796 that "it was so Exceeding Cold we were not able to stand it." Still, work had to go on, but to do so he "was obligd. to give the

---

30 Roberts identified the following skilled occupations on the Middlesex Canal: blacksmiths and apprentices, stone- and bricklayers, blasters, stonecutters, boatbuilders and boat painters, teamsters, painters, millers, millhands, stewards, overseers, cooks and clerks. *Middlesex Canal* (see n. 8 above), 75.
31 For example, the initial workforce on the Potomac was split into two groups of fifty hands, each under a superintendent, assistant and three overseers. La Rochefoucault-Liancourt noted that the 250 workers on the canal at Little Falls, New York, were organized into companies, and the Northern Company planned to separate 300 labourers into twelve gangs of twenty-five men. POT/PRO, 30 May 1785 (A 1); La Rochefoucault-Liancourt, *Travels through the United States* (see n. 4 above), 362; *Albany Gazette*, 22 Nov. 1792.
32 Roberts, *Middlesex Canal* (see n. 8 above), 75–76; Bacon-Foster, "Potomac Route to the West" (see Introduction, n. 2 above), 185.
33 *Albany Gazette*, 19 Nov. 1792.

Hands one Shilling an Hower."[34] Exposure to the elements caused a variety of physical problems and illnesses, like common colds, flu, heatstroke and frostbite. The wet, swampy areas where much of the work took place also brought more serious health risks in the form of insect-borne diseases like malaria and yellow fever. As a result, workers were often ill, and some companies provided medicines in an effort to keep them going.[35]

The work also led to many accidents. In addition to the normal minor injuries associated with manual labour, there were more serious casualties, usually associated with blasting, a most imprecise science at this time. James Rumsey, engineer on the Potomac works, reported such an accident in 1785. "One of our best men had the misfortune this morning of haveing both his hands most horridly maimed by a Charge of powder going of [sic] that he was attempting to Bore out, the hammer & auger was blew quite out of sight." Similarly, Michael Bowman, a blaster for the Potomac Company at Shenandoah Falls, had just finished drilling and charging a hole when it took fire and went off. "His situation is scarcely to be described," reported the Maryland Gazette, "having had the fore part of his head blown to pieces, one of his eyes blown out, and his breast and limbs shockingly bruised and mangled." A surgeon was called in and Bowman's wounds were dressed, but it was four weeks before he could be moved to his friends' shanty.[36] Such accidents could not but have an impact on canallers, and were a likely spur to absconding servants. In 1786 Rumsey blandly noted, "we had our Blowers, One Run off the other Blown up."[37]

Labour power was bought, rented and bartered for in canal construction. Unfortunately, no evidence remains of the cost of purchasing indentured servants, but slaves were hired annually at an average of £20 (or $60–70) and "found" (food and lodging) for common labour and £25–30 for skilled.[38] The cost of free labour was approximately the same when the irregularity of their employment is taken into consideration (work usually ranging from May to November). Common labourers on the Potomac in 1785 were paid £2 per month, and the average wage in the mid-1790s was

34 Thomas Bell to President and Directors, 30 Dec. 1796, POT/COR.
35 James Rumsey to William Hartshorn, 20 Sept. 1785: Hartshorn to Richardson Stuart, 2 Oct. 1785; Stuart to Hartshorn, 24 Jan., 10 July 1786, POT/COR.
36 Rumsey to Hartshorn, 26 Sept. 1785, POT/COR; Maryland Gazette, 10 Aug. 1786.
37 Rumsey to Hartshorn, 3 July 1786, quoted in Bacon-Foster, "Potomac Route to the West" (see Introduction, n. 2 above), 164.
38 POT/PRO, 18 Oct. 1785 (A 14), 5 Nov. 1792 (A 42), 22 Dec. 1795 (A 66), 17 Dec. 1800 (A 207–08); Virginia Journal, 7 Dec. 1786; Rumsey to Hartshorn, 26 Nov. 1785, POT/COR; Porcher, Santee Canal (see n. 11 above), 6; Phillips, History of Transportation (see n. 6 above), 36–40; Wayland Fuller Dunaway, History of the James River and Kanawha Company, Columbia University Studies in History, Economics and Public Law, no. 236 (New York, 1922), 31.

$8–12.[39] Skilled workers were paid 25 to 100 percent more than common labour.[40]

Wage rates were high compared with those in Europe, but it is a mistake to assume that scales necessarily translated into earnings. Many factors intruded in canal construction to ensure that a person made but a portion of the rate at which he or she was paid. Although wage labourers were normally hired by the month for the season, they were only paid according to the number of days worked. Interruptions due to the weather, injury, illness or company financial problems were common. Not knowing when or for how long they would be working, free canallers constituted a casual workforce that came and went with demand, a pattern that would become the norm for most manual labour in the industrial age. Many had other work that they could fall back on at this time, but for those without alternatives unemployment was a new, perplexing and threatening experience. Workers on the Delaware & Schuylkill, for example, averaged only 106 work days over a fifteen-month period in 1794–95, or seven days per month. Of course, this included many workers who only stayed a part of the time, but this in itself gives an indication of the amount of work available. Even the regular workers, those with more than 200 days of employment, averaged only seventeen and a half days per month (Table 2).

The casual nature of the work meant that an individual's earnings usually fell substantially below wage rates. Delaware & Schuylkill workers earned an average of $77 for the fifteen months covered by the payroll, or $5 a month. Those with more than 200 days made $169 for an average of $11 a month (Table 3). Regular workers thus earned only a little over half of their wage rates, which then stood at $18–20 a month. For temporary workers, the irregularity of work and consequent diminution of earnings was not a crucial factor as they could always return to the home farm or find another job elsewhere, but those dependent on the industry could be pushed below the subsistence line. This situation was compounded by the possibility that financially strapped companies would be unable to pay cash wages for work done. When construction dragged to a halt on the Chesapeake & Delaware Canal in 1806, for example, the company owed workers almost $16,000 in outstanding promissory notes.[41]

---

39 Payroll for work at Seneca Falls, 15–29 Oct. 1785, file 4, box 4, Miscellaneous Accounts, Potomac Company Papers, series 179, NA/RG79; *Albany Gazette*, 6 Dec. 1792; Delaware & Schuylkill Minute Book, 14 Dec. 1792 (see n. 21 above); POT/PRO, 5 Oct. 1796 (A 85); Reports of Laommi Baldwin, 17 Oct.–1 Dec. 1795, 31 March 1797, and Baldwin to James Sullivan, 7 Feb. 1797, Middlesex Reports (see n. 21 above).

40 Memoranda of Persons who enter and Rate of Pay, April 1795, Middlesex Canal – Memoranda, 1794–1803, file 1, box 3, Mss. 7, Baldwin Collection (see n. 21 above); Report of Baldwin, 17 Oct.–Dec. 1795, Middlesex Reports (see n. 21 above); Roberts, *Middlesex Canal* (see n. 8 above), 81; *Albany Gazette*, 22 Nov. 1792; POT/PRO, 5 Oct. 1796 (A 85).

41 Chesapeak [*sic*] & Delaware Accounts, 1804–1806, filed with Joshua Gilpin, *A Memoir on the Rise, Progress, and Present State of the Chesapeake and Delaware Canal . . .* (Wilmington, De., 1821), in Uncatalogued Canal File uder Chesapeake and Delaware Canal, American Antiquarian Society.

The irregularity of work persisted throughout the Canal Era, swinging as it did to the natural rhythms of the weather and the seasons. From a management perspective, it meant that labour would have to be made as responsive as possible to fluctuating demand, a strong argument for free labour. To wage workers it meant that much of their potential earning power was washed away. In the early years they were protected somewhat by the provision of subsistence by canal companies, but as employers were forced to economize and as labour supply increased, these protections would be stripped away, exposing workers to the harsh realities of the weather and the market.

The purchase of hire price or cash payment was but one component of the wage bill. Free labour, as well as slaves and servants, received part of their earnings in kind, being "found" by their employers. This was a reflection of tradition but also a practical recruitment strategy in an underdeveloped labour market where full-time workers were not expected to provide food and shelter for themselves. Incorporation of subsistence rights was thus meant to attract labour, and to this extent was in workers' interests, but it also made them more dependent on their employers. Thus, before construction could begin canal companies had to make arrangements to provide for the workforce. This could entail the creation of a new settlement with housing, stores, bakeries, smithies and mills because of the often-secluded position of the work site. Benjamin Henry Latrobe faced such a situation when initiating construction on the Chesapeake & Delaware Canal in 1804, as only "two miserable huts" were available in the area. "The country affords little convenience for lodging men," he wrote. "The best plan will be to fix upon some elevated spot, and to build sheds: to lay in a stock of beef pork and potatoes, and perhaps of liquor for the men, and to establish a careful person to manage the provisions & take care of the utensils on the spot. The men had also better lodge in the sheds."[42]

Few employers took such care with the niceties of camp life. Labourers on the Potomac had initially to settle with more rudimentary surroundings. Washington wrote that "as they will be frequently moving, we have provided Tents as most convenient and least expensive, for their accommodation." These were the two guiding principles in company housing, although on the Potomac they could soon allow for the construction of huts. The hands were still living in shanties six years later, but by 1796 the company planned to erect a plank-covered bunkhouse measuring seventy-two feet by eighteen by seven at Great Falls.[43] A shortage of

---

42 Latrobe to Joseph Tatnall, 15 April 1804, Memorandum for Mr Randall, 29 March 1804, Latrobe Collection, MHS.
43 Washington to Edmund Randolph, 16 Sept. 1785, in *Writings of George Washington*, ed. Fitzpatrick (see n. 5 above), v. 28, 267; POT/PRO, 10 Nov. 1785 (A 13); Jacob Hackney's Petition & Account, 9 Dec. 1791, POT/COR; Bacon-Foster, "Potomac Route to the West" (see Introduction, n. 2 above), 182–83.

housing was reported on the southern section of the Middlesex in 1795, but a mess house was built that would shelter fifty men, and the next year a framed barracks was erected in the "great Swamp," where the hands slept on bunk beds filled with straw and covered with tow cloth in these spartan surroundings.[44] For part-time workers who lived at home or boarded with local families, living conditions would be similar to those with which they were familiar. For others who were dependent on company housing, living in virtually all-male barracks housing tens of workers with few amenities would make for an unusual arrangement, in effect a place to sleep when they were not working.

Most labourers also had their food provided by the company. Free and unfree labour on the Potomac received similar daily rations: one pound of salt pork or one and a half pounds of salt beef or one and a half of fresh beef or mutton; one and a half pounds of flour or bread; and "a reasonable quantity of spirits."[45] Alcohol was structured right into the labour exchange, being served out at intervals during the day; labourers for the Potomac Company in the 1780s were promised three gills of rum a day.[46] Company responsibility did not stop with food and drink. Hired slaves and servants had to be provided with clothing, shoes, hats and bedding, as well as given medicine when ill.[47]

Companies had to take special measures to keep so many hands fully provided for, a duty that caused many headaches and led management to seek ways of avoiding the responsibility. Not only was it an onerous task, it was also quite expensive. Boarding alone usually cost almost as much as the wage of common labour. In 1786, when wages on the Potomac were about £2 a month and slaves were being hired at the equivalent of £1 13s., boarding cost £1 11s. Similarly, wages stood at $9 on the Middlesex in 1795, while board was the same amount; two years later it was $11 versus $9.[48] These figures do not include the cost of housing, clothing, blankets or medicines, which would have pushed provisioning costs up to and beyond wage rates. It is clear that this was an expensive arrangement for management, but the subsistence bill was the price that had to be paid for doing industrial business in an essentially commercial world.

Slaves and servants gained little from this system, but it worked more in the interests of free labour. When work and wages came to a standstill food

---

44 Reports of Baldwin, 15 June–15 July, 15 July–15 Aug. 1795, 25 Nov. 1796, Middlesex Reports (see n. 21 above); Roberts, *Midddlesex Canal* (see n. 8 above), 76.

45 POT/PRO, 14 July 1785 (A 6), 18 Oct. 1785 (A 14); *Virginia Journal*, 7 Dec. 1786.

46 POT/PRO, 14 July 1785 (A 6), 1, 2 Feb. 1786 (A 15–16). A gill was usually a quarter-pint, but sometimes a half-pint.

47 Rumsey to Hartshorn, 12, 16 June 1786, POT/COR; Hartshorn to Stuart, 2 Oct. 1785, POT/COR; Stuart to Hartshorn, 10 July 1786, POT/COR; POT/PRO, 18 Oct. 1785 (A 14).

48 POT/PRO, 15 April 1786 (A 17); *Virginia Journal*, 7 Dec. 1786; Report of Baldwin, 17 Oct.–1 Dec. 1795, Middlesex Reports (see n. 21 above); Baldwin to James Sullivan, 7 Feb. 1797, Middlesex Reports (see n. 21 above).

and shelter usually continued, thereby insulating workers from under-employment. At the same time, it bred a dependence on one's employers. Control of the necessities of life is a powerful weapon to hold over the head of another. Unlike part-time workers who split their world into subsistence and monetary segments, and could retreat to the land when desired, true canallers had no control over the means of production, were usually without a home, and would have to think twice before moving on. Like slavery and indentured servitude, "mixed" payment for free labour indicated that this was not a wholly capitalistic productive system.

The way in which canal construction was carried on shaped the lives of its labour force. Relatively large bodies of men working side by side during the day, often sharing the same sleeping and eating quarters, made for an intimate environment. Similarly, the relationship between canal companies and their labourers appeared close on the surface. Officials could have personal knowledge of their men, as did Benjamin Latrobe, who wrote that fifty were employed at Elkforge, "all of them hands who have formerly been under my direction."[49] Whether known or not, the provision of food, shelter and clothing cemented a bond between master and hand. But paternalism's human flourishes merely cloaked the exploitation inherent in slavery, indentured servitude and, to a lesser extent, free labour. The difficulty of the work, the harshness of living conditions, the absence or irregularity of payment, all bred tensions in the production relationship that were blunted and redirected but never wholly eased by the coercion or conciliation of unfree and free labour. From the beginning, early canals experienced difficulties that led them to experiment with different labour types, to tighten up and systematize discipline, and ultimately to wash their hands of the problem.

The labour problem

"Riots and quarrels are now becoming so frequent that the exercise of legal power has become absolutely necessary – not only to cheque but to secure offenders of the public peace", wrote C. Meyers, the Potomac Company's engineer in the mid-1790s. Meyers was not alone in his view of the workforce. Years earlier, the company had noted in its Proceedings that "the Hands employed on the work of opening the Navigation of the River are irregular and disorderly in their Behaviour," leading it to decide to purchase sixty servants to use instead of free labourers. James Rumsey, engineer at Seneca Falls, complained that he had "a Bulleying Sett" of hands who drove off another labourer and had to be dismissed, and Thomas Johnson wrote of several "disorderly Fellows" who had to be discharged,

49   Latrobe to Isaac Hazlehurst, 14 May 1804, Latrobe Collection, MHS.

suggesting hired slaves be used instead.[50] The problem of unruly workers was not confined to the Potomac and did not only involve free labourers, although they tended to be more volatile.

Servants and slaves, unlike free labourers, did not have the option of changing jobs if the conditions were not to their liking, but they did the next-best thing by absconding. The Potomac Company was plagued with runaways and this was an important factor in their decision to rely more heavily on free labour. Absconding was an individualistic response to bondage, an attempt to extricate oneself from an institution rather than a collective attempt at resistance, which the power of masters made unlikely. Slavery studies have indicated that running away was a means of eluding work for a while or of visiting family who lived on another plantation more often than a serious attempt to escape slavery, and this was probably the case on canals.[51]

Indentured servants fled more often because they had a better chance of success, their white complexion and the willingness of employers elsewhere to ask no questions acting in their favour. Information gathered from runaway servant advertisements from the Potomac Company gives a sense at least of who they were if not specifically why they fled.[52] Of twenty-five individuals, twenty were Irish, one Scottish, and the nationality of four was not given (although their names appear to be Irish). The mean age was twenty-five. Physically, they averaged about five and a half feet tall, and twenty were said to have distinguishing features: scars, pockmarks, lameness. One man's face was pitted with gunpowder from a blast going off in his hands, and another could be identified by a bite mark on his cheek. A number also had been disfigured by the company, their eyebrows and strips of scalp having been shaved for earlier episodes of flight. Whether due to their current occupation or not, it is clear that servants bore the scars of a difficult life. No direct evidence of motivation exists, but it is not hard to fathom why they ran away. The bonds of servitude naturally chafed people who had experienced freedom, and the good chance that they could get away was an everpresent incentive. The difficulty of river improvement work itself must have made the thought of freedom even more appealing. Still, servants did not usually flee on their own. Of twenty-five cases from the Potomac Company, two servants fled singly (although one of these went off with a free labourer and the other was expected to join up with another party of absconders), and there were two groups of two, two of three, one party of six and one of seven. Whatever their rationale, absconding servants

50 C. Meyers to Governor of Virginia, n.d. [1796?], reproduced in *Plantation and Frontier*, ed. Phillips (see Introduction, n. 2), v. 2, 178; POT/PRO, 9 Sept. 1785 (A 10); Rumsey to Hartshorn, 11 Sept. 1785, POT/COR; Johnson to Washington, 21 Sept. 1785, McPherson-Johnson Papers, MHS.
51 *Virginia Gazette*, 5 Aug. 1790.
52 *Maryland Gazette*, 16 Feb. 1786; *Virginia Gazette*, 22 June, 13, 27 July 1786; *Virginia Journal*, 1 Feb., 21 June, 17 July, 11 Oct. 1787.

were a thorn in the side of the company. Their light-footedness cancelled out the advantage of white bonded labour – its immobility – and if successful meant that the company was not only losing a manpower source but also the capital invested in the indenture purchase.

Free labourers were even more of a nuisance, but conditions in the industry undoubtedly contributed to their discontent and disorder. Workers stole but not always for thieving's sake. They took medicine, food and tools for their own use, cut wood to heat their huts, filched gunpowder to sell, and stole money to buy things they could not afford.[53] Their depredations and rowdiness often brought them into conflict with local residents, as happened on the Schuylkill & Susquehanna Canal in 1783 when Irish labourers clashed with the German residents of Myerstown, Pennsylvania. Some twenty years later, Irish canallers from the Chesapeake & Delaware fought with jockies and gamblers, as well as the residents of Elkton, Maryland, at a fair. Seemingly just a brawl among different ethnic groups – Irish, natives and blacks – it came at a time when the company was experiencing financial difficulties and there had been problems paying the workers.[54] These two examples highlight a pattern that was to persist throughout the Canal Era: canallers, separated and differentiated by the work they did, fought all and sundry out of frustration as much as for the hell of it.

Free labourers also came into conflict with their employers. Disputes in these years tended to be over nonpayment of wages rather than rates, a problem rooted in canal companies' recurring financial troubles. When investors did not pay up on their stock and construction costs exceeded estimates, canals were strapped to meet their commitments. This could lead workers to join together to make a collective protest, although often one more akin to assault than a strike.

The Potomac Company had worker troubles from very early on. In 1785, wages were held back because it was reluctant to send the payroll from Georgetown through the near-wilderness to the work camps upriver, fearing robbery. Washington complained that "paying the workmen every fortnight" was "rather troublesome," and suggested "some once a month would do better." The hands, many of whom were owed "a hole month's pay," had another perspective. Rumsey reported: "the men are much Dissatisified that they Do not get the money as Soon as it is Due, and Every time that they get a Little Drunk, I am cursed and abused about their money." He had managed to escape injury thus far, but feared "bad

53 See Hartshorn to Stewart, 2 Oct. 1785, 24 Jan. 1786, POT/COR; Jacob Hackney's Petition & Account, 9 Dec. 1791, POT/COR; Bacon-Foster, "Potomac Route to the West" (see Introduction, n. 2 above), 164.
54 Alvin F. Harlow, *Old Towpaths: The Story of the American Canal Era* (New York: D. Appleton & Co., 1926), 54; Latrobe to Joshua Gilpin, 26 Aug., 2, 8, 12 Sept., 7 Oct. 1804, Latrobe Collection, MHS; Latrobe to Adam Farquair, 24 Oct. 1804, ibid.

consequences in Such frequent attacks." The company felt that the workers should not complain about being paid once a month when it was feeding them. This probably was little consolation to Rumsey at the front lines. Laommi Baldwin confronted a similar situation on the Middlesex in 1795. When work was suspended at Woburn, he did not have enough money to pay the men, who "grew unruly and clamorous." Baldwin confided that "during this period my situation was rather uncomfortable." And in the spring of 1804, Benjamin Latrobe wrote that no wages had been given on the Chesapeake & Delaware, and "the men must work upon hope." This was a prophetic statement, for by late summer they were doing just this, as contractors were in financial distress and unable to pay their hands. Only the company's intervention prevented "a very general mutiny," and one of the contractors was in fact taken hostage by several workers. Latrobe calmed the situation with $8,000 expressed from Wilmington.[55]

Canallers occasionally joined together to assert their rights. This was the case on the Middlesex Canal in 1798 when a number of hands demanded that wages be raised beyond $8; Baldwin refused, however, and they departed. Two years earlier, when New York's Western Company hired additional labourers to be paid on the basis of how much soil they excavated, the older hands, who were paid by the day, threatened them and refused to let them work. This turnout worried Philip Schuyler, the Western's president, who feared that "the most pernicious consequences will certainly result from such daring and unwarrantable attempts," the company being "left so entirely to their mercy" in the future if it acquiesced this one time.[56] Schuyler's refusal to bargain would become the gospel of later canal managers when strikes were a common occurrence.

Most labour unrest in this period was reactive, responses to the breaking of established relations rather than demands for additional benefits, but occasionally unrest became assertive. In either case, reactive or assertive, protesting canallers were more threatening to companies because they could shut down work, whereas runaway slaves and servants only weakened manpower. As well, free workers could not be herded together for a collective head shaving. To solve their labour problems, companies had to come up with the money or ride out the storm. To head off future disorder, a number of companies eventually implemented a stricter regimen of discipline and attempted to routinize the payment system.

55 Washington to Edmund Randolph, 16 Sept. 1785, in *Writings of George Washington*, ed. Fitzpatrick (see n. 5 above), v. 28, 267; Rumsey to Hartshorn, 26 Sept. 1785, POT/COR; Hartshorn to Rumsey, 30 Sept. 1785, POT/COR; Report of Baldwin, 12 Sept.–17 Oct. 1795, Middlesex Reports (see n. 21 above); Latrobe to Thomas Vickers, 3 May 1804, Latrobe Collection, MHS; Latrobe to Gilpin, 26 Aug., 2, 8, 12 Sept., ibid.
56 Baldwin to President and Directors, 30 March 1798, Middlesex Reports (see n. 21 above); Schuyler cited in Miller, "Private Enterprise in Inland Navigation" (see n. 21 above), 400–01; Carp, "Erie Canal and the Liberal Challenge to Classical Republicanism" (see n. 10 above), 101–02.

Whether running away, rioting and brawling, or merely not working as hard as the company would like, canal workers caused problems for their bosses. Pressed from above by financial pressures and from below by recalcitrant navvies, canal companies attempted to hone production, moving to establish complete control over the labour process by cutting costs and tightening discipline. Their effort to create a stable, dependable, flexible, manageable workforce met with mixed results. It would only be some fifty years later, when conditions within the industry had altered markedly, that this ideal came within reach.

The obvious way to cut costs was to spend less on labour. This could be done in several ways: by paying lower wages, by making hands provide for themselves and by getting them to work longer and harder. It was difficult to implement any of these policies, however, as labour shortages meant that slaves, servants and wage workers alike were in great demand. This did not keep employers from seeking the grail of cheap labour, though. Officials of Pennsylvania's transportation companies thought the silver chalice could be found in New England, and sent an agent there to hire 1,150 men. He went offering unchristian terms: 3s.–3s. 6d. a day (roughly 40–47¢) without food and shelter. But it was found that wages there stood at 3s. 9d. (50¢) in summer. The company then determined to offer $5–6 a month plus provisions and shelter. The agent returned in several months with only a few hands and the news that New England workers were receiving $7. The initiative to cut wage costs was an abject failure, and two years later the Delaware & Schuylkill was paying $18–20 a month for its common labour.[57]

One advantage free labour had over slave and indentured from the perspective of a cost-cutting management was that the food chain that linked labourer to boss could be uncoupled, a fact soon grasped by both New York canals. In 1792, the Northern Company advertised for hands at half a dollar a day. Workers had to provide their own bedding; wooden bowls, kettles and tools were supplied. The company also tried to commercialize the subsistence relationship. "The overseers, laborers and cooks to find their own provisions," blandly noted the ad in the biggest departure from common practice, "but as they may not conveniently be able to procure them, the company will lay in a stock of provisions . . . which will be sold them at prime cost, with the charges of transportation only added." This stripping away of subsistence shifted an added burden onto workers' shoulders that would have to be paid for out of unchanged wages. The roots of truck payment, which was to anger canallers in later years, can be seen in this move. The company also sought to keep hands in

---

57 Delaware & Schuylkill Minute Book, 22 Oct., 16, 17, 20 Nov., 14 Dec., 1792, 13 Feb. 1793 (see n. 21 above); Delaware & Schuylkill Workmen's Time Book, 1793–94 (see n. 22 above).

place by withholding fifteen days' wages until the end of the season, "unless they shall forfeit it by quitting the service without being discharged before the time is expired for which they shall engage."[58] The Northern clearly wanted the best of both worlds: limited responsibility and maximum control. How successful it was is not apparent. But three years later its sister company, the Western, called for workers with essentially the same terms, although wages for labourers could vary from 50¢ to 75¢ "according to their respective abilities."[59]

Another way of bringing down expenses was to get more work from labourers by implementing a drive system powered by coercion or incentive. Changing the time-based mode of payment to a job-based, piece-rate system could have the desired effect. People paid by the day tend to do the minimum amount of acceptable work and to look busy without being busy, always a sore spot with employers. It was thought that paying by task increased speed and exertion, an implicit goal that workers resisted. This was the cause of conflict on the Western in 1796. Similarly, the Potomac early on tried to get its miners to accept pay by performance rather than by day, but they demanded one shilling a foot, "which we think too much." No agreement appears to have been reached. The company's common labourers, paid a monthly wage, were still spurred to added effort by liquor.[60] Finally, the Middlesex decided in 1795 to abandon time-based pay. Work was suspended, the hands were paid off (mostly with promises as there was not enough money), and new employment was offered on a job basis. The men refused and threatened Baldwin, but within a few months the engineer could report that there were no more day or month hands in company employ.[61] The victory was short-lived, however, as time wages were soon again in place. Faced with periodic labour shortages, canal companies found it difficult to implement policies that were disliked by workers.

The same forces were working on the employer–slave relationship. Whereas when the Potomac hired slaves in 1785 they were totally provided for, eight years later it required that owners supply good clothing and a blanket. As well, the company stipulated that any time lost through either sickness or elopement would be discounted from the hire price or made

---

58 *Albany Gazette*, 22 Nov. 1792. The Middlesex Canal sought to achieve the same ends by offering a higher wage rate for workers who stayed the whole season than for those who left before their term was up. Articles of Regulations for the workmen on the Middlesex Canal, 1799, Middlesex Canal – Instructions to Workmen (see n. 25 above).

59 *Albany Gazette*, 15 June 1795.

60 Washington to Edmund Randolph, 16 Sept. 1785, in *Writings of George Washington*, ed. Fitzpatrick (see n. 5 above), v. 28, 267; Bacon-Foster, "Potomac Route to the West" (see Introduction, n. 2 above), 185.

61 Reports of Baldwin, 12 Sept.–17 Oct. 1795, 2 Dec. 1795–6 Jan. 1796, 14 Jan.–22 Feb. 1796, Middlesex Reports (see n. 21 above).

good through labour.[62] The Potomac wanted to put as much of the burden of illness and accident as possible on the slaveowner.

Alternatively, some companies tried to increase efficiency by tightening their grasp on production. This involved increasing their control over their workers, first by imposing a strict code of labour discipline and second by systematizing all aspects of camp life so as to create a factorylike model of work organization in a distinctly unfactorylike setting. The directors of the Chesapeake & Delaware Canal summed up this goal when they prematurely congratulated themselves on their progress in 1805, reporting that "a body of workmen have been formed and reduced into system," which would "carry on the undertaking with as much expedition, and as compleat a control over the workmen and expenditure" as possible.[63]

The superintendent or overseer became a key figure in enforcing labour discipline. "The overseer," according to the Northern Company, "shall constantly attend the men when at work, and he and they shall obey all the reasonable commands of the person or persons employed by the directors to superintend and direct the works." The Middlesex determined to hire a number of overseers "well calculated for driving work on," and with very specific duties. They were to "see that they [the men] are all out to work in season that they are all imployed to the best advantage that they have their drink without hinderonc [sic] to the business . . . that they do not linger at meal times." And workers were to be fired when they did not abide by these wishes. The Middlesex, for example, made money available to superintendents for immediate dismissal of hands who did "not answer their wished for industry & attention."[64]

Enforcing discipline was a productive strategy that required supervision. Overseers served this purpose, but direction without system is pointless. Some companies went halfway, establishing rules and regulations to be followed, and a few attempted to impose order on the entire production process encompassing all aspects of workers' lives. The expedients adopted were gang labour and barracks accommodation, which drew on slavery and military models and promised maximum supervision both during and after work.

Matildaville, the construction camp at Great Falls on the Potomac in the late 1790s, most closely approximated this ideal.[65] Matildaville was one of the first planned towns in the United States. Its main promoter, Light-Horse Harry Lee, sought to take advantage of the canal and water power

62 POT/PRO, 18 Oct. 1785 (A 14), 5 Nov. 1792 (A 42); William Deakans to Hartshorn, 29 Dec. 1793, POT/COR.
63 Second Report of the Directors of the Chesapeake & Delaware Canal Co., 1805, in Gilpin, *Memoir on the Rise, Progress, and Present State of the Chesapeake and Delaware* (see n. 41 above), Appendix, 63.
64 *Albany Gazette*, 22 Nov. 1792; [Rough sketch on copy of a letter to directors] Baldwin, 1 Jan. 1798, Middlesex Reports (see n. 21 above); Report of a Committee, 6 May 1797, ibid.
65 See, Garrett, "Washington's Potowmack Canal" (see n. 11 above), especially the illustrations of the settlement, pp. 720–23, 743.

to set up a thriving commercial centre. An inn, sawmill and store were among the businesses that sprang up at the site. In addition, it was the headquarters for the Potomac Company works at the falls, a spectacular flight of locks cut through rock cliffs overhanging the river. Workers' quarters and the superintendent's house were erected in close proximity to the construction site. An old black man butchered the meat for a central eating house set up in a converted smithy that could accommodate thirty men at a time. Two women were kept busy there cooking the beef and baking bread in an oven nine feet by nine. Hands were given ration tickets to trade for food at the mess hall.[66]

A system of regulations was also adopted to impose order. C. Meyers, the engineer, had experienced discipline problems with the hands, and had sought magisterial powers to deal with the situation. Frustrated with this request, he tried to lay down his own law.[67] The day was parcelled out according to an industrial time discipline, and every effort was made to wring as much work as possible out of the day. "The Bell must be rung every morning $\frac{1}{4}$ before Six OClock – exactly at 8 OClock for breakfast $\frac{1}{4}$ before 9 – exactly at 1 OClock $\frac{1}{4}$ before 2 and exactly before 6 OClock each day." The foreman had to make sure that the men were working when they should be; a company snoop could appear anytime and the foreman would have to account for absentees or face fines of one dollar for a missing "artifiser," 50¢ for a borer and 25¢ for a labourer. Overseers also had to account for all gunpowder used. Labourers who missed part of a day would be charged for their rations in proportion to the amount of time they were absent; for example, a quarter-ration for a quarter-day missed. And rations had to be drawn at the set times or the hand would go hungry. Meyer also sought to extend the company reach into the barracks. It was required "that the Huts & Cook houses be kept clean and in good order duly washed and sprinkled the better to preserve health and avoid infection." The women hired to cook and care for the men were subject to fines for a roster of offenses: "for not having the meals ready for the men at the stated hours $\frac{1}{4}$ dollar – for not having the Hutts clean swept out beds made house sprinkled $\frac{1}{2}$ dollar." Although to the advantage of the men living there, these sanitary regulations were symptomatic of management's desire to poke its nose into every nook and cranny of their lives.[68]

Other canals implemented discipline packages piecemeal, but with the same goal: the systemization of the labour process in an effort to cut costs and increase efficiency. They turned to the examples of plantation slavery and the military. Slavery had pioneered gang labour, communal accommodations and the use of overseers. The military, one of the few earlier

66 William Darke to John Goulding, 29 Aug. 1796, POT/COR; John Templeman's observations of orders, 2 Feb. 1797, ibid.; Richard Kennedy to John Goulding, 28 March 1797, ibid.
67 Regulations of C. Meyers, 6 June, 5, 17 Aug., 1, 3 Sept., 3 Oct. 1796, POT/COR.
68 See also Mary Stetson Clarke, *The Old Middlesex Canal* (Melrose, Mass.: Hilltop Press, 1974), 36.

institutions to confront the same problems of a large labour supply and the need for an efficiently functioning administration, had relied from time immemorial upon a hierarchy of ranks, each with its specific functions. It was an army's abilities in mobilizing, provisioning, transporting, and executing maneuvers that made the difference between winning and losing. Given the Revolutionary background of many canal promoters, it is not surprising that work camps had a martial air to them. Slavery and the army also shared a fundamental concern for discipline and order. Work was overseen by middle-level managers, employees supervising lower-level employees. The needs of internal improvement projects paralleled those of these two institutions, and canals attempted to ape their success by establishing a system of gang labour, barracks living and rigid discipline.

Plantation quarters and military barracks were transformed into work camps on canals. Hands lived in bunkhouses – large open-plan structures containing rows of beds or pallets of straw, perhaps a hearth, a door and windows with no covers – or congeries of smaller buildings. Food was prepared in the shelters or at a central kitchen from which rations would be distributed in exchange for ration tickets. Hands would eat, rest and sleep at the camp in the interlude between bouts of toil. Proximity to the work site blurred the line between labour and the rest of life. Bunkhouses in no way approximated a household, but were meant to meet the minimum requirements for shelter. The barracks system became a production line for replenishing energy necessary to prop up the more serious business of digging, wheeling, blasting and mortaring. A chain of command was established to ensure that it ran efficiently, with the board of managers as high command, engineers as generals and overseers as the sergeants in this canal army. Labourers were the grunts.

The toll

Despite their best efforts to get a grip on finances and tame their workers, early river improvement companies were only partially successful. Really nothing more could be expected, given the nature of the capital and labour markets. Most projects experienced quite a few problems that slowed completion or led to a total shutdown. A few were pushed to a close – notably the Middlesex, Santee, Dismal Swamp and James River projects – but others had to scale back their design or close their books entirely. The Potomac, dogged from the first by defaulting investors, had to discharge its hands and sell its servants in 1796. Work was suspended for two years, and only resumed after the company mortgaged its stock for a loan and the Maryland government subscribed in the company – a pattern of state involvement that was to characterize later public works. Most of its projects were completed by 1802, but work progressed fitfully until 1816. The life of the Chesapeake & Delaware was much briefer. Work began in May 1804 and by December 1805 financial problems forced the company to close the books; all employees were released, and the company's tools, equipment and land were sold.[69] In their striving to remain afloat, however, early canals charted a course to be followed by their successors.

A period of quiet ensued in the canal business, partly born of weariness with the struggle, partly a result of war with Britain. A new era opened in the late 1810s with the beginning of the Erie Canal, a time of much more grandiose schemes than early promoters would have attempted. Yet the first canals had never successfully solved the riddles of how to secure enough money, marshall an adequate labour force and control their workers. Cost-cutting by the reshaping of the labour contract had been resisted, as had tightening the screws of labour discipline. When parsimony and system failed, canals decided to get rid of responsibility entirely, to pass the day-to-day handling of construction costs and labour management to an independent contractor, a practice used in these early years that really took hold only with the Erie Canal. This way they hoped to sit back and anticipate the profits from tolls on a finished artificial waterway, while builders bore the brunt of construction and engineers acted as middlemen. As we shall see, this arrangement did not solve the problems but merely shifted them onto the shoulders of contractors. Inadequate capital remained a reality, as did labour shortages and disciplinary troubles. Not all builders could cope with the responsibility and many ended up dumping the burden on their workers by running away. Contractors had to cut corners to make a living and, as before, this was done at the expense of labour.

69 Washington to Tobias Lear, 12 Jan. 1795, in *Writings of George Washington*, ed. Fitzpatrick (see n. 5 above), v. 34, 85–87; Bacon-Foster, "Potomac Route to the West" (see Introduction, n. 2 above), 186–91; Walter S. Sanderlin, *The Great National Project: A History of the Chesapeake and Ohio Canal*, Johns Hopkins University Series in Historical and Political Science, v. 64 (Baltimore, 1946), 29ff; Ralph D. Gray, *The National Waterway: A History of the Chesapeake and Delaware Canal, 1769–1965* (Chicago: University of Illinois Press, 1967), 20–24.

CHAPTER 2

"As low as labor and capital can afford": the contracting system, 1817–1840

More lasting than Brass, I've accomplish'd a monument,
And higher than Regal pride fashion'd the Pyramids;
Not showers corrosive, not violent winter winds,
Not numberless ages, nor time ever fugitive
Can sap, or destroy this immortal memorial.[1]

I being an entire stranger, be sure I had not much to say,
The Boss came round in a hurry, says, boys, it is grog time a-day.
We all marched up in good order, he was father now unto us all,
Sure I wished myself from that moment to be working upon the canal.[2]

"To subdue the earth was . . . one of the first duties assigned to man at his creation" by "the Lord of the Universe," declaimed President John Quincy Adams at the groundbreaking ceremony for the Chesapeake & Ohio (C&O) Canal on the Fourth of July, 1828. "To subdue the earth is pre-eminently the purpose of the undertaking" at hand. After this peroration, Adams plunged the ceremonial shovel into the earth, only to have it deflected by stubborn roots. Rolling up his sleeves to the delight of the spectators, he bent his back and rammed the blade home again, finally turning up a meagre measure of soil to initiate a project that aimed to link the Atlantic with the Mississippi.[3] Adams's gesture at canal building, with the ground refusing to be subdued, can be read as an omen of the C&O's future and a warning of the troubles that would besiege canal construction in general.

The East's great rivers tantalized merchants with the promise of untold trade nestling in the Ohio and Mississippi valleys, while the mineral riches

---

1 Isaac Briggs's translation from Ode 30 of Book 3 of Horace, as recorded in his Diary, 17 Aug. 1817, Isaac Briggs Papers (MS. 1716), MHS. Briggs, a surveyor and engineer for the Erie Canal at the time, later worked on the James River & Kanawha Canal.
2 From "Paddy on the Canal," in *Irish Emigrant Ballads and Songs*, ed. Robert L. Wright (Bowling Green, Ohio: Bowling Green University Popular Press, 1975), 533. This and ensuing excerpts are reprinted by permission of the publisher.
3 *Bedford* [Pennsylvania] *Gazette*, 25 July 1828.

of the Appalachian Mountains and upper Great Lakes taunted budding industrial entrepreneurs. Yet the promise was illusory. The mighty St. Lawrence was rendered impassable by rapids shortly after issuing from Lake Ontario. The Great Lakes choked on Niagara's torrents and the falls and rapids of the St. Mary's River. The Hudson, Delaware, Susquehanna, Potomac, James and Savannah rivers, sired by mountains, were likewise shielded from the interior. Beginning with the Erie Canal, the great projects of the Canal Era confronted these imposing obstacles and sought to improve nature. As a result of their herculean efforts, canals reshaped the map of North America, laid the foundation of trade for fifty years, and created a labour force that dwarfed other sectors of nonagricultural production.

National and commercial interests made transportation development seem imperative. In his *Report on Roads and Canals* of 1808, U.S. Secretary of the Treasury Albert Gallatin set out a plan for a comprehensive network of artificial waterways and roads to integrate most of eastern North America. Gallatin justified his plan in national terms that would become familiar refrains among canal promoters: any savings in transportation costs would naturally accrue to the country as a whole; improved transportation would assist in spreading civilization and strengthening state and national ties by enhancing communications; and an inland waterway system would serve national defense by facilitating the movement of men and munitions and freeing the country of dependence on oceans, which could be blockaded by foreign naval powers. "No other single operation, within the power of Government," concluded Gallatin, "can more effectually tend to strengthen and perpetuate that Union which secures external independence, domestic peace, and internal liberty."[4] Naturally, the federal government should play an important part in an area of such grave national concern. Unfortunately for Gallatin and other civic-minded promoters, the War of 1812 intervened, and after the war the country's politicians were still not prepared for the degree of government involvement that such a plan would entail. Instead, the main impetus for canals came from the merchant class and state politicians with an entrepreneurial vision of their region's commercial potential and a keen sense of personal profit.

In the early decades of the nineteenth century domestic trade was reaching its natural limits, given the existing transportation network and resulting high cost of moving goods. Commercial interests proposed various internal improvement projects to overcome these barriers. "The primary object of undertaking these works," reported the Ohio Board of Canal Commissioners, "was, to furnish the means of transporting the

---

4 *Selected Writings of Albert Gallatin*, ed. E. James Ferguson (Indianapolis: Bobbs-Merrill, 1967), 228–40 (quotation is on p. 232).

surplus productions of our agriculture, our forests, and our mines to market, at a cost which would not consume their whole value at the place of sale, and leave nothing to compensate the labour and the capital employed in their production."[5] Canals were designed to skim off a portion of this profit by providing overland rights-of-way on which tolls could be charged.

Compared to the river improvement schemes of the previous century, the canal projects of the early nineteenth century were monstrous in scale. Seeking to breach the Appalachian barrier, the East's transmontane canals aimed to overcome seemingly insuperable obstacles by inching hundreds of miles up sparsely settled river valleys, arching over or burrowing through the cordillera to tap the river systems beyond. Midwestern states, raw territories in all but name, eagerly sought to draw the whole of vast, still largely virgin regions to the embrace of the East. Canadian colonies, but a littoral smudge on the St. Lawrence and Lakes Ontario and Erie, nonetheless were similarly poised to tame this watery leviathan.

A brief outline of the main projects of this era clearly indicates the magnitude of the tasks confronting promoters (see Map). Of the Eastern canals, the largest were those that sought to traverse the mountains. The Erie Canal, stretching from Albany to Buffalo, was 350 miles in length; the other main canals of New York State amounted to another 225 miles.[6] The Pennsylvania Main Line ran over 270 miles from Columbia in the east to Pittsburgh with the assistance of a short rail link over the Alleghenies; the state branch lines added more than double that amount. Maryland's Chesapeake & Ohio paralleled the Potomac from Georgetown to Cumberland for 180 miles, and Virginia's James River & Kanawha combined 200 miles of canal with nearly 50 of slackwater navigation in its march from the Chesapeake over the Blue Ridge. Farther south, Georgia had the Savannah, Ogeechee & Altamaha, a 15-mile coastal waterway, and the Brunswick Canal, running from the Altamaha River to the coast south of Savannah. A number of other important Eastern canals supplemented the coastal river network. The Chesapeake & Delaware, though only 13 miles long, was a crucial tidewater link, and the Union Canal spanned 80 miles between the Susquehanna and Schuylkill rivers. More important to the industrial future were canals that pierced the mountain shield to tap the anthracite coal-

5 *Eleventh Annual Report of the Ohio Board of Canal Commissioners* (Columbus, 1833), 37.
6 The following information is drawn from the table "Canal Companies: Basic Organizational Information," in the Appendix of Baer, *Canals and Railroads of the Mid-Atlantic States* (see Introduction, n. 12 above); Richard G. Waugh, Jr., "Canal Development in Early America," in *The Best from American Canals*, ed. William H. Shank (York, Pa.: The American Canal and Transportation Center, 1980), v. 1, 4; Michael Chevalier, *Society, Manners, and Politics in the United States: Letters on North America* (orig. ed. 1836; Gloucester, Mass.: Peter Smith, 1967), ch. 22; Shaw, *Canals for a Nation* (see Ch. 1, n. 12 above); Robert Passfield, "Waterways," in *Building Canada: A History of Public Works*, ed. Norman R. Ball (Toronto: University of Toronto Press, 1988), 113–42.

fields of Pennsylvania and New York: the Delaware & Hudson (105 miles) bringing coal from the upper Delaware to New York City; the Lehigh Coal & Navigation Company (35 miles), running from Easton on the Delaware River to Mauch Chunk and the coal fields at the head of the Lehigh River; the Delaware & Raritan (44 miles), giving New Brunswick, New Jersey, access to the Delaware and the coal fields beyond; the Morris Canal (about 100 miles), linking Newark to Easton, and again supplying New York's anthracite requirements; and the Schuylkill Navigation, 62 miles of canal 46 miles of slackwater uniting Philadephia with Port Carbon and the coal beds at the head of the river.

Midwestern states soon responded with enthusiasm to the public works of the East. Both the Ohio & Erie (309 miles) and the Miami & Erie (249 miles) joined the Ohio River with Lake Erie. Indiana's Wabash & Erie was the largest of all, measuring almost 400 miles and bisecting the state from west to east, and the Illinois & Michigan connected the Illinois River at Joliet with Peru/La Salle, a distance of 97 miles. To the north, the relatively short Canadian canals were meant to remove the few barriers and make the St. Lawrence and the Great Lakes navigable from the top of Lake Superior to the Atlantic Ocean. The Lachine and Beauharnois were small canals that bypassed rapids on the St. Lawrence near Montreal, as did the Cornwall canals further upriver. The Rideau combined canals with slackwater navigation to cover the 120 miles from the head of the St. Lawrence to the Ottawa River, thereby giving Canada an alternative route of transportation in case of war with the United States. Finally, the 27-mile-long Welland Canal circumvented Niagara Falls, allowing passage between Lakes Erie and Ontario.

These projects in their sheer scale and number posed novel problems of organization. The task was enormous: mobilizing adequate capital, somehow getting thousands of canallers together, providing for them, and directing their labour in an efficient fashion, all for an enterprise extended over a large, often unsettled, territory. Institutional business studies have described canal development in surprisingly bloodless fashion. Anthropomorphized canal companies dug the beds, laid the stone locks, blasted the tunnels, and straddled rivers with aqueducts, as they marched inland with narrative ease; in the process, national interests were served and a transportation revolution wrought. Yet, if the early experience of waterway projects taught anything, it was that construction was a troublesome process powered by human energy and bedeviled by problems of organization and control. For public works to work, these waters had to be calmed, and the twin rocks that had scuttled earlier efforts – shortages of capital and labour – circumnavigated.

Novel forms of organization were pioneered to address these problems, which for the first time brought the state into partnership with business on a grand scale and erected a management bureaucracy that foreshadowed that of railroads.[7] The professional engineer was the key figure in this hierarchy. More importantly, canal promoters adopted a business stratagem born of early industrial production – contracting – to disseminate both the risk of failure and the responsibility for construction. Independent builders contracted to complete sections of the larger project, assuming the immediate control of finances and labour management. This system was crucial in shaping labour relations on the canal, linking workers with contractors in personal ties of mutual dependence that both generated and contained the strains inherent in the relationship between employer and employee.

Management by engineers and contract building prevailed at the height of the Canal Era, which began with the building of the Erie Canal (1817–25), the project that started the boom in the industry. This system created a split world of production. On one level, large-scale business organizations directed public works projects, established a management team, crafted ties with local, regional and central governments, and handled finances that increasingly relied on European investors. The engineer was the foundation of this edifice. On another level, construction was carried on in a myriad of small, face-to-face work environments, with navvies living on site or nearby in shanty camps provided by contractors. This bifurcated realm of production resulted from the immature nature of the economy. The scale and cost of such projects required a large administrative structure and government involvement, but the nature of the labour market and contemporary business practices made the smallness of contracting attractive. Contracting (initially at least) was a strategy to contain industrial growth within a familiar framework and to free the embryonic corporate structure from the worries of the direct cost of construction and labour control. It was never fully successful in either role, and the traditional organization of labour it echoed was an illusion that was maintained only as long as labour shortages persisted.

Working capital

It was clear that traditional methods would be inadequate to the task of the proposed canals, especially that of funding. The prevailing form of business organization, the partnership, could not generate the requisite capital and expertise to support such schemes.[8] Investment capital was scarce in this

---

7 Alfred Chandler argued that railways were the first modern business enterprises – that is, large-scale, corporately owned, multiunit, bureaucratically managed organizations. Alfred D. Chandler, *The Visible Hand: The Managerial Revolution in American Business* (Cambridge, Mass.: The Belknap Press of Harvard University, 1977), esp. Part II. In terms of scale of capitalization, business organization and labour mobilization, however, canals provided an important model for later railroads.

8 An idea of the amount of investment required is given by George Taylor's estimate that $125 million was spent on canal building in the United States between 1816 and 1840. *Transportation Revolution* (see Introduction, n. 12 above), 52.

era of primitive accumulation and tended to the invested conservatively, in local banks or trading ventures, for example. Few businesses other than banks and insurance companies could get capital from abroad. To overcome funding problems canal projects were organized either as private companies, as chartered corporations with a mix of public and private investment, or as public agencies. Incorporation, with its limited responsibility provision, enabled the mobilization of credit that smaller canals needed.[9] But although private capital was an important component in construction financing, canals came increasingly to rely on public funding.

Federal government aid was limited. Secretary Gallatin's assertion that the "general government alone can remove these obstacles" had failed to stir Congress to action. Washington did provide land grants to planned projects: over 500,000 acres to Indiana in 1827 and another 260,000 acres in the early 1840s, 400,000 acres to Alabama in 1828, 5 sections to Wisconsin in 1838, and 750,000 acres to Michigan in 1852.[10] It also subscribed stock in canal companies: $300,000 in the Chesapeake & Delaware in 1825 plus a further $150,000 four years later, and $1 million in the C&O Canal in 1828, among others.[11] But, for the most part, the U.S. government left canal promotion to others. The British government was more forthcoming in its Canadian colonies. It subscribed stock in the Lachine Canal in the 1820s, granted over £16,000 in 1827 and loaned £50,000 the following year to the Welland Canal Company, and it was directly responsible for the construction of the Rideau and Ottawa River canals. And in the early 1840s, it gave a £1.5 million loan guarantee for the United Province of Canada's plans to complete the St. Lawrence and Great Lakes canal system.[12] The relatively undeveloped Canadian economy necessitated greater imperial participation in the promotion of public works, and the British belief in strong central government made the role natural. This set Canada apart from the United States, where the ideology

9 Chandler, *Visible Hand* (see n. 7 above), 8–9; Carter Goodrich, Introduction to *Canals and American Economic Development*, ed. Goodrich (orig. ed. 1961; New York: Kennikat Press, 1972), 6; Harvey H. Segal, "Cycles of Canal Construction," in ibid., 177–79; H. Jerome Cranmer, "Improvements Without Public Funds: The New Jersey Canals," in ibid., 115–16, 145–46; Harlow, *Old Towpaths* (see Ch. 1, n. 54 above), ch. 21.

10 *Report of the Secretary of the Treasury, on the Subject of Public Roads and Canals* (orig. ed. 1808; New York: Augustus M. Kelley, 1968), 7; Paul Fatout, *Indiana Canals* (West Lafayette, Ind.: Purdue University Studies, 1972), 39; Shaw, *Canals for a Nation* (see Ch. 1, n. 12 above), 135–40; W. E. Martin, *Internal Improvements in Alabama*, Johns Hopkins University Studies in Historical and Political Science, v. 20 (Baltimore, 1902), 39–44; "An Act to grant a quantity of land to the Territory of Wisconsin, for the purpose of aiding in opening a canal to connect the waters of Lake Michigan with those of Rock River," 18 June 1838, in *A Documentary History of the Milwaukee and Rock River Canal*, ed. I. A. Lapham (Milwaukee, 1840), 60–63; John N. Dickinson, *To Build a Canal: Sault Ste. Marie. 1853–1854 and After* (Columbus: Ohio State University Press, 1981), 29–30.

11 Gray, *National Waterway* (see Ch. 1, n. 69 above), 63–64; Sanderlin, *Great National Project* (see Ch. 1, n. 69 above), 56.

12 Boily, *Les Irlandais et le canal du Lachine* (see Introduction, n. 11 abvoe), 16; *The Annual Report of the Welland Canal Company, 1832* (St. Catharines, Ont., 1833); Passfield, "Waterways" (see n. 6 above), 117–19.

of states' rights and the Jacksonian reluctance to federally fund public works that were not national in character limited Washington's financial involvement in canal building.

Not only was the federal government opposed to underwriting construction, but the municipal governments that stood to prosper from canals did not have enough revenues to get too involved in their financing.[13] As a result, most of the initiative and funding for canals came from state governments. Although states intervened reluctantly in other areas of the economy, many went to the extent of establishing public agencies to build, operate and finance public works. Promoters argued that the magnitude of the job and the common good that they would serve called for running canals as public enterprises, and that only in this way could the threat of monopoly be headed off. New York, Pennsylvania, Virginia, South Carolina, Ohio, Indiana, Illinois and the Province of Canada, among others, established canal commissions or boards of public works, and money for the massive projects came from their coffers or as a result of public credit. Early on, then, states assumed a central role in what were essentially business ventures, anticipating and even exceeding in some ways later government intervention in the economy.

State governments further obscured the line between public and private by repeatedly feeding funds into incorporated canals to the extent that they became virtual state enterprises. The Ohio Loan Law of 1837, for example, enabled the state to act as financing partner with private investors. When costs rose and the money market collapsed, Ohio faced bankruptcy. Similarly, the C&O Canal Company was rescued so many times by Maryland that it was forced to mortgage all its property to the state, and the Welland had to turn repeatedly to the Upper Canadian government for financial support of one sort or another. States also assisted public works companies by granting them special privileges to aid their capital accumulation. Connecticut chartered the "Mechanics' Bank" to help finance the Farmington Canal, and also subscribed $100,000 in stock. The government of Maine incorporated the "Canal Bank" in 1825 to underwrite the Cumberland & Oxford Canal; two years earlier it had granted the company the right to run a lottery to raise $50,000 for construction costs.[14] Between publicly built projects and cash handouts to private

---

13   One exception was the C&O, which was promised $1.5 million each by Washington, Georgetown and Alexandria, although it never saw all of this amount. Shaw, *Canals for a Nation* (see Ch. 1, n. 12 above), 99.

14   Dickinson, *To Build a Canal* (see n. 10 above), 19; Sanderlin, *Great National Project* (see Ch. 1, n. 69 above), ch. 5; George Washington Ward, *The Early Development of the Chesapeake and Ohio Canal Project*, John Hopkins University Studies in Historical and Political Science, v. 17 (Baltimore, 1899), 107–10; *Annual Report of the Welland Canal Company* (1832); Charles Rufus Harte, *Connecticut's Canals* (Reprinted from the 54th Annual Report of the Connecticut Society of Civil Engineers, Inc., n.d.), 13–14; Philip I. Milliken, *Notes on the Cumberland and Oxford Canal and the Origin of the Canal Bank* (Portland, Me.: Bradford Press, 1935), 24–30.

businesses, the canal industry was largely the creature of state governments. Harvey Segal estimated that 73 percent of the money invested in American canals before 1861 ($137 million of $188 million) was provided by state and municipal governments. Another $22 million came in the form of government stock subscriptions and loans to mixed enterprises.[15]

Public financing came to dominate canal construction because of governments' ability to borrow large amounts on foreign and domestic money markets. There was a relative scarcity of investment capital in North America at this time and canal commissions came to rely on Europe as a source of loanable funds, but their cost was very volatile. Bonds (usually government-secured) were sold to investors payable with interest after a set number of years. In the late 1830s, as depression set in, these money markets dried up and public works found it increasingly difficult to meet financial obligations to their bondholders. As a result, there were few investors willing to take a risk, capital evaporated, construction slowly ground to a halt, and governments were stranded. A crisis of canal construction ensued as a number of states defaulted on canal loans, effectively closing off foreign investment.[16] A partnership had been forged between the public and private sector that blurred the distinction between the common good and the promotion of business interests and, eventually, dragged some states into financial ruin.

Canal construction also had an insatiable appetite for workers. The labour market had not developed significantly from the time of early internal improvements, and the industry's needs had swelled with the size of projects.[17] Although difficult and necessarily crude, informed estimates can be made about the workforce's changing dimensions. At the peak of the first wave of river improvement projects in the mid-1790s, 3,000–4,000 people were employed. This figure tailed off in the early nineteenth century as financial problems curtailed work. Construction on the Erie from 1817 and the imitators it spawned caused a mushrooming of the labour force. By the late 1820s, roughly 35,000 were employed on such canals as the Ohio & Erie, the Miami, Canada's Rideau and Welland canals, the Pennsylvania system, the Chesapeake & Delaware, the Delaware & Hudson, and the Morris. Another wave of development peaked in the mid-1830s as the Illinois & Michigan, Wabash & Erie, C&O, Cornwall, and James River & Kanawha canals, as well as enlargements of New York's and Pennsylvania's existing lines, kept the number of industry workers at about the same level as the previous decade. The panic of 1837 and ensuing depression caused a

15 Segal, "Cycles of Canal Construction" (see n. 9 above), 179.
16 Ibid., 179–83; Chandler, *Visible Hand* (see n. 7 above), 34.
17 Segal estimated 30,000 full- or part-time canal workers in his ten canal-building states in 1840, or 5.5% of the total nonagricultural workforce. "Cycles of Canal Construction" (see n. 9 above), 206. The fact that one in twenty workers was employed in the industry certainly made canallers important to the overall labour experience in this period.

downturn in the industry as companies tightened belts, many eventually suspending construction in the early 1840s. Although work opened in Canada on the Welland, Lachine, Beauharnois and Williamsburg canals, it was not enough to staunch the hemorrhaging of the workforce. Only about 7,000 people were employed in the years 1841–46, as gaunt, unemployed labourers haunted the line in hopes of finding crumbs of work. The labour force swelled to about 10,000 as construction partially revived in the late 1840s, but tailed off as lines like the Wabash & Erie, C&O and James River & Kanawha were completed early in the next decade. By 1855, as the Canal Era drew to a close, only about 5,000 were still at work.

At its height canal construction had marshalled a large army of workers that was an important element of the broader workforce, an army that made inordinate demands on canal management. Whereas a canal's workers had previously numbered in the tens or hundreds, now the larger canals required thousands. Such numbers daunted employers, especially as labour shortages persisted throughout much of the period. All available sources of labour were exploited. Southern internal improvement projects still relied primarily on slaves, though they were increasingly supplemented by free labour. With the demise of indentured servitude, free labour was the rule in the North, yet competition from other public works, agriculture and the building industries meant canals had to fight for men into the late 1830s. Companies sent agents out to scour the interior for hands, offering transportation money, ample food and drink, good wages and the promise of steady work as a lure. Advertisements were placed in newspapers laying out the terms of employment and stipulating the number of men needed, which was generally exaggerated in an attempt to flood the labour market and drive down wages.[18] The experience of the C&O Canal illustrates the degree of the problem. The company competed with other industries and agriculture's harvest demands for wage workers, but their main competitors were public works in other states and in Canada. C&O President Charles Mercer lamented during the first of many labour shortages that "labourers are difficult to be had, at high prices, that is, 10 and 12 dollars the month, besides their board and whiskey and a supply of necessary tools." The board of directors advertised for workers, sent out recruiting agents, and petitioned Congress unsuccessfully for one thousand federal troops to work on the canal's mountain section. They also toyed with the idea of hiring or purchasing slaves, but nothing came of this.[19] The desperate company even

18 The Illinois & Michigan Canal, for example, circulated a notice at the opening of construction calling for at least three times as many workers as it required. *Chicago American*, 11 June 1836.
19 Charles Mercer to James Barbour, 18 Nov. 1828 (A 4), Letters Sent by the Office of the President and Directors, Chesapeake and Ohio Canal Company Papers, series 194, NA/RG79 (hereafter C&O/LS); Proceedings of the President and Directors of the Chesapeake and Ohio Canal Company, Chesapeake and Ohio Canal Papers, series 182, NA/RG79 (hereafter C&O/PRO), 27 May 1829 (A 230–31), 15 July 1829 (A 309–10); John Ingle to Thomas Bender, 1 March 1837 (D 72–73), C&O/LS; John

imported indentured workers from Europe to meet their demands, an experiment that sadly misfired, as will be shown in the next chapter. Despite such initiatives, the industry as a whole was generally unable to fill its labour needs completely until the early 1840s when, not coincidentally, most construction had shut down.

Not only did companies have to get enough men in the field, but they had to provide for them once there. Accommodation had to be found or built, and precautions taken to ensure that food, clothing and bedding were available. And to get work under way, tools, powder, dray animals and workshops had to be in place. Thus, the military engineer for the Grenville Canal wrote in 1819 that most of his time since arriving at the work site had been spent in erecting physical plant and procuring materials. In the same vein, the engineer for Maine's Kennebec Locks & Canals Company had to build five houses "for the convenience of the workmen," an office and several shops before the job could start.[20] With the expansion of canals, the resulting supply line of purchasing, transportation and distribution resembled nothing as much as that associated with military campaigns. Needless to say, it was an expensive exercise. Provisioning was a responsibility that early canal companies had been unable to shed; later projects were more successful.

Management

Early canals had been relatively small private companies that got by with a limited management structure, but bigger projects meant greater organizational problems. Construction did not take place within a mill's closed walls but in numerous workplaces over a large territory, and the labour process resisted rationalization because of the work's unenclosed, dispersed and diversified nature. To take on the imposing tasks of mobilizing sufficient capital and labour, and to implement the actual plan of construction, canal projects adopted a management structure that anticipated modern business corporations in its hierarchical, functionally diversified organization.

The canal commission or board sat at the top of canal organization in the case of public agencies, while a board of directors headed private companies. The representative agents of the state or investors respectively, these bodies oversaw administration, set policy, directed officers, and reported back to the government or stockholders through the work of full-time clerks, treasurers and other personnel.

Nelson to Mercer, 13 Jan. 1829, Mercer to Ingle, 23 Jan. 1832, Letters Received by the Office of the President and Directors, Chesapeake and Ohio Canal Company Papers, series 190, NA/RG79 (hereafter C&O/LR); *Second Annual Report of the Chesapeake and Ohio Canal Company* (Washington, 1830), 29.
20 Capt. W. J. Mann to Maj. Bowles, 30 Sept. 1819, v. 39, Canal Papers, British Military and Naval Papers, series C-1, RG8, Public Archives of Canada, Ottawa (hereafter PAC/RG8); *Report of Colonel William Boardman, Engineer of the Kennebec Locks and Canals Company* (Augusta, Me., 1837), 6.

A corps of engineers linked upper management and construction. Ostensibly disinterested professionals charged with ensuring the quality and economy of the work, engineers also functioned as enforcers of the board's will, often at the expense of contractors and labourers. At the apex of this command structure stood the chief engineer, who directed the work and advised the board. He was responsible for establishing the canal's route, providing overall estimates, ensuring that construction continued on apace, and directing the network of underlings and contractors. The chief was assisted by a number of resident engineers, each of whom supervised a specific "residency" or division of the canal line, a contiguous group of sections. They surveyed their residencies, prepared cost estimates and construction specifications and oversaw the work, aided by assistant engineers, rodmen and chainmen. Resident engineers were middle-managers in close contact with contractors and their men. And once a portion of the canal came into service, completed sections were divided up and placed under the care of maintenance superintendents who reported to the chief engineer. These officers, sometimes engineers in their own right, performed regular upkeep and emergency repairs, usually operating from a scow with a force of ten to twenty men, direct employees of the canal. Engineers played a fundamental role in canal building, providing expertise and directing an unwieldy production process, but their contributions transcended the technical. As the main representatives of capital, located at the point of production and in contact with the builders and their men, they came to play an important part in formulating policy and shaping the nature of labour relations.

Engineering as a profession in North America traces its roots largely to the era of canal construction. There were few, if any, qualified individuals available when the first projects were undertaken in the late eighteenth century, and most jobs were entrusted to European professionals. The lack of talent persisted well into the Canal Era, and canals had to promote native ingenuity. Michael Chevalier observed how Ohio, "with its population of farmers, which has not a single engineer within its limits," had "with the aid of some second-rate engineers borrowed from New York, constructed a canal [the Ohio Canal] longer than any in France."[21]

As Chevalier noted, the Erie Canal was the source of technical know-how for most canal building. When the Erie was in its planning stages, it was evident that native talent would have to be found. Professional men with an interest in the mechanical arts were attracted to the project and joined it as engineers, while young men from families of standing were drawn to a developing profession that increasingly came to embody the nineteenth-century ideals of ingenuity and industry. Thus Benjamin Wright, a judge in upstate New York with some experience in surveying property lines,

21 Chevalier, *Society, Manners, and Politics in the United States* (see n. 6 above), 234–35.

worked on the inland lock companies of the 1790s, and by the opening of construction on the Erie in 1817 was one of its three head engineers. Wright went on to work for the Chesapeake & Delaware, Blackstone, C&O, Delaware & Hudson and Farmington canals, as well as various railroads in New York. As a practical school of engineering, the Erie produced the nation's first generation of professionals, including James Geddes, Canvass White, John Jervis and Nathan Roberts. These individuals became chief engineers on other canals where they shared their experience with others; many went on to illustrious careers in civil engineering.[22]

Beneath these luminaries were individuals from more humble backgrounds, who were self-taught or learned on the job, moved from place to place, and often found themselves out of work or out of the profession.[23] They might have worked their way up the hierarchy from chainman to rodman to assistant engineer and beyond, or they could have come to engineering from related work. For example, Daniel Teer claimed skill in surveying, mapping and sketching, as well as knowledge of metals, mining, engineering and bookkeeping when he wrote the C&O from Ireland asking for a job. He had also worked in "the Clock and Watch Making business" but found it "too sedentary for my taste and constitution." Similarly, Christian Custer outlined his experience when seeking employment from the Wabash & Erie; he had first been a millwright, then managed a foundry and machine shop, followed by stints building anthracite furnaces, improving rolling mills and erecting machinery for crane works. He also claimed knowledge of "Damb building lock building and building bridges of iron or wood." William Gooding was equally versatile, having taught school and farmed in Bristol, New York, before being apprenticed to the chief engineer on Canada's Welland Canal in 1823 at the age of twenty. He remained there six years, then ran a general store in Lockport, New York. In 1831, he was hired as a junior assistant engineer on the Wabash & Erie Canal, working there two years before moving on to Illinois. Gooding did some surveying for the Indiana Board of Canal Commissioners, then made the big time in 1836 when he was hired as chief engineer of the Illinois & Michigan. He stayed in this post over ten years.[24]

22 Shank, *Towpaths to Tugboats* (see Ch. 1, n. 12 above), 15–22, 31–35; Harlow, *Old Towpaths* (see Ch. 1, n. 54 above), ch. 6; Shaw, *Erie Water West* (see Ch. 1, n. 21 above), Parts I and II; Gray, *National Waterway* (see Ch. 1, n. 69 above), 44–45; Harold Kanarek, "The U. S. Army Corps of Engineers and Early Internal Improvements in Maryland," *Maryland Historical Magazine*, v. 72 (Spring 1977), 99–109.
23 Most engineers took a keen interest in their profession. For example, Isaac Briggs read texts by the French engineers P. C. Lesage and General D'artillerie Andreossy when working on the Erie, as well as Fulton's *Treatise on Canal Navigation*. Briggs Diary, n.d. (entry preceding 4 Jan. 1819), Briggs Papers, MHS.
24 Daniel Teer to Mercer, 12 Jan. 1829, C&O/LR; Christian Custer to Commissioners of Wabash & Erie Canal, 10 May 1848, Wabash & Erie Canal Correspondence (hereafter W&E/COR), Internal Improvement Papers, Records of the Auditor of the State, Archives Division, Indiana Commission on

Engineers played a crucial role in directing public works construction in this period. As the eyes, ears and minds of management, they were responsible for melding men and technology into a well-oiled excavating engine. Yet their actual power was moderated by the anomalous position created for them by upper management. Given the glitches that dogged construction from the early years, canal companies increasingly backed away from immediate control of production, ultimately deciding to give responsibility for building canals to an army of independent contractors, petty entrepreneurs attempting to eke out a profit on a small stretch of the line. Engineers were to orchestrate this motley crew, with authority only over technical matters and little say in the organization of production and handling of the workforce.

Contractors

James Clark, superintendent of the Pennsylvania Main Line's Juniata Division, outlined to the state canal commissioners his priorities when selecting contractors: secure the most faithful and competent; choose the lowest bid; do not give too much work to any one individual or company; require that a contractor personally supervise his work; and forbid any transfer of contracts without the superintendent's permission. Following these rules, Clark claimed, would protect management from "that pernicious species of speculator who may be denominated *canal jobbers*" and (more importantly) would attract honest men who would finish their jobs at prices "as low as labor and capital can afford."[25]

Clark's recipe for canal construction encapsulated the attraction contracting held for promoters. Boards could hem builders in with contractual provisions and police their competence with an engineering corps, yet make them financially liable for any construction costs above set figures and burden them with labour mobilization and discipline. If correctly implemented, contracting offered a maximum of control with a minimum of responsibility. A good contractor, as Clark enthused, promised the dream of all canal builders: near-effortless, economical completion of public works. With such allure, it is not surprising that virtually all construction from the time of the Erie Canal was the domain of contractors. More often than not, however, the ideal of efficiency was shattered by the reality of shoddy work, clashes with management, fiscal insolvency and labour conflict.

Contracting was a business strategy born of the transition from merchant to industrial capitalism. Many investors in the early nineteenth century

---

Public Records, Indianapolis (hereafter IN/II); Gooding to Board of Trustees, 4 Nov. 1847, in *Report of a Majority of the Board of Trustees of the Illinois and Michigan Canal* . . . (Washington, 1847), xxv; John M. Lamb, *William Gooding, Chief Engineer I. and M. Canal* (Lockport, Ill.: Illinois Canal Society, n.d.), 1–2.

25 *Report of the Canal Commissioners of Pennsylvania* (Harrisburg, 1827), 128.

were undoubtedly interested in profit, but hesitant to take on the whole burden of production; contracting allowed them to expand the scope of their business without soiling their hands. Contractors thus filled a void in the undeveloped capital and labour markets. Part master builder and part entrepreneur, they straddled both worlds, traditional and industrial.[26]

Some of the first waterway companies, the Potomac and the Dismal Swamp Canal among them, had experimented with contracting, and much of the work on the Middlesex was carried out by contractors, mostly local people with a smattering of foreigners. But the Chesapeake & Delaware Canal (1804–05) was the first canal to rely entirely on contractors.[27] With the gigantic schemes after the War of 1812, contracting became virtually the sole mode of carrying on construction. Even in the South, where projects were smaller and slave labour predominated, contractors did much of the work.[28] The pattern was set by the New York Canal Commission. Originally the commissioners put aside $75,000 to buy equipment and build the Erie themselves, but, faced with a planned 350-mile canal, they decided on the "more economical course" of giving the job to contractors who would supply their own tools.[29] The arguments for such a move were persuasive. Contractors' limited capital resources would promote cost efficiency, whereas direct state or company construction threatened bureaucracy, political patronage and waste. Simply put, it was believed that contracting would be cheaper. Theoretically tidy, these assumptions did not always work in practice. The interests of canal board and contractor often diverged. The former, driven to cut costs where possible, passed much of the risk of financial failure onto the latter. Expenses often overran contractors' resources, and, with little hope of aid from the canal administration, insolvent builders occasionally fled the line and their debts.

The nature of payment under the contracting system severely circum-

26 Contracting was used in Britain's transportation and mining industries. In North America, the system was quickly adopted by railroad builders, the construction and building industry, the machine and tool trades, and the garment industries. Raphael Samuel, "Mineral Workers," in *Miners, Quarrymen and Saltworkers*, ed. Raphael Samuel (London: Routledge & Kegan Paul, 1977), 33–34; Chris Fisher, *Custom, Work and Market Capitalism: The Forest of Dean Colliers, 1788–1888* (London: Croom Helm, 1981), ch. 4; David Brooke, *The Railway Navvy* (Newton Abbot, England: David and Charles, 1983), 32; Terry Coleman, *The Railway Navvies: A History of the Men Who Made the Railways* (London: Hutchinson, 1965), 52–53; Walter Licht, *Working for the Railroad: The Organization of Work in the Nineteenth Century* (Princeton: Princeton University Press, 1983), 19–24.

27 Thomas Bealle to Potowmack Company, 1 Aug. 1796, POT/COR; Charles Clinton Weaver, *Internal Improvements in North Carolina to 1860*, Johns Hopkins University Studies in Historical and Political Science, v. 21 (Baltimore, 1903), 71; Contract between Thomas Harvy, Richard Oak, James Leigh, Schofield [obscured] and John Penny, 15 Nov. 1794, Middlesex Canal – Memoranda (see Ch. 1, n. 40 above); Roberts, *Middlesex Canal* (see Ch. 1, n. 8 above), 67–68, 71; Gray, *National Waterway* (see Ch. 1, n. 69 above).

28 "Report of the Superintendent of the Public Works for 1828," in *Internal Improvements in South Carolina 1817–1828*, ed. David Kohn (Washington, 1938), 583.

29 *Report of the Commissioners of the State of New York, on the Canals. . .* (Albany, 1818); Minutes of the New York Canal Commission and Superintendent of Public Works, v. 1, p. 1 (16 April 1817), New York State Archives, Albany.

scribed contractors' ability to make a profit. Proposed canal routes were divided into sections – usually about a half-mile in length or based on specific jobs like lock making – on which bids were made by prospective contractors. Typically, pricing schedules were drawn up setting the cost of different kinds of work: per cubic yard or chain for grubbing and clearing, embankment or excavation, and per perch for masonry. This system was not as prevalent in Canada, where a total price for the contract was often set. It was difficult to estimate the final cost of the work in either case. Moreover, common canal policy was to accept the lowest responsible bid, which pressured contractors to cut estimates to a minimum. Keen competition for contracts prevailed. In 1826, for example, 110 sections on the Ohio Canal received six thousand bids, an average of fifty-four bids per section.[30] Competition forced bids down and created a situation in which luck as much as skill was required for contractors to complete their sections at a profit.

This system was further complicated by subcontracting, in which builders parcelled out portions or all of their contract. This inevitably led to problems, as subcontractors had to do the work for prices beneath the original contract so the contractor could have his profit. Some canals outlawed subcontracting, having had enough problems making builders follow orders without dealing with independents twice removed from their authority. This practice appears to have been more prevalent in later years and in Canada.[31]

Contractors occupied an anomalous position in the industry, neither canal employees nor truly independent, bound in important respects by their contractual relation with the company. A specific date of completion was included in the contract, as well as provisions for quality of work. Breaking these rules could result in a contractor losing the job. Their pay rested on satisfying the engineer that work was progressing according to schedule and in the prescribed fashion. Given prevailing labor shortages and their chronic financial problems, contractors found it difficult to satisfy management.

To ensure they were getting honest builders and not *"canal jobbers,"* some public works required that contractors post a financial bond up front. It was also common practice for the company to retain a percentage (usually 15 to 20%) of the monthly estimate, which would be repaid upon satisfactory completion of work. Thus, contractors on the Chesapeake &

---

30 Bleasdale, "Unskilled Labourers on the Public Works of Canada" (see Introduction, n. 11 above), 52–53; C. P. McClelland and C. C. Huntington, *History of the Ohio Canals* (Columbus: Ohio Archaeological and Historical Society, 1905), 23.
31 Articles of Agreement form [Chenango Canal], box 50, John Bloomfield Jervis Papers (on microfilm), originals held at Jervis Public Library, Rome, N.Y.; William C. Bouck to Jervis, 18 Aug. 1834, box 48, ibid.; Bleasdale, "Unskilled Labourers on the Public Works of Canada" (see Introduction, n. 11 above), 53–56.

Delaware in 1804 had to put up a security "for the due performance of their Contracts," and were required to complete "a considerable quantity of work before they [became] entitled to receive any money, thus leaving a part of their earnings as security in the hands of the Company." Similarly, the Milwaukee & Rock River Canal held back 10 percent of builders' earnings, and Illinois & Michigan contractors were expected to give a personal bond of 5 percent of the contract's worth and forgo 15 percent of their estimates until completion.[32] Posting of securities and retention of payment meant that aspiring contractors had to have their own capital to invest in the work.

Contractors were paid on a month-to-month basis according to their established scale of prices, based on the engineer's estimate of the amount of work done. Thus their financial well-being rested largely in the hands of the board's direct representative. How many feet of earth had been dug or how much stone had been blasted away in the last month was a matter of opinion. Friction inevitably developed. As petty entrepreneurs, contractors strove to minimize costs and maximize profits. As management figures, engineers enforced quality control and sped construction in an economical fashion. A strategy for distancing capital from direct involvement in production, contracting increasingly broke down under the pressures of competition and rising expenses. Men with little capital were caught in the vise of diminishing income and expanding production costs. In the end, it was usually their workers who suffered the consequences.

North America initially had few experienced canal builders. At first work was often carried on by local merchants, professionals and farmers out to make a profit. The latter, in particular, with their experience in ditching, draining fields, stump pulling and use of animal teams, made an easy transition to canal work. Thus "yeomen" accounted for most contractors on the Middlesex at the turn of the century.[33] And New York's canal commissioners reported early in the construction of the Erie that "the greatest part of the contractors are men of property and respectability, whose reputations are intimately connected with a faithful performance of their contracts." These individuals were "native farmers, mechanics, merchants and professional men, residing in the vicinity of the line."[34] As often as not, however, builders were men of small means who saw an opportunity to earn some hard cash and perhaps fill in the slack periods of the agricultural season. The fact that the canal might pass right though

32 Latrobe to Thaddeus O'Hara, 2 Sept. 1804, Latrobe Collection, MHS; *Milwaukee and Rock River Canal*, ed. Lapham (see n. 10 above), 77–78; *Chicago American*, 28 Jan. 1837.

33 Of the fifty-two contractors on the Middlesex for whom he could establish occupation, Christopher Roberts found thirty-six yeomen, eight labourers, five clothiers, one weaver, and two partnerships pairing a seaman with a housewright and a yeoman with a gentleman. *Middlesex Canal* (see Ch. 1, n. 8 above), 71.

34 *Report of the Commissioners of the State of New York* (1818), 11; *Annual Report of the Canal Commissioners, Communicated to the Legislature* (Albany, 1819), 10.

AS LOW AS LABOR AND CAPITAL CAN AFFORD"

their land made the job easier, while offering the promise of enhanced property value when completed.[35] Inexperienced, with other commitments pulling at them, these individuals were not always the most efficient builders.

Professional contractors who had acquired their skills in England emigrated to New World canals. In 1794, the Middlesex Canal Company signed a contract with a number of individuals "late of the Kingdom of Great Britain." John Hay had been a subcontractor on Waterloo Bridge in London and had also helped build an abbey and stables before finding work on the C&O.[36] Contracting soon became associated with Irishmen, however, at least for those individuals who followed it full-time. Benjamin Latrobe made this connection in 1804, when he advised an applicant for work to form a partnership with some *"honest, sober, & industrious,* though perhaps illiterate Irishman."* A number of Irish contractors and their men were brought over from England to work on the Erie Canal, the commissioners noting in 1819: "A very few of the contractors are foreigners, who have recently arrived in this country." When this project was completed, these men spread out across the Northeast to wherever canals were being built. When the Erie engineer Benjamin Wright was chosen to oversee the Blackstone Canal in Massachusetts, for example, he brought with him several veteran Irish builders, who prospered and laid the foundation of Worcester's Irish community.[37] As time went on and construction mushroomed, a pool of talent developed and professional contractors became the norm, with the Irish providing the backbone of canal construction, at least until the 1840s when contracting started to become big business run by men with ample capital.

Contractors moved from job to job as one was completed and another opened. They could be recruited by engineers they had worked with in the past, as on the Chesapeake & Delaware Canal where Latrobe gave contracts to "good honest men" he had known for a number of years.[38] In later years, such personal contacts were less likely. Contractors would hear by word of mouth where work could be found, but increasingly canal companies advertised the letting of contracts in newspapers. For example, notices were placed in Ohio, Pennsylvania and New York newspapers, as well as those of Indiana, when some work was planned on the Wabash & Erie in 1849.[39]

35 For example, contractors Murry, Doyle and Kirby asked the Trustees of the Wabash & Erie to be awarded the section of canal that traversed their land. T. J. Bourne to Messrs. Blake and Palmer, 5 Aug. 1847, W&E/COR.
36 Contract between Harvy, Oak, Leigh, Schofield [obscured] and Penny, 15 Nov. 1794, Middlesex Canal – Memoranda (see Ch. 1, n. 40 above); John Hay, 14 Feb. 1832, C&O/LR.
37 Latrobe to H. W. Swin, 7 May 1804, Latrobe Collection, MHS; *Annual Report of the Canal Commissioners* (Albany, 1819), 10; Vincent E. Powers, "Invisible Immigrants: Pre-Famine Irish Community in Worcester, Massachusetts, 1826–1860," Ph.D. diss., Clark University, 1976, 107–09.
38 Latrobe to Joseph Tatnall, 15 April 1804, Latrobe Collection, MHS.
39 J. L. Williams to T. H. Blake, 23 April 1849, W&E/COR.

And often their migration was preceded by written inquiries about job opportunities. "I have been on the Canall at lockport this 2 years and my two brothers," wrote Hugh McNamara, a New York contractor, to the Ohio Canal's chief engineer, "and we being well acquainted with that work we taking Small Jobs but we are out of employ now and I considered of going to the Ohio Canall to try to get a Job me and my Brothers." And William Mason, "being out of employment," wrote Indiana's Whitewater Canal to see if assistance was needed "of a man who has had much experience in the construction of Canals and R. Roads both in this country and in spane and the management of Labourers."[40] In lieu of prior communication, builders often carried a letter of recommendation from officers on canals where they had worked as evidence of their skill.

Professional contractors could be highly mobile. Of the contractors given jobs on the C&O in October 1828, five hailed from New York, five from Pennsylvania, two from Virginia, and only one from the city of Washington. Nor did the U.S.–Canadian border act as any barrier to these roving builders; for example, in 1829 a contractor by the name of Osborn arrived at the C&O from Canada, and McCullough and Clark at work on the Welland in 1844 were from Pennsylvania.[41] A synopsis of two contractors' careers gives an idea of the diversity, mobility and growing professionalism of builders. George Barnet, onetime master mechanic and one of the largest contractors on the Illinois & Michigan in the 1840s (as well as an important investor in the company), had worked as a contractor for twenty to thirty years on canals in the States and Canada. John Black, a contractor on the Beauharnois in 1843, testified that he had been a contractor for about sixteen years: first on the Pennsylvania Canal, then for the Philadelphia Railroad, the Susquehanna River improvement, the Columbia Dam across the Susquehanna, the towing path to the Columbia Bridge, and the Croton Dam, before moving to Quebec.[42] Such long careers and geographical mobility increasingly came to characterize contracting during this period. The constraints of capital and labour ensured that only the fittest survived, and the shifting locus of production made contractors migratory beasts. They were necessarily followed in their wanderings by large herds of workers.

40 Hugh McNamara to Alfred Kelley, 8 March 1825, Board of Canal Commissioners Correspondence, Canal Commission and Board of Public Works Papers, Ohio State Archives, Columbus (hereafter OH/CC); William Mason to Thomas H. Blake, 15 July 1847, Whitewater Canal Correspondence, IN/II.

41 Schedule 5, "Report of the President of the Chesapeake and Ohio Canal Company to the General Assembly of Maryland," in *A Communication from the Executive Department of the 16th February, 1829* (Annapolis, 1829); C&O/PRO, 25 Sept. 1829; *St. Catharines Journal*, 20 Sept. 1844.

42 *Report of a Majority of the Board of Trustees of the Illinois and Michigan Canal*, 9, Appendix Q (Evidence of George Barnett); Deposition of John Black (No. 7), "Beauharnois Report" (see Introduction, n. 3 above).

Contractors were also employers responsible for getting enough labourers together, keeping them on the job, providing for them and remunerating them. In the undeveloped labour market of the period, traditional personal relations between worker and employer persisted. The former, whether slave or free, confronted the latter with certain expectations of rights and duties, as the dynamics of class and race were played out within petty fiefdoms where contractors directed life and labour. These relationships were rarely as balanced or reciprocal as recent literature on slavery and labour would lead one to believe. They resulted from structural flaws in the system of production rather than from tradition, and should not be idealized as indicative of a kinder, gentler past. Still, canal construction at this time took place in a smaller setting where the master–worker relationship was less commercial and more ruled by mutual needs than it would be in later years.

The nature of the industry had changed from the early years when Benjamin Latrobe, chief engineer of the Chesapeake & Delaware, could say that the company had fifty labourers at Elkforge, "all of them hands who have formerly been under my direction." By the time of the Erie, management disavowed any knowledge of the workers. Josiah White, proprietor of the Lehigh Navigation, observed that "the hands come from all nations and [are] stranger[s] to us." With this anonymity went a lack of responsibility, as was made clear by President Charles Mercer of the C&O Canal Company: "All the works on the canal are executed in pursuance of contracts between the company and certain individual contractors. The labourers whom these contractors employ, are irresponsible and unknown to the company and its officers." Significantly, Mercer was responding to a claim for expenses from local charitable organizations for feeding and sheltering sick and indigent canallers.[43]

Despite such disclaimers, canal administrations did retain ultimate authority for workers in some important areas, primarily concerning discipline. Contracts on Pennsylvania's public works in 1831, for instance, enjoined contractors to dismiss "every quarrelsome disorderly person, and such as shall be addicted to habits of intemperence, or who shall wantonly commit any unnecessary trespass, either upon the person, land or property of citizens living, travelling, or working upon or near the works of the said canal, or be guilty of other offensive conduct."[44] The presence of liquor on the line was of most concern to canal administrators, who believed it was responsible for the vice and violence they associated with the workforce,

43 Latrobe to Isaac Hazlehurst, 14 May 1804, Latrobe Collection, MHS; "Josiah White's History Given By Himself," Josiah White Papers, Manuscript Division, William R. Perkins Library, Duke University, Durham, N.C.; Mercer to Susan Decatur, 13 Dec. 1830, C&O/LR.
44 Copy of contract form, in *Report of the Canal Commissioners of Pennsylvania* (Harrisburg, 1831), 35.

and many moved to rid the line of its malign influence. The C&O prohibited contractors from passing out "ardent spirits" in 1832, and contractors caught doing so faced having their contracts declared abandoned. Similar provisions were adopted on most canals but rarely had the desired effect.[45] Morality clauses in contracts were weakly enforced as, for the most part, companies wanted as little as possible to do with workers.

Contractors first had to get a body of workers together numbering in the tens to hundreds. They faced the problem of labour shortages here directly, competing with small-scale manufacturing, the day labour needs of urban areas, and agriculture's expanding requirements for workers, as well as with other public works.[46] Some builders sought to circumvent the problem by maintaining a stable of regular workers, supplemented with local labourers. The chief engineer on the C&O asserted "every contractor has his followers, labourers who go with him from one part of the country to another." Such was the case with one contractor who brought 100 men with him from Canada to the C&O in 1829.[47] Others relied fully on the market, picking and discarding unknown workers as need dictated. To secure hands, contractors spread the word that they were hiring and advertised in local or regional newspapers. An ad in the *Cleveland Herald*, for example, promised "$14 a month will be given for labourers, on Lock No. 44 at Cleveland, work dry and good fare." Blandishments of high wages and healthy conditions were the norm, as were exaggerations of the number of workers needed. In the South, other inducements had to be offered. Contractors on the Muscle Shoals Canal in Alabama advertised their desire to hire slaves, with the unreassuring promise they would "be responsible to slave holders who hire their negroes to us, for injury or damage that may hereafter happen in the process of blasting rock or of caving in of banks."[48]

Once an adequate supply of men had been collected, contractors had to try to keep them together. Hands were hired by the year, season (from spring to fall) or month. Only later did day labour become common. Wages were paid fortnightly, monthly or (very rarely) annually. Hands were paid only for days worked, and, with the regular seasonal and weather-related interruptions, this usually averaged only two out of three days. Labour was exchanged for housing, provisions, and often the use of tools and washing of clothes, as well as for cash. These services accounted for a significant portion of the entire wage bill. In 1829, a contractor on

45 C&O/PRO, 11 July 1832 (C 185–86); Mercer to Ingle, 23 Jan. 1832, C&O/LR; Alfred Cruger, 7 July 1832, C&O/LR; George Bender to Ingle, 27 Aug. 1835, C&O/LR.
46 See Canal Commission Minute Books, v. 1, 336, Ohio Canal Commission Papers, Ohio State Archives, Columbus; Jesse Williams to Ethan Allen Brown, 13 June 1826, Ethan Allen Brown Papers, Ohio Historical Society, Columbus; Richard Howe to Kelley, 3 Dec. 1831, OH/CC; *Plantation and Frontier* (see Introduction, n. 2 above), ed. Phillips, v. 2, 347.
47 Charles Fisk, 24 Nov. 1835, C&O/LR; C&O/PRO, 25 Sept. 1829.
48 Cleveland *Herald*, 14 May 1829; *Plantation and Frontier*, ed. Phillips (see Introduction, n. 2 above), v. 2, 348.

the C&O calculated his daily costs per worker to be 96.5¢. Of this, roughly half was for wages (46.5¢); the rest went for board (30¢) and for whiskey, use of tools, superintendence and buildings (20¢).[49] Although the men usually did not receive pay for days lost due to inclement weather, board and shelter continued. Labourers also usually lived in shanties thrown up by the contractor at the work site, either bunkhouses shared by fifteen or twenty men or huts where men lived with their families. Set off on its own in tangled woods bordering rivers, each section or group of sections constituted a community of workers and assorted family members. Together they ate, slept, caroused and worshiped, but mostly worked, with the contractor involved in most facets of his workers' lives. Combined with persistent labour shortages, this closeness bred a situation in which employer paternalism flourished.

Philemon Wright was the archetypal paternalist. Founder of Hull, Quebec, Wright was involved in commercial farming and the Ottawa timber trade as well as contracting on the Rideau. He crafted firm ties with his mainly French-Canadian workers, hiring them by the year and switching them from one business concern to another to make the most of their labour. While a Wright might be a distant figure looming over an entire community, other builders lived in much closer contact with their men, like Abram Garfield, father of President James Garfield. A contractor on an Ohio canal, he boarded his hands in his own log cabin, where of an evening his wife entertained the labourers with sweet songs. This account, undoubtedly embroidered, suggests the intimacy that could exist between master and men. But close personal ties are not always positive. Sharing the same house with one's boss could breed conflict as much as camaraderie. Perhaps some nights Garfield's bone-weary hands would much rather have been drinking than have been a captive audience for his wife's dulcet tones. Such closeness also gave employers greater control over their hands. For instance, Josiah White drew up a "cob law," a set of regulations meant to order his workers' lives even when not at work. "Any hand that took more victuals on his plate then he could eat, was to be cobed; he was also to be cobed for running or going any way incivil to his meals. For any hand going into the kitchen without due liberty, an centinel was placed at the door as guard."[50] Such a situation was more likely to create friction than conviviality.

Still, it was not surprising that some builders inspired respect and

49 H. W. Campbell to Mercer, 30 Aug. 1829, C&O/LR.

50 H. C. Pentland, *Capital and Labour in Canada 1650–1860* (Toronto: James Lorimer & Co., 1981), 56; Jaime Valentine, "Supplying the Rideau: Workers, Provisions and Health Care During the Construction of the Rideau Canal, 1826–32" (Research Publication Section, Research Division, National Historical Parks and Sites, Environment Canada – Parks, Microfiche Report Series No. 249, 1985), vii, 25–26, Table I; Wylie, "Poverty, Distress, and Disease" (see Introduction, n. 11 above), 13; Anonymous, *The History of Tuscarawas County, Ohio* (Chicago, 1884), 387–88; "Josiah White's History" (see n. 43 above), 12.

friendship in their men. Many came from the same ethnic background, had worked with them for some time, ate the same food and slept under the same roof. Sharing such experiences could naturally bind men together. When a deceased contractor on one of Indiana's canals was buried, his wife recorded that "crowds thronged," including "men of all ranks from the most gifted, most honoured citizens down to the unlettered labourers on the public works."[51] The small scale of production allowed individual personalities to colour labour relations for good or ill.

The contractor was like the "padrone" of later years, recruiting among his fellow immigrants, representing them to canal management and looking after their needs. But he did not necessarily serve their interests. Contractor paternalism arose out of conditions of labour shortage. To keep men at work they had to satisfy workers' demands – good wages, the provision of food, shelter, clothing and certain services chief among them. To a degree, canallers were protected from unemployment and want when there was no work; from this perspective, paternalism worked in their interests. At the same time, the fact that the contractor controlled their subsistence as well as their labour made them dependent on him. Locked into a long-term employment agreement, with the roof over their heads and food on their table put there by the boss, workers' freedom of movement was potentially limited. Power the contractor derived from this arrangement enabled him to enforce stronger labour discipline when so desired, as the threat of lost subsistence rights could be held over the heads of his employees. Labour shortages buffered workers against outright abuse of the system, but the potential was there and real.

The intimate relations between contractor and hands masked opposing class lines that lay beneath. Their differing interests, the very inequality of the structured relationship despite its elements of mutuality, contained the threat that the cozy facade of contractor paternalism would be sundered if subjected to impersonal market forces. As economic pressures intensified during the depression years after 1837, contractors' worsening financial condition eroded the personalism of labour relations. Forced underbidding, a result of competition exacerbated by the industry's growing inability to pay for work done, pressured contractors to complete their jobs as quickly and cheaply as possible. Strains developed within the relationship, primarily over questions of income and the availability of employment, and conflict increasingly burst into violence. From the convulsions of the late 1830s would emerge a new form of labour relations based more purely on cash for work. The nature of contractor payment was an important ingredient in hastening this transformation.

---

51 Catharine H. Lowry to Elizabeth Wines, 10 Oct. 1842, Charles James Worden Papers, W. H. Smith Memorial Library, Indiana Historical Society, Indianapolis.

The economics of contracting

In 1829, the president and directors of the C&O instituted a system of incentives "to stimulate the just pride of the contractors." They announced that a silver cup worth $50 would be awarded for the completion of the best lock, a $10 silver medal for the best culvert, and less precious silver medals for various other jobs.[52] But too often those who reached for the promised baubles of contracting only ended up with dross.

Contractors were the essential link in the chain of canal construction. Given the tremendous pressures these individuals were subject to, it is not surprising that the chain periodically snapped and gave way. The competitive nature of the bidding system pared profitability to the bone, and problems with collecting, managing and providing for sufficient numbers of labourers proved a persistent headache. Builders often fled the line when debts grew too large to be redeemed by future construction, abandoning their contracts and leaving creditors and unpaid workers to scramble for whatever property and outstanding money were left behind.

Underbidding was the main cause of financial problems among contractors, competition ensuring that they bid as low as feasible. Although most canals would not accept an obviously uneconomical proposal, instead settling for the lowest "responsible" one, the possibility of profit was so narrow that any alterations in optimum conditions could render it null. Unforeseen rises in wages and provision prices could make a mockery of initial calculations. H. W. Campbell, a contractor on the C&O, noted in 1830 that wages, $8 a month when he bid, ranged from $10 to $14 less than two years later, while provisioning costs had also risen. Bad weather and epidemics played havoc with a work schedule as well. Contractors' miscalculations of the difficulty of work protracted the time involved and shrank the likelihood of finishing the job. Builders for two sections on the Wabash & Erie, for example, complained they were excavating "a kind of soft sand stone" and not sand as expected. "[W]e are prepared to do the work as low as any Body," they maintained, "but we are not willing to loos any more." Contracting partnerships also ran into problems, as personal disputes could develop over business matters or individual conduct. A recurring complaint was that one partner was not doing his share of the work or contributing promised capital. Sometimes the falling-out could be more serious, as in the case of a contractor named Gunn who was jailed for debt when his partner absconded from the C&O with their monthly estimate.[53]

---

52 *Third Annual Report of the Chesapeake and Ohio Canal Company* (Washington, 1829), lxiv – lxvi.
53 H. W. Campbell, 13 July 1830, C&O/LR; J. J. Vest, S. Vest, and R. Brasher to the Trustees of the Wabash & Erie, 15 June 1850, W&E/COR; William J. Ball to Col. T. H. Blake, 10 July, 11 Sept. 1848, Abandoned Sections no, 1 – Eal River Division, W&E/COR; Thomas Purcell, 24 Aug., 16 Sept. 1833, C&O/LR.

Even if he had been discerning in his evaluation, had scrupulously pursued his work and had an honest partner, a builder was still at the mercy of canal management. He could be shortchanged by an engineer who did not agree with the extent or difficulty of the work done. In 1839, for example, several contractors on the C&O complained that the engineers of their division practiced "cutting down" estimates by hundreds of dollars – that is, undervaluing the work that had been done – "thereby trammelling these contractors – causing them to be unable to meet their engagements with their laborers, and seriously overthrowing their credit." A number had gone bankrupt as a result.[54]

If engineers felt that builders were not meeting the terms of their contract, they had the authority (with the board's authorization) to declare it abandoned and re-let it to a more acceptable candidate. This was the case with contractors Ennis and Hanchett, who, "having entirely neglected to attend to their work," lost their contract on the Wabash & Erie.[55] The erstwhile contractor lost his posted security, whatever money had been retained from his estimates, and investments in housing, tools and provisions.

Late payment or nonpayment of estimates by management was more damaging to a contractor's purse. When not getting the money due him, a contractor on the Ohio Canal took the expedient of refusing to pay his men for work done as long as a year before. This could have frightening consequences, however. Often, if a builder did not have enough cash to pay off his hands, he faced being confronted by an angry, impoverished mob.[56] Management malpractice could have a more serious effect. A contractor on New York's Chenango Canal was not given his estimates nor paid for thirteen months, yet kept at work believing his account would soon be settled. Instead, he went bankrupt and had to sell off his tools to meet his creditors; only upon petition to the state canal board were his losses made good.[57] Contractors thus faced a variety of economic pressures, any one of which could be the difference between successful completion and financial ruin.

Some builders looked to management when things went wrong. M. S. Wines, $3,000 in debt with his property under several attachments and confined by law to Washington County, asked the C&O to release his outstanding earnings to his creditors, saying all he wished was his liberty. And when W. W. Fenton got hopelessly in debt, owing his forty men an

54 Petition of Contractors Near Fifteen Mile Creek, Alleghany County, n.d. [25 Sept. 1839], C&O/LR.
55 Ball to Blake, 15 March 1849, Abandoned Sections, W&E/COR.
56 Robert Creighton to Kelley, 5 May 1827, OH/CC. See also Timothy Cunningham, 21 Dec. 1837, C&O/LR; Henry Smith, 26 Dec. 1837, C&O/LR; George Grier, 24 Nov. 1838, C&O/LR; Richard Howe to Kelley, 9 Jan. 1832, OH/CC; C. Carter to E. F. Lucas, 27 March 1844, Mary J. Aborn Collection, Indiana Division, Indiana State Library, Indianapolis.
57 Report of the Select Committee, upon the petition of Crossitt and others, for relief, New York State, In Assembly, 9 May 1836.

average of $19, he asked the company's aid to help pay them off "for the benefit of their familys." There is no record of the C&O's response. Others were forced to request that their contracts be declared abandoned to avoid getting further in debt.[58]

At least these individuals accepted their condition with honour, notifying company officials and seeking to satisfy their creditors. Other builders were not so scrupulous. Too far in debt ever to hope to escape, with merchants and labourers demanding their money and perhaps with a fat packet of cash drawn for the last month's estimate, many merely took to the road without warning.[59] In May 1829, the contractor on section 19 of the C&O absconded with the last estimate, leaving his unpaid labourers "in a pitiable condition . . . sick, without money, medicine, provisions or the power of attaining any." When Ford and Company abandoned the line, they owed their workers and masons $150–200 in total, in some cases $15–20 to married men with families dependent on the wages. Contractor Thomas Walsh fled "poor, common labourers," each of whom he owed between $15 and $42.[60]

Workers were outraged at such behaviour. When R. A. Clements abandoned his contract on the C&O the company still owed him $270, and his labourers claimed that the money should be handed over to them before going to his creditors, "in as much as they performed the labor which produced the money." Workers on the Chesapeake & Delaware, whose contractors absconded with their wages, refused to return to work for the canal company after it took over construction unless guaranteed they would be reimbursed. And when a C&O contractor died in 1830 leaving debts of $200 to his men, his hands hired an attorney to represent their claims.[61] Often canallers took the law into their own hands, a fact that struck fear in the hearts of insolvent employers, and perhaps hastened their flight. The head of a maintenance crew on the Juniata Division of the Pennsylvania system voiced his apprehension about discharging forty men without money to pay them. To do so would mean "treating them with great injustice," but, more importantly, would "be nearly as much as my life would be worth, for they are all Irish and already begin to shew some rebellious symptoms." When a contractor on the Delaware & Hudson absconded, leaving "about 150 men who had confidence in a villain, not even the means of paying for a dinner," they seized his supply of

58 M. S. Wines, 36 March 1830, C&O/LR; W. W. Fenton, 14 Aug., 20 Sept. 1830, C&O/LR; Ball to Blake, 15 May 1849, Abandoned Sections, W&E/COR.
59 See James Costigan & Co. to Ingle, 7 April 1830; J. S. Nicholls, 27 April, 20 July 1830; Clement Cox, 4 May 1831; William Price, 25 May 1838, C&O/LR.
60 C&O/PRO, 16 Dec. 1829 (A 425); Cruger to Ingle, 8, 12 Nov. 1829; Daniel Van Slyke to Mercer, 24 July 1830; D. Weisel to Ingle, 19 March 1833, C&O/LR.
61 Ingle to Richard S. Coxe, 2 April 1830 (A 197), C&O/LS; *Eighth General Report of the President and Directors of the Chesapeake and Delaware Canal Company* (Philadelphia, 1827), 12–17, 27; Ingle to Coxe, 2 April 1830 (A 196), C&O/LS.

gunpowder and threatened to blast the property, if not the owner, to hell. The militia had to be called out to quiet them.[62]

The threat to peace and continued production on the line was magnified when generalized financial problems caused a wave of contractors to take the money and run. Rising expenses were a key factor. The cost of wages and provisions had been on an upward trend through the 1820s–30s. For instance, prevailing labour shortages on the C&O Canal caused wages to rise from $10–12 a month without board (or roughly $23–25 a month with room and board costs included) at the opening of construction in 1828 to $15–17 by 1833 and to $1–1.25 a day without board (or $26–32.50 a month based on twenty-six working days per month) by 1839.[63] The story was the same wherever wage labour prevailed on canals.

Although aid was occasionally forthcoming when conditions were bad, the common stated policy of canal administrations precluded upward revisions of prices. The Ohio Canal Commission, for example, made it clear in 1826 during a time of some financial difficulties among contractors that no more than the contracted price would be paid, whatever the case.[64] In the midst of a general crisis during 1836, contractors on Ohio's Miami Canal north of Dayton drew up a memorial to the state legislature asking for relief. Prices had risen greatly since they had taken their contracts in 1833–34: wages for common labourers had gone from $8–10 a month to $12–14. The commission recommended that relief be given only in cases of extreme hardship, otherwise "all inducement to a vigilant and economical prosecution of work on the canal will cease." Rising costs and illness were to be expected and allowed for when making a bid. "If extra allowances become general," the commissioners worried, "the contract will soon become a nullity."[65]

For all practical purposes, that was exactly what contracts had become by the mid-1830s, as they were frequently abandoned, either through management action or by absconding builders, and canals were occasionally forced to revise prices upward to head off a general collapse of contractors.

62   W. B. Mitchell to James Stevenson, 27 March 1831, Juniata Division Reports and Miscellaneous Documents, Divisional Records, Board of Canal Commissioners Records, Canal and Public Works Papers, Part I, Division of Internal Affairs, Bureau of Land Records, Record Group 17, Pennsylvania Historical and Museum Commission, Harrisburg (hereafter PA/RG17; *Ulster Sentinel*, 19 July 1826, quoted in Dorothy Hulburt Sanderson, *The Delaware and Hudson Canalway: Carrying Coals to Rondout* (orig. ed. 1965; Ellenville, N.Y.: Rondout Valley Publishing Company, 1974), 109, 110.

63   Chesapeake & Ohio, Ledger for Labor Accounts, 1829–30, Chesapeake and Ohio Canal Papers, series 291, NA/RG79; Hagerstown [Maryland] *Torchlight*, 21 May 1829; Purcell, 4 May 1833, C&O/LR; *Eleventh Annual Report of the President and Directors of the Chesapeake and Ohio Canal Company* (Washington, 1839), 16.

64   "Fourth Annual Report of the Ohio Canal Commission, 1826," in *Public Documents Concerning the Ohio Canals*, ed. John Kilbourne (Columbus, 1832), 188–89; Samuel Rosseter to Kelley, 3 Oct. 1826, OH/CC; Samuel Granger to Kelley, 7 Dec. 1826, OH/CC.

65   [Picqua, Ohio] *Western Courier*, 9 Jan. 1836; Ohio Canal Commission Minute Books (see n. 46 above), v. 1, 331–39.

Boards could deny builders an elevation of their prices, but could not halt climbing costs of labour and provisions. As new sections of the canal were open for letting, they were forced to grant higher contract prices than had been foreseen at the commencement of construction. And, in light of the everpresent danger of labour unrest and angry local creditors caused by defaulting contractors, management was repeatedly forced to break its code of nonresponsibility and take measures to prevent contractor fraud, if only to keep work going. As early as the end of the first season of construction on the Erie, for example, advances had to be made to contractors.[66] Despite such remedial action, business failure was a very real presence for builders. Harry N. Scheiber estimated that 12−15 percent of contracts were abandoned on Ohio's canals, for instance.[67] And this does not take into account the many more who barely eked out their contract with little in the way of profits, or even some residual debts to show for all their effort.

The C&O's experience shows the quandary in which both builders and management were placed. The company believed the wave of contractor failures in the late 1820s was the result of an increased wage bill "attributable to various causes – as the ill-health of the Potomac Valley, in the autumnal months; and the vicinity of other public works, offering higher wages to the laborer, and a country better calculated for the accommodation of his wants, in sickness as well as in health." Contractors could not cope on the basis of their bid. "The truth is," admitted the chief engineer, Benjamin Wright, "that *we know* the prices of these contractors are very low, and that it yet remains doubtful whether they can sustain themselves – and therefore any little favorable circumstances should not be turned against them." In what became a common response on canals when contractors were in trouble, the C&O released the retained percentage to those they trusted in hopes this would suffice. As a final solution, the president was empowered to increase contract prices for future work, again for "deserving" builders.[68] Canals were forced to make such allowances throughout the Canal Era. The alternative of declaring contracts abandoned and going through the bidding process once more would have achieved nothing, as higher costs would have made for higher prices anyway. The Pennsylvania Board of Canal Commissioners, for example, re-let many contracts on the Erie Extension because of rising costs and adverse conditions, but had to do so again when these prices too proved

---

66 Minutes of the New York Canal Commission and Superintendent of Public Works (see n. 29 above), v. 1, p. 5 (10 Dec. 1817). See also ibid., v. 1, p. 50 (11 Jan. 1825); ibid., v. 2, p. 142−67 (21 May 1838), 183−92; *In Senate, State of New York, Report from the Commissioners of the Canal Fund of allowances made to contractors on the Chenango Canal, 27 March 1837* (N.p., n.d.).

67 Harry N. Scheiber, *Ohio Canal Era: A Case Study of Government and the Economy, 1821−61* (Athens, Ohio: Ohio University Press, 1969), 72.

68 *Second Annual Report of the Chesapeake and Ohio Canal Company* (Washington, 1830), 5; Benjamin Wright to Mercer, 9 Feb., 25 March 1830, C&O/LR; C&O/PRO, 8 April 1829 (A 196), 22 April 1829 (A 205), 27 May 1829 (A 230−35).

inadequate.[69] Price revision was thus not a case of company welfare but the least harmful business strategy.

Such tactics stemmed the tide of abandoned contracts but could never eliminate the problem, which was rooted firmly in the nature of contracting. Builders on the C&O, for example, were again caught in a spiral of inflation and failures in the mid-1830s, and the company was repeatedly forced to release retained monies and increase prices. "'The laborer is worthy of his hire' is an old saying, both just and true," a committee of directors said of contractors, "and it is equally so, that it is *to the interest . . .* of all who compose this great Company, that he should receive it." They felt certain that the board "would revolt" at the idea of achieving "this great undertaking, through the means of unrequited labor, or, of benefitting or profiting, at the expence of the ruin of the poor & laboring man." As we shall see, management's concern did not extend to the true "poor & laboring man."[70]

Price revisions were palliative at best from an industry perspective. They might solve a number of contractors' problems for the time being but did not erase the source: canal construction usually did not draw in enough capital or finish quickly enough to be successful. This was understandable given the constraints of the developing industrial economy. Only more capital (with the federal government the only viable source) and labour could have solved the problem. Canal companies had adopted contracting to get rid of responsibility for solving this conundrum but it was no solution, only a holding tactic until the spread of a capitalist labour market largely did the job for them.

Contractors were petty entrepreneurs. They risked initial capital outlay against the possibility of making a profit at the completion of the job. The contractor was both independent and dependent. He was fully responsible for the work and men, but was contractually linked with a canal management that asserted executive control in important areas. Also, he was enmeshed in a payment system that increasingly became a credit network, the state paying irregularly and in scrip, the builder scratching out his work, often indebted to hands. As it operated for much of the Canal Era, it was clear that the contracting system did not work for a significant minority of builders. Many were forced to abandon their contracts, yield themselves up to the mercy of the company or courts, or flee the line. As a result, canallers were left without jobs, were owed money for work, and often were short of food, shelter and clothing, for all of which they had

69 *Pennsylvania Board of Canal Commissioners Report* (Harrisburg, 1836–37), 128.
70 Report of a Committee of Directors on an Increase in Prices, 4 Feb. 1837, C&O/LR; C&O/PRO, 20 Aug. 1836 (E 126–28); Michael Smith, 19 Aug. 1836, C&O/LR; Fisk to George Bender, 22 AUG., 14 Sept. 1836, C&O/LR; George Bender, 23 Aug. 1836, C&O/LR; Anthony Loftus, 28 Oct. 1836, C&O/LR; Fisk's Estimate for increase of price, Dec. 1836, C&O/LR; Report of C. B. Fisk, 5 Feb. 1838, C&O/LR.

relied on their bosses. Such incidents destroyed the illusion of contractor paternalism, showing it up as the commercial relationship it was and highlighting the dependence of workers, however cocooned they were in the apparent shelter of shanty society. The contractor, as middleman between capital and labour, became a lightning rod for all the grievances inherent in that position. This connection between labourer, contractor and capitalist, and the strains that inevitably developed within it, lay at the heart of the severe labour unrest that periodically convulsed canals.

For all its problems, the managerial and contracting system developed in canal construction usually got the job done. The completion within eight years of such a massive undertaking as the Erie Canal was testimony to its practicality. At the same time, the arrangement always experienced problems and often seemed to be on the verge of disarray, even when economic conditions were favourable. The system would increasingly break down in the mid-1830s, as financial problems intensified, canals' ability to pay builders on schedule declined and it was not unusual for estimates to be one or two months in arrears. Contractors operated on their retained percentage (if the company would release it) or on credit and their workers' sufferance, in this way passing on the financial risk of construction. The canal industry's continuing problem with funding and labour supply had been subsumed by the contracting system, but instead of disappearing, it fragmented into a thousand little difficulties. The economic climate of the late 1830s crudely forged the myriad pieces into a monstrous whole that brought the industry to its knees. Out of the crisis would emerge a stronger contracting system with its paternalistic trappings dissolved by the solvent of labour surplus. At last, contracting would approximate its ideal and become a business run "as low as labor and capital can afford."

CHAPTER 3

"Human labor, physical and intelligent"

Let Prosperity be excited to perpetuate
our
Free Institutions,
and to make still greater efforts than
their ancestors, to
promote
Public Prosperity
by the recollection that these works of
Internal Improvements
were achieved by the
Spirit and Perseverence
of
Republican Freemen[1]

When I landed in sweet Philadelphia, the weather was pleasant and clear
I did not stay long in the city, so quickly I shall let you hear.
I did not stay long in the city, for it happened to be in the fall,
I never reefed a sail in my rigging, 'till I anchored out on the canal.[2]

As a child in Ireland, Richard Kelley was orphaned and left in the care of his uncle, who apprenticed him to a shoemaker. Soon tiring of the work, Kelley stowed away in 1811 on a ship to Newfoundland. There he worked on a fishing smack. At one point he was caught in a forest fire while ashore on the Miramichi River in New Brunswick, and only escaped by crawling into a hole on the riverbank. The next year he survived a shipwreck and, with the aid of an Indian boy, made his way to Quebec where he set up shop as a shoemaker. After several years, Kelley left with a contractor for the Welland Canal to make and repair shoes for the labourers, meeting and marrying his wife on the Rideau Canal along the way. He eventually

1 Inscription on plaque placed on completed locks on Erie Canal at Lockport, from *Picqua Gazette*, 16 July 1825.
2 From "Paddy on the Canal," *Irish Emigrant Ballads*, ed. Wright (see Ch. 2, n. 2 above), 533.

settled at Split Rock, New York (where the Welland had a quarry), and, after working on the Oswego and Chenango canals, Kelley established a successful shoe shop and grocery store.[3]

The Fry family made a journey of seventy-four days by wagon, ship and canal boat from Bavaria to Buffalo in the mid-1830s. Sixteen-year-old Fred soon was recruited by an agent of Ohio's Walhonding Canal with the promise of a wage of 50¢ a day plus board, as well as passage and provision on the way there. Fred left for Cleveland but soon found the food allowance was not forthcoming. With but 18¢ to his name, he went hungry for three days before he bought bread for himself and five friends at Massillon on the Ohio Canal. This barely blunted the sharp edge of their hunger, and the companions were forced to leave the canal boat to forage for food along the towpath. Luckily they stumbled upon a potato patch and orchard. Fred reached Roscoe on the Walhonding that night and went straight to work the next day. His family soon followed and the Frys took up residence in a log cabin provided by the contractor, which they temporarily shared with a French labourer and his wife. The nine people lived together in one room for a winter until the French woman died and her husband left. The Frys were not left untouched by death either, as four of them had been laid to rest within ten years. Life along the canal could be costly.[4]

The stories of Richard Kelley and Fred Fry are unusual in that they can be pieced together into relative wholes. Other canallers tended to leave just fragments of their lives, yet these also are revealing of the experience of those who dug canals. Cornelius Coleman, twenty-five years old, was an Irish indentured labourer working for the Potomac Company in the mid-1780s who had already served in Kentucky. Coleman was soon on the move again, running away from his canal master. Benjamin Mace of Indiana worked in a hopyard but in the spring of 1826 put in some time on the canal around the falls of the Ohio River at Louisville, Kentucky, where he caught a fatal fever. Two nameless Irishwomen dressed in men's clothing came to work as quarriers on the Chesapeake & Delaware line, but quickly left when they discovered the lack of accommodations for workers there. William Thomas had left his home in Wales for America and found work on the Erie Canal near Utica, New York, but soon grew homesick and disheartened by canalling and warned others from following. At the age of nine, Richard Farrell was already working as a waterboy on the Welland Canal. Baptiste Dorion, a French-Canadian mason from Montreal, worked on the Rideau Canal as well as the Union Bridge, did farmwork and skippered a lumber raft for his boss, entrepreneur Philemon Wright. Sam, a slave in North Carolina, was twenty when his master sold him for $900

3 Teresa Bannan, *Pioneer Irish of Onondaga (about 1776–1847)* (New York: Putnam & Sons, 1911), 175–78.
4 Terry K. Woods, *Twenty Five Miles to Nowhere* (Coshocton, Ohio: Roscoe Foundation, 1978), 23–25.

to the Cape Fear and Deep River Navigation Company, which quickly took out an insurance policy on his life.[5]

A runaway apprentice shoemaker, a Bavarian youth and his family, an indentured servant, a native-born, part-time canaller, two women quarriers, a homesick Welshman, an Irish waterboy, a French-Canadian mason, and an African-American slave: by very different paths in very different circumstances these individuals (and thousands more like them) arrived at canal work. A more motley crew than the republican freemen immortalized in the commemorative plaque on the Erie at Lockport, they shared the status of canal worker. Who these people were, where they came from, and how and why they came to be on public works are questions that shed light on the canal labour force but also on the rise of capitalism and the wage labour system that lies at its heart.

Roots of the workforce

Speaking at the commencement ceremony for the Ohio Canal on the Fourth of July, 1825, Thomas Ewing, Esq., admitted that the state of Ohio did not have much gold or silver. "But money is not wealth, it is merely its representative, and . . . it is not the quantity of the precious metals which it [Ohio] contains, that is the criterion of its power, but the excess of human labour and human sustenance, which remains after supplying the people with the ordinary comforts of life." Ewing thus rejected traditional measures of affluence in favour of a labour theory of value, convinced that "the only efficient agent is human labor, physical and intelligent, and gold and silver are but the means in the hands of government to call forth that labor and give it direction."[6] Yet the problem remained of finding enough natural human wealth to make the state prosperous by digging its canal system. Just as it was impossible to play the alchemist and transform dirt and rock into gold and silver, an army of workers could not be conjured up where a stand of trees or field of corn stood. Early industry developed within such a barren terrain, starved of human labour, but it was not a wasteland, as people surged in from a variety of sources to make the economy rich and verdant. And canal companies harvested where and when

5 *Virginia Journal*, 11 Oct. 1787; Herschel Hurdy to Benjamin Mace and all friends, 16 Aug. 1826, Benjamin Mace Papers, Indiana Division, Indiana State Library; Latrobe to Thomas Vickers Mason, 15 April 1804, Latrobe Collection, MHS; Latrobe to Stephen Hayes, 27 Oct. 1804, ibid.; William Thomas to His Father et al., 17 Aug. 1818, in *The Welsh in America: Letters from the Immigrants*, ed. Alan Conway (Minneapolis: University of Minnesota, 1961), 60–61; Bannan, *Pioneer Irish of Onondaga*, (see n. 3 above), 47; Valentine "Supplying the Rideau" (see Ch. 2, n. 50 above), 25–26; Mr. McKay's Bill of Sale for Sam, 30 Jan. 1856, and Insurance Policy on the Life of Sam for H. A. London, 19 Feb. 1856, London Family Papers (No. 2011), Southern Historical Collection, Wilson Library, University of North Carolina at Chapel Hill (hereafter SHC).
6 *Commencement of the Ohio Canal at the Licking Summit. July 4th, 1825, Lancaster, Ohio* (Columbus, 1826), 20–21.

they could – slaves, servants, wage workers, women, children and, increasingly, immigrants – making for a highly differentiated and largely
anonymous group. A workforce had to be drawn from existing scarcity and
it mirrored the pockets of labour scattered across the Noth American
landscape.

The president of the Chesapeake & Ohio, like other canal officials, had
no personal knowledge of those digging his canal. "The greater part of
them are transient foreigners; sometimes on the Pennsylvania Canals; sometimes on the Baltimore and Ohio Rail Road; sometimes at work on our
canal."[7] At this time, it was still novel to have an army of labourers
roaming from work site to work site, a situation that became normal in the
industrial age. And canallers were people on the move. The first workers
tended to be native-born Americans who journeyed to public works from
farms on a casual or seasonal basis. As time passed, the majority of canallers
came to be European migrants. And for most, canal construction was just a
passing stage in their work career. From a historical perspective, navvies
were changing from unfree to free, indentured and slave labour playing a
significant role in early construction but gradually yielding to wage workers.
Thus canallers were people in motion, with different personal pasts but
shared experiences, a faceless mass caught in the current of history flowing
in canals.

The story was much the same in Europe and in North America. The
emergence of industrial capitalism set in train a series of changes that
uprooted a previously agrarian people and transformed them into wage
workers. In a drawn-out process, market forces redirected production from
subsistence to commercial exchange, redefining and streamlining agricultural
and craft practices to make them competitive, thereby liberating the labour
power of a significant proportion of the population to be used where
demand dictated. Discussed in terms of factors of production, these changes
seem to work in an impartial way, clockwork in which the various gears fit
neatly together, but flesh and blood fed into this machinery could be
maimed and mutilated. The scenario on canals was but a reflection of class
formation in larger society. It was a history of movement from the land or
petty production to wage work, the hallmark of proletarianization, that
best captures the navvies' story and infuses a study of canal construction
with historical importance. It was not a tale of unalloyed decline for those
who ended up working on canals; the lives of dependent people of all eras
have been difficult. But for most free people at least, it amounted to a
qualitative loss in the important sense of controlling the results of their
labour. In the past, feast or famine, they consumed the immediate products
of their efforts; now they were dependent on their employer and the market
as the arbiters of their fortune, which lay beyond their control. So it was

7 Mercer to Susan Decatur, 13 Dec. 1830, C&O/LR.

that the breakdown of household production and the emergence of wage labour altered the essence of existence for many. People with some control over the fruits of their toil were reconstructed into individuals who purchased their subsistence with labour power. For most this entailed a movement from farmland to free labour, and whatever the starting place – Irish village or Yankee cabin in the woods – the trek to a canal shanty town was an arduous one.

In Canada and the northeastern United States a household form of production was the norm into the early nineteenth century. Craft production took place within the home or small workshops, and was for local consumption. Farm families produced the bulk of their own needs while a few commodities, like butter, cheese and spun goods, were used to exchange for necessary items and minor luxuries the household could not produce itself. However, market participation was clearly subsidiary to subsistence. Over time, development placed pressure on the land. Natural increase led to intergenerational subdivision, continual cropping made the soil decreasingly productive, and the spreading market drew farmers into a competitive system that required specialized production of commercial crops rather than the subsistence ideal of mixed agriculture. A crisis of household production developed in which the only way to perpetuate the family's hold on the land was to recast its priorities. Further shrinkage of farm acreage had to be prevented, land being the source of both subsistence and saleable commodities. Primogeniture became a more common form of inheritance. As a result, provisions had to be made for the other children, such as partial support to go with wage labour, training in nonagrarian occupations, and marriage of daughters to propertied males. Fewer opportunities on the land meant postponement of marriage and increasing spinsterhood or bachelorhood.[8]

While such strategies were often successful in perpetuating the family farm, a surplus of labour was naturally spun off, consisting of individuals who could no longer be provided for in the new agrarian order. The choice offered these people was wage labour at home or migration, and the final decision tended to be delayed as long as possible. People worked for wages part-time, either locally or following harvests around the region, while doing their share on the home farm in return for room and board. Many in the North relocated to large urban centres where jobs were opening. Eventually, the move away would become permanent and the farmer fully a

8 Henretta, "Families and Farms" (see Introduction, n. 6 above); Palmer; "Social Formation and Class Formation" (see Introduction, n. 6 above), 241–44; Clark, "Household Economy" (see Introduction, n. 6 above); Mary P. Ryan, *Cradle of the Middle Class: The Family in Oneida County, New York, 1790–1865* (Cambridge: Cambridge University Press, 1981), 19–34; David Gagan, *Hopeful Travellers: Families, Land, and Social Change in Mid-Victorian Peel County, Canada West* (Toronto: University of Toronto Press, 1981).

worker. The western frontier did allow displaced farmers the chance of again establishing themselves on the land, as tenants as well as farmowners, but the same problems snapped at their heels. The process would start again as dwindling land, population pressures, higher capital costs to remain competitive, and a greater subjection to the market would squeeze the farm families, once more forcing some from the land. For many, then, migration only prolonged the move into wage labour.[9]

Canal work, because of its relatively high cash wages and seasonality, was an attractive option to people set adrift from the land but still pulled by its republican promise, at least into the 1830s. Most farmers would be acquainted with the basic skills needed, such as digging, cutting trees, pulling stumps and driving teams, and some would be able to do some blacksmithing, carpentry or stonework. Particularly in more recently settled areas, farmers looked to the cash wages canal work offered as a means of supplementing agricultural income, paying off the farm and meeting taxes. Massachusetts farmers in the 1790s, with farms shrinking and soils depleted, were thankful for the opportunity to dig the Middlesex. Similarly, labourers on the canals of New York, Pennsylvania, Ohio and Indiana were first drawn from the local farm population. On Pennsylvania's Delaware & Schuylkill Canal in the 1790s, individuals worked for a few days only to disappear, presumably returning to their farms, while others brought along their teams to haul for 15s. ($2) a day, a princely sum for cash-hungry yeomen when common labourers earned 5s. 6d. Naturally farmers were rarely available during planting and harvesting. The military superintendent at the Grenville Canal complained in 1824 that hands, impossible to get all spring, were too numerous in other seasons. And on the Ohio Canal in 1831, rising wheat prices meant that farmers and their sons stayed on the farm, thereby creating labour shortage and high wages on the canal.[10]

Many of the locals who worked on canals were farm labourers and not owners, which, given prevailing labour shortages, placed companies in competition with farmers, especially during the planting and harvesting seasons. Higher wages resulted. Loammi Baldwin, the Middlesex Canal's engineer, had a problem with labourers who signed on for the season and

9 Jeremy Atack, 'Tenants and Yeomen in the Nineteenth Century," *Agricultural History*, v. 62 (Summer 1988), 6–32; Gavin Wright, "American Agriculture and the Labor Market: What Happened to Proletarianization?" *Agricultural History*, v. 62 (Summer 1988), 182–209; Joy Parr, "Hired Men: Ontario Agricultural Labour in Historical Perspective," *Labour/Le Travail*, v. 15 (Spring 1985), 91–103.

10 Baldwin Report, 15 July–15 Aug. 1795, Middlesex Reports (see Ch. 1, n. 21 above); Peter A. Wallner, "Politics and Public Works: A Study of the Pennsylvania Canal System, 1825–1857," Ph.D. diss., Pennsylvania State University, 1973, 74; Ernest M. Teagarden, "Builders of the Ohio Canal, 1825–1832," *Inland Seas*, v. 19 (1963), 95–96; William Cooper Howells, *Recollections of Life in Ohio From 1813 to 1840* (Cincinnati: Robert Clark, 1895), 138–39; Harlow, *Old Towpaths* (see Ch. 1, n. 54 above), 247; Delaware & Schuylkill Time Book, 1793–94 (see Ch. 1, n. 22 above); Captain Henry DuVernet, 4 Nov. 1824, v. 41, Canal Papers, PAC/RG8; Richard Howe to Kelley, 3 Dec. 1831, OH/CC.

then left when farm wages went up during haying in early summer. Despite the holding back of their wages, men still left. When construction began on Ohio's Miami Canal in the late 1820s local farmers paid wages partly in trade, which enabled the company to attract labourers at a lower cash rate. But farmers soon began paying cash, which forced the canal to give higher wages, as native labourers preferred agricultural work.[11] By the 1830s, native-born workers were declining as a segment of the canal labour force. Canalling was never really an attractive job for those with some options, and its increasing identification with immigrant labour, violence and drunkenness appears to have redirected the native-born into farm labour or industrial work or onto the frontier as more fitting opportunities for American sons.

In Quebec similar forces were conspiring to sever *habitants* (the French-Canadian peasant farmers) from the soil and thrust them into wage labour. It is a story that is less akin to the rest of the American Northeast and more closely approximates that of Ireland with its shared themes of British dominance, the breakdown of a peasantry and religious and cultural conflict. The seigneurial system in which peasants farmed the land of their lords was transformed as the former French colony was drawn more firmly into the British Empire. After the British market was opened to Canadian agricultural products in 1793, a shift from near-subsistence to commercial production ensued. Land under cultivation expanded and the population grew to meet increased labour demands. In the early 1800s, however, French-Canadians turned away from growing wheat for the British market to production for local consumption. Although a prolonged historical debate has been waged over whether this shift resulted from the *habitants'* innate conservatism or their burgeoning market mentality, certain common features of transforming French-Canadian society are agreed upon.[12] The population was swelling, placing pressure on the land, traditional relationships with seigneurs (the French-Canadian landed gentry) were crumbling and life was increasingly influenced by market forces. Families evaded laws enforcing partition of inheritance so as to concentrate landholding. Necessarily, those kept from the land as a result of this strategy had to look elsewhere for a

11 Baldwin to President and Directors, 23 July 1798, Middlesex Reports (see Ch. 1, n. 21 above); Ohio Canal Commission Minute Books (see Ch. 2, n. 46 above), v. 1, 336.
12 See Fernand Ouellet, *Economic and Social History of Quebec, 1760–1850: Structures and Conjunctures* (French edition 1966; Ottawa: Carleton University, Institute of Canadian Studies, 1980), ch. 7–14; Ouellet, "Le Mythe de 'l'habitant sensible au marché': commentaires sur la controverse LeGoff – Wallot et Paquet," *Recherches Sociographiques*, v. 17 (1976), 115–32; Gilles Paquet et Jean-Pierre Wallot, "Crise argricole et tensions socio-ethniques dans le Bas-Canada, 1802–1812: éléments pour une ré-interpretation," *Revue d'Histoire L'Amerique Français*, v. 26 (1972), 185–237; T. J. A. LeGoff, "The Agricultural Crisis in Lower Canada, 1802–1812: A Review of a Controversy," *Canadian Historical Review*, v. 55 (March 1974), 1–31; Paquet and Wallot, "The Agricultural Crisis in Lower Canada, 1802–12: mise au point. A Response to T. J. A. LeGoff," *Canadian Historical Review*, v. 56 (June 1975), 133–61; Paquet and Wallot, *Lower Canada at the Turn of the Nineteenth Century: Restructuring and Modernization* (Canadian Historical Association, Historical Booklet no. 45, 1988).

means of support, and they found it in the growing colonial timber industry, on the docks of Montreal and Quebec City and as farm labourers. In mid-century an exodus began to New England's industries among the colony's redundant labour force, a disturbing development to insular French-Canadian society.

Canal construction was an attractive alternative as it offered *Canadiens* an opportunity to remain at home near to family and church, and its seasonality allowed *habitants* to maintain connections to the land by working part-time on the family farm or as agricultural labourers. Thus the French played a small but important role on Canadian canals. The Rideau's two main contractors, Philemon Wright and Sons of Hull, and McKay and Redpath of Montreal, employed significant numbers of *habitants*, considering them more controllable than Irish. French-Canadians constituted 75 percent of the former's and 66 percent of the latter's common labourers, and 50 percent of skilled workers for both contractors.[13] Yet they never amounted to the numbers one would expect on Quebec canals. Their dislike for the work, job competition with the Irish, and prevailing ethnic stereotypes that characterized *habitants* as insufficiently hardy for such demanding work limited their participation.[14] A variety of cultural factors thus contoured and limited the French-Canadian experience with canalling.

Women were doubly disadvantaged by the commercialization of agriculture, as they had derived some authority in the household economy from their role in producing surplus goods that brought needed cash into the home. Labour shortages assured that wage work opened up for them, but their secondary status in patriarchal society meant they could be more fully exploited than men. Jobs they were able to get as domestics, teachers and mill workers had attractions – like freeing them from the direct supervision of parents and providing the independence that wages could confer – but they were always treated as second-class producers solely because of their gender. In the sweating trades even these benefits did not accrue as the household was adapted and moulded to the needs of industrial capital, women working at home and their wages going directly into the household pot. Movement into wage labor thus came at a cost for women, their gender being used as justification to situate them at the bottom of the economy. Capitalist development thus offered women choices similar to those faced by all labouring people: transformation into free labour even more disadvantaged by their gender, or retreat into the home either as subjugated sweated labour or, for the more well-off, as pampered and protected but ultimately powerless madonnas. Women developed defenses to parry these cruel thrusts, and to a degree converted the force to their

13   Wylie, "Poverty, Distress, and Disease" (see Introduction, n. 11 above), 12.
14   Bleasdale, "Unskilled Labourers on the Public Works of Canada" (see Introduction, n. 11 above), 89–91.

own ends, but inevitably they were in the end pinioned by their sex to a disadvantaged and subordinate position in society. Socially, this meant that they were the inferiors of their male relatives; economically, women were dependent appendages of male breadwinners, no matter how crucial they were to household finances.[15] This double exploitation is clearly apparent in the rather limited evidence on women in the canal industry.

The two women quarriers mentioned at the opening of this chapter who appeared on the Chesapeake & Delaware Canal were unusual in their involvement in actual construction. Because of the physical demands of the work and prevailing attitudes toward females, few participated in either digging or skilled work. Such considerations did not always protect slave women; the Santee Canal purchased equal numbers of both sexes in the 1790s, and the Cape Fear & Deep River Navigation Company also owned women in the 1850s.[16] These women worked alongside men in the swamps and river channels as they did in the rice and cotton fields. Conversely, white women in the North filled service jobs in the industry, hired by the company or contractors or paid directly by the hands. Nellie Butler and Susan Jackson, for instance, worked as cooks for the C&O, as did Mary Adlum and her daughter Rachael. Allice Daw cooked for twenty hands on a maintenance scow for the Wabash & Erie. Laundering was another major source of employment for women on canals.[17] Several women also worked as locktenders on the C&O, a position of authority inherited when their husbands died. This situation caused some consternation among company officials. One superintendent complained, "It is very plain that they are not as competent as men," even though they had been performing the job for some time. The company moved to strip these women of their jobs but relented, settling for female labour specifically because it was cheaper than that of men, a consideration that usually won out against moral concerns in industry.[18] Women, typically wives of canallers, also worked for themselves, setting up boarding shanties, cooking, mending and cleaning for a fee, or

---

15 Julie Matthaei, *An Economic History of Women in America: Women's Work, the Sexual Division of Labor, and the Development of Capitalism* (New York: Schocken Press, 1982); Faye E. Dudden, *Serving Women: Household Service in Nineteenth-Century America* (Middletown, Conn.: Wesleyan University Press, 1983); Christine Stansell, "The Origins of the Sweatshop: Women and Early Industrialization in New York City," in *Working-Class America: Essays on Labor, Community, and American Society*, ed. Michael H. Frisch and Daniel J. Walkowitz (Urbana: University of Illinois Press, 1983), 78–103; Marjorie Griffin Cohen, *Women's Work, Markets, and Economic Development in Nineteenth-Century Ontario* (Toronto: University of Toronto Press, 1988); Gordon, Edwards, and Reich, *Segmented Work, Divided Workers* (see Ch. 1, n. 13 above), 67–73; Thomas Dublin, *Women at Work: The Transformation of Work and Community in Lowell, Massachusetts, 1826–1860* (New York: Columbia University Press, 1979), ch. 3.

16 Porcher, *Santee Canal* (see Ch. 1, n. 11 above), 6; London Family Papers (no. 2011-B), 1855, folders 7, 8, SHC.

17 C&O Ledger for Labor Accounts, 1829–30 (see Ch. 2, n. 63 above), 135, 158, 165; Check Roll of William Elgin for September 1834, C&O/LR; Amount due and paid on the Division of the Wabash and Erie Canal from Peru to Carrollton, Aug. 1847, Abstracts of Labor Due, IN/II.

18 Mary Ross, 24 March, 1835, C&O/LR; Elizabeth Burgess, 31 March 1835, ibid.; John Young, 15 March, 15 April, 30 Sept. 1835, ibid.

selling liquor. Given the disproportionate male population on canals, prostitution must have been a factor as well.

Those wives and daughters who lived off the canal had to work to provide subsistence for the family as canal wages on their own were inadequate. The man might not be home for months at a time, would find it difficult to send money by the mails and rarely would have much left over after his own expenses. For much of the year then, these households would be female-dominated, with most decisions being made by the mother. But this was hardly a position of strength given the nature of women's work. One justification for paying women less was that their income was additional to that of the real earner. Here, however, with the man hardly a household fixture and only able to contribute to the family income intermittently, his wife and children had to make do with the crumbs bought with their devalued labour. Despite working as seamstresses or domestics, these women (and their children) were an extension of the canal economy. As a result, women were ensnared in the industry and proletarianized simultaneously with their husbands and fathers, although rarely doing the actual excavation. Canal digging and women's work were different manifestations of the same phenomenon, and it is revealing to find them connected here, cultivated dependence necessitiating and propping up other forms of exploited labour.

Children experienced similar changed conditions with the emergence of industrial capitalism. While they had always toiled on farms and in craftshops, often involving hard work, children were usually not exposed to the exacting and dangerous regimens found in factories or construction sites. Their experience in these fields was not at all like farming where a future stake in the land gave the work some personal meaning, nor like apprenticing where tutelage and craft pride imbued tasks with some social value and offered a promise of future advancement. Wage work meant for children a premature and unsympathetic immersion in a mature world where they were treated as so much labour – smaller, weaker, but labour nonetheless.

Richard Farrell, the nine-year-old waterboy mentioned at the beginning of the chapter, was just one of many youths who worked on canals, a fact borne out by an advertisement proclaiming "stout industrious boys will be employed" on the Pennsylvania Canal near Pittsburgh. The situation on the C&O Canal in 1829 indicated the extent of child labour; one in nineteen labourers (113 of 2,113) were "boys."[19] Youths were more directly involved in construction than women, performing a number of light tasks that freed the more expensive adult labour to do heavy work. Boys carried water for

19 *Bedford Gazette*, 3 Aug. 1827; *Third Annual Report of the Chesapeake and Ohio Canal* (Washington, 1829), 24. See also Check Roll of William Elgin for September 1834, C&O/LR; John Young, 30 Sept. 1835, ibid.

men and beasts, acted as servants to engineers and contractors, were powder monkeys and helped lockkeepers, but most often drove the many horses, oxen and mules that hauled rock, dirt and timber to and from the work site.

John Campbell's experience was perhaps typical of child labourers. He worked on the Wabash & Erie Canal as a boy, tending horses for an Irish teamster and hauling fill from the excavation site to dumping pits. The contractor, with whom he boarded, took advantage of Campbell's youth by bullying and blustering him rather than paying the boy's wages. Campbell felt he had little recourse considering he was the only "hoosier" among a horde of Irish. His helplessness was driven home every day at noon, he recalled, when he was beaten by two Irish boys solely for the delight of his fellow labourers.[20] Although Campbell's account may be somewhat embroidered, it does show that children played an important role in the work process and that their tender age exposed them to persecution. As with women, their devalued social status was exploited by the industry, making them a cheap source of labour.

At the same time petty agriculture was undergoing a crisis of production, its apparent antithesis, plantation slavery, was experiencing similar pressures. An anachronistic and by nature noncapitalistic labour system, American slavery was nonetheless yoked to capitalism. Its raison d'être was the production of staples for an international market. As cotton prices declined then stabilized in the antebellum period and the cost of labour per unit of production rose, productivity had to be expanded so that a profit could be made. The only ways to do this were to find a cheaper source of labour – something very difficult since the closure of the international slave trade – or to aquire more land. The problem was compounded in the border and coastal states by soil exhaustion from continual cropping and failure to adopt improved agricultural techniques, problems not unlike those of domestic agriculture in the North and Canada. These regions naturally looked to the territories opening in the West, seeing in their vast fertile soils the only solution for the problems of slavery production.[21] For slaves in the affected regions this crisis had two effects – forced migration or increasingly commercialized slavery – "choices" similar to those faced on the land elsewhere, although the degree of coercion was obviously more profound. The first and most dreaded was sale to the Deep South where still fertile lands and large plantations created an insatiable demand for labour. A second result of declining productivity in the border and coastal states was a shift of labour into nonagricultural production, with masters

20 *Indianapolis Star*, 26 July 1907, in Scrapbook, John TenBrook Campbell Papers, Indiana Division, Indiana State Library.
21 Eugene Genovese, *The Political Economy of Slavery: Studies in the Economy and Society of the Slave South* (New York: Pantheon Books, 1965), Introduction, parts 3 and 4; Palmer, "Social Formation and Class Formation" (see Introduction, n. 6 above), 237–39.

hiring their slaves out to the urban craft and service sectors, while a small but not insignificant industrial sector absorbed some of the redundant plantation labour. Heavily capitalized ventures like factories and public works also sought to exert greater control over production by purchasing and training their own slaves.[22] A different type of slave emerged as well, a slave/worker whose labour power was hired or bought on the market not unlike a free labourer, with the fundamental difference that these were unfree workers and the fruits of their toil went to their master. In a unique fashion a slave peasant had been transformed into a slave proletarian, "freed" from the soil to satisfy the labour demands of commercial and industrial production.

Such "proletarianization" tended to work in favour of slaves, conferring more freedom from the scrutiny of masters and putting them in a position of skill and responsibility that sometimes even brought cash payment. But it also removed slaves from the protective web of paternalism and placed them in a situation where their labour was viewed more explicitly as a commodity to be exploited as fully as possible as the social responsibilities of ownership were subjugated to the demands of commercial production. This potential danger was recognized on Southern public works (in those states south of Maryland and Delaware) where hired slaves were the typical labourers. "This hiring out of Negroes is a horrid aggravation of the miseries of their condition," Fanny Kemble wrote of Georgia's Brunswick Canal in the mid-1830s, "for if, on the plantations, and under the masters to whom they belong, their labour is severe and their food inadequate, think what it must be when they are hired out for a stipulated sum to a temporary employer, who has not the interest which it is pretended an owner may feel in the welfare of his slaves, but whose chief aim it must necessarily be to get as much out of them, and expend as little on them, as possible."[23] Similar considerations made some owners hesitate to let their slaves out to public works.

Some canal companies in the South avoided the problem by buying their own slaves. In 1807, the Dismal Swamp Canal owned six slaves; in 1829 the state of Georgia owned 190 that it used on its roads and rivers. In the 1850s, the Cape Fear & Deep River Navigation Company was buying both male and female slaves; the commercial nature of the relationship was revealed in 1856 when the company president estimated that the money invested in human chattel had paid 35 percent a year.[24] Purchasing slaves

---

22 Robert S. Starobin, *Industrial Slavery in the Old South* (New York: Oxford University Press, 1970).
23 F. A. Kemble, *Journal of a Residence on a Georgia Plantation* (orig. ed. 1863; New York: Alfred Knopf, 1961), 105.
24 Brown, *Dismal Swamp Canal* (see Ch. 1, n. 16 above), 46; Phillips, *History of Transportation* (see Ch. 1, n. 6 above), 114–15; London Family Papers (No. 2011-B), 1855, folders 7, 8, SHC; Payrolls, 1859–60, London Family Papers (No. 2011), SHC; Alexander Murchison to the Directors, 14 March 1856, London Family Papers (No. 2442), SHC.

ensured a labour supply, but also meant that hands had to be cared for even when their labour was not needed. Some companies avoided the problem by hiring out their slaves in slack time, as Virginia's Upper Appamattox Company did in 1816. Contractors with their own slaves might also own a farm to which they could be shifted when needed. This was the case for one builder on the James River Canal who occasionally sent his bondsmen from the line to harvest wheat or plant "Irish Potatoes." Slave labour's seeming inflexibility was also offset by its value as property. In dire circumstances, slaves could be sold for a quick infusion of cash, as the Cape Fear & Deep River Navigation Company was forced to do in the late 1850s. An official on the Kanawha River Improvement in Virginia, after experimenting with local white labour, made clear this advantage. "The negroes being your own (or hired) you can command their service when you please – when your work is completed, if you have not further occasion for them, they can be sold for nearly as much, or probably more than they cost you."[25]

Although slave labour was the norm in the South throughout the period of canal construction, local whites and free labourers from the North were increasingly used from the 1820s. Southern yeomen farmers were wedged into a slavery system that offered few opportunities for wage labour, but this system altered as agriculture became more commercialized and the ability of petty producers to compete declined.[26] A few found their way onto public works, but like farmers in the North, they appear to have done so only on a temporary basis, working a few days here and there for cash wages. This was the case for whites who worked on a section of the James River & Kanawha during 1851.[27] Perhaps because of their casual attitude toward the work, or maybe as a result of already developing stereotypes about "poor white trash," they were usually not seen as a satisfactory labour source. The Kanawha River Improvement used locals at first, but found them slow workers, so the company built in an incentive system whereby bonuses were paid for yards of earth dug. "Although free men should not require such a stimulus to the performance of their duty," moralized the

25 Journal A, p. 59, Journal B, p. 99, Journals of the Board of Public Works, entry 6, Virginia Board of Public Works Records, Archives, Virginia State Library, Commonwealth of Virginia, Richmond (hereafter VA/BPW); Time Charts for Workers on the James River and Kanawha Canal 1848–57 (Ms. 25), June 1849 and March 1851, in Austin-Twyman Papers, Earl Gregg Swem Library, The College of William and Mary, Williamsburg, Va.; Account, 15 April–31 Oct. 1856, Cape Fear and Deep River Navigation Co. Papers (No. 2992), SHC; Thomas Bragg to Henry London, 9 April 1857, London Family Papers (No. 2442), SHC; Payrolls, 1859–60, Cape Fear and Deep River Navigation Company Records, Internal Improvements Papers, State of North Carolina Treasurer's and Comptroller's Records, North Carolina Archives, Raleigh (hereafter NCA); John Bosher to Robert Pollard, 11 Nov. 1822, Kanawha River Improvement, Letters, Accounts, Contracts, box 194, James River Company Records, VA/BPW (hereafter JRCR).
26 Steven Hahn, *The Roots of Southern Populism: Yeomen Farmers and the Transformation of the Georgia Upcountry, 1850–1890* (New York: Oxford University Press, 1983).
27 Time Chart for Workers on the James River and Kanawha Canal, Jan.–Dec. 1851, Austin-Twyman Papers (see n. 25 above).

superintendent, "the great bulk of labourers here are very illiterate, and without much sense of that kind of honour, which makes men desirous to earn their wages before receiving them."[28] The Kanawha ultimately depended upon slaves to supply Southern honour.

Elsewhere free labour was imported from the North to provide missing skills. A stream of Irish immigrants flowed from New York to New Orleans, some of whom found their way onto the Crescent City's canals. In 1820, about 1,000 Northern workers, probably Irishmen, were employed by South Carolina's Board of Works. Contractors for that state's Catawba and Saluda canals imported men from Philadelphia, Boston and Connecticut, providing passage, food, medical attention and sometimes advanced wages as inducements. Northern workers seemed to have spent only the work season in the South, returning north during winter. Some workers were brought down only to be left unemployed after a short period in a region without many other job opportunities. Such was the case of the hundred Irishmen brought in by the contractors Kirksey, Cotton & Co. for the Cape Fear & Deep River Navigation works in 1856.[29] Considerable traffic thus existed between North and South, but it appears to have been composed of Irish immigrants rather than native-born Northerners. Along with local labourers, this made for a significant contingent of free white workers on Southern canals. It is impossible to estimate the proportion of whites to blacks on Southern canals, but scattered evidence shows slaves almost always predominated.

The experience on Southern canals, as in Southern society in general, was set apart by the presence of slavery. For the bulk of the workforce it meant a more restrictive labour regime than that confronted by their white co-workers. And although moving off the land, in the sense that they slaved off of plantations, blacks by no means were moving toward the free status of most canallers. Even for white labour, slavery meant fewer job opportunities. Still, with a growing number of white wage workers, both natives and migrants, the South was inching toward a world of work that already was fast overtaking labourers elsewhere.

The forces uprooting North Americans were but continuations of changes transforming Europe that had the same effect of setting people in motion,

28 Bosher, 5 Nov. 1821; Bosher to Pollard, 11 Nov. 1822, Kanawha River Improvement Letters, JRCR.
29 Earl F. Niehaus, *The Irish in New Orleans, 1800–1860* (Baton-Rouge: Louisiana State University Press, 1965), 35; "Report of the Board of Public Works to the Legislature of South Carolina, 1820," in *Internal Improvements in South Carolina*, ed. Kohn (see Ch. 2, n. 28 above), 50; "Report of the Board of Public Works, 1821," in ibid., 131–37; Clipping from Camden, South Carolina, Newspaper, March 1820, in ibid., 67; Phillips, *History of Transportation* (see Ch. 1, n. 6 above), 85–86; "Report of the Board of Public Works, 1822," in *Internal Improvements in South Carolina*, ed. Kohn (see Ch. 2, n. 28 above), 165–66; Report of the Superintendent of Public Works for 1825, in ibid., 425; D. G. McDuffie to President and Directors, 7 June 1856, London Family Papers (No. 2442), SHC.

blazing the most important pathway to canals. The great transatlantic migrations of the sixteenth through twentieth centuries took place at a time when Europe was changing from feudal to capitalist society. Movement, internal and external, was a result of the process by which people were cut from the land or the craft and directed into the labour market. This obviously was a long-term and piecemeal development. The transformation from peasant to proletarian stretched over hundreds of years, was intergenerational rather than personal for most, and was at its essence an economic metamorphosis, not simple cultural flight. Necessarily, what happened in Europe was important to what happened in North America. Immigrants were fragments of European society carrying with them the seeds of social and economic transformation, unfinished business that would be transacted on canals where immigrants made up much of the labour force.

The importance of immigration to public works was made clear early on. An Irish-American newspaper maintained that "so long as necessary canals, roads, and bridges, remain unfinished or unattempted, so long must we feel the necessity of increasing the population by adding thereto the laborious and scientific foreigners. Then let emigration be encouraged, and this most solid of all riches flow in without interruption."[30] It was largely natives of Ireland who performed these public services. "The Irish labourers are found uncommonly handy and active, and for years have a large portion of the work on canals and turnpikes," Mathew Carey, the Irish-American printer and pamphleteer, wrote in the 1820s. More to the point, Ralph Waldo Emerson maintained, "the poor Irishman, the wheelbarrow is his country," while Charles Dickens asked rhetorically, "who else would dig, and delve, and drudge, and do domestic work, and make canals and roads, and execute great lines of Internal Improvement?"[31] These few literary examples hint at the emerging truism in the mid-nineteenth century that where there was scut work you would find the Irish. This relationship fed an emerging stereotype that the Irish were more suited to strenuous work than their Anglo peers, a rationalization of labour exploitation reminiscent of the assertion that blacks were built to work under a broiling sun or in fetid rice swamps. What led the Irish to canals, and how they came to be considered so handy with a spade – rather rudimentary technology in itself – is a fragment of a larger story in which a traditional peasant culture was broken down and capitalist society put in its place.

The Great Famine has been seen as the watershed in Irish history, with

---

30 *Shamrock*, 17 Aug. 1816, quoted in Svejda, *Irish Immigrant Participation in the Construction of the Erie Canal* (see Ch. 1, n. 11 above), 16.
31 Mathew Carey, *Reflections on the Subject of Emigration from Europe* (Philadelphia, 1826), 22; Emerson quoted in Richard D. Borgeson, "Irish Canal Laborers in America: 1817–1846," M.A. thesis, Pennsylvania State University, 1964, 24; Dickens quoted in Max Berger, *The British Traveller in America, 1836–1860* (Gloucester, Mass.: Peter Smith Publishers, 1964), 68.

what went before irretrievably changed by this abrupt and catastrophic holocaust. Recent literature has moderated this position, however, tracing many of the phenomena associated with the Famine – the dissolution of the peasantry, the reformulation of family life and massive emigration – back into the eighteenth century, portraying this event as the culmination of a longstanding process.[32] Into the eighteenth century, most Irish rural dwellers lived communally, with the most common arrangement being the *clachan*, a cluster of dwellings in which groups of families, usually related, lived. The land they farmed was leased and worked in common in a system known as *rundale* in which each household was assigned a share of tillage and pasture land, while the land was always changing hands to ensure that no one family monopolized the best holdings, the emphasis being on subsistence not profit.[33] From the late seventeenth century, this communal system came under pressure as Ireland was drawn into the British market. Landlords confiscated land, evicted peasants and converted it to commercial production, a process facilitated by the government which chipped away at tenants' rights within the clachan system. After 1750, Irish market involvement accelerated as English demand grew apace and landlords shifted production to meet it. The Irish government promoted this growing commercial orientation, and the construction of the Grand and Royal canals was among its most significant initiatives. Ireland was a colonial appendage of the British economy, manipulated by the needs of English capital, and those drawn from the land into commercial production were reduced to pauper status, the wealth they produced transferred across the Irish Sea or into the hands of the Protestant Ascendancy at home. This process – what Kerby Miller calls commercialization – was a protracted one, not being completed until the Famine.[34] Most clung tenaciously to the land, adopting a variety of strategies to prevent complete amputation of traditional agrarian life.

The scarcity of land caused by its conversion to commercial production meant family strategies had to be altered to maintain access. The partible inheritance pattern that characterized the clachan, defining its familial and communal structure, was replaced by impartibility, conferring ownership on the oldest male offspring. Siblings were thus reduced to dependent status at home, wage labour or emigration. This classic shift in family priorities generally occurs when land is scarce. Farmers moved into the market gradually, more pushed by the need of cash for provisions, taxes,

32 "General Introduction," *Irish Peasants: Violence and Political Unrest 1780–1914*, ed. Samuel Clark and James S. Donnelly, Jr. (Madison: University of Wisconsin Press, 1983).
33 Kerby Miller, *Emigrants and Exiles: Ireland and the Irish Exodus to North America* (New York: Oxford University Press, 1985), 27–28.
34 Ibid., 28–33; Michael Beames, *Peasants and Power: The Whiteboy Movements and their Control in Pre-Famine Ireland* (New York: St. Martin's, 1983), 8–13; Joel Mokyr, *Why Ireland Starved: A Quantitative and Analytical History of the Irish Economy, 1800–1850* (London: George Allen & Unwin, 1983), 144–47.

rents, tithes and other demands, than pulled by perceived profit-making opportunities. As changes in the land squeezed tenants from their relatively secure leases, they entered more temporary agreements where rents fluctuated with the market and caused greater turnover. Population pressures and high rents shrank the amount of land people could afford and many were reduced to a *conacre* system, renting small plots for one season's potato crop that barely allowed them to keep a toehold on the land.[35]

Peasants gradually were transformed into labourers. The lucky found steady employment in one place, but many had to turn to migrant or *spalpeen* work part of the year. Some shipped for the season to fish the Grand Banks off Newfoundland. Others left the land for part of the year to work the harvests in Ireland; in particular, those from the poor West poured into the South leading to resentment among local residents (and sowing the seeds of the Cork–Connaught feud that flared along North American canals). By 1816, steamboat service made passage to England and Scotland affordable, and many followed the harvests across the Irish Sea. Public works in Ireland and Britain also drew many from the land, spurring their conversion to wage work. Tramping from job to job, trying to piece together enough wages with the potatoes on the small plot at home to keep alive, spalpeeners were neither wholly of the land nor of the labour market. Eventually, most would stay on at wage work although this step was not usually taken until all other options had been exhausted.[36] Most fought their displacement from the land; it was not a mystical relation but a practical realization that access to the soil meant greater control over subsistence. The stick not the carrot prodded peasants into becoming proletarians. Tired of being pushed along, they increasingly turned and fought.

By the early nineteenth century, Irish society was resolving into two classes with diverging interests, the landed and the landless. Widespread social disorder was the result.[37] The most common form of conflict in Ireland, the faction fight, pitted kinship or community networks against each other in ritualized combat that served recreative functions while playing a crucial role in controlling access to land and jobs.[38] In a more systematic fashion, peasants formed secret societies and waged a war of

35 Powers, "Invisible Immigrants" (see Ch. 2, n. 37 above), 61–63; Miller, *Emigrants and Exiles* (see n. 33 above), 34, 217–18; Beames, *Peasants and Power* (see n. 34 above), 6–8.
36 Barbara M. Kerr, "Irish Seasonal Migration to Great Britain, 1800–38," *Irish Historical Studies*, v. 3 (Sept. 1943), 365–80; Arthur Redford, *Labour Migration in England 1800–1850* (orig. ed. 1926; New York: Augustus Kelley, 1968), 141–49; James E. Handley, *The Navvy in Scotland* (Cork: Cork University, 1970), 16–20; Miller, *Emigrants and Exiles* (see n. 33 above), 34.
37 Beames, *Peasants and Power* (see n. 34 above), 13, 16–17; Miller, *Emigrants and Exiles* (see n. 33 above), 53–54.
38 Paul E. W. Roberts, "Caravats and Shanavests: Whiteboyism and Faction Fighting in East Munster, 1802–11," in *Irish Peasants*, ed. Clark and Donnelly (see n. 32 above), 64–101; Miller, *Emigrants and Exiles* (see n. 33 above), 60–61.

violence to resist the collapse of traditional agricultural production. Michael Beames's study of Whiteboyism traces the economic roots of a representative agrarian protest movement. Originating in the 1760s and spreading to all of Ireland outside Ulster by the end of the century, the movement was a response to the commercialization of social relations and the proletarianization of many peasants. The Whiteboys' overriding goal was maintaining access to the land, thereby ensuring subsistence, the central concern of peasantries. In the process, they developed an alternative vision of social relations to that of the market. While there were other types of movements, all different in some way, they all shared certain features with the Whiteboys. They were secret societies, some of a religiously sectarian nature, that grew out of economic grievances and used force and violence – terrorism – to achieve their ends; as such, they were indicative of the degree of social turmoil caused in Ireland by the transition to capitalism.[39] They also provided an important historical precedent for canallers caught in the same vise of dwindling means and narrowing options.

Collective violence was a stopgap measure, not a solution, and the Irish ultimately faced a tough decision: landless status at home always on the edge of poverty, or emigration abroad, which also meant proletarianization for most. In fact, there was little choice in the matter. Options like conacre and spalpeen labour gave the illusion of volition, but these also were products of diminished expectations. The social and economic changes undergone by Irish society as a result of its integration into the marketplace narrowed opportunity. An individual could not choose to remain a peasant on a clachan, but was instead left with the pick of two lesser evils, partial or complete separation from the land. To characterize emigration, then, as a rational decision made in light of prevailing social and economic conditions is to miss the fact that conditions for two centuries and more had been increasingly stacked against those involved and imposed an ultimatum more than a free choice. People exerted some control over their immediate condition and this was of significant personal importance. Yet seen as a whole, this was but a patina of volition overlaying the rock-hard imperatives of historical forces propelling people into emigrating. Emigration was a daunting experience, filled with both terror and anticipation. Whatever their future prospects, most would-be North Americans found the transition a painful one.

Unlike those of Richard Kelley and Fred Fry, the emigration experience of most canallers cannot be reconstructed; yet there is little reason to suspect that it diverged greatly from that of other migrants. Moving from

---

39 Beames, *Peasants and Power* (see n. 34 above); James S. Donnelly, Jr., "The Whiteboy Movement, 1761–5," *Irish Historical Studies*, v. 21 (March 1978), 20–54; *Secret Societies in Ireland*, ed. T. Desmond Williams (Dublin: Gill and MacMillan, 1973); *Irish Peasants*, ed. Clark and Donnelly (see n. 32 above); Gale E. Christianson, "Secret Societies and Agrarian Violence, 1790–1840," *Agricultural History*, v. 46 (July 1972), 369–84.

the land, some got their first taste of navvying on Ireland's canals, and quickly learned the lesson of wage labour.[40] Led by work at potato harvesting or lured by the promise of higher wages, many Irish made the jump to Britain's public works, where they constituted a significant component of the labour force.[41] From there it was but another step to North America. Engineers from the Erie Canal made a fact-finding trip to England in 1816, and news of opportunities in North America percolated among the navvies. The following year, Canvass White, a New York engineer, returned to England and recruited a force of experienced Irish workers. By the end of the 1818 season there were significant numbers of Irish on the Erie.[42] The seeming plethora of jobs and higher wages in North America made migration an attractive proposition for both experienced canallers and labourers in general, especially as Ireland and Britain slid into agricultural crisis in the 1820s. To tap this labour supply, canal companies and contractors sent over recruiting agents, and several states set up immigration commissions.[43]

From one instance of orchestrated immigration it is possible to get a sense of the experience of some canallers. Facing an endemic labour short-age, the C&O Canal sought to exploit Europe's depressed economic situation. "Meat, three times a day, a plenty of bread and vegetables, with a reasonable allowance of liquor, and light, ten, or twelve dollars a month for wages, would we have supposed," wrote Charles Mercer, the company president, "prove a powerful attraction to those, who, narrowed down in the circle of their enjoyments, have at this moment, a year of scarcity presented to them." Mercer argued that emigration would relieve Great Britain "of a wretched surplus population, by transferring it to America, where its presence is much needed, and its labour would be amply rewarded." Agents were sent to Europe and notices placed in Irish and Dutch news-papers of the wonderful opportunities available. The C&O claimed it would take three to four thousand Irish and their priests, while ten thousand job openings in all, over three times what was needed, were advertised.[44]

---

40 For instance, workers on the Shannon link of the Grand Canal several times struck for higher wages. Ruth Delaney, *A Celebration of 250 years of Ireland's Inland Waterways* (Belfast: Appletree Press, 1986), 87.

41 Terry Coleman estimated that one-third of Britain's railway navvies were Irish. David Brooke found the Irish concentrated in the West Midlands and Scottish border region. In his study of a Yorkshire railway navvy gang in 1851, J. A. Patmore determined that 26% were Irish-born. Coleman, *The Railway Navvies* (see Ch. 2, n. 26 above), 83–84; Brooke, *The Railway Navvy* (see Ch. 2, n. 26 above), 21, 26–29; Patmore, "A Navvy Gang of 1851," *Journal of Transport History*, v. 5 (May 1962), 185.

42 The Canal Commissioners reported that one-quarter (roughly 1,000) of the workforce were foreign-born, presumably mostly Irish. *Annual Report of the Canal Commissioners* (Albany, 1819), 10.

43 Powers, "Invisible Immigrants" (see Ch. 2, n. 37 above), 89–90; George E. Condon, *Stars in the Water: The Story of the Erie Canal* (Garden City, N.Y.: Doubleday, 1974), 63, 67; Robert Ernst, *Immigrant Life in New York City 1825–1863* (New York: King's Crown Press, 1949), ch. 1.

44 Mercer to James Maury, 18 Nov. 1828 (A 38–40), C&O/LS; Mercer to James Barbour, 18 Nov. 1828 (A 41–43), ibid.; Circular to U.S. Consuls at Cork, Belfast and Dublin, 18 Nov. 1828 (A 43), ibid.; Mercer to Thomas P. Cope, 18 Nov. 1828 (A 40–41), ibid.; Mercer to Maury, 7 March 1829 (A

Those who took up the C&O's offer signed a limited-term indenture of two to three months in return for passage to America. In all, several hundred men entered into this scaled-down indenture and emigrated, some with their families. Skilled hands were especially desired, and a number of colliers and miners from England and Wales, "men of good character steady and industrious," made the move. "Some few Irishmen are among them," noted the agent, "but all these have worked sometime in England, amongst Englishmen and are good workmen and peacable."[45] The desperation of prospective employees was made clear by the case of an Irish civil engineer who travelled to New York with his wife on faith of the advertisements. He wrote to Mercer expressing his desire for work, "I care not how fataguing [sic], or how low the wages."[46]

The move to the New World for these economic migrants was not a smooth one. A number of willing labourers were swindled by a man posing as the agent of the C&O who directed them to Liverpool in return for a £1 fee.[47] During the passage, the labourers were fed too little and what they got was often rotten, leading them to threaten the company's agents and attempt to break into the ship's storeroom to "gratify their own ingovernable appetites."[48] It was no surprise, then, that many were in sorry shape on landing. Contractors complained that they arrived "destitute of the comforts of life, and we have been compelled to clothe them." Other employers were not so solicitous; one in particular saw his hands abandon the line because he refused to provide adequate food and shelter. A number of the immigrants needed medical attention, provided by the company but at the ultimate expense of the individual, while others appealed to charitable organizations for relief.[49] Disenchanted with the situation and lured by the possibility of immediate wages, many soon ran off to nearby cities or to work on the Baltimore & Ohio Railroad. The company prosecuted a number of these runaways, but the Baltimore court ruled that the indenture did not constitute a master-and-servant relationship. Instead, it was determined to be an ordinary contract and therefore could only be enforced by an action for damages. The company decided to let the matter drop.[50] The

---

60–61), ibid. The Illinois & Michigan also recruited labourers from abroad. *Second Annual Report of the Commissioners of the Illinois and Michigan Canal* (Vandalia, 1837), 10.

45 Henry B. Richards, 21 Aug. 1829, C&O/LR. Also Mercer to Maury, 8 July 1829 (A 82–84), C&O/LS; Mercer to Richards, 8 July 1829 (A 84–87), ibid.

46 Daniel Teer to Mercer, 12 Jan. 1829, 19 Aug. 1830, C&O/LR.

47 [Baltimore] *Niles' Register*, v. 37, 169 (7 Nov. 1829).

48 George Gill, 18 Nov. 1829; Peter Powell, 18 Nov. 1829, C&O/LR.

49 Boteler & Reynolds to John P. Ingle, 5 Nov. 1829, C&O/LR; C&O/PRO, 6 Oct. 1829 (A 367–68); Ingle to M. S. Wines, 3 Oct. 1829 (A 112–14), C&O/LS; Ingle to Dr. Joshua Riley, 21 Oct. 1829, ibid.; Stewards of the "Society of the Sons of St. George" to Ingle, 17 Feb. 1830, C&O/LR.

50 Peter Powell, 18 Nov. 1829, C&O/LR; William Wirt to Ingle, 28 Oct., 4, 6 Nov. 1829, ibid. Ingle to M. S. Wines, 3 Oct. 1829 (A 112–14), C&O/LS; Ingle to Phineas Janney, 26 Oct. 1829 (A 122–24), ibid.; Ingle to Wirt, 29 Oct., 6, 7, 13, 25 Nov. 1829 (A 125–29, 138), ibid.; Ingle to

C&O's attempt to resurrect indentured labour showed how difficult the move was for prospective navvies, even in cases of assisted immigration.

Traditionally, it has been assumed that the Irish arrived as peasants and collected in city slums as a floating proletariat. The first part of this assumption must be seen as largely false. The majority of emigrants had prior experience with commercial relations and wage labour, and thus cannot be viewed as peasants, at least not in the pure sense; in fact, emigration was largely a result of the breakdown of the peasantry. What evidence there is for canallers bears out this revision. Of the 635 signators on a petition from Rideau canallers in 1829, 428 (67%) were from the provinces of Ulster in the North and Leinster in the East, the two most commercialized parts of Ireland at the time, as opposed to the less developed South and West. This breakdown reflected contemporary immigration patterns.[51] The second part of the assumption – that the Irish became an urban proletariat – would not apply to most canal labourers, who would probably have been considered rural dwellers given the location of shanty camps, yet they were as much members of a proletariat as if they lived in a city slum.[52] Although it is impossible to determine exactly, it is not too far-fetched to say that the overwhelming majority arrived as labourers and remained so for some time.

It was certainly the view of contemporary observers that the Irish worked on canals not by choice but by necessity. For example, an official on Canada's canals noted that "the labour is invariably performed by Irishmen, who . . . having no other mode of gaining their livelihood seem to monopolize all the labour of the public works, both here and in the United States."[53] What evidence there is points to the fact that canallers often arrived with but the barest essentials and in a weakened physical state. Many moved right onto public works; for example, the Cleveland *Herald*

Glenn, 1 April 1830 (A 194–95), ibid.; *Second Annual Report of the Chesapeake and Ohio Canal Company* (Washington, 1830), 5–6; *Niles' Register*, v. 37, 150 (31 Oct. 1829).

51 Lt. Col. By, petition on behalf of the Irish working on the Rideau Canal, Canada, to the Colonial Office, 5 Feb. 1829, p. 64, v. 22, C.O. 384, Colonial Office Records, Public Records Office, London, England. I would like to thank Dr. Kerby Miller of the University of Missouri at Columbia for drawing this document to my attention, and for kindly providing his data for my use.

52 In a study of Ontario's Irish, Donald Akenson found that the overwhelming majority of Irish people and two-thirds of Catholics lived in rural areas. The crucial question missed by his urban–rural dichotomy is whether these people were labourers or proprietors. Mere rural residence did not provide one with independence; some control over the means of production was necessary. One would suspect that many of these were indeed farm labourers, perhaps insulated from the worst conditions of a ghetto but no more in control than an urban worker. Even those who rented or owned farm property were not necessarily in a favourable position, as the pressures on land and creeping soil exhaustion in Ontario at this time made many holdings marginal at best. See Akenson, "Ontario: Whatever Happened to the Irish?" *Canadian Papers in Rural History*, v. 3, ed. Akenson (Gananoque, Ontario: Langdale Press, 1982), 231–33; John McCallum, *Unequal Beginnings: Agriculture and Economic Development in Quebec and Ontario until 1870* (Toronto: University of Toronto Press, 1980); Gagan, *Hopeful Travellers* (see n. 8 above); Parr, "Hired Men" (see n. 9 above), 93–97.

53 Memorandum of Charles Wetherall, 3 April 1843, Lachine Canal – Riots on the Canal 1842–45, file 9, v. 60 (hereafter Lachine Riots), Records of the Department of Public Works, series A1, Record Group 11, Public Archives of Canada, Ottawa (hereafter PAC/RG11).

noted the arrival of some Irish on the Ohio Canal in 1825 who had come directly from landing at Quebec. Colonel By, chief engineer of the Rideau, wrote of recent arrivals that "at present the poor fellows lay with nothing but their rags to cover them." And in 1854, a director of the St. Mary's Canal described the workers scoured from upstate New York as "sick, starved, lean, lank, slim, light of build, fallow, and about half of them will weigh under 100 lbs. They look as if they had come from abroad or an emigrant ship lately."[54] The pitiful condition of newly arrived canallers certainly became worse after the depression of the late 1830s and the famine seized Ireland.

John Mactaggart, an official on the Rideau, did not agree that the Irish were necessary for the public works. Stating a preference for French workers, he felt that migrating to Canada meant only misery for the Irish. "Let some plan, therefore, be found to keep these people in bread at home. . . . Emigration only increases their distress, and they may just as well die in Ireland as in Canada." William Thomas, our Welsh immigrant, echoed Mactaggart's dyspeptic view of immigration. Lured across the Atlantic by fellow Welshmen who spoke glowingly of the opportunity to be met there, Thomas found work on the Erie near Utica in the late 1810s. His experiences were less than rewarding, as he revealed in a letter home to his family. "These men sent back a lot of lies. . . . If it were not for the canal, many of the Welsh would be without work. I beg all of my old neighbors not to think of coming here as they would spend more coming here than they think. My advice to them is to love their district and stay there. I am thinking of coming home myself this spring if I have the support of the Lord." Whether Thomas was expressing just a natural homesickness or a more profound discontent with his reduced condition as a canal labourer, it is clear that he did not consider the New World a land of milk and honey. Of course, some canallers improved their condition by immigrating. A group of Irish workers on the Rideau maintained that "on the whole we most certainly conclude that the Poor Man's situation is bettered by emigrating to Canada, as our own personal experience has fully convinced us." The fact that they deemed themselves to have attained "a state of comfort and happiness we never could have hoped to meet had we remained in Ireland" shows that the peasant-to-proletarian pathway could lead up as well as down.[55]

For good or ill, most canallers were Irish by the 1830s. "For some years

54 Cleveland *Herald*, 16 Sept. 1825; By quoted in Wylie, "Poverty, Distress, and Disease" (see Introduction, n. 11 above), 9; John Brooks quoted in Dickinson, *To Build a Canal* (see Ch. 2, n. 14 above), 81.
55 John Mactaggart, *Three Years in Canada; An Account of the Actual State of the Country in 1826−7−8* (London, 1829), v. 2, 249; William Thomas to His Father et al., 17 Aug. 1818, in *The Welsh in America*, ed. Conway (see n. 51 above), 60−62; Petition on behalf of the Irish working on the Rideau Canal, 5 Feb. 1829 (see n. 51 above).

past, the Public Works, both in the United States & in Canada, have been carried on almost exclusively by Irish Labourers, who have been accustomed to flock in Masses from work to work," affirmed the engineer Charles Atherton, "& thus a large proportion of the Labourers on the Lachine Canal Improvements are men of unsettled habits, having no established home, & consequently not bound by the moral ties which influence a settled population." Martin Donnelly, a labourer on the Beauharnois, at least concurred on the transiency of his fellow workers: "The larger portion of these men are Irishmen who have worked in the United States. The remaining portion are with very few exceptions, Emigrants from Ireland, recently arrived in this Province."[56] They swarmed public works sites, making them virtual Irish villages – at least in demographic terms, for the transient, competitive nature of shanty camps would never delude a navvy into thinking he was in a peasant clachan back home.

For immigrant canallers there is no question that the end of their journeys, however different their backgrounds, was much the same: wage work in a notoriously rough occupation. They may have moved on again in a short time, but most would have been likely to remain in wage work. We see here the connection between European industrial development, class formation and North American labour demand, a chain with immigration as the crucial link. The changes begun over a century before were concluded on the shores of North America. Irish peasants had been made into proletarians. Their story – gradual separation from the land, transfer to wage labour and migration to where the market dictated – was played out around the world in varying renditions. Representatives of the many people set in motion by the transition to capitalism, among them Africans, Germans, Swiss and Welsh, found their way onto canals. The story of canallers, then, is one small thread in this tapestry.

The canal construction industry built a labour force that mirrored North America's developing social landscape. The makeup of this army of workers and the conditions they experienced on canals were moulded by the nature of the labour market, which into the late 1830s was understocked. No rock was left unturned in an attempt to fill this insatiable demand. Labour agents were sent to Europe and large Eastern U.S. cities, notices posted, ads placed in papers, immigrants rounded up, slaves hired or bought, farmers drained from the soil, and women and children harnessed to production. Still this was not enough. Canal boards looked to other sources of untapped labour. In 1818, Secretary of War John C. Calhoun unsuccessfully recommended that the military be used on transportation projects. The C&O's bid to Congress to have federal troops dig its proposed

56 Atherton to Hope, 29 March 1843, Lachine Riots (see n. 53 above); Deposition of Martin Donnelly (No. 3), "Beauharnois Report" (see Introduction, n. 3 above).

mountain section proved equally fruitless. New York exempted labourers on the Erie Canal from militia duty in 1819 so that construction would not be interrupted, and Canada's Rideau and Ottawa River canals were built partly by the British military.[57] Canals also turned to convict labour. In 1821, Governor DeWitt Clinton pardoned prisoners from New York's Auburn State Prison who agreed to work for contractors on the Erie Canal at prevailing wage rates, a practice renewed the next year. Indiana's state prison was located in Jeffersonville in anticipation of using its prisoners to build a canal around the falls on the Ohio River. And Ohio released a number of prisoners from its state penitentiary in 1827 to work on the Columbus feeder of the Ohio Canal.[58]

In the process, canal companies constructed a workforce divided by ethnic and cultural background and by freedom and bondage, and riddled throughout by differences of gender and age. This segmentation was further compounded by the physical separation imposed on the labourers by the nature of the industry, strung out as it was between two countries. Despite its heterogeneity and diffuse nature, however, the canal workforce was unified by its common condition. Free or unfree, man, woman or child, canallers had a weak grip on the fruits of their labour, and one that was being progressively loosened by the growing power of the market.

Markets and human capital

The tens of thousands of workers employed in the canal construction industry at its peak in the 1820s and 1830s collected into distinct yet overlapping regional labour markets marked by different types of workers with divergent wage rates. The one true dividing line was that between North and South, which bisected North America into prevailing free and unfree forms of labour. Nonetheless, the tramping Irish canaller acted as a solvent that blurred even this distinction.

Quebec and Ontario constituted the northernmost labour market. The international boundary separated Canada and the United States into distinct social and political systems with different currencies, yet did little to stop

---

57 Forrest G. Hill, *Roads, Rails and Waterways: The Army Engineers and Early Transportation* (Norman: University of Oklahoma Press, 1957), 41; Ward, *Early Development of the Chesapeake and Ohio Canal* (see Ch. 2, n. 14 above), 35–36; *Second Annual Report of the Chesapeake and Ohio Canal* (Washington, 1830), 17, 25–27; Noble E. Whitford, *History of the Canal System of the State of New York* (Albany: Brandow Printing Co., 1906), v. 1, 91; Wylie, "Poverty, Distress, and Disease" (see Introduction, n. 11 above), 10–12.

58 Minutes of the New York Canal Commission, 16 July 1821 (v. 1, 23), 7 Feb. 1822 (v. 1, 25) (see Ch. 2, n. 29 above); Shaw, *Erie Water West* (see Ch. 1, n. 21 above), 129; Condon, *Stars in the Water* (see n. 43 above), 64; *Indiana Gazetteer* (Indianapolis, 1833), 135; State of Ohio, "An Act to commute the punishment of certain convicts in the Penitentiary, for labor on the Columbus feeder of the Ohio Canal, 30 Jan. 1827," in *Public Documents Concerning the Ohio Canals*, ed. Kilbourne (see Ch. 2, n. 64 above), 266–67; State of Ohio, General Assembly, *Journal of the House of Representatives* (Columbus, 1827), 19–20; [Chillicothe, Ohio] *Scioto Gazette*, 10 May 1827.

labour migration, canallers moving back and forth as the vagaries of employment dictated.[59] This market was also set apart by the use of French-Canadians, at least on the St. Lawrence and Ottawa Valley canals. Other local farmers also found employment, but Irish immigrants from the 1820s increasingly dominated the workforce, and by the 1840s were reported to have a virtual lock on canalling jobs. The second market was the northeastern states, stretching from Maine to Maryland. In the late eighteenth century, this market utilized a mix of indentured and free labour, with a small component of slaves on the southern fringe. Beginning with the Erie Canal, local and bonded labour was quickly supplanted by Irish immigrant wage workers. As early as 1818, it was reported that already at least one-third of the Erie labour force was foreign-born.[60] The Midwest – Ohio, Indiana, Illinois, Michigan and Wisconsin – constituted the third market. Canal building began here in the mid-1820s when these areas were still part of the frontier. Labour shortages were more of a problem than back east and wages were consequently higher into the 1840s. Local farm labour was used here for a longer period, but immigrant workers appeared on the scene quite early, Irish as well as Germans, soon squeezing out their native predecessors. For instance, it was reported that Germans arrived on the Miami Canal near Dayton in 1833–34 and accounted for three-quarters of the workforce between that city and Piqua by 1837.[61] The final and most distinctive market was the American South below Maryland, in particular Virginia, North and South Carolina, and Louisiana, although some canal construction went on elsewhere. Obviously, what set this region apart was its reliance on slaves. Still, wage labour was always a factor, either surplus farm workers or migrating immigrants, linking Southern canal construction to its Northern partner.

These were by no means discrete markets, as considerable movement occurred between them. Canal work meant that people were always on the move. Canallers travelled in groups – following favoured contractors and gang leaders or accompanying a few mates – and on their own, often with their families in tow. Work would draw to a close on one section, but was always opening up down the line or on another canal. Conflict with those in charge, the difficulty and remoteness of the work, dismissal for drunkenness or poor job performance, or the inevitable seasonal, weather-influenced or financial interruption of work all contributed to the itinerancy of the tramping canaller. The high transiency rate on the Delaware & Schuylkill Canal in the 1790s has already been detailed, a fact of navvying

---

59 For instance, in 1838 it was reported that 150 men had been brought from Canada to the Illinois & Michigan Canal and that two more contractors were recruiting there. *Report of the Board of Commissioners of the Illinois and Michigan Canal* (Vandalia, 1838), 37.

60 *Annual Report of the Canal Commissioners* (Albany, 1819), 10.

61 Ohio Canal Commission Minute Books, (see Ch. 2, n. 46 above), v. 1, 334–36; *First Annual Report of the Board of Public Works of the State of Ohio to the Assembly* (Columbus, 1837), 8–9.

life that remained the case throughout the Canal Era. For instance, workers on the Western Division of the Illinois & Michigan Canal came and went with great frequency in 1838–39, the force shifting up or down by as much as 87 percent every three months (Table 4). Clearly, this made for great flux both at work and in the shanty camps, a situation similar to that found on the Rideau Canal by Jaime Valentine. He noted a high level of movement among the hands employed by Philemon Wright at Dow's Swamp in the late 1820s: 57 percent stayed for less than three months, 20 percent for four to six months, and only 10 percent for more than a year. Valentine found similar results at Smith Falls: 40 percent were employed for one month or less, and only 6 percent stayed more than four months.[62]

Lack or irregularity of work were common spurs that pushed canallers on the road. "It was want of employ which induced me to return here in the hope of finding work on the Canal," confessed John Ford, an aspiring worker on Canada's Beauharnois. "I have hitherto found none and have been supporting myself out of the money which I earned as well on this Canal as in the States where I wrought during two years or thereabouts on the Erie Canal." Labourers also moved on if conditions were not to their liking. Desertion was a continuing problem on the military projects of Canada, for instance. The commanding officer on the Grenville Canal reported that "some of our best workmen" had deserted in 1820, and on the Rideau 35 of the 160 Royal Sappers and Miners who arrived from England in 1827 fled the line before the canal was completed. Other concerns also played a part, such as the desire to avoid harsh weather. An engineer on the Illinois & Michigan, commenting on the seasonal swelling and shrinking of the labour force, noted that the "migratory character of the men is also a main cause of this variation, as many of them go to the south at the setting in of winter, to return in the spring."[63] Clearly the prospect of water work during December was more appealing in Virginia than in Illinois.

Canal companies played an important role in directing the flow of traffic. When labour was in short supply, as for most of the period under study, canal companies actively searched out workers. While all did not go to the extent of sending agents to Europe like the C&O, they did have men in the large Eastern cities to direct immigrants to their works, a practice occasionally perverted by individuals posing as agents and defrauding unwary labourers. For instance, in 1829 a man pretending to represent the C&O in Boston fraudulently took money from labourers in return for promised passage to and employment on the canal. Similarly, a number of Irish stonecutters

---

62 Valentine, "Supplying the Rideau" (see Ch. 2, n. 50 above), 23–25.
63 Deposition of John Ford (No. 2), "Beauharnois Report" (see Introduction, n. 3 above); Capt. DuVernet, 30 Nov. 1820, v. 40, Canal Papers, PAC/RG8; Valentine, "Supplying the Rideau" (see Ch. 2, n. 50 above), 26–27; *Report of the Board of Commissioners of the Illinois and Michigan Canal* (Vandalia, 1838), 52.

from New York paid a fee to a man claiming to be the agent of contractors on the Wabash & Erie. When they arrived in Toledo with their families they discovered the man had been an imposter, leaving then with "no money and no jobs."[64]

Companies also sent men into the countryside looking for hands and promising travel costs, food and shelter, good wages and steady work. In 1833, when workers were few and wages high, the Wabash & Erie sent an agent to Buffalo to recruit German and Irish labourers and dispatched another into the state's interior counties and to the Ohio River in search of indigenous labour.[65] Increasingly, the most common means of labour recruitment was through newspaper advertisements, which laid out the terms of employment and stipulated the number of men needed, generally exaggerated in an attempt to flood the labour market and drive down wages. For example, the Illinois & Michigan circulated a notice calling for 10,000 labourers at the opening of construction (when the canal never employed more than 3,000), promising high wages and opportunities for investment in the "healthful climate of Northern Illinois." Similarly, Indiana's Central Canal called for 2,000 workers, offering them $20 a month and "fare and lodgings . . . of the most comfortable character."[66] Such blandishments must have been an incentive to head west to recent immigrants and unhappy Easterners.

Professional canallers learned from experience not to believe the milk-and-honey stories they saw in newspapers. When Frederick Marryat asked Irish labourers at Mohawk Falls on the Erie why they did not go to Ohio and Indiana where wages were said to be $2 a day, he was informed that workers never found such advertised wages once there. Canallers had their own sources of information, a network of first-hand accounts carried by tramping workers that let them know what the actual conditions of employment were on other projects, where they were hiring, which canals paid the best wages, and who were the best contractors. The literate would write about conditions to their friends and family, which would act as a spur or brake on migration. Immigrants brought to the Wabash & Erie in 1833, finding a good thing, were soon sending letters back east to encourage others to make the trip. Conversely, after sickness, unemployment and late wage payments soured the situation on the Illinois & Michigan in 1846, the disaffected hands were reported to "have written to their friends the most false and discouraging accounts of frauds practiced upon the laborers

64 C&O/PRO, 7 Dec. 1829 (A 414); *Niles' Register*, v. 37, p. 301 (2 Jan. 1830); *Fort Wayne Sentinel*, 27 Aug. 1842, quoted in Charles R. Poinsatte, *Fort Wayne During the Canal Era, 1825–1855: A Study of a Western Community in the Middle Period of American History* (Indianapolis: Indiana Historical Bureau, 1969), 60.
65 *Report of the Commissioners of the Wabash and Erie Canal* (Indianapolis: Indiana House of Representatives, 1833), 163–64.
66 *Chicago American*, 11 June 1836; "2,000 Laborers Wanted on the Central Canal of Indiana," 1 May 1837, Broadside Collection, Indiana Division, Indiana State Library.

here, the sickness of the country etc. etc." And letters of reference occasionally played a part in the job-seeking process, as they did with engineers and builders. "Donel Dougherty and patrick kegan are particular Friends of mine," wrote a superintendent of masonry on the C&O. "I recommend them to your service as men of sutible abilityes the have been frequently imployed on publick works be fore. I hope you will find them a Job By doing so you will much oblige your most humble servant."[67]

Transiency was thus not directionless or pointless, and (at least until the 1840s) usually not born of desperation. Canallers even used their mobility as a bargaining tool with employers. "The migratory disposition of the labourers operated injuriously to the contractors in various ways," complained the managers of the Lehigh Coal & Navigation Company, "for they would not be urged at work beyond their own inclination; knowing that their services were in demand, they would take up a line of march at the least supposed provocation." Such tactics resulted from an understocked labour market, as the managers concluded with a capitalist axiom: "under this state of things, not as much work is performed by the same number of hands, as when they are plenty and employment scarce."[68] Labourers' use of this strategy should not be overstated, as they were held in place by contracts and delayed wage payment, although never very effectively. More importantly, experience taught canallers that conditions were unlikely to be significantly better elsewhere, as the Erie hands had made clear to Marryat. In later years, sheer need would act as a glue holding them in place. Nonetheless, for much of the Canal Era and for most workers, navvying was a peripatetic occupation.

This made for a highly mobile workforce, but not all components moved. Transiency was a function of a free labour market, and slaves on Southern canals were obviously much more stable, although they would be moved from plantation to canal and on to other jobs. Labour drawn from local farms tended to be sedentary as well. The people who moved were those who did not have alternatives to keep them in place, but kept on the move chasing jobs – that is, people dependent on wage work. While this described most segments of the canal labour force to a degree, it most closely captured the experience of the Irish. Whereas native-born workers tended to be part-time and live locally, and even other immigrants like the Germans were more likely to settle near the canal as they did in northwestern

---

67 Frederick Marryat, *Diary in America* (orig. ed. 1839; Bloomington: Indiana University Press, 1960), 93; *Report of the Commissioners of the Wabash and Erie Canal* (Indianapolis, 1833), 163–64; William Gooding to William H. Swift, 6 July 1846, William Henry Swift Papers, Chicago Historical Society, Chicago; Christopher Lawn to Fisk, 27 July 1837, C&O/LR.

68 *Report of the Board of Managers of the Lehigh Coal and Navigation Company, presented to the Stockholders* (Philadelphia, 1829), 12. The use by labourers of transiency as a means of bettering job conditions was noted by Jonathan Prude in New England textile workers. "Social System of Early New England Textile Mills: A Case Study, 1812–1840," in *Working-Class America*, ed. Frisch and Walkowitz (see n. 15 above), 19–27.

Ohio, most Irish descended on an area when a job opened, did the work, and moved on. The *Cleveland Herald* reported that "36 hardy sons of Erin," recently employed on the Erie, had arrived on the Miami Canal, and the *New Orleans Picayune* noted the arrival of a boatload of "Irish, green as shamrocks," anticipating what "a valuable acquisition they will prove in carrying out internal improvements."[69] When they moved it was from one canal to another, or into similar work. As a people whose presence in North America was an affirmation of their separation from the land, who were isolated and pushed into undesirable jobs because of their ethnic background, the Irish found work where they could. Tramping for them was a continuation of the immigrant experience. Many funneled into canal work, becoming "professional" canallers for all practical purposes. To follow such a calling meant to pursue the ever-moving lines of internal improvements. It is difficult to see how this fluidity had other than a corrosive effect on worker community, as impermanence mixed with oppression simultaneously bred divisions and internecine conflict among workers.

Tramping was shaped by labour concerns as much as by the promises of canal companies. But as labour surplus came to be the norm in the 1840s, transiency increasingly became a necessity, with more workers searching for fewer jobs, hiking hundreds of miles on the strength of a rumour. No longer did canals have to offer inducements, appoint agents or advertise widely; they could let the workers come to them. And on Canadian canals in the 1840s, as will be shown, too many workers, not too few, became the problem.

The success story of a Richard Kelley, rising from runaway orphan to independent businessman, with canals but a passage in his life, was not the norm. For most, canalling was an irrevocable step along the way to wage work. The migration that had begun long before in peasant clachan, African village, seigneury, or in the fields or at the loom of a family farm was drawing to a close, a journey on which perhaps a canaller's grandparents had first set out. Spalpeening, delayed marriage and immigration were steps along this path, drawing canallers closer to proletarian status. Digging canals was one of the final stops along the way, as is caught by the irony of canallers working every day in earth, often in ditches with it rising up over their heads, but with no claim to it; it was dirt, not soil, and provided no food. Instead, they had to cut their hunger with wages. For most, subsistence had been transformed from the tangible – consuming what you grew, selling what you made – to the legerdemain of wage labour. Canallers laboured for others under harsh conditions. This exacted a price that no wage could meet.

69 *Cleveland Herald*, 9 Sept. 1825; *New Orleans Picayune*, 7 Nov. 1841, quoted in Niehaus, *Irish in New Orleans* (see n. 29 above), 35.

CHAPTER 4

Payment "fit for labouring people"

I entered with them for a season, my monthly pay for to draw,
And being in very good humor, I often sang Erin Go Bragh.
Our provision it was very plenty, to complain we'd no reason at all,
I had money in every pocket, while working upon the canal.[1]

Common labourers working on the Kanawha River for the James River Company in 1821 had to sign a contract outlining terms of employment. For its part, the Company promised to pay the agreed wages and to furnish "substantial & wholesome food, fit for labouring people, and such reasonable accommodations for lodging, he finding his own beding, as the season of the year may require." In return, labourers agreed to work at least one month, and "to conduct themselves diligently, orderly & soberly, & with due & proper obedience to the manager or managers, Foremen, or directors of the work, so that the same may go on with regularity & dispatch." If a labourer failed to behave in an acceptable manner he could be discharged at any time, while ten days' worth of his wages were retained as a security, "it being all important to the Company not to be impeded in their operations by improper conduct, or sudden desertions from their employment." Similarly, the company managers wished to "secure the services of diligent and orderly mechanics in whom they can depend to remain steadily in their employment for such term as they may stipulate." Skilled workers also gave their word to serve "diligently, orderly and soberly," and to perform any job required when there was not enough work in their particular trade. In return, they received a set wage, "substantial and comfortable boarding . . . and such shelter and accommodation for lodging." Mechanics had one month's wages retained, however, and were equally subject to discharge for misconduct.[2]

1 From "Paddy on the Canal," in *Irish Emigrant Ballads and Songs*, ed. Wright (see Ch. 2, n. 2 above), 533.
2 Form of Contract to be made with labourers on Kanawha, 21 May 1821, Kanawha River Improvement Letters, JRCR; Memorandum of agreements with mechanics, May 1821, ibid.

It is evident from these contracts that more was involved in the relationship between employer and employed than mere wages. The exchange of labour power for value in these cases was between wage workers and employers, but alienation of labour spanned the spectrum from free to slave – casual, contracted, indentured and coerced – and was rarely a simple bargain of wages for work, at least not until late in the canal-building era. Contractual obligations, the provision of food and shelter (the practice of "finding"), expectations of moral conduct, and the accumulated weight of a system of chattel bondage all complicated labour relations. Any evaluation of the bond between master and labourer on canals, then, must look beyond the purely monetary dimension to the material and social essence of the "wage."

On the whole, earning power was relatively high in the first decades of canal construction, offering workers a chance to make a living, albeit one shorn of luxury. But income declined from the late 1830s, largely as a result of an increasingly overstocked labour market. Wages dropped, unemployment rose and most contractors ceased to find for their workers. The labour relationship was commercialized and at a monetary value discounted by the market. These factors combined meant real suffering for many canallers and their families later in the Canal Era.

A dollar earned

The problem with using wage-based models for establishing workers' standard of living is that they generally posit a labour market in equilibrium with uniform pay structures and steady employment. The reality in canal construction was starkly at odds with this ideal, involving, as it did, a fair degree of unpaid labour done by slaves and servants, marked wage differentials, payment in kind through the provision of food and shelter, irregular employment and continuing problems with nonpayment of wages for free labour. The seemingly good wages earned by canallers obscured a net income that grew increasingly anemic as the mid-nineteenth century approached. Subsistence, not the "competence" of the stereotypical artisan republican, was the practical goal of canallers, and when this goal was denied, as it was frequently after the mid-1830s, it provoked crime and violence as well as outbursts of worker protest.

General trends in wages over time are apparent. Pay for common canal labour in the northeastern United States (from Maryland northward) averaged around $8–10 a month in the 1790s, but could dip to $6 or rise to $12 depending on local circumstances. These rates persisted into the mid-1820s when expanding construction strained manpower resources and inflated prices. For example, common labour was paid $8–10 a month on the C&O when construction began in 1828, rising to $14–16 by 1831. And between 1835 and 1839 day wages jumped from 75–87¢ to $1.12–1.25. Some contractors were forced to abandoned their contracts, and the company sometimes increased payments to contractors to allow them to continue work.[3] Pay was higher to the west where land was in greater and labour in even shorter supply. In Ohio wages started artificially low in the mid-1820s at $5–8 a month (an explicit policy of the Canal Commission that soon foundered on labour shortages), steadily rising to $18 in 1832. Between 1833 and 1836 labour costs increased again by a third, causing two out of three contractors on the section of the Miami & Erie above Dayton to abandon their jobs in 1836 alone.[4] In Canada, daily wages rose from 1s. 3d. to 1s. 6d. in the early 1820s to 2s. 3d. by the next decade, and up to 3s. 4d.–4s. by the later 1830s. These years on the whole were thus favourable to workers, with decent wages and regular employment, but any sudden lessening of competition could burst the bubble.

The bloom left canal construction with the panic of 1837 and the long depression that followed. States that had borrowed heavily to finance projects were now beset by querulous creditors demanding repayment, and were ultimately forced to scale back work severely or even suspend it entirely. Thousands of canallers were thrown out of a job, thus solving the labour shortage problem and leading to a drop in wages. On the Illinois & Michigan Canal, for example, wages that stood at $26 in 1836 (with even a report of $40) had dropped to $20 by 1837 and down to $16 six years later. Similarly, day wages averaged 3s. 4d. on Canadian canals in 1836, but dropped to 2s. 6d. by the early 1840s. The situation did not get better for canallers, despite a slight resurgence in construction on U.S. projects in the late 1840s, as labour demand dwindled in the twilight of the Canal Era during the 1850s.[5] This decline (coupled with concurrent loss of subsistence provision by the contractor) meant a substantial drop in canallers' earnings. The pattern was thus one of a period of stable wage rates during small-scale construction, followed by steady growth as the number of projects expanded, then contraction as work dropped off during the depression.[6]

3 *Report of the President of the Chesapeake and Ohio Canal Company to the Legislature of Maryland* (Annapolis, 1831), 7–8; B. and J. Gorman, 18 Jan. 1837, C&O/LR; *Annual Report of the President and Directors of the Chesapeake and Ohio Canal Company* (Washington, 1839), 30; *Eleventh Annual Report of the Chesapeake and Ohio Canal Company* (Washington, 1839), 16.

4 John Dillon to Micajah Williams, 21 July 1825, Micajah T. Williams Papers, Ohio Historical Society; J. L. Williams to Micajah Williams, 13 May 1831, ibid.; Scheiber, *Ohio Canal Era* (see Ch. 3, n. 66 above), 45–48, 73, 124–25; Teagarden, "Builders of the Ohio Canal" (see Ch. 3, n. 10 above), 100–01.

5 *Report of the Board of Commissioners of the Illinois and Michigan Canal* (Vandalia, 1838), 30; Borgeson, "Irish Canal Laborers" (see Ch. 3, n. 31 above), 42–44; Ralph Ellis, "Labourers, Contractors and Townspeople: The Economic, Social and Demographic Impact of the Cornwall Canal 1834–1843," paper presented at the 1983 Canadian Historical Association conference in Peter Way's possession, 13–14; Bleasdale, "Unskilled Labourers" (see Introduction, n. 11 above), 84–87, 103.

6 For wage rates in similar groups, such as farm workers, common day labourers and canal maintenance hands, see Donald R. Adams, Jr., "Prices and Wages in Maryland, 1750–1850," *Journal of Economic History*, v. 44 (Sept. 1986), 625–45; Stanley Lebergott, *Manpower in Economic Growth*,

Demand was the motor that drove wages over the long term. The North American labour market as a whole was short-staffed in the early nineteenth century, which pushed up wage levels compared to those in Europe. This pattern is evident on canals, where shortages, persisting into the late 1830s, kept wages high and supplemented by the provision of food and shelter. Within this general trend there were fluctuations of supply and demand that pushed wages up and down. Employers occasionally reported a labour surplus that depressed wages, as on the Licking Summit section of Ohio's Miami & Erie Canal in the fall of 1825, when workers were abundant and available at "fair" rates.[7] More often, it was a matter of insufficient numbers and inflated wages.

The general condition of labour shortage that underlay this situation was exacerbated by a number of forces. One inescapable factor was illness, which was endemic on public works construction sites. The months July through September were known as the sickly season, when epidemics were wont to break out, sending labourers scattering away from canals, which they not unnaturally saw as the source. Sickness strained labour supply and drove up wages as companies sought to lure workers back to the line with financial inducements. It was reported that cholera epidemics on the Miami & Erie Canal in the summers of 1832 and 1833 inflated wages from an average of $16 to $19.50. And when sickness struck the Pennsylvania Canal in 1828, inflating wages from $11–12 a month to $16–18, many contractors had to abandon their jobs.[8]

Competition from commercial agriculture, manufacturing and other public works had a more sustained impact on wages. Contractors always had to be mindful of local agricultural wages and tended to peg their rates slightly higher than those offered by farmers. When construction began on Ohio's Miami Canal in the late 1820s, the company was able to attract labourers at a lower cash rate because local farmers paid wages partly in trade. They soon began paying in dollars, however, forcing the canal to give higher wages, as most native labourers preferred agricultural work. By 1839, monthly wages near Lima were $17–20 on the canal and $12–16 on local farms.[9] Even so, during harvest time when it was absolutely essential to get enough hands, farmers set wages at levels with which most contractors could not compete, prompting seasonal shortages. This pattern is clearly evident in an 1823 labour account book for the James River Canal, which noted that the workforce shrank during the late spring and early fall while

Tables A–23 and A–25, ch. 6; Walter B. Smith, "Wage Rates on the Erie Canal, 1828–1881," *Journal of Economic History*, v. 23 (Sept. 1963), 303–04; Taylor, *Transportation Revolution* (see Introduction, n. 12 above), 295.

7 Micajah Williams to Isaac Minor, 28 Sept. 1825, OH/CC.

8 John Laughry, 15 Jan. 1834, OH/CC; Elizabeth Miller Pratt, "The Building of the Pennsylvania Canal, 1826–1834," M. A. thesis, Columbia University, 1949, 53.

9 Ohio Canal Commission Minute Books (see Ch. 2, n. 26 above), v. 1, 336; T. L. Spaulding to Gravill Whitney, 25 May 1839, Spaulding Papers, Indiana Division, Indiana State Library.

wages for common labour rose, presumably as a result of competition during planting and harvesting.[10] Canal construction also competed with traditional handicraft production and emerging manufacturing and building industries for the numerous masons, carpenters, blacksmiths, stonecutters and other skilled workers that it required. Given the rough nature of the work and persisting pull of the craftshop, public works often had to pay relatively high wages to get skilled workers. For instance, contractors on the Lachine Canal complained in 1843 that, whereas daily wages for skilled workers in Quebec City averaged around 1s. 8d., they had to pay between 2s. 6d. and 3s. 6d.[11] On the whole, canal wages for "artificers" tended to be just above going rates in other industries. Canals most directly competed with other public works for labour. During the 1820s and 1830s when construction mushroomed, companies frequently complained that they could not get enough men on their lines because of other projects. Wages rose quite markedly as a result. On the Ohio canal system, for instance, competition from Pennsylvania's public works and the National Road made it impossible to get workers at the established rate of $5 a month in 1825.[12]

Even when wage rates dwindled, labourers on North American canals were better rewarded than their European peers.[13] Such comparisons seem to lend credence to the contention that the wealth of the New World made for a better standard of living for workers, but actually say more about the depression of European labour. To infer from such contrasts that North American workers were comfortable, cosseted and therefore co-opted by capitalism would be a mistake. Standard-of-living comparisons among various national working classes is a matter of splitting hairs over degrees of disadvantage. North American workers may have been better off than British and certainly Irish labourers, but this did not ensure a life of luxury or even comfort. They were still workers who had to scratch and claw to get by. Even during the relatively balmy days for canallers during the 1820s–30s, seemingly high wages on canals masked a variety of factors that meant real earnings were significantly less than rates appeared to indicate. These "variables" must be illuminated before a realistic portrait of canallers' material conditions can be painted.

10 Accounts of Labor on Canal, 1823, box 193, JRCR.
11 Scott and Shaw to Maj. Gen. Sir James Hope, 31 March 1843, Lachine Riots (see Ch. 3, n. 53 above).
12 John Dillon to Micajah Williams, 21 July 1825, Williams Papers, Ohio Historical Society.
13 For example, Irish unskilled labourers on the Erie Canal were paid about 50¢ a day in 1818 compared to the approximately 10¢ per day they could earn at home in Ireland at this time. And the Poor Law Inquiry of 1836 reported that Irish labourers earned 4–8d. a day for most of the year and no more than 10d. to 1s. 2d. during harvest. This was at a time when common labour on Canada's Cornwall Canal was paid 3s. 4d. to 4s. a day and 1s. 3d. during winter. Condon, *Stars on the Water* (see Ch. 3, n. 43 above), 66; Samuel Clark, *Social Origins of the Irish Land War* (Princeton: Princeton University Press, 1979), 37–38; Ellis, "Labourers, Contractors and Townspeople" (see n. 5, above), 13–14.

Wage differentials

One of the most fundamental variables influencing wages was the term of employment. Canallers occasionally were hired by the year, a system that guaranteed a steady supply of labour but had the drawback of leaving hands idle in slack times. Wages were lower for annual hirings because the company had to account for the costs of weather-enforced layoffs.[14] More common was monthly hiring, in which a labourer's wage was calculated on the basis of a set number of workdays (usually twenty-four to twenty-six) and shrank in relation to days lost through inclement weather, sickness or lack of work. This method benefited employers by keeping men on the line but without wages when they could not work. Both annual and monthly hiring usually included room and board. There were also day labourers who, working by the day or part thereof, earned what was at first glance a higher wage, but out of this sum they had to provide their own food and shelter and they were much more susceptible to unemployment.[15] Day labour, although not uncommon, did not become the norm in hiring until the 1840s when a glut made it unnecessary for contractors to provide inducements to tie workers to them. The piece rate, whereby hands were paid according to the amount of work they did, was another mode of payment. This allowed industrious workers to maximize earnings but contained the implicit employer goal of driving work along at the fastest pace possible. It was resented by most workers because of its latter dimension, and was not very common.[16] Finally, some contractors offered incentives for work that exceeded the expected daily amount, a system that many workers took advantage of but others disliked for the competitiveness it bred.[17] At any given time, these various hiring practices could coexist, and consequently wage rates were anything but uniform.

The seasonal wage shift was another significant factor. Joseph McIlvaine, secretary to the Pennsylvania Board of Canal Commissioners, complained that "it is difficult to answer with precision . . . as to the *average wages* of Canal Labourers. They vary with the seasons, and are still more dependent upon the proportion of Labourers to the work required to be done." Wages

14　Philemon Wright, a big contractor on the Rideau Canal, paid canal labourers £20 per annum and between £1 15s. and £2 5s. per month (£21–27 if they worked a full year). Valentine, "Supplying the Rideau" (see Ch. 2, n. 50 above), Table 1.

15　J. Lackland to President and Directors, 25 May 1832, C&O/LR.

16　In 1818, a team of three Irishmen on the Erie Canal took advantage of the pecuniary rewards possible within piecework. They earned the equivalent of four times the daily wage by digging at a prodigious rate, an achievement that won the praise of state canal commissioners, who hoped it would be an example to their countrymen. *Report of the Commissioners of the State of New York, on the Canals* (Albany, 1818), 13; Condon, *Stars in the Water* (see Ch. 3, n, 43 above), 66–67.

17　Hands on Virginia's Kanawha River, for instance, were offered 10¢ for every yard over four yards dug each day, or roughly a quarter of a day's wage (as they were paid $10–12 a month). The superintendent noted that this had a considerable effect, some hands gaining five to six days' wages in one month. John Bosher, 5 Nov. 1821, Kanawha River Improvement Letters, JRCR.

were lower in winter when there was less work to do and more men to do it, and higher in summer when expanding construction created a labour demand exacerbated by seasonal illnesses. Writing in 1831, McIlvaine reported that during winter $5 per month was a common wage compared to $10–12 in the summer. Similarly, the summer day wage for common labour on the James River Canal in 1823 was 4s. 6d., but fell to 3s. 6d. in the winter; on the Cornwall Canal in 1837 summer pay hovered around 4s. and plummeted during winter to 1s. 3d. Those who could afford it left in the fall looking for better wages. Thus free labourers on Lock 20 on the James River left virtually en masse in October 1851 when pay was rolled back from 6s. 9d. to 6s. Others did not have the wherewithal to leave or feared being unable to find other jobs, and thus were at the mercy of contractors. In fact, McIlvaine confessed, men could be held in virtual bondage by seasonal demand. "In some cases I have known them work a whole winter for merely their food."[18]

Skill also made for a broad spectrum of wage levels, with common labourers earning a base wage rate and artisans paid according to the value attached to their particular expertise. On Virginia's James River Canal in 1823, for example, waterboys earned 2s. 6d., common labourers 3s. 6d.–4s. 6d., drillers 4s. 6d., carpenters 4s. 6d.–7s., the whiskey carrier 5s., blasters 7s. 6d., and blacksmiths and overseers 9s.[19] There might also be gradations of pay within common labour according to task, as on the Ohio Canal in 1831 where the wage for common wheeling was $14 while that for ditching was $18.[20] Even within skill divisions there was often no standard wage, with a variety of individualized pay levels dependent on a worker's competence, experience, prior relationship with the employer, and a number of other factors. Thus, although there were prevailing tendencies, for the most part there were no set pay scales.

Apart from skill, wages often were shaped by the appeal of a particular job. Danger drove up the remuneration for blasting, and discomfort and untraditional work patterns had the same effect. Thus sustained labour in water often brought higher wages, as did work at night, on Sundays or during the Christmas vacation, in effect constituting overtime pay.[21]

18 McIlvaine's letter is found in Mathew Carey, *Address to the Wealthy of the Land, Ladies as Well as Gentlemen, on the Character, Conduct, Situation, and Prospects, of those Whose Sole Dependence for Subsistence, is on the Labour of their Hands* (Philadelphia, 1831), 4; Accounts of Labor on Canal, 1823, JRCR; Ellis, "Labourers, Contractors and Townspeople' (see n. 5 above), 13–14; Time Charts for Workers on the James River and Kanawha Canal, October 1851, Austin-Twyman Papers (see Ch. 3, n. 25 above).
19 Accounts of Labor on Canal, 1823, JRCR.
20 J. L. Williams to Micajah Williams, 13 May 1831, Williams Papers, Ohio Historical Society.
21 See James River Company Receipts, 23, 25 Oct., 8, 20 Dec. 1823, box 197, JRCR; John Bosher, 5 Nov. 1821, Kanawha River Improvement Letters, JRCR; J. K. Moorhead to F. R. Shunk, 6 June 1831, Reports and Miscellaneous Documents, Juniata Division Records, PA/RG17; *Report of the President and Managers of the Schuylkill Navigation Company to the Stockholders, 1831* (Philadelphia, 1831), 9; John Flyn's time, 22 Nov., William O'Connor's time, 20 Dec. 1847, Abstracts of Labour Due, Wabash and Erie Canal, IN/II.

A worker's earning power was also subject to social influences, such as gender, race, ethnicity and age. Devaluation was quite apparent in the case of women. When they moved into wage labour women performed work sexually segregated from and undervalued relative to that of men. Women thus received lower wages, which made them dependent on men for survival; in this way, patriarchy was perpetuated under the potentially destabilizing conditions of capitalist production. Rarely directly involved in canal construction, women nonetheless played an important role in cooking, cleaning and caring for men in the shanty camps. This labour was sometimes unpaid, considered part of wifely duties. At other times, women were paid either directly by canallers or by contractors who included these services as part of the wage. For example, Mrs. Mary Adlum worked twenty-three days as a cook and servant on the C&O in September 1834 at 15¢ per diem. Rachel Adlum, presumably her daughter, worked three days as a cook at a rate of 25¢. At the same time, the men the Adlums served were paid at least twice as much, 50¢ being the norm. Even Mrs. Adlum's son Henry got the princely sum of a half-dollar a day for work as a servant boy. The average monthly wage for a hand on the C&O at this time was $15–17 plus room and board, whereas the total earning of the Adlum family (a husband not being evident) for September were just $14.70.[22] Clearly the efforts of women were devalued, a young boy being rewarded considerably more than his older sister and mother for roughly the same work.

Wage studies often err by viewing income solely in individual terms, when more accurately the family was the basic economic unit, and the married man's earnings became essentially a family wage out of which food, shelter and fuel for several people had to come. A canaller's family was thus pushed into wage work to make up the difference.

Sup and shelter

The issue of real earnings was also complicated by the practice of "finding." The nexus between labourer and employer on canals was never fully monetized in the period under study. Slave and indentured labour were the most obvious exceptions to monetization, and for free labour wages were but one component of payment. Most commonly, food, shelter and clothing were supplied to these workers just as they were to slave and indentured hands. Workers' desire to be provided for was a measure of their need, which resulted from their having moved off the land and away from home. At the same time, employers derived benefits from the practice, as lack of control over subsistence kept workers in place as much as any contractual relation. Finding became a form of paternalism in which the master's

22 Check Roll of William Elgin for September 1834, C&O/LR.

dominance and the worker's dependence were daily played out, thus rein-forcing the relationship. In effect, a bargain was struck in which workers yielded their immediate freedom of movement in exchange for the promise that their material needs would be met.

Before work began, a contractor had to make sure there was adequate shelter and food for his hands. Shanties would be thrown up, crude cabins of all sizes and materials, and often a variety of other goods and services were offered. A cook frequently prepared food for the hands, and a laundress washed their clothes. Perhaps a canaller's wife would be responsible for these and other tasks associated with womanhood, such as mending and making clothes, nursing injuries and minding children.[23] Having these time-consuming tasks performed for them released men to work longer hours, while some semblance of traditional domestic life was maintained. Some canal companies also provided their workers with clothing, bedding and household utensils. The James River Company distributed shirts, winter clothes and hats in 1828, and hands on the Wabash & Erie received bedding, pots, pans, knives and plates. And to heat the draughty shanties without loss of worker time or depredations on local residents' trees and fences, contractors and canal companies sometimes found it advantageous to provide wood or coal as fuel. Employers also commonly supplied tools to spare labourers initial expense and to ensure that work went on with minimum interruption. By no means a universal practice, this became less common with time. Labourers were held financially responsible for lost or broken company-supplied implements.[24]

Liquor was another customary work benefit on canals, and the job's difficulty and harshness reinforced its perceived need. Despite management's growing dissatisfaction, contractors doled out liquor on a daily, fixed basis quite remarkable by today's standards. Canallers were literally drunk with the fermented fruits of their labour. Yet alcohol consumption was a vice that was rooted as much in the economic exchange between employer and labourer as it was in the past; in effect, alcohol must be seen as a component of real earnings, inevitably factored into labour costs and at times explicitly evaluated as part of the wage. On sections 30 and 31 of the C&O in 1829, for example, whiskey amounted to 4 percent of daily construction costs (including labour, board, tools, superintendence and buildings).[25] And it could be a cheap alternative to cash wages. Rum at times was issued to Rideau hands working in water in lieu of extra wages;

23 For example, the Western Company of New York provided one cook for each company of thirty-three labourers. *Albany Gazette*, 15 June 1795.
24 James River Company – Receipts and Warrants, Oct. 1828, JRCR; J. L. Williams to Thomas Dowling, 9 Dec. 1850, W&E/COR; Delaware and Schuylkill Minute Book (see Ch. 1, n. 21 above), 16 Nov. 1792; Roberts, *Middlesex Canal* (see Ch. 1, n. 8 above), 65–67; *Albany Gazette*, 15 June 1795.
25 H. W. Campbell to Mercer, 30 Aug. 1829, C&O/LR.

and when money ran out on the Ohio Canal in 1839 some contractors offered their hands whiskey to stay on. When not explicitly part of wages, liquor could be exploited as a commodity to help defray labour costs. Philemon Wright bought whiskey from local settlers for 2s. per gallon and passed it on to his Rideau workers at 2s. 9d., thus making a tidy profit while satisfying his obligations.[26] For a variety of cultural and economic reasons alcohol was a key ingredient in canal construction, but, given its addictive nature, the practice was open to abuse by employers.

Goods and services were not always provided for canallers. Men with families on the C&O in the winter of 1829–30 received a purely cash wage from which they had to pay board and washing bills. Skilled workers often received higher wages with no allowance for their board, and common day labourers' pay exceeded that of monthly workers because they had to find for themselves.[27] And, while room and board normally continued as long as the job, some contractors saved money by making hands pay a portion of their keep on days lost due to inclement weather, as was the case with the C&O contractor Thomas Kavanagh & Co. After losing half of November 1830 to rain, it made its men pay half-board on bad days in December.[28] Nonetheless, workers saw provisions contributed by contractors as their due. As long as canallers had real choice for whom and under which conditions they worked, these perquisites were a predominant feature of labour relations.

Room and board constituted a significant part of a canaller's real earnings (seen as a combination of wages and boarding expenses). Scattered evidence suggests roughly half of a contractor's labour bill went toward providing for his hands. (Table 5 shows that board alone usually accounted for 40–50% of the wage bill.) In effect, this meant that wage scales for common labour masked an almost equal component of income, and must not be taken as a complete indicator of standard of living. The provision of food and shelter was a crucial element in the canaller's budget, one of equal importance to the wage when considering employment. It was thus not surprising workers were reluctant to work for companies that sought to thrust the burden of subsistence onto their shoulders. A bedrock of material necessities

26 Katherine M. J. McKenna, "Working Life at the Isthmus, Rideau Canal during its Construction 1827–1831: The Human Cost of a Public Work," Research Publication Section, Research Division, National Historical Parks and Sites, Environment Canada – Parks, Microfiche Report Series No. 34, 1981, 21; Lee Newcomer, "Construction of the Wabash and Erie Canal," *Ohio State Archaeological and Historical Quarterly*, v. 46 (1937), 203; Wylie, "Poverty, Distress and Disease" (see Introduction, n. 11 above), 15.
27 Ingle to J. Powell, 8 Dec. 1829, C&O/LR. During the winter of 1829–30, labourers were paid $9–10 plus board a month and skilled workers got $1–1.50 a day without board. In May 1832, common hands received $12 a month with board, which worked out to 66¢ a day in combined earnings, while day labourers had to be paid 75–80¢ to defray their boarding and provisioning expenses. Chesapeake and Ohio Canal Ledger (see Ch. 2, n. 63 above), Dec. 1829–March 1830; J. Lackland, 25 May 1832, C&O/LR.
28 Thomas Kavanagh & Co. to Mercer, 8 March 1831, C&O/LR.

was particularly essential to workers in an occupation subject to frequent weather-induced work interruptions, as they were assured of support (for the most part) even when not earning their keep. Thus, the system worked in the interests of canallers, easing their worry about where the next meal would come from and whether they would have a roof over their heads.

Canallers thus worked for much more than mere wages, their labour being directly exchanged for the stuff of life: food, shelter, cleaning, fuel, even clothing. Single labourers benefited most from this system; without a family to support and with most of their needs met within the labour relationship, they essentially could do what they wanted with their wages, which by the standards of common labour were fairly good. If work was steady and they managed to avoid illness or injury, canal digging could be a remunerative occupation, at least until conditions changed during the 1840s.

Nonetheless, although provision of subsistence worked in labourers' interests, their need was a measure of their dependence. The canal construction industry reconstituted the domestic economy according to its productive needs. Essential components of sustaining existence heretofore ordered around the family – building a house, providing food and clothing, laundering, cleaning, cooking, putting fuel in the fire – had been taken from the control of labourers and then returned to them as part of an economic exchange. Because the building blocks of subsistence amounted to half their earnings yet were out of their hands, canallers became dependent on their employer. The system tied boss to hands, at the same time obscuring and reinforcing the unequal relationship between capital and labour.

Time is money

Beneath the rise and fall of wages, behind the advantages of room and board, lurked a variety of threats that ate away at the net income of canallers. Even in the best of times high wage rates distorted reality. Canal work tended to be casual labour, hired by the job and constantly on the move. Outdoor work was subject to the vagaries of nature, halting for inclement weather and often shutting down for winter. Illness or injury also had a tendency to gnaw away at a worker's income. Thus underemployment and unemployment rendered canal work highly irregular and were the most significant factors in the failure of earnings to live up to the promise of wage scales.

Alexander Keyssar in his study of unemployment in Massachusetts has shown that, although never endemic in the early nineteenth century and often blunted by various economic options, it was always a factor in labourers' lives. "Idle" workers would shift back into agriculture or pursue other forms of household production to tide them over slack times. But by mid-century (largely as a result of massive Irish immigration), these options were eroding, making more and more people totally reliant on wages. The merely idle – individuals between jobs – became the unemployed, a large labour reserve that was in place by 1870. Pervasive unemployment for Keyssar was a badge of the new working class, marking their dependence.[29] In effect, a market-driven economy had emerged. If anything this shift occurred earlier in canal construction, as precisely the people who catalyzed the process in Massachusetts – Irish immigrants – had formed the bulk of the workforce for years. By the 1840s, the "industrial disease" was a constant threat to canallers, and even before it was by no means uncommon if usually short-term. Yet, with few other employment opportunities to exploit, canallers were not the "merely idle."

Seasonal and weather-induced work interruptions were the main cause of redundancy. The winter cessation or slowdown of construction meant that most canallers lost many days each year as a matter of fact. In Canada and parts of the northern United States this could mean that virtually the entire workforce was laid off for spells if not the whole winter. Labourers would stay nearby hoping to pick up scraps of work, head for the lumber camps, or go to the city in search of odd jobs such as woodcutting and snow shovelling or perhaps charity. Even those who got work on canals found their income shrunk by the fact that many days were lost to snow, sleet or a hard freeze,[30] and winter pay rates were substantially below those of summer. With both wages and days worked cut in half, winter meant that canallers lucky enough to get work could be earning but a quarter of peak prevailing rates. Loss of income from seasonal wage shifts and work slowdowns was more pronounced in northerly regions, but it was a factor wherever canals were dug. Similarly, daily shifts in weather throughout the year profoundly shaped income. Heavy rain or sharp frost could mean not only missing a day of work but also losing wages, as workers' pay was docked accordingly. Thus, when the hands of the C&O contractor Kavanaugh & Co. could only work sixteen days in November 1830, they received only two-thirds of their $9.50 wage for that month.[31]

Many clear days were lost to personal illness, a constant worry to canallers. Even when they escaped disease, work was often missed when labourers fled the line to avoid the epidemics that struck with varying severity every summer. A different danger threatened them on the job, as accidents were ordinary features of the occupation. Strained muscles, cuts and bruises meant lost days; severed fingers and limbs, blinded eyes and broken bones caused by explosions, rock falls or cave-ins laid men up for

29 Alexander Keyssar, *Out of Work: The First Century of Unemployment in Massachusetts* (New York: Cambridge University Press, 1986), ch. 2.
30 For example, workers at Smith Falls on the Rideau averaged only eleven days of work per month in the winter of 1830–31. Valentine, "Supplying the Rideau" (see Ch. 2, n. 50 above), 17.
31 Kavanaugh & Co. to Mercer, 8 March 1831, C&O/LR.

much longer periods if not emphatically ending their careers. Companies and contractors accepted no legal responsibility for accidents on the job, although room and board could be continued and modest compensation paid in compelling situations.

Time had a more subtle effect on real earnings. Canallers commonly worked from dawn to dusk, twelve to fourteen hours in the summer and about ten in winter. Employers sought to squeeze as much work out of the sunlight as possible by implementing a strict industrial-time regimen. On the Chesapeake & Delaware Canal, for example, "the men are summoned to meals and work by a bell, which must be punctually obeyed or forfeiture is incurred." And an engineer on the Ohio Canal made the corporate case clear: "If hands are negligent, you must dock them in proportion to the time they loose by shirking, and pay them only the fair value of their work."[32] Canallers resisted such strategies by working at their own pace. Management more aggressively attacked the workday in the 1840s when they extended the accepted hours of work without a commensurate wage increase. This prompted a backlash from workers, which will be examined in Chapter 8.

Thus for a variety of reasons, canallers lost time on the job, which cut into the heart of their working year and made the ideal of employment – 26 days a month – a pipedream. A few examples give a sense of the gap between illusion and reality. Regular labourers on the Delaware & Schuylkill Canal in the mid-1790s averaged 212 days' work a year, or about 18 days a month (Table 2).[33] Stephen Gaines, a mason on the James River, averaged almost 17 days per month in 1823, while Tom Abrahams, a labourer on the same canal, could only manage just under 12 days' work. Similarly, Martin Donnelly only averaged 11 days a month on the Beauharnois Canal during a stretch in 1842–43. Lawrence Kennedy, a worker on the Wabash & Erie, did considerably better, working 254 days during the year from July 1847 to June 1848, for a monthly average of 21 days. But the workers as a whole on Kennedy's section only managed $8\frac{1}{2}$ days a month in 1848 (over 14 days for those who worked at least four months).[34]

During the heady days of the 1820s and 1830s construction was at a peak and there was a general labour shortage. When a contract ended, hands tended to be out of work only until they journeyed to the next job. But chronic unemployment became a recurring problem as depression set in, public works were scaled back and continuing immigration flooded the

32 [Pottsville, Pennsylvania] *Miner's Journal*, 28 May 1825; Byron Kilbourn to T. Plummer, 24 June 1829, OH/CC.
33 The Delaware & Schuylkill figures were calculated on a monthly basis for labourers who had worked 200 or more days during the period May 1794–July 1795. Delaware and Schuylkill Workmen's Time Book (see Ch. 1, n. 22 above).
34 Accounts of Labor on the Canal, 1823, JRCR; Deposition of Martin Donnelly (No. 3), "Beauharnois Report" (see Introduction, n. 3 above); Pay Rolls, 20 Dec. 1847, 31 Oct 1848, Abstracts of Labor Due, Wabash & Erie Canal, IN/II.

market. Despite fluctuations of supply and demand in ensuing years, unemployment was a continuing and imminent threat to canallers and fundamentally shaped their earning power. Thus, while receiving what perhaps could be considered fair value for their work, canallers rarely received a fair chance at steady employment, and when they did, they faced the possibility of not getting paid for their toil.

John Campbell, an orphan boy, was working as a farm labourer at $4 a month when at the age of fourteen he took a job on the Wabash & Erie for the promise of a $7 wage from his Irish boss. "When I had worked four and a half weeks . . . I asked Burns if my month was up," recalled the aged Campbell. "He stormed out with boy-scaring oaths – 'that time is not up yet.'" The youth asked again at six weeks, then at the end of seven, but still the contractor refused to pay him and prompted his Irish hands to chase the native-born Campbell away with nothing to show for his many weeks of labour.[35] Too often this happened: if getting and keeping a job was not difficult enough, canallers also had to contend with a variety of situations in which wages were misdirected, delayed or disappeared. The most benign of wage problems, monthly instead of weekly payment, usually only proved a nuisance for workers, but the truck system (or company store pay) and the high incidence of absconding contractors seriously threatened workers' ability to earn a living. The latter problems also undermined public confidence in the canal, and sometimes forced officials to take measures to protect workers, all the while maintaining their lack of responsibility.

The length of the pay period was a recurring canaller complaint. Wages were paid retroactively and at long intervals. At the extreme end of the spectrum, some contractors like Philemon Wright of the Rideau had their workers sign contracts one to two years in length, stipulating wages would not be paid until the end. More common was the monthly pay period, although there usually was a lag between the completion of work and disbursement of wages, as was the case on G. W. Rodgers's section on the C&O where earnings were released on or about the fifteenth for the previous month's work. This system was specifically meant to keep labourers in place and at work. Canallers being a highly transient group, it effectively meant that wages were left behind when they moved on, and contractors got work for free. The long gap between wage payments placed workers in the position of having to buy provisions on credit to tide them over, a situation that became more pronounced as subsistence rights were taken away in the 1840s. Goods bought on credit tended to cost more, even when not coming from a contractor's store. Another alternative for canallers

35 *Indianapolis Star*, 26 July 1907, in John T. Campbell Scrapbook (see Ch. 3, n. 20 above).

was to get an advance on their wages, for which they had to pay a fee.[36] Either way, delayed payment meant a shrinkage of earnings, and was disliked by workers who favoured fortnightly (or, ideally, weekly) periods for greater flexibility in providing for themselves.[37]

Workers lost even the certainty of payment as the crisis of the late 1830s deepened. Unable to meet their loans, canal companies and state authorities could not pay contractors who naturally passed the debt on to their labourers. In lieu of cash, wages were paid in scrip, paper notes backed by state treasuries or company capital, technically redeemable at par. Inevitably, the shaky financial condition of both government and business meant scrip was devalued significantly, and canallers ended up with wages worth on paper twice what they were worth in reality. The C&O Canal first used this expedient in 1834 when it paid its contractors with company scrip that was soon discounted up to 33 percent, a practice they had to resort to several times later in the decade. Similarly, Indiana contractors issued notes backed by canal commission lands; known as White Dog scrip, it circulated at discounts of 10–60 percent, and was refused by some local merchants. As a result, the estimated real value of some workers' wages fell to $3 a month.[38] Scrip made a mockery of wage rates and forced workers into poverty.

Contractors manipulated workers' earnings more perniciously with the system of truck pay in which wages were given in the form of vouchers redeemable in provisions at a store owned by their employers. The rationale for this arrangement was that when work sites were far from settled areas where goods could be bought from merchants, contractors made essential items available, nominally at cost. For example, Whitacre and Avery, contractors on the Ohio Canal and owners of a general store in Dover, allowed their men goods on credit which was subtracted from their wages.[39] The scarcity of alternative vendors and the tacit pressures to deal with one's employer caught canallers in the web of this ostensibly voluntary system. And for contractors it was hard to resist the opportunity to profit from the relationship, so as to recoup the money lost through their pared-down estimates. Truck was uncommon before the 1840s as most workers were still provided for as part of the labour contract, but thereafter labour surplus allowed contractors to take subsistence rights away from their

36 Valentine, "Supplying the Rideau" (see Ch. 2, n. 50 above), 16; G. W. Rodgers, 4 May 1836, C&O/LR; Bleasdale, "Unskilled Labourers" (see Introduction, n. 11 above), 163–65.

37 See the testimony of labourers given before the Beauharnois riot commission in "Beauharnois Report" (see Introduction, n. 3 above).

38 Ingle to John D. Grove, 18 April 1834 (B 215), C&O/LS; Ingle to William Price, 18 April, 4 June 1834 (B 215–16, 240–41), ibid.; Ingle to Boteler and Reynolds, 26 Aug. 1834 (B 299–300), ibid.; Purcell, 1 April 1834, C&O/LR; W. Easby, 23 June 1834, ibid.; Adam Young, July 1834, ibid.; Poinsatte, *Fort Wayne During the Canal Era* (see Ch. 3, n. 64 above), 71–72; Carter to Lucas [26 July 1844], Aborn Collection, Indiana State Library.

39 Thorton Whitacre & Hyde T. Avery Ledger, 1827–28 (v. 202), Ohio Historical Society.

employees and convert provisioning into a commercial relationship in which store pay was the most extreme manifestation. Because of the timing, it was also more a factor in Canada.

The everpresent danger that they would not be paid at all was an even greater threat to canallers' unsteady grasp on their earnings. Contracting even at the best of times was a risky business, cutthroat competition ensuring that bids for work were as low as possible and often insufficient to cover costs. Bad weather, epidemics and other unforeseen factors could cause contractors' profits to disappear, just as they could consume workers' earnings. When disaster struck, bankrupt contractors fled the line with a trail of debt in their wake and sometimes the last cash estimate in their carpetbag as seed money to set up on some other project. For canallers it meant lost wages and imminent poverty.

Some canal companies took measures to prevent contractor fraud, but these initiatives failed to eliminate the problem. A spate of incidents on the Ohio Canal system in 1826 and 1827 angered creditors and workers, many of whom were local residents, thereby tarnishing the reputation of the Canal Board. Two contractors on the Miami Canal fled without paying their subcontractors or labourers any of the $4,000 they had received from the commissioners, and two others absconded from the same canal the day after they had drawn $700. In June 1827, a contractor's agent left the Ohio Canal without fully paying the hands, causing a suspension of work "and quite a *blow up*." This was unsurprising, given that employers were trifling with workers' livelihood. A blacksmith confided, "i am a poo man work for my living went on the canal for the purpus of making some money to helpe myself to a small farm to make a home," but alas, he was owed over $300 by an insolvent contractor for work done by himself and his men, and his dream of petty proprietorship took flight with his debtor.[40]

Such incidents discouraged local residents from taking jobs on canals, and led to a reported labour shortage on the northern section of the Ohio Canal during the spring and summer of 1826. The Ohio Board of Canal Commissioners reported: "The suffering and losses in many cases, brought upon individuals who have furnished these men with supplies, and upon the labourers employed upon their jobs, have tended in some degree, to bring the work into disrepute, and to destroy the confidence of the laboring community in the certainty of receiving their wages." Every effort had been taken to "guard against this evil, and to secure to the labourer, as far as may be practicable, the just reward of his exertions." The board included in contracts a provision giving it the right to withhold payment from contractors suspected of intending to defraud labourers of their wages, and payments were to be made in checks so they could not abscond before

---

40 *Piqua Gazette*, 25 Oct. 1826; Micajah Williams to Kelley, 3 Nov. 1826, 21 June 1827, OH/CC; Reuban Hill to Kelley, 13 March 1827, ibid.

paying workers. It was later reported that these measures led to "greater punctuality in the payment of laborers," but had not eliminated fraudulent contractors. Tellingly, the board lay part of the blame for this failure on the shoulders of the workers for failing to take "the necessary measures to insure the payment of their wages" by not notifying company officials about nonpayment.[41]

This philosophy of worker guilt was fully expressed by the Ohio Board of Canal Commissioners in a "Notice to Labourers on the Canal." Although problems with payment sometimes stemmed from fraudulent contractors, "it is more frequently caused by the negligence of the laborers in not taking the proper measures to secure their pay, or by their not laboring faithfully so as to earn their wages." The board developed guidelines for the workers to follow to prevent the evil from continuing.

First, To enquire as to the character and responsibility of the persons for whom they propose to work; and not to work for any one who does not sustain a good character for honesty and responsibility:

Second, Not to work for a sub-contractor unless the original contractor will agree *in writing* to be accountable for the wages agreed on:

Third, Not to work for any person who suffers his hands to be idle, inattentive to their work, do the work unfaithfully, or who does not attend to his business himself; for such a man will probably be unable to pay his laborers:

Fourth, To be industrious and sober and careful to earn the wages that the contractor agrees to pay; remembering that the surest way to get your pay is first to earn it:

Fifth, To settle with your employer as often as once a month and demand your pay; and if not paid, to give immediate notice of such failure to the Acting Commissioner, or the Engineer, who has charge of the work, who will inform the Commissioner.

The notice then offered a piece of advice in which Adam Smith seemed to meet Confucius. "He who will take *promises* instead of *payment*, should be contented with promises; and not grumble if he gets nothing else." And in case this aphorism was lost on rough canallers, the Commission made clear its position. "The Commissioner will not interfere in procuring payment to laborers who are idle, unfaithful, insolent, or disobedient to their employer – such men do not deserve their wages."[42]

These nostrums for labour seem just the tonic for capital, as they spoke more to the interests of the industry than out of concern for the workers. In addressing the issue of wages, they implicitly summed up ongoing changes

41 "Fifth Annual Report of the Ohio Board of Canal Commissioners, 1826," in *Public Documents of Ohio*, ed. Kilbourne (see Ch. 2, n. 64 above), 236, 248; "Report of the Canal Committee of the Senate, 18 Jan. 1827," in ibid., 263; "Sixth Annual Report of the Ohio Board of Canal Commissioners, 1827," in ibid., 287–88; [Columbus] *Ohio State Journal*, 29 June 1826; *Canton Ohio Repository* 11, 18 Jan. 1827, 1 Feb. 1828. Such provisions were regularly inserted in contracts on canals in this period, once they had experienced problems with contractor failures. See *Report of the Commissioners of the Wabash and Erie Canal* (Indianapolis, 1833), 9.

42 "Notice to Labourers on the Canal," June 1827, signed Alfred Kelley, Acting Commissioner, Williams Papers, Ohio Historical Society. I thank the State Library of Ohio for permission to quote from this document.

in labour relations. The hierarchical yet personal relationship between contractor and hand, best expressed in the subsistence connection, was breaking down under market forces. The "Notice" articulated the emerging ideal of free labour: canallers were independent agents in the labour marketplace, making rational economic decisions based on an evaluation of options. They chose whether to enter into an agreement with an employer according to prevailing conditions, such as wages and his character, and should abide by that agreement. Back in reality, contractors, screwed down by the economics of canal building, periodically bored through the rights and interests of labourers. Late payment of wages, nonpayment or payment in paper assaulted the basic right of wages for work, as workers were made to bear the brunt of the irrational economics of the industry. The Ohio Commissioners encouraged canallers to protest any irregularities in payment and promised to police defaulting contractors, but they, like other canal officials, could never prevent the problem and would never accept basic responsibility for the workers or the system. Instead, the board sought to shift blame onto the victims' shoulders. The price of being a free labourer was living with the danger of losing the price of labour. To misappropriate the logic of the Ohio Board of Canal Commissioners: he who took the *promises* of free labour instead of *payment*, too often had to be content with promises.

A penny saved

"In the general," wrote C&O President Charles Mercer of canallers, "they are extremely improvident; wasting in dissipation their daily wages nearly as fast as they receive them. Scarcely one has yet been known to lay up anything for winter or for sickness and infirmity."[43] Such attitudes led Mathew Carey, the Irish-American journalist, to publish a pamphlet in 1831 defending the labouring poor. In particular, he wished to dispel the "erroneous opinions" that jobs could be found by all willing to work, that those who worked hard could always support themselves comfortably, and that the poor's sufferings resulted from "their idleness, their dissipation, and their extravagance." Carey made a budget analysis of a canal labourer with a wife and two children to show that common working people, through no fault of their own, lived in the shadow of want. Using the prevailing summer and winter rates on the Pennsylvania system as his model, the husband earning $12 a month for ten months and $5 for two while the wife made a half-dollar a week at such work as seamstressing, Carey generously estimated $156 as the family's annual earnings. He assessed their yearly expenses at $171.02, calculating $40 for clothing and shoes, $6.60 for washing at the canal, $26 for rent (at 50¢ per week), $3.12 for soap and candles, $7.80 for fuel, and $87.60 for food for wife

43 Mercer to Decatur, 13 Dec. 1830, C&O/LR.

and children (the husband being provided for at work). This left a deficit of $15, even though "there is no allowance for a single day in the whole year lost by accident, by sickness, or by want of employment – no allowance for expense arising from sickness of wife or child – no allowance for the contingency . . . of working, during the winter months, for board alone. It is assumed that no unfavourable circumstance has taken place."[44] In the best scenario, Carey believed canallers could just about scrape by, but even here often found themselves dependent on public charity at some point during the year.[45] When something went wrong – like injury, ill health or unemployment through bad weather or the completion of work – the family economy could be completely overturned.

The case of the canaller family represented to Carey the situation of the labouring poor, those at the bottom of the working class whose wages were not enough to support themselves, yet who must labour merely to stay alive. Carey affirmed:

There is no occupation, however deleterious or disgraceful, at which there is any difficulty in procuring labourers, even at inadequate wages. The labour on canals in marshy situations, in atmospheres, replete with pestilential miasmata, is full proof on this point. Although the almost certain consequence of labouring in such situations, is a prostration of health, and danger of life – and that no small portion of the laborers return to their families in the fall or winter with health and vigour destroyed, and labouring under protracted fevers and ague, which in many cases undermine their constitutions, and return in after years, and . . . too often hurry them prematurely into eternity – their places are readily supplied by other victims who offer themselves upon the altars of industry.[46]

Carey may have exaggerated the Malthusian workings of the marketplace, but the marginality of canal labour, tottering along the line of subsistence between employment and the chasm of the almshouse, was an experience shared by many at the lower reaches of the workforce. With days limited by forces of nature and acts of God, and work irregular and uncertain even for those who laboured on a steady basis, lost income was the obvious consequence. And as work became more fitful and less remunerative in the later decades of construction, it became increasingly difficult for canallers to survive on their earnings.

Obviously there was great variation between individuals, from place to

---

44 Carey, *Address to the Wealthy of the Land* (see n. 18 above), 2, 4–7. Carey allowed his hypothetical family the following weekly household purchases: bread, meat, potatoes, butter, tea, sugar, milk, salt, pepper, vinegar, fuel, soap, candles, etc., for a total of $1.79 1/2. He believed that this estimate was too low, and compared it unfavourably to the cost of rations in prisons and almshouses.
45 Scattered evidence bears Carey out. See Cases of John Fitzgerald (admitted 21 Oct. 1824), William Daily (14 Dec. 1824), John Welsh (10 Feb. 1825?), Michael Horgan (18 Dec. 1825), Baltimore Almshouse, Admission and Discharge Book, 1814–26, MS. 1866.1, MHS; Case of Michial Mullen (admitted 12 June 1833), Baltimore Almshouse, Medical Records, 1833–37, MS. 2474, MHS; Jos. Brigum[?] to Dr. John Little, 10 Oct. 1829, C&O/LR; Little, 13 Oct. 1829, ibid.; J. Geo. Whitwell to Mercer, 9 March 1830, ibid.
46 Carey, *Address to the Wealthy of the Land* (see n. 18 above), 9.

place, and over time. For example, regular labourers on the Delaware & Schuylkill Canal in the mid-1790s with 200 or more days of works over fifteen months made an average annual income of $169, or $11 monthly, a fair amount at the time. When all those who had worked more than 30 days are taken into consideration, however, average income dropped markedly – $77 a year, $5 a month – but many, of course, had other economic resources (Table 3).[47] By comparison, Tom Abrahams, a labourer on the James River Canal, worked just over 100 days and earned $72 (or an average monthly income of $8) between April and December 1823. With his wage varying from 60¢ to 80¢ a day, he earned less than half what steady work would have brought him. A mason on the same line, Stephen Gaines, prospered by comparison, the higher wages his skill demanded and regular employment (almost 17 days a month on the average) bringing him almost $180 during these nine months, or $20 monthly. Lawrence Kennedy was another example of the up side. He worked 254 days on the Wabash & Erie during the year from July 1847 to June 1848, for a monthly average of 21 days and a projected annual income of $259. During this time at least, Kennedy was one of the more fortunate canallers, with steady employment giving him a satisfactory income. The experience of Martin Donnelly, a labourer on Canada's Beauharnois Canal, gives an idea of canal construction's more capricious nature. Donnelly worked only 112 days during ten months in 1842–43, but 11 days a month on average.[48] Donnelly's case reflected the sharpened exigencies of the 1840s. Working less than every other day at a time when wages had declined and labourers had to provide for themselves, Donnelly found it hard to cope financially. Although there were exceptions, his experience reflected the prevailing trend.

Work was irregular even in the early decades of canal construction, but the gap between canal wages and subsistence earnings was often made up by working elsewhere, as farm labourers or on other construction projects. For farmers who worked part-time on canals it was but a secondary source of income and the loss of a job only meant a return to the land. Periodic interruptions of work were also usually bridged by contractors' provision of food and shelter. Particularly for young, single males these were years when a living could be made from canalling. With no family ties, a place to live and food on the table, not to mention comparatively good wages, money could even be saved.[49] It was different for married men, for when the

47 These figures were calculated for the period May 1794–July 1795. Delaware & Schuylkill workmen's Time Book (see Ch. 1, n. 22 above).
48 Accounts of Labor on Canal, 1823, JRCR; Pay Rolls, 20 Dec. 1847, IN/II; Abstracts of Labor Due [1848], Wabash and Erie Canal, IN/II; Deposition of Martin Donnelly (No. 3), "Beauharnois Report" (see Introduction, n. 3 above).
49 Jaime Valentine argued that "frugal" workers on the Rideau Canal in the late 1820s were able to save up to half their wages as down payment for land on Upper Canada's frontier, but offered no solid evidence to prove his case. Valentine, "Supplying the Rideau" (see Ch. 2, n. 50 above), 18.

subsistence needs of the father-husband were met by a canal wage, those of the family often were not. Wives and children were either pushed into poorly paid and harshly exploited employment or relegated to a marginal existence in the shanty camps collecting scraps of work.

Beginning in the late 1830s, alternative employment became scarcer as a result of the depression, workers became more dependent on internal improvement jobs, the gap between supply and demand widened to the detriment of labour, and wages dropped. And, as was more often the case, there was now no safety net of guaranteed accommodation and provisions. Canallers' economic existence was commercialized and fully subjected to the market. As a result, they had less control over subsistence and lived with the threat of abject poverty. Neither contractors nor canal officials accepted responsibility for their workers, believing in the fairness of the market and the sanctity of free labour. The economy recovered somewhat in the late 1840s, but things were never the same again. Construction was but a shadow of its former dimensions, there was commonly a labour surplus, wages rarely returned to their earlier higher levels, and guaranteed subsistence was a thing of the past. Poverty was a continuing threat, maybe not as imminent as during the bad times but ever lurking in the background, even more so than in the bleak world of the labouring poor captured by Carey in the early 1830s.

Slave wages

The experience of slave labour on canals has been an unstated and obvious exception to most of what has been discussed so far in this chapter. As property, the issue of wages did not usually involve unfree blacks. Nonetheless, they were enmeshed in a system where labour was exchanged for value that was increasingly determined by market forces.

Slaves were usually hired by the year or half-year, although quarterly, monthly and even daily terms became more common as the desire for a more flexible labour force developed in the later decades of construction. The fee paid to the master was set by prevailing local conditions, including labour supply and cycles of agricultural production, but was also influenced by fear for the safety of valuable property. The job was considered dangerous and canal companies had to pay more than the going agricultural rates, 50 percent higher in the case of the James River Company during the late 1790s.[50] In 1785–86, slaves were hired by the Potomac Company for £20 and found for the year. By the mid-1790s, the annual price was $60 and the owner had to provide good clothing and a blanket; time lost to sickness or elopement would be discounted. And by the turn of the century, the company paid $60–70 for a slave's labour. On South Carolina's Santee Canal, common slaves were hired at £15–16 per annum in 1793 and £18

50 Dunaway, *James River and Kanawha Company* (see Ch. 1, n. 38 above), 31.

three years later when skilled bricklayers were worth £25–30. By 1800, common hands brought their owners £24 for men and £20 for women. At this time, slaves were hired to work on the James River Canal for £15 a year. In 1821, $120 was the annual price on Georgia's public works, while assistant lockkeepers on the Dismal Swamp Canal were hired at $168 in 1842, falling to $120 the next year. There was a general rise in the price of hired labour over time, and by the late 1850s it cost $150–200 to hire slaves on the Cape Fear & Deep River Navigation.[51]

Public works found it difficult to get enough workers, as they competed with slavery's agricultural base and suffered from a reputation as a dangerous line of work in which to invest slave capital. Some canal companies got around shortages by purchasing their own slaves.[52] The cost was largely set by the state of the agricultural slave market, and obviously involved a considerable investment. In 1856, the Cape Fear & Deep River purchased Sam, a twenty-year-old slave, for $900, and later that year sold seven slaves for $6,900, or an average of $986 each. Buying was a long-term investment as the annual hiring price stood at around $150–200. Purchasing slaves ensured a labour supply, but it also meant that hands would have to be cared for even when their labour was not needed. Some canals avoided the problem by hiring out their slaves in slack time, as the Upper Appomattox Company did in 1816. In dire circumstances, slaves could be sold for a quick infusion of cash, a course taken in 1823 by the James River Company that realized a profit of $458 on a slave bought the year before, and as the Cape Fear & Deep River Navigation Company was forced to do in the late 1850s.[53]

Whether owned or hired for the long term, slaves had to be provided for, and the cost of food and shelter formed a significant component of the labour bill. In the 1780s, hired slaves on the Potomac Canal received 1–1.5 pounds of meat and a ration of bread each day, with "a reasonable quantity of spirits," the same diet provided free workers. In the 1830s, contractors for the Brunswick Canal in Georgia promised masters their

51   POT/PRO, 18 Oct. 1785 (A 14), 5 Nov. 1792 (A 42), 22 Dec. 1795 (A 66), 17 Dec. 1800 (A 207–08); Rumsey to Hartshorn, 26 Nov. 1785, POT/COR; *Virginia Journal*, 7 Dec. 1786; Porcher, *Santee Canal* (see Ch. 1, n. 11 above), 6; Phillips, *History of Transportation* (see Ch. 1, n. 6 above), 26–40, 114–15; Dunaway, *James River and Kanawha Company* (see Ch. 1, n. 30 above), 31; Analysis of Accounts, 30 Sept. 1842, 18 Feb., 30 Sept. 1843, Dismal Swamp Canal Company Records, entry 81, VA/BPW; Accounts and Records of Negro Hire, 1859–60, Cape Fear and Deep River Navigation, NCA.
52   Brown, *Dismal Swamp Canal* (see Ch. 1, n. 16 above), 46; Phillips, *History of Transportation* (see Ch. 1, n. 6 above), 114–15; London Family Papers (No. 2011-B), 1855, folders 7, 8, SHC; Alexander Murchison to the Directors, 14 March 1857, London Family Papers (No. 2442), SHC.
53   Mr. McKay's Bill of Sale for Sam, 30 Jan. 1856, London Family Papers (No. 2011), SHC; Account, 31 Aug. 1856, Cape Fear and Deep River Navigation, SHC; Journal A, p. 59, Journal B, p. 99, Journals, VA/BPW; Receipts and Warrants, June 1831, p. 82[b], JRCR; Accounts, 15 April– 31 Oct. 1856, Cape Fear and Deep River Navigation, SHC; Thomas Bragg to Henry London, 9 April 1857, London Family Papers (No. 2442), SHC; Payrolls, 1859–60, London Family Papers (No. 2011), SHC.

slaves would "be provided with three and a half pounds of pork, or bacon, and ten quarts of gourd-seed corn per week, lodged in comfortable shantees, and attended constantly by a skilful physician."[54] As with slavery in general, this was the extent of slaves' wages for their labour: enough food and shelter to keep them at work. There is some indication that chattel did in fact receive wages in special instances, however. For example, on the Cape Fear & Deep River in 1859, slaves were paid for working on Sunday or for doing more than was expected of them.[55] These exceptions indicate a consensus on the mutual obligations involved in the slave–master labour relationship – obligations that would be set out contractually in wage labour – but they were merely customary and left to the master.

As in the North, employers moved away from long-term labour commitments when it became apparent that the most economical worker was the one who could be hired and fired at will. In the late 1820s and early 1830s, hiring by the quarter-year was the norm, with the going rate $15–16 on the James River Canal and $17.50 on the Black River Canal. Monthly hiring also emerged as an option, bringing such prices as $12 per month on the James River in 1823, $18 on Georgia's Brunswick & Altamaha Canal in 1838 and $24–35 on the Cape Fear & Deep River Navigation in the late 1850s.[56] By the mid-1830s, day hiring of both whites and slaves was becoming more frequent. The James River Company paid a day rate of 50¢ for slaves, and free labourers were paid 50¢ to $1 for work on the Blue Ridge Canal. By the late 1850s, slaves hired to work on the Cape Fear & Deep River Navigation cost $1–1.50 a day; carpenters and blacksmiths brought their masters $2–2.50.[57] Prices for slave labour were thus roughly comparable to the wages of free labour, as when free blacks worked on canals.[58]

This shift to shorter periods of hire paralleled changes in free labour elsewhere on canals, and indicated a desire for a rationalized labour force that could be used when needed and let go when not. In effect, slavery on public works was aping capitalist labour and slaves were becoming as much workers as slaves, although obviously still chattel. Despite the growing

---

54 POT/PRO, 18 Oct. 1785 (A 14); *Virginia Journal*, 7 Dec. 1786; Copy of contractors' notice in J. S. Buckingham, *The Slave States of America* (London, n.d.), v. 1, 137.

55 Accounts and Records of Negro Hire, 1859, Cape Fear and Deep River Navigation, NCA.

56 Receipts and Warrants, 1828–31, JRCR; Journal B, 30 June 1833, box 188, JRCR; Minute Book D, 18 July 1835, JRCR; Kanawha Road and Navigation Receipts, 25 Aug. 1835, box 197, JRCR; Receipts, June–August, 1823, box 197, JRCR; Buckingham, *Slave States of America* (see n. 54 above), v. 1, 137; Accounts and Records of Negro Hire, 1859–60, Cape Fear and Deep River Navigation, NCA.

57 Kanawha Road and Navigation Receipts, 27 July 1835, JRCR; Accounts and Records of Negro Hire, 1859–60, Cape Fear and Deep River Navigation, NCA; Monthly Payroll, Nov., Dec. 1860, London Family Papers (No. 2011), SHC.

58 Free black carpenter Abel Payne was paid $35 a month, and Rufus Lane and Jack Powell, also carpenters, received daily wages of $1 and $1.25 respectively. Monthly Payroll, Nov., Dec. 1860, London Family Papers (No. 2011), SHC.

similarity of labour use, fundamental differences, besides that of liberty, separated slaves and wage workers. Unfree canal labourers tended to be more fully exploited, working more steadily in all sorts of conditions. A comparison of work on Locks 19 and 20 of the James River Canal in 1851 highlights the disparity between the two forms of labour. The slaves, both hired and owned, worked regularly (some had been with the contractor since 1838 and most toiled regularly between 1847 and 1851).[59] By comparison, white workers came and went with alarming frequency. During 1851, twenty-seven slaves worked 261 days on the average, or almost 22 days a month. In 1855, slaves working for the same contractor averaged 267 days for the year and just over 22 per month. Eighty-seven free labourers only managed an average of almost 18 days' work in 1851, or a paltry 1.5 days a month (Table 6). White workers tended to be hired on a day or part-day basis and for specific jobs; a number were wagoners. Clearly they were marginal to the canal and had some other primary line of work, while slaves constituted the heart of the workforce. And when compared to Northern free labour of the 1850s, beset by an overstocked market and dwindling construction, slaves appeared models of consistency.

Nonetheless, steady work did not translate into steady earnings, only more work. And although slaves benefited from continuing subsistence (something that free canallers after the 1830s could appreciate), they were also expected to work in conditions whites would not accept without extra pay. Thus, slaves on the James River toiled through the unpredictable Virginia winter, in all but torrential downpours and on through the summer fever season for which the James River was notorious.[60] Blacks were treated as if they were immune to these forces that ate away at a free labourer's work year; after all, this had always been a main selling point for slavery, and made perfect sense on canals when work was guaranteed.

Not surprisingly, slave canallers' lives were difficult. Never receiving much more than a roof over their heads and food in their bellies for their hard work, their labour was increasingly treated like a market commodity, yet they never received its growing value as they drudged year by year in conditions that were believed to fell the strongest whites. As Fanny Kemble saw it; "The Negroes are hired from their masters, who will be paid, of course, as high a price as they can obtain for them – probably a very high one, as the demand for them is urgent – they, in the meantime, receiving no wages, and nothing more than the miserable Negro fare of rice

59 Time Charts for Workers on the James River and Kanawha Canal, 1837 (MsV. 22), Austin-Twyman Papers (see Ch. 3, n. 25 above); Time Charts for Workers on the James River and Kanawha Canal, 1848–57, ibid.; Time Book for Gwynn Dam and Lock, 1855-56, folder 164, ibid.
60 When it rained one day in October 1850, free labourers broke off but it was noted that "negroes worked in rain"; during another downpour slaves shifted to cutting stone in a shed. Oct. 1850, Feb. 1851 payrolls, Time Charts for Workers on the James River and Kanawha Canal, Austin-Twyman Papers (see Ch. 3, n. 25 above).

and corn grits." James Silk Buckingham agreed that "it is a positive robbery of their only natural wealth, the labour of their hands, to steal it from their pockets, and place it in that of their owners."[61] Free workers could leave, riot or strike, but slaves' options were limited. As on plantations, however, they did register their dislike for the lifestyle, a fact that comes through in scraps of information. Most commonly, slaves could just be useless or truculent at their job, as seemed to be the case with Henry, whom the contractor deemed "the most worthless [illegible] negro I have seen." More serious, they could take flight from the canal, like Amos and Fleming who ran away from the works at Gwynn Dam for a week in July 1855, and Harrison who eloped for a month and a half the next year.[62] These were all individualized forms of protests, limited assertions of self, by people who had no hope of changing their condition. Slaves who found themselves on canals, as elsewhere, could only make the most of a bad situation: eat their wages, take whatever liberties they could devise, and do the work. Free labourers had it better, obviously, but the unpredictability of their earnings made want a real possibility.

The bottom line

Slavery, indentures, annual and monthly hirings, the provision of food and shelter were all strategies born of prevailing manpower shortages, and were traditional, nonmonetary aspects of labour relations meant to guarantee supply in an increasingly capitalistic world. In confronting the conundrum of commercial labour relations, canal builders – both employers and employed – were not merely responding to market dictates but were actually engaged in constructing this world. By trial and error they sought to erect levees to direct the current of change, but in the process altered the landscape itself. Paternalism was one such bulwark, and for a time it served its purpose. It answered capital's labour needs by drawing workers more securely within the production process, but saddled it with unwanted responsibilities that would be jettisoned as soon as possible. Similarly, the system worked in canallers' interests, offering job security and a means of subsistence, but it also bred dependence, workers being tied to and reliant on employers. Nonetheless, for the free labourer these early decades were the most rewarding. Despite the irregularity of work and problems with payment, relatively high wages and a degree of choice in where they worked gave them a subsistence existence and some control over their lives.

The depression of the late 1830s altered the material world of canal

61 Kemble, *Journal of a Residence on a Georgia Plantation* (see Ch. 3, n. 23 above), 104–05; Buckingham, *Slave States of America* (see n. 54 above), v. 1, 137.
62 July 1849 payroll, Time Charts for Workers on the James River and Kanawha Canal, Austin-Twyman Papers (see Ch. 3, n. 25 above); Time Book for Gwynn Dam and Lock, July 1855, June 1856, ibid.

construction. Labour surplus allowed contractors to monetize the relationship by moving away from traditional practices: they hired day labour, stripped away subsistence rights and drove down wages. In the process, canallers would be "freed," made fully dependent on their labour for support. The randomness of work and uncertainty of pay that resulted reflected workers' changed condition as members of an individualized, casual labour force separated from poverty only by the sweat of their labour and the whims of the market. In this changed environment canallers had few options. They could move on in search of better opportunity; they could stay, work when able and eke out an existence, with some eventually "making it" while others experienced despair and deprivation; or they could resist the erosion of their standard of living by fighting each other for jobs, and by rioting and striking for better wages and work conditions. The cost exacted by canal work, what with its rough conditions and assorted dangers, was another factor that had to be figured into this equation.

CHAPTER 5

"The greatest quantity of labour"

When I came to this wonderful rampire [*sic*], it filled me with the greatest surprise,
To see such a great undertaking, on the like I never opened my eye.
To see a full thousand brave fellows at work among mountains so tall,
To dig through the vallies so level, through rocks for to cut a canal.[1]

"The walk along the embankments is not only highly interesting, but exciting," wrote a correspondent for the *Detroit Advertiser* while visiting the St. Mary's Canal at Sault Ste. Marie, Michigan, in 1854.

The frequent processions of barrowmen toiling their slow and weary way up the narrow plank to the sides of the cut – the high platforms erected for the cars used in moving the heavy masses of rock – the horse-drills keeping up their continual buzz as the poor, jaded animals tread to the ceaseless music, and the heated steel descends into the almost impenetrable rock – the noise of the blast which is so loud and frequent as to make one think he is going through the uproarious salute of a grand military reception, or that the 4th of July is perpetuating itself – the stampede among the men as word is passed that a fuse is fired – the scattering of the rock which follows the explosion, sometime shooting innumerable masses of all sizes into the heavens, giving you no bad idea of Ætna and Vesuvius – the voices of the overseers and the louder utterings of the cataract, which all this scene of animation is preparing to overcome for the uses of man.

The reporter was clearly impressed by the "industry" of the scene, and returned to write a second account with images drawn from the cult of improvement. "The men upon it are as thick as bees, there being fourteen hundred in all, and the work is going on bravely. Everything seems to be like clock work."[2] This "scene of animation," with its singing drills, volcanic explosions and rocketing cascades, certainly gave a colourful impression of canal work. But behind this seeming "clock work" there seethed a small army of workers, exerting and hurting, daring dangerous tasks

1 From "Paddy on the Canal," in *Irish Emigrant Ballads and Songs*, ed. Wright (see Ch. 2, n. 2 above), 533.
2 From [Sault Ste. Marie, Mich.] *Lake Superior Journal*, 9, 16 Sept. 1854.

for higher wages and a manly reputation, whose experience belied the symmetry of production conveyed in these reports.

Tyrone Power, the Irish actor, looked beyond the whirl of activity to the human dimension of canal work. While visiting New Orleans during his tour of America in the mid-1830s, he made a detour to inspect the canal being dug by his expatriate countrymen through swamps from the city to Lake Pontchartrain. He was confronted by the sight of "hundreds of fine fellows labouring here beneath a sun that at this winter season was at times insufferably fierce, and amidst a pestilential swamp whose exhalations were fœtid to a degree scarcely endurable even for a few moments." In the midst of this hostile environment, canallers were "wading amongst stumps of trees, mid-deep in black mud, clearing the spaces pumped out by powerful steam-engines; wheeling, digging, hewing, or bearing burdens it made one's shoulders ache to look upon." Nor did day's end mean welcome escape, as the men were "exposed meantime to every change of temperature, in log-huts, laid down in the very swamp, on a foundation of newly-felled trees, having the water lying stagnant between the floor-logs, whose inter-stices, together with those of the side-walls, are open, pervious alike to sun or wind, or snow." Life in this Irish mudsill was tenuous. "Here they subsist on the coarsest fare," Power continued, "holding life on a tenure as uncertain as does the leader of a forlorn hope; excluded from all the advantages of civilization; often at the mercy of a hard contractor, who wrings his profit from their blood; and all this for a pittance that merely enables them to exist, with little power to save, or a hope beyond the continuance of the like exertion." This bleak portrait was made even more grim by health conditions. "Next comes disease, either a sweeping pestilence that deals wholesale on its victims, or else a gradual sinking of mind and body; finally the abode in the hospital, if any comrade is interested enough for the sufferer to bear him to it; else, the solitary log-hut and quicker death."[3]

Strenuous, body-sapping work, crude, deleterious conditions, ubiquitous disease, the lurking spectre of death – not a hive of industry or precision clockwork as the *Advertiser* reporter would have it – these were the charac-teristics of canal construction Power sketched. It was a play acted out with passion on all canals, perhaps melodramatically at New Orleans as scripted by the Irish thespian, but with greater or lesser pathos elsewhere. And everywhere, the plot was driven by work, the very nature of the job.

Such a negative reading of canal work does not mean that navvies, the "brave fellows" of the ballad at the head of this chapter, did not take a certain pride in such a "great undertaking." In fact, the very difficulty of the job and harshness of shanty life, not to mention the magnitude

3 Tyrone Power, *Impressions of America, during the years 1833, 1834, and 1835* (orig. ed. 1836; New York: Benjamin Blom, 1971), v. 2, 239, 241.

and public import of many canal projects, contributed to their sense of specialness. They thus could display a degree of satisfaction with their work, a jauntiness of spirit; but, for unskilled workers at least, this had to be outweighed by the substance of their existence.

For both good and bad reasons then, work was central to canallers' lives. It was the mortar that bound together slaves, Irish and German immigrants, French *habitants*, and Anglo-Americans. Whatever factors isolated and pulled these groups apart, as canal workers they shared a common fate.

Dredge and delve

Canal construction had as much to do with the past it was helping to bury with every shovelful of dirt as with the urban-industrial world for which it was preparing the way. It took place outdoors, often in areas some distance from settlements and their amenities. The work environment was quite different from that of mill hands who laboured within walls, the staccato rhythm of machines in their ears, and from the closed, claustrophobic garret of sweated workers. For canallers, the vault of the sky was their roof and the murmuring of the ubiquitous river their constant companion. But this did not make for an idyllic pastoral existence. Rain made their clothes sodden, the dampness seeming to seep into their bones, and heat blistered and blackened their skin, making sweat pour from their brows. And as in farming, there was always something to be done during winter, though construction often ground to a halt outside the South. For workers the onset of winter promised numbing cold that robbed hands of their dexterity and threatened frostbite. Contractors on the Erie whose sections involved deep cutting or embanking where frost was not a factor, or passed through earth fed by hot springs or covered by vegetation that resisted the cold, worked through the winter of 1819. Similarly, while the frost was severe on the summit of the Delaware & Hudson in December 1825, deep cutting, embanking and blasting continued.[4] Still, this world of work was a familiar one.

Like earlier patterns of labour, work on the canal was described by the arc of the sun through the sky; canallers laboured from dawn to dusk, twelve to fourteen hours in summer, and eight to ten in winter for those lucky enough to get work. In shanty camps on the Erie Canal the cook's helper blew the wake-up horn a half-hour before sunrise, called "All out Mush in the kettle," and the men stumbled bleary-eyed from their plank bunks for breakfast.[5] A full day of labour followed, interspersed with breaks for lunch and supper and periodic timeouts for dispensing the liquor ration.

4 *Annual Report of the Canal Commissioners* (Albany, 1819), 4; *Annual Report of the Board of Managers of the Delaware and Hudson Canal Company to the Stockholders, 1825* (New York, 1826), 10.
5 Ralph K. Andrist, *The Erie Canal* (New York: American Heritage Publishing, 1964), 38–41.

The continuity with prior patterns of labour was also borne out by everpresent livestock, as on farms a necessary factor of production. Thus, on the Second Residency of the C&O there were 87 horses to 565 men in December 1829, and on the Western Division of the Illinois & Michigan during 1838 there was an average of 38 teams of horses and oxen to over 500 men. On the Lachine, 760 hands were matched by 254 horses.[6] Yet the sheer number of animals and men involved, as well as the concerted organization of their efforts, belied any initial impressions of a bucolic world.

The similarity with preindustrial agrarian practices also falls away in the pace of work. Whereas a farmer's day could be filled with different pursuits, social as well as productive, canallers were driven at an industrial pace. Contractors were paid piece rates – so much per yard of excavation – and therefore had incentive to speed completion, in effect to implement a system of discipline that promoted steady, at times extraordinary, labour. Slaves on the James River were expected to work through the night when the situation demanded it. This became the norm for Irish labourers on the C&O's Paw Paw tunnel, where work proceeded day and night with three shifts of eight hours, although the labourers' resistance made this system work less efficiently than clockwork.[7] Such a regime, although unusual, set canal work apart from even the most labour-intensive agricultural work, and won the enmity of those who laboured under it. One canaller, resenting his bosses' time consciousness, complained that they only "give you twenty-one minutes to eat/ . . . scream, threaten, and shout at you/While forcing you back to work."[8] Industrial discipline belied canalling's seemingly traditional nature, and became stricter in later years.

Canal construction was an industrial machine driven by animal flesh and blood with the aid of tried and true implements: picks, axes, shovels, mattocks, wheelbarrows and carts.[9] Still, there were a number of mechanical innovations to speed work. On the Erie Canal, for example, a tree feller was invented. "By means of an endless screw, connected with a roller, a cable, a wheel and a crank, one man is able to bring down a tree of the largest size, without any cutting about its roots," boasted the canal commissioners. A stump puller was also invented but was found too expensive, and a special

6 Daniel Vanslyke to President and Directors, 26 Dec. 1829, C&O/LR; *Report of the Illinois and Michigan Canal* (Vandalia, 1838), 52; Return of the Number of Mechanics, Labourers and Horses Employed on the Lachine Canal, 31 Aug. 1844, Lachine Riots (see Ch. 3, n. 53 above).

7 Time Charts for Workers on the James River and Kanawha Canal, 5 May 1849, Austin-Twyman Papers (see Ch. 3, n. 25 above); *Ninth Annual Report of the President and Directors of the Chesapeake and Ohio Canal Company* (Washington, 1837), 8; *Report of the General Committee of the Stockholders of the Chesapeake and Ohio Canal Company* (Washington, 1839), 16.

8 Quoted in Miller, *Emigrants and Exiles* (see Ch. 3, n. 33 above), 270.

9 Raphael Samuel examined British industries in which similar conditions of production prevailed. "The Workshop of the World: Steam Power and Hand Technology in Mid-Victorian Britain," *History Workshop Journal*, no. 3 (Spring 1977), 6–72, and "Mineral Workers," in *Miners, Quarrymen and Saltworkers*, ed. Samuel (see Ch. 2, n. 22 above), 3–97.

plough was developed for cutting roots. More common were the various cranes used to lift rocks, from the simple tripods employed at quarries, to bigger versions lining rock cuts as at Lockport on the Erie, to "the monster crane" that lifted the huge chunks of the Canadian Shield blasted from the bed of the St. Mary's Canal. In addition, horse- or steam-driven pumps were jerryrigged to combat the inevitable problem of either too much or too little water. For instance, Pennsylvania's Union Canal, faced with an inadequate water supply at the summit of the line, purchased a 100-horsepower steam engine to drive a pump, but the engine failed on its first day in operation, and a backup engine had to be bought. Still, most companies stuck with the traditional, so that bigger jobs merely meant more men. Not until mid-century did steam dredges make their appearance, and then only a few large contracting firms could afford them.[10] Canal digging thus maintained a facade of traditional labouring practices, while a developing industrial organization of work recast it into modern mass production.

Not only did canal construction evoke a traditional agrarian past, it transcended most forms of contemporary industrial production in its sheer size and distended nature. Work distances ranged from a few to hundreds of miles, the size of the workforce from fifty to five thousand. Canals snaked across miles of territory, but were divided into numerous sections under the direction of different contractors, each at a different stage of completion, some just getting under way – recruiting men and amassing supplies – others winding up the job with men and contractors fanning out to a variety of other jobs. Although canallers were thrown into close contact on individual sections, they were hedged off from workers on other parts of the line. All these factors made for a segmented labour force and a varied work experience, and provided a blueprint for the massive national industries that arose in the late nineteenth century.

Digging canals was hard manual work, rough labour as it was sometimes known. At the same time it required many skills. Canals were not mere ditches; they had to overcome the fundamental problem of cutting through miles of rock-studded territory, often extending from mountains to low-lying swamps, while maintaining a manageable descent in altitude – no more than two inches per mile. Reservoirs had to be built, hills cut through, tunnels dug or railways laid, and aqueducts arched over broad rivers. Through all these obstacles canals had to retain a uniformity of design. The canal's *prism*, or channel, required exact specifications with its

---

10 *Annual Report of the Canal Commissioners* (Albany, 1819), 11, 12–13; *The Journal of Increase Allen Lapham for 1827–1830*, ed. Samuel W. Thomas and Eugene H. Conner (Louisville, Ky: G. R. Clark, 1973), 107; *Lake Superior Journal*, 9 July 1853, 15 July 1854; *Annual Report of the President and Managers of the Union Canal Company of Pennsylvania, to the Stockholders* (Philadelphia, 1826), 6–7; *Annual Report of the President and Managers of the Union Canal Company of Pennsylvania, to the Stockholders* (Philadelphia, 1827), 4; Bleasdale, "Unskilled Labourers on the Public Works of Canada" (see Introduction, n. 11 above), 23–30.

sloping sides and bottom waterproofed, or *puddled* as it was called, so as to retain water. Canal dimensions varied, but averaged thirty to forty feet across at the surface, twenty to thirty feet across on the bed and ten feet in depth (so as to hold four feet of water).[11] Masonry locks with their wooden gates had to be watertight while accounting for drops in elevation, necessary links in the chain of canals.

Grubbing was the first step in construction. A strip of land was cleared of trees, brush and rocks to make way for the canal. The grubbed area's dimensions usually amounted to the canal's width plus twenty feet on either side.[12] This work, involving levelling what was often virgin bush, required the strenuous use of axes and picks, as trees were felled and rocks pried from the soil to be dragged away in carts. As in pioneer farming, stumps posed a particular problem, having to be pulled by oxen, undercut by digging or, for the more unyielding, blasted. Another way to get rid of stumps was called "pooling-in," whereby roots were cut and an excavation made under the stump for it to cave into; many workers were smothered or lost limbs performing this risky procedure.[13] With the land cleared, it was ready for either *embankment* or *excavation*, the former where the canal was to lie above the natural surface of the ground and the latter when below.

When building embankments the contractor was in effect making the sides of the canal; thus great care had to be taken to make it firm and watertight. All wood, roots, plant matter and rubbish had to be mucked out to the width of at least ten feet under each bank, so it would have a solid base and not settle with time, thus undermining the canal. The work itself was rather simple but time-consuming. Contractors looking to cut corners and costs stinted by doing a shoddy job of this *mucking* and *ditching*, for instance using improper fill from their excavations as the base of embankments. When such shortcuts were discovered by engineers, contractors would be ordered to do the work over or face not being paid for the job. Embankment usually constituted a small part of canal construction, often let as a separate contract, but more than half of the Middlesex's twenty-seven miles rose above ground.[14]

Excavation involved digging through any type of material from the loosest soil to the hardest rock. Canallers on the Erie worked their way through hard-pan (a mixture of earth and stones), quicksand, breccia

11 Powers, "Invisible Immigrants" (see Ch. 2, n. 37 above), 100–02.
12 On the Erie Canal, for example, grubbing was sixty feet wide with trees cleared at least an additional thirty-three feet. Minutes of the New York Canal Commission (see Ch. 2, n. 29 above), v. 1, p. 2, 5 June 1817.
13 Andrist, *Erie Canal* (see n. 5 above), 34–35; McClelland and Huntington, *History of Ohio Canals* (see Ch. 2, n. 30 above), 24; Mactaggart, *Three Years in Canada* (see Ch. 3, n. 55 above), v. 2, 248; Wylie, "Poverty, Distress, and Disease" (see Introduction, n. 11 above), 16–17.
14 McClelland and Huntington, *History of Ohio Canals* (see Ch. 2, n. 30 above), 24; Lewis M. Lawrence, "The Middlesex Canal," unpublished typescript dated 1920 in possession of American Antiquarian Society, 20.

(gravel), marl, gypsum and limestone. Where the earth to be removed was common dirt, dry and no deeper than four to five feet, it could be broken by ploughs, then planed by scrapers, both pulled by oxen or horses.[15] The way prepared, men set to with their picks and shovels. The simplest type of excavation was earth removal, with dirt shovelled into wheelbarrows or horse-drawn carts to be hauled over to the fill. Captain Campbell, who worked on Indiana's Wabash & Erie Canal as a boy, reminisced many years later about the process:

All the dirt was moved in carts and wheelbarrows. Each teamster led two horses, one at a time, from the shovel pit to the dump, or tow path, where a dump boss directed to "haw gee and back." That was the command whether the turn to be made was haw or gee. The boss would throw his weight on the back end of the cartbed when it would tip down and shoot the dirt out backward and down the embankment, or on the level ground, or in a hole or sink according to the progress of the embankment. Then drives [sic] (or leader, more properly) would lead the horse and cart back to the shovel pit and turn and back the cart to the pit and lead the other horse and cart to the bank. While one horse was being led to the bank or towpath, six to eight shovelers would be filling the other cart.

A production line of sorts was thus set up, often with a contractor's assistant keeping a tally of the volume of earth removed. "Empty teams continually take the place of those which go off with their loads," the *Free Journal* reported of the Chesapeake & Delaware, "and by means of copper tokens given to each driver as he takes away a load, the precise number is ascertained by the overseer." This system helped both in making an estimate of work done for the engineer and in keeping account of labour performed by common wheelers, who were occasionally paid by the barrow load.[16]

Whether digging or carting, excavation meant constant effort for the canaller. Sand was removed on the Blackstone Canal by ox-drawn carts, "six of these muscular wielders of the 'pick axe, spade and shovel,' loading the vehicle 50 times in one hour." In an unusual feat of labour (prompted by economic incentives) three Irishmen on the Erie Canal dug three rods in a four-foot cutting, or 249.5 cubic yards, in five and a half days of work. This amounted to approximately fifteen cubic yards a man per day, or about three times the normal average. By comparison, slaves were expected to move two cubic yards (or about fifty-four wheelbarrows) of dirt a day on the Santee Canal in the 1790s.[17] When all this exertion had produced a channel through the earth, cattle and men tramped down the soil to make it into a firm canal bed.

15 *Annual Report of the Canal Commissioners, Communicated to the Legislature* (Albany, 1820), 3–5, 9–10.
16 *Indianapolis Star*, 26 July 1907, in John T. Campbell Scrapbook (see Ch. 3, n. 20 above); *Free Journal* in *Miner's Journal*, 28 May 1825.
17 [Worcester] *Massachusetts Spy*, 19 Oct. 1825; *Report of the Commissioners of the State of New York* (Albany, 1818), 13; *History of the Old Santee Canal* (Monck's Corner and Columbia, S. C.: South Carolina Public Service Authority, n.d.).

Earth removal became more difficult where a cut was being made through a hill. Planks were laid up the bank to give a solid surface to the barrow men who wore metal cleats on their feet for traction, and, in cases of steep inclines, pulley systems at times were rigged on the lip of the cut with ropes running down around the belts of men scaling the hill. This was potentially dangerous work, both for the barrow man, who if he lost his footing could be crushed by the heavy load, and for those in the pit below who would then be exposed to an avalanche of dirt, rock and rampaging wheelbarrow. As work progressed the whole labour force concentrated on the floor of the excavation, working at close quarters mindful of others' elbows and shovel handles. A contractor on the Beauharnois Canal, for example, reported that with work drawing to a close on section 1, there were 200 men and ninety horses crowded into a space about 500 feet in length, working ankle-deep in water.[18]

Excavation became more problematic in wet areas, when the men had to stand in water sometimes up to their waists, shovelling muck from the murky stew at their feet. Water excavation was one of the least desirable jobs as it meant being wet and miserable all day. Josiah White, who directed the improvement of the Lehigh River, remembered that workers had to wear "strong shoes with holes cut in the toe to let out the water, as our work was generally in the water 7 to 8 months in the year." Mathew Carey reported that construction on the Chesapeake & Delaware was carried on in flooded meadows during the winter of 1824–25, where the "labourers had to work in the water, and sometimes in the ice."[19] The discomfort of such toil was compounded when carried on in swampland. The Erie Canal was dug though the notorious Montezuma marshes at the outlet of Cayuga Lake near Syracuse. The Irish labourers worked in six to twelve inches of water, legs swelling from the inescapable dampness, leeches fastening onto them, and mosquitoes driving them to distraction while infecting them with diseases. The situation was so bad that excavation was scheduled for the winter, when the ground was frozen and mosquitoes were blissfully absent.[20] It is no surprise then, that canallers on the Erie sang this ditty:

> We are digging the ditch through the mire;
> Through the mud and the slime and the mire, by heck!
> And the mud is our principal hire;
> Up our pants, in our shirts, down our neck, by heck![21]

18 Teagarden, "Builders of the Ohio Canal" (see Ch. 3, n. 10 above), 99–100; W. Shanly to Thomas Begly, 4 Aug. 1845, Riots on the Beauharnois, file 26, v. 54, PAC/RG11 (hereafter Beauharnois Riots).
19 "Josiah White's History" (see Ch. 2, n. 43 above), 16; Mathew Carey, *Exhibit of the Shocking Oppression and Injustice Suffered by John Randel of the Chesapeake and Delaware Canal* (Philadelphia, 1825), 3.
20 Shaw, *Erie Water West* (see Ch. 1, n. 21 above), 125; Andrist, *Erie Canal* (see n. 5 above), 45; Harlow, *Old Towpaths* (see Ch. 1, n. 54 above), 54.
21 Quoted in Fatout, *Indiana Canals* (see Ch. 2, n. 10 above), 58.

"No person without experience can be fully aware of the disadvantages of laboring in wet earth," the New York Canal Commissioners remarked. "The laborers who work in it destroy more clothes, live more expensively, are more exposed to sickness, and require higher wages, than other laborers." Not only did contractors often have to pay higher wages for this sort of work, but it was usually hard to get men to stay on past October at any price, at least while alternative jobs were available.[22] Quicksand posed even greater difficulty, as an employee of an Erie contractor made clear:

The quicksand, after being drained in the best manner, was still a fluid and would run; and it would hold the shovel fast, so as to make it difficult sometimes to pull out; the workmen would often sink in and stick fast, so as to render it rather difficult to extricate themselves.

The only away to avoid this messy fate was for the workers quickly to dig a trench and lay in a bed of stones, which would sink "to a considerable depth before they found bottom."[23]

Rock excavation was the most dangerous task, as blasting was the only way to cut through solid stone. The procedure seemed deceptively simple: a hole was hand-drilled and packed with powder, and a fuse was inserted at the top. Yet it took three men using a rock chisel and a sledgehammer a day to drill a one-and-three-quarter-inch hole twelve feet deep, or a three-inch hole four feet deep.[24] Fuses were a matter of guesswork, strips of match-paper soaked in a saltpeter solution that when dried would burn according to the strength of the solution. A blaster would light the fuse and run for cover. Some charges failed to go off or merely rumbled the ground, but if all went well, rock fragments would fly into the sky and then rain down, and when the dust had settled the rock bed would have receded several more feet. Overcharging could propel boulder-sized rocks hundreds of yards through the air to land on cowering labourers and crash into shanties or nearby communities. The rock cut on the Erie Canal at Lockport, New York, involved carving a channel twenty-seven feet wide and thirteen to thirty feet deep through a mountain ridge, in all two miles of solid rock. Blasting went on almost without stop. Horse-operated cranes lined the lip of the cut at seventy-foot intervals, drawing up baskets filled with rock fragments from the excavation floor to be hauled to nearby fill areas. Rocks, some weighing up to twenty pounds, fell without warning on the little hamlet of Lockport that had sprung up at the canal site. The townspeople cut down small trees, stripped them of their branches, and leaned them against their houses, their tops extending over the roofs as a

22 With wages of $15–17 a month, well above the going rate, men resisted working in the water at Johnson shoals on the Kanawha River Improvement during the cold November of 1821. Five hands hired one day quickly tired of the chilling toil and deserted the next. Bosher, 5 Nov. 1821, Kanawha River Improvement Letters, JRCR.
23 Testimonies of Albert Story, p. 11, and James Howard, p. 17, *Report of the Select Committee, upon the petition of Crossitt and others* (see Ch. 2, n. 57 above).
24 Valentine, "Supplying the Rideau" (see Ch. 2, n. 50 above), 20.

shield against the unnatural hail.[25] Blasting was of course more of a threat to the workers themselves, and because of this danger contractors had to pay higher wages for the job. The chance to earn extra money unfortunately led some men to proclaim a proficiency that they did not possess, with dire consequences.

Tunnelling, involving working at great depths under the earth as well as blasting, was equally difficult and dangerous, as the digging of the C&O Canal's Paw Paw tunnel proved. Bored through a mountain, the tunnel was 3,118 feet long with another 200 feet of deep cut at its southern end. Construction was expedited by sinking shafts down from the mountainside 8 feet wide and from 122 to 188 feet deep, with excavation to proceed from there as well as the exterior. Rock was blasted out, reduced to rubble by sledgehammers and picks, then hauled up the shafts by winches and carted away by horse-drawn railcarts to nearby spoilsites.[26] As in mining, cave-ins were an imminent threat.

When the banks had been raised, hills levelled, swamps forded and mountains pierced, the finishing touches were put on the rough bed of the canal. The sides had to be set at an angle (commonly 33 degrees) and, with the bottom, puddled to make them waterproof. William Weston, English consulting engineer to the Middlesex Canal in the 1790s, outlined the proper method. "[T]he whole *interior part* exposed to the action of water must be covered with a stratum of Clay about six inches in thickness, and then the same must be well rammed with Rammers . . . and then another course of the same thickness, and so on untill the whole has received a Coat at least two feet in thickness."[27] Only in this way could the finished canal be expected to retain its precious flow of water. Reservoirs were constructed by damming creeks at points where water would build up in natural hollows, ensuring a steady supply of water even in drier areas. Basins were built at either end and at choice ports along the canal. These acted as harbours, allowing for boats to turn around and providing wharfage for merchants and producers who transported their goods on the waterway. Finally, towpaths paralleling the entire course of the canal had to be level and firm, made from choice fill compacted into place, able to support the incessant tread of horses, mules and drivers that would power barges to their destination. On the Erie Canal towpaths had to be ten feet wide and at least two feet above the water line.[28]

Locks were key pieces in the overall puzzle of canal building. Stone-

25 Shaw, *Erie Water West* (see Ch. 1, n. 21 above), 130–31; Condon, *Stars in the Water* (see Ch. 3, n. 43 above), 88–91.

26 *Report of the General Committee of the Stockholders of the Chesapeake and Ohio Canal* (Washington, 1839), 16; Thomas F. Hahn, "The Paw Paw Tunnel," in *Best from American Canals*, ed. Shank (see Ch. 2, n. 6 above), v. 1, 25–26.

27 Weston to Directors, 23 Jan. 1796, quoted in Lawrence, "Middlesex Canal" (see n. 14 above), 20.

28 Minutes of the New York Canal Commissioners (see Ch. 2, n. 29 above), v. 1, p. 2, 5 June 1817.

walled with wooden gates at either end, and up to 100 feet long by 18 wide, locks were watertight chambers that acted as steps overcoming rises and falls in the natural terrain. Their construction required the expertise of masons, stonecutters, quarriers and blasters. A suitable rock site was rarely convenient to the canal line, so separate work camps often were set up with their own workforce and living accommodations. These quarries could be quite distant from the canal; for instance, the Welland got its stone from Split Rock, New York, at the other end of Lake Ontario, and the St. Mary's, perched at the junction of Lakes Superior and Huron, had to ship rock from Marblehead on the shores of Lake Erie in northwestern Ohio. Wherever it came from, the procedure was much the same. Rock was blown from the bed by blasters. Split stone of suitable size was then dressed with chisels by stonecutters and lifted by winches into carts or boats to be hauled to the canal. Each stone was pulled into position in the waiting lock bed by block and tackle; the mason would further shape it to get an exact fit, then grout the joints with a hydraulic cement mixture (which required magnesian limestone, a commodity not always close at hand)[29] and puddle the back of the wall. Master masons often carved their personal insignia into the stonework as a lasting testament to their craftsmanship, a rite their forebears had performed for centuries. Carpenters and blacksmiths completed the lock by building and installing wooden and iron-hinged gates with sluices to regulate water flow.[30]

The stonework techniques of lock building held for culverts, dams and aqueducts. Culverts fed streams under the canal, and dams regulated water flow in rivers and diverted a supply into the canal. Aqueducts were arched causeways that carried canals across rivers or maintained a level when crossing valleys, thus obviating the need for a set of locks. Some of these were quite impressive: one near Schenectady, New York, was almost 1,200 feet in length. The aqueduct crossing the Allegheny River at Pittsburgh was only marginally shorter, and there was even a steel suspension aqueduct on the Delaware & Hudson designed by the famous bridge engineer Jan Roebling.[31]

Canals facing significant rises over short distances sometimes opted for an alternative to an expensive series of locks. Inclined planes, such as on the Morris Canal, were levelled slopes on which were constructed rudimentary railways. Barges were floated into a carriage resting on a truck set on railway car wheels. The carriage was pulled up the incline by a rope-and-pulley system powered by horses, water or steam engines. At the top, the boats would be refloated into a lock and let into the canal. This system

29 Shank, *Towpaths to Tugboats* (see Ch. 1, n. 12 above), 39.
30 Wylie, "Poverty, Distress, and Disease" (see Introduction, n. 11 above), 17–18; Robert Harris, *Canals and their Architecture* (London: Hugh Evelyn, 1969), 74–75.
31 Waugh, "Canal Development in Early America (Part 2)" (see Ch. 2, n. 6 above), 6; "Roebling Aqueduct Restored," *American Canals*, no. 58 (Aug. 1986), 1–3.

could become quite sophisticated. On the Allegheny Portage Railroad, for example, an actual engine and train ferried canal barges for the Pennsylvania Mainline across the mountains in a series of ten inclined planes, a journey that impressed Charles Dickens among others.[32]

Canal construction thus involved a lot of skilled labour, including quarriers and stonecutters, blasters, masons, brickmakers and layers, carpenters and blacksmiths. The number of craftsmen varied with the type of work to be done. On sections where excavation or embanking predominated, there would be fewer craftsmen relative to common labourers, but "artificers" could amount to over half the workforce where quarrying, a flight of locks or a tunnel was the work at hand.[33] Skilled work brought higher pay and a degree of independent status, and it was an area where the native-born and German, English or Scottish immigrants were likely to be overrepresented, whereas the Irish dominated unskilled positions (Tables 7 and 8). These factors naturally led to divisions among the workforce as skill was reinforced by wage differentials and social cleavages. Still, the exposed and gruelling nature of the work, the absence of craft tradition in an essentially new industry, the fact that many craftsmen would be Irish by their sheer weight of numbers (at least by the 1830s), and the promiscuous mixing of the skilled and unskilled in shanty camps narrowed the gap between the two. As a result, there is little evidence of "aristocratic" airs among these more privileged workers, and they tended to join their "common" mates in revelry and protest, just as they did in work and rest.

This is by no means a comprehensive examination of the technical side of canal building. Construction was always on the move and every new section brought new natural conditions that made novel demands. Nonetheless, from the crest of the Blue Ridge to the depths of the Montezuma marshes certain characteristics prevailed that shaped canal workers' lives. The work took place out in the open, usually in remote locations, exposed to the elements and isolated from civilization. It was by its very nature seasonal and impermanent. Most importantly, canal construction was hard work in often trying conditions. From sunup to sundown there was toil, interspersed with breaks for lunch and dinner and the periodic visits of the "jiggerman." Labor was uniformly backbreaking: cutting trees and brush, drilling, stone crushing, and digging, always digging. Men would spend much of their day in ditches, hacking at the dry earth with dust in their throats, mired in mud or up to their waists in water, bending, thrusting

---

32 Waugh, "Canal Development in Early America (Part 2)" (see Ch. 2, n. 6 above), 6; Charles Hadfield, "Evolution of the Canal Inclined Plane," *American Canals*. no. 58 (August 1986), 4–7; Charles Dickens, *American Notes, and Reprinted Pieces* (orig. ed. 1842; London, 1870), ch. 10.

33 For example, there were twenty stonecutters and two labourers at the quarries for the Monocacy Aqueduct on the C&O in 1830, while 150 stonecutters were swamped by 3,000 labourers on the Welland Canal in 1842. A. B. McFarland, 13 Sept. 1830, C&O/LR; Power to Begly, 24 Dec. 1842, Welland Canal Letterbook, v. 2097, series C-VI, Records of the Department of Railways and Canals, Record Group 43, PAC (hereafter PAC/RG43).

the shovel home, straightening and tossing the muck aside to be wheeled away later. Craftsmen were spared some of the dull routine and granted a degree of pleasure in their effort, but their work was only marginally less strenuous: attacking stone with sledge, hauling the roughened blocks with hawser, horse and human prodding, shaping a fitted block by endless but considered blows of hammer and chisel, then hoisting the finished product into position with a grunt, a smile of informed pleasure vying with opened-mouth huffing and puffing from exertion. At work, the canaller was a digging, clawing, tunnelling, lock-building machine – a pumping and pulling piston, fuelled by bread and meat, lubricated by shots of raw liquor, but driven by pride of endurance or prowess and the need to survive.

After hours

As the sun dipped beneath the horizon, the men would knock off work and head for home, which was usually not far from the work site, set off in a thinly settled wilderness, nestled alongside a river or creek. The canal was a natural focus for community life. Work dictated when the navvy rose, how he spent his time, the food he ate, the liquor he drank, the clothing he wore and, in a more capricious fashion, what illnesses or accidents were to wrack and maim his body. Canal work was not just a job but also a lifestyle, one that exacted very real social costs from the people who lived it.

Contractors often provided shelter for their hands as a means of keeping a stable of workers; and "stable" is the right word, as the accommodations often did not differ significantly from those given the horses and oxen. For example, Canada's Grenville Canal, built by a joint military and civilian force, was "situated in a remote and uncleared part of the country where the Detachment is encamped in the Woods and exposed to many privations and inconveniences." Elementary preparations were required before work could begin. "From the uninhabited state of the Country," reported the military commander, "the first thing done was to clear a space for an encampment of the Trees & the place fixed upon as the most convenient . . . is so Rocky that it was with great difficulty a place could be found to fix a Tent upon."[34] In tents or crude shanties, the makeshift walls provided a virtually opaque barrier to the future historian. Workers left few records of their living arrangements. What remains are descriptions of these evanescent settlements made by travellers through the area, usually well-off Britons slumming it on their New World tour, whose accounts, while colourful and revealing, drip with condescension for the overwhelming Irishness and

---

34 DuVernet to Major Bowles, 8 Dec. 1819, v. 39, Canal Papers, PAC/RG8; DuVernet, 30 Nov. 1820, v. 40, Canal Papers, ibid.

definite proletarian character of shanty dwellers. Thus their representations of canal life must be tempered with an awareness of their innate biases.

James Silk Buckingham archly recalled encountering a colony of Irish navvies on the Illinois & Michigan Canal near Utica, Illinois ("and a more repulsive scene we had not for a long time beheld"). "The number of persons congregated here were about 200, including men, women, and children, and these were crowded together in 14 or 15 log-huts, temporarily erected for their shelter." Buckingham decried the "dirtiness and disorder" of these individuals, but stripped of its moralizing his account gives us some idea of the crude, cramped, yet communal character of such work camps. Frederick Marryat, another British traveller, dared venture where Buckingham would not, and provided a glimpse into one such shanty. At Mohawk Falls, near Troy, New York, Marryat stumbled on

a few small wooden shealings, appearing, under the majestic trees which overshadowed them, more like dog-kennels than the habitations of men: they were tenanted by Irish emigrants, who had taken work at the new locks forming on the Erie canal. I went up to them. In a tenement about fourteen feet by ten, lived an Irishman, his wife, and family, and seven boys as he called them, young men from twenty to thirty years of age, who boarded with him. There was but one bed, on which slept the man, his wife, and family. Above the bed were some planks, extending half way the length of the shealing, and there slept the seven boys, without any mattress, or even straw, to lie upon.

Marryat needed but one more sign to complete his portrait of Irish debasement: "I looked for the pig, and there he was, sure enough, under the bed." Charles Dickens had a similar impression when he came across an Irish shanty settlement for railway workers near Lebanon, Pennsylvania, in the early 1840s.

With means at hand of building decent cabins, it was wonderful to see how clumsy, rough, and wretched, its hovels were. The best were poor protection from the weather; the worst let in the wind and rain through wide breeches in the roofs of sodden grass, and in the walls of mud; some had neither door nor window; some had nearly fallen down, and were imperfectly propped up by stakes and poles; all were ruinous and filthy. Hideously ugly old women and very buxom young ones, pigs, dogs, men, children, babies, pots, kettles, dunghills, vile refuse, rank straw, and standing water, all wallowing together in an inseparable heap, composed the furniture of every dark and dirty hut.

Dickens's celebrated concern for the common people of English industrial cities does not seem to have extended to these orphans of American progress. Such accounts, while condescending, certainly convey the flavour of living conditions on canals, and in substance do not differ much from Power's more sympathetic portrayal of "log-huts, laid down in the very swamp" on the canal at New Orleans.[35]

35 J. S. Buckingham, *The Eastern and Western States of America* (London, n.d.), v. 3, 222–24; Marryat, *Diary in America* (see Ch. 3, n. 67 above), 92–93; Dickens, *American Notes* (see n. 32 above), 126.

In fact, canallers would live in virtually any type of shelter. Mactaggart claimed of the Irish "that if they can get a *mud-cabin*, they will never think of building one of wood." This was obviously more a matter of necessity than of choice; nonetheless, he reported that at Bytown on the Rideau, canallers "burrow into the sand-hills; smoke is seen to issue out of holes which are opened to answer the purpose of chimneys." Like the workers on the Grenville Canal, the Irish diggers of the Suffolk Canal in East Cambridge, Massachusetts, lived in tents. Josiah White, director of the Lehigh River improvement, "Had riged 2 scows 30 to 35 feet long by about 14 feet wide for lodging and eatting room of our hands about 70 in number." Maintenance crews on completed sections of canals tended to live on boats as well. Some serendipitous labourers for the James River Company of Virginia luxuriated in two-story brick houses with fireplaces in every room, and workers on the section of the Miami & Erie that passed through Dayton, Ohio, had a rowhouse built for their use. Where possible, canallers would board with local farmers or townspeople, generally at the expense of contractors. And temporary local workers, of which there were a large number early on, would have their own, presumably more comfortable, home to return to at night.[36]

Two settlement patterns emerged on public works: the urban shanty town and the work camp on the canal. In shanty towns workers and their families lived in rented accommodation or buildings of their own construction in so-called bog settlements, home to other working-class immigrants. Here, navvies managed some semblance of family life, patronized their taverns and practiced their religion; in effect, they had the building blocks of community, albeit ones always threatening to crumble. The husband was often away at the canal or in work camps, but had a home to return to. Such Irish communities sometimes became permanent neighbourhoods outlasting the canal, like Corktown at Bytown (present-day Ottawa) at the north end of the Rideau and Paddy's Land in Rochester, or formed the basis of towns themselves, such as "Dublin," which developed into Akron, Ohio, and "Irish Row," soon transformed into Lockport, New York.[37]

36 J. Lackland to President and Directors, 25 May 1832, C&O/LR; Mactaggart, *Three Years in Canada* (see Ch. 3, n. 55 above), v. 2, 243; DuVernet, Memorandum respecting the Tents, n.d. [Nov. 1820], v. 40, Canal Papers, PAC/RG8; Dennis Clark, *Hibernia America: The Irish and Regional Cultures* (Westport, Conn.: Greenwood Press, 1986), 81; "Josiah White's History" (see Ch. 2, n. 43 above), 12; Robert Pollard to Bernard Peyton, 12 Dec. 1818, Journal B, p. 85, VA/BPW; a picture of the Dayton rowhouse appears in Raymond Boryczka and Lorin Lee Cary, *No Strength Without Union: An Illustrated History of Ohio Workers 1803–1980* (Columbus: Ohio Historical Society, 1982), 14; Copy of letter to *Montreal Gazette* from Henry Mason, 23 March 1843, Lachine Riots (see Ch. 3, n. 53 above); State Dr.[?] to Stephen Pitts, 18 Feb. 1845, Central Canal Pay Rolls, IN/II.
37 Wylie, "Poverty, Distress, and Disease" (see Introduction, n. 11 above), 21–23; Valentine, "Supplying the Rideau" (see Ch. 2, n. 50 above), 45–46; Borgeson, "Irish Canal Laborers" (see Ch. 3, n. 31 above), 54; Shaw, *Erie Water West* (see Ch. 1, n. 21 above), 131–32; Svejda, *Irish Immigrant Participation in the Construction of the Erie Canal* (see Ch. 1, n. 11 above), 44–45; Condon, *Stars in the*

More common were work camps, rude collections of shanties that mushroomed along the canal line, home to a population numbering from the tens into the hundreds. These makeshift villages were predominantly male enclaves, but the resident population was inflated by family members, unemployed workers and assorted hangers-on. Working and living at such close quarters made for an intimate setting.[38] Housing took the form of either barracks-like bunkhouses or small family-centred buildings. Bunkhouses in which congregations of men lived communally prevailed when work sites were some distance from settlements, or when the majority of the workforce were young and single. The men slept in bunks arranged in tiers around the walls, shared a communal hearth, and had their cooking and cleaning performed for them. The number per shanty could vary widely. "The workmen live in companies of fifteen and twenty in *Shantees* — frame buildings along the canal, provided with a cook, or boarded in more private houses, erected for the purpose," it was reported of the Chesapeake & Delaware Canal. At Nob Shoal on the Kanawha River there were thirty to forty men per house. The six shanties at the Isthmus on the Rideau Canal, each measuring twenty feet by twenty feet, were capable of holding 150 men. And on the St. Mary's Canal in 1853, 100 labourers were living in a shanty measuring 100 by 22 feet.[39]

Some shanties were family dwellings, a husband, wife and children living with a number of boarders, somewhat like the traditional farm household. Yet unlike the latter, production wholly lorded it over reproduction, and unrelated boarders often outnumbered their hosts. The result was a distorted reflection of domestic life. John Campbell when a boy worked for the Irish teamster Tom Burns on the Wabash & Erie in such a "family" shanty. Burns lived in a "double or long cabin" with a partition in the middle. "The horses were stabled in the east part and the family in the west," recalled Campbell. "An Irishman and I slept in the lower bunk next to the horses, and the hired girl and two children in the bunk above us. Burns and his wife slept in a bunk at the south side."[40] This arrangement was intimate and personal but hardly congenial, as Campbell found himself frequently subjected to the capricious wrath of his employer. The domestic shanty became more common after the 1830s as the result of

Water (see Ch. 3, n. 43 above), 91; Teagarden, "Builders of the Ohio Canal" (see Ch. 3, n. 10 above), 96; C. O. Bartlett, "The Ohio Canal," typescript, n.d., 7 (VFM 2204) Ohio Historical Society; Oscar Olin, Ada Allen, Edwin Brouse, and James Braden, eds., *A Centennial History of Akron* (Akron: Summit County Historical Society, 1925), 30–31.

38 For example, forty-seven hands per section was the average on sections 7–18 of the C&O in 1829, and a mean of thirty-three workers per section on the canal's ninety contracts ten years later. Daniel Vanslyke to President and Directors, 26 Dec. 1829, C&O/LR; *Eleventh Annual Report of the Chesapeake and Ohio Canal Company* (Washington, 1839).

39 *Miner's Journal*, 28 May 1825; John Bosher to Robert Pollard, 2 June 1822, Kanawha River Improvement Letters, JRCR; McKenna, "Working Life at the Isthmus" (see Ch. 4, n. 26 above), 4; *Lake Superior Journal*, 11 June 1853.

40 *Indianapolis Star*, 26 July 1907, John T. Campbell Scrapbook (see Ch. 3, n. 20 above).

the growing rarity of company housing and the increasing number of married men wholly dependent on canal work. Workers had to put up their own shelters, and these tended to be simple and arranged around a married couple.

The common feature linking bunkhouse and family shanty was their spartan character. Those that had windows rarely had glass or screening, an open invitation to mosquitoes and blackflies. A cooking pot or crude hearth usually sat in the centre of the building, with a hole in the roof overhead as a chimney. Beds were usually mere planks, sometimes cushioned with straw. "The first 2 Or 3 years we had no feather bed or matras on our work, the managers as well as all hands, slept in bunks, of unplained pine boards, and blankets, some had straw, and others the plain board, to sleep on," recounted Josiah White. These workers were relatively well off compared to canallers on the Sandy & Beaver Canal, who had to sleep on the floor.[41]

The crowded, meagre conditions of shanty life were relieved to a degree by a hearty diet. Working strenuously for hours on end required large food intake, and outdoor labour was believed to necessitate intermittent consumption of alcohol. Before the 1840s, contractors often provided basic provisions; luxury items, like coffee, tea, sugar and eggs, when not provided, were purchased by the hands themselves from local merchants or the contractor. Staple fare for canallers included flour, beef, bacon, potatoes and beans, supplemented by wild game like turkey, deer and rabbit. They consumed large quantities of whatever was available.[42] Breakfast and supper were prepared in the shanties, but lunches were often packed and eaten at the work site, bread and cold meat being the staple midday fare, although pots of cooked food could be brought out to the workers. Meal preparation was handled by a cook, usually a hand's wife or a labourer known to be good at the kettle. That this could be done in a most rudimentary fashion is clear from the following account:

A large iron kettle, capable of holding from two to three bushels, was kept hanging over the fire. A cart load of potatoes was piled at one side of the fire, and a barrel of mackerel at the other side. A layer of potatoes, just as they came from the ground, without the benefit of knife or water, was tumbled into the kettle and a layer of mackerel from the barrel without a rinse, and so on alternately till the kettle was full, and when boiled was dished up.[43]

Life within these shanties is not hard to imagine. Morning was a welter of confusion, men crawling from their plank beds, fumbling in the grayness of false dawn for boots, groaning as yesterday's labour was stretched out of

41 "Josiah White's History" (see Ch. 2, n. 43 above), 16; R. Max Gard and William H. Vodrey, *The Sandy and Beaver Canal* (East Liverpool, Ohio: East Liverpool Historical Society, 1952), 65.
42 See POT/PRO, 14 July 1785 (A 6); Andrist, *Erie Canal* (see n. 5 above), 38–41; C. J. Forbes to Peter Turquand, 30 June 1827, v. 43, Canal Papers, PAC/RG8; J. Lackland to President and Directors, 25 May 1832, C&O/LR; Gard and Vodrey, *Sandy and Beaver Canal* (see n. 41 above), 65.
43 *Indiana* [Pennsylvania] *Times*, quoted in Borgeson, "Irish Canal Laborers" (see Ch. 3, n. 31 above), 55.

sinewy muscles or cursing as last night's liquor recoiled in the stomach. The atmosphere was a mixture of stale breath, cooking meat and the musty dampness that seeped into every niche of the cabin overnight. During the day a bunkhouse could be a virtual tomb — dust blowing in through the window, flies and bees noisily meandering in and out, shadows inching across the floor — while a family shanty rang with the shouts of children and the clang of cooking pots. In the evening the men — some stonily tired, others boyish at the end of work — piled inside looking hungrily to the hearth. The few hours before sleep passed in a whirl of eating, joking, drinking, quarreling, gambling or even quiet meditation. One by one they drifted to their beds and peace slowly descended. The night churned quietly: straw rustling, bodies tossing and turning, murmurs, sighs, breaking wind, muffled curses, slapping at mosquitoes or scratching at bedbugs, the buzzsaw of snores. Outside, small animals scratched in the leaves, deer made their way to the creek, owls called, water burbled along a rocky bed, frogs croaked and, underlying it all, the industrious clicking of insects warning of the morrow's labour.

"The king of terrors"

"I have been informed that they generally live about eighteen months after coming to this country, and work and drink most of the time," wrote Anne Royall of "the *Teagues*." "In many instances, on some of the canals, they die so fast, that they are thrown into the ground from four to six together, without coffins."[44] Although Royall emphasized the "drink" part of her account rather than the "work," it is clear that canal construction had a strong element of occupational hazard. Injuries abounded, from such minor ailments as cuts, bruises and strained muscles to maimings, loss of limbs and loss of life. The setting and the elements also played a role. Hot weather could cause heat stroke, winter work led to frostbite. The fates could be capricious. A canaller named Connelly working on the C&O near Williamsport, Maryland, was struck and killed by lightning; on the same canal John Wiley, a Scot from Dumfries, drowned.[45]

The most common cause of accidents was the very nature of the work. Blasting in particular was a dangerous business and probably the main cause of accidental injury or death among canallers. Three Irish workers were killed while blasting rock on the C&O Canal in June 1830. They had lit the slow fuse to a powder charge and retreated to a safe distance, but,

---

44 Anne Royall, *Mrs. Royall's Pennsylvania, or Travels Continued in the United States* (Washington, 1829), v. 1, 126.
45 Hagerstown *Torchlight*, 31 July 1834; Unsigned note, n.d. (found with Henry Boteler to Mercer, 14 June 1830), C&O/LR; C&O/PRO, 11 Nov. 1829 (A 395). In the case of Wiley there appears to have been a possibility of suicide, as his wife had died the year before, leaving him to care for their three children.

not hearing the blast as soon as expected, they returned just as it exploded. A blaster was killed on the Rideau Canal in the same way. "It appears that the blast hung fire and when he ran forward to ascertain the cause it suddenly exploded while he was in the act of examining it – he has left a wife and family to deplore his melancholy end." Not long after, "another person was struck by a falling stone from a blast and his skull so badly fractured that he lies without hope of recovery."[46]

Part of the problem was that blasting's higher wages attracted the eager but inexperienced with fatal consequences. John Mactaggart, Clerk of the Rideau Works, bemoaned the fate of such "poor, ignorant, and careless creatures."

Some of these, for instance, would take jobs of quarrying from contractors, because they thought there were *good wages* for this work, never thinking that they did not understand the business. Of course, many of them were blasted to pieces by their own *shots*, others killed by stones falling on them. I have seen head, arms, and legs, blown about in all directions; and it is vain for overseers to warn them of their danger, for they will pay no attention. I once saw a poor man blow a red stick, and hold it deliberately to the *priming* of a large shot he had just charged. I cried out, but it was of no use. He seemed to turn round his face, as if to avoid the smoke; off went the blast, and took away his arm, and the half of his head: he was killed in a moment. As the blocks of stone fell, one of them broke the leg of another poor man, who knew nothing of such a shot being fired.[47]

While Mactaggart laid the blame on the navvies, canal contractors and companies were equally responsible for not adopting adequate safety precautions. The rudimentary technology of blasting at this time made accidents inevitable, but the number could have been reduced with greater care.[48] Benign neglect, not blatant disregard for worker safety, characterized employer policy, but the result was the same.

Some who were not blasted to the great beyond returned to land less than whole, and faced the possibility of being unable to provide for themselves and their families in an era with few social safety nets to cushion their fall. James Broughton, a stonecutter and mason on the C&O's Seneca Aqueduct, was nearly blinded in one eye by a premature explosion; being already sightless in the other, Broughton was no longer able to do manual labour and asked the company for help. Felix O'Neal, a labourer on the same canal, was "by the will of the Almighty god disabled by a blast, which unables me at the present to support meself, which said Blast, broke my thigh bone, and injured my hand most surprising." O'Neal also

---

46 Hagerstown *Torchlight*, 1 July 1830; *Brockville* [Ontario] *Gazette*, 26 Feb. 1830, quoted in McKenna, "Working Life at the Isthmus" (see Ch. 4, n. 26 above), 28–29.
47 Mactaggart, *Three Years in Canada* (see Ch. 3, n. 55 above), v. 2, 245–46.
48 Mactaggart implicitly acknowledged this by eventually getting blasting procedure "so systematized, that a number of shots were always prepared to be *fired* at once; a person stood at a distance, and kept blowing a horn, so that all quarriers got out of the quarry to a respectable distance before the mine was sprung." Ibid., v. 2, 246.

requested some form of aid. Another stonecutter and mason on the C&O, John Miller, met with an accident "without fault of his owen" while quarrying stone in October 1838, making it necessary "that his limb was on the spot amputated." Miller felt sure that "with the aid of an artificial foot he should be enabled to do something again for the support of his family," but lacking the means to buy one, asked the company for aid. Canallers north of the border met with similar accidents. James Butler and Peter Stormont were injured falling from scaffolds; the former broke his breastbone, and the latter had his "Scalp laid open nearly from ear to ear." David Cardey, a miner on the Grenville, "blew himself up on the works . . . and is still in Hospital here having lost both Eyes and got his Scull fractured." Cardey, who was but twenty-one, had arrived with his younger brother two years before from Ballantry, County Antrim, Ireland, to find work on the canal. Now his brother was somewhere in America and there was no one to look after David.[49]

Compensation was a touchy subject. Contractors shared in the prevailing belief among employers that they were not responsible for injuries sustained on the job, maintaining that the work's inherent risk was assumed by the labourer when he decided, as part of the free labour bargaining process, to take the job. For their part, canal companies and boards of works argued they were not the employers of labour and were in no way culpable for any mishaps. One reason contracting had been adopted was to ensure that management would be "irresponsible" for the workers. Capital's stance was undergirded by the law, which held that neither contractors nor companies were liable for workplace injuries.[50]

Nonetheless, companies showed a degree of concern for workers' suffering; it was also sometimes in their interest to make some form of compensation, however paltry, to maintain morale and keep an adequate workforce on the line.[51] Thus Felix O'Neal, confined to bed with his broken thigh, was awarded a pension by the C&O of $5 a month (when going wages for labourers were $10–12) for five months if he remained disabled, and John Miller was given $50 out of the company's contingency fund with which to purchase his artificial leg. Similarly, Butler and Stormont, the men injured on the Grenville Canal, were paid one shilling per day as well as given food rations as long as they were incapacitated. David Cardey, in an anomalous position as a civilian employee of the British Army, was granted a pension of 1s. 6d. per diem from His

49 Richard Holdsworth for James Broughton, 15 Oct. 1831, C&O/LR; Felix O'Neal, 13 April 1831, 15 Oct. 1831, ibid.; John Miller, 29 June 1839, ibid.; DuVernet to Col. Darling, n.d. [May 1823], v. 40, 22 Aug. 1821, v. 39, Canal Papers, PAC/RG8.

50 Bleasdale, "Unskilled Labourers on the Public Works of Canada" (see Introduction, n. 11 above), 148.

51 The same conditions of inevitable injury and reluctant, inadequate compensation were found on the railways in Britain and America. Brooke, *Railway Navvy* (see Ch. 2, n. 26 above), 149–50; Licht, *Working for the Railroad* (see Ch. 2, n. 26 above), 197–205.

Majesty's Treasury. In this instance, military paternalism offered significantly more protection than that of contractors or companies. Unfortunately, Cardey soon died of his injuries and had little time to live off the Crown's largesse.[52]

Fatal or maiming accidents were so common on public works that everyone would have been mindful of the hazards. Canal construction was not unique in such dangers; occupations from farming to factory work all had their own peculiar perils. But, as in railroad construction, the building industries and mining, there was a higher risk involved in canal digging, and it was the workers who suffered the consequences.

Benjamin Mace of Jefferson County, Indiana, went to work on the canal around the falls of the Ohio River at Louisville, Kentucky, in the spring of 1826. He stayed for one month, went home, then returned in July when he "was put to work in a ditch in the bottom of the canal knee deep in mud and water." This time, Benjamin remained only two weeks before he returned home, but shortly after "was taken with chills and fever." A friend vowed Mace "was in the most severe distress that ever I saw a poor mortal. . . . He was in such pain and anguish that he cried to the Lord to send him out of the world or abate his misery." The room in which he lay reeked of fever and it was evident to those caring for him that he was dying. "We went up and behold he was in the agonies of death he was struggling with the king of terrors – the ratles of death were upon him – he groaned and strugled for life." Ben's wife, "far gone in pregnancy," watched hysterically as he died that morning. His death was believed to be a result of "billius remittant or a kind of malignant fever" that he caught while "working in the mud and water on the canal." Michial Mullen, twenty-six years of age, was admitted to the Baltimore Almshouse in June 1833 with a case of paralysis. Mullen, his spine deformed since birth, had come to the United States from Ireland several years before, working on canals and roads. His deformity had not been a serious impediment to his work until he was struck with an intermittent fever a year earlier, and paralysis began to affect his lower extremities. The almshouse doctor reported that he "could neither feel pinching, puncturing or cauterization." The treatment prescribed was galvinism, the administration of an electric current through electrodes attached under Mullen's skin on the back of the neck and left leg. This method failed to stimulate a recovery.[53]

52 Extract from the Journal of the President and Directors, Ingle to C. Smith, Treasurer, 25 May 1831, C&O/LR; C&O/PRO, 3 July 1839 (F 85); DuVernet to Darling, 22 Oct. 1823, v. 40, Canal Papers, PAC/RG8; [Geo.?] Harrison to Lord Dalhousie, 7 Feb. 1822, v. 40, Canal Papers, ibid.; DuVernet to Darling, 12 June 1822, v. 40, Canal Papers, ibid.; D. Chisholm, 7 April 1822, v. 40, Canal Papers, ibid.
53 Herschel Hurdy to Benjamin Mace and all friends, 16 Aug. 1826, Benjamin Mace Papers, Indiana State Library; Case of Michial Mullen, admitted 12 June 1833, Baltimore Almshouse Medical Records, MHS.

Mace was a native of Tewksbury, Massachusetts, who had immigrated to Indiana where he worked in a hopyard producing for the Louisville breweries. His first wife had died of the ague, but he quickly remarried. Canal work appears to have been an opportunity to earn good cash wages that proved fatal. Mullen, a poor immigrant, was forced to eke out a living on public works projects despite his physical handicap, which worsened under the strain of hard labour; ultimately he was subjected to contemporary "doctoring" in a poorhouse infirmary. Despite their dissimilar experiences, the cases of Mace and Mullen provide some insight into the health of canallers and illuminate the costs exacted by their occupation. Death, if not imminent, was never far away.

"They absolutely die by the dozen, not of hunger, but of disease," affirmed John Mactaggart of Irish labourers on the Rideau. Typically, he blamed the victims, who "will not provide in summer against the inclemencies of winter. Blankets and stockings they will not purchase; so the frost bites them in all quarters, dirt gets into the putrid sores, and surgical aid is not called in by them, until matters get into the last stage." Moreover, "by living as they do, and drinking *swamp waters*, if there be none nearer their habitations, instead of spring or river water, [they] bring on malignant fevers of all kinds." Like other critics, Mactaggart ignored the diminished physical and financial conditions of most canallers, and, more importantly, underplayed the pathological conditions that made public works sites mazes of morbidity. As in the case of work-related injuries, such attitudes allowed management to wash its hands of the consequences of its actions, and exposed canallers to much "sickness and mortality," a situation lamented by the more sympathetic Mathew Carey:

It is not all improbable, indeed it is almost certain, that among the whole number employed, five percent return to their families in the winter, with broken constitutions, by fevers and agues, one-half of whom are carried off to an untimely grave. Those that escape this state, often linger for years in a state of debility, subject to occasional returns of their painful and enervating disorder.[54]

In either case, it is clear that a multitude of ailments stalked canals, and few navvies were lucky enough to receive medical attention; most were left to their own devices, often with fatal consequences.

Frances Trollope wrote poignantly of the case of one debilitated labourer. While staying with friends near the C&O Canal, she received word that a man lay dying a quarter-mile away.

The spot was immediately visited by some of the family, and there in truth lay a poor creature, who was already past the power of speaking; he was conveyed to the house, and expired during the night. By enquiring at the canal, it was found that he was an Irish

---

54 Mactaggart, *Three Years in Canada* (see Ch. 3, n. 55 above), v. 2, 244; Carey, *Address to the Wealthy of the Land* (see Ch. 4, n. 18 above), 6.

labourer, who having fallen sick, and spent his last cent, had left the stifling shantee where he lay, in the desperate attempt of finding his way to Washington, with what hope I know not. He did not appear above twenty, and as I looked on his pale young face, which even in death expressed suffering, I thought that perhaps he had left a mother and a home to seek wealth in America. I saw him buried under a group of locust trees, his very name unknown to those who laid him there, but the attendance of the whole family at the grave, gave a sort of decency to his funeral which rarely, in that country, honours the poor relics of British dust: but no clergyman attended, no prayer was said, no bell was tolled.[55]

Despite its bathos, Trollope's account captures the danger and ultimate impersonality of canal labour. Not everyone was struck dead and left in an unmarked grave, but few escaped the ravages of illnesses that seemed to ooze out of public works sites.

Canals were a breeding ground of severe infectious diseases, often masked by generic names such as ague and bilious fever. Typhoid, spread by food or water contaminated by excreta, thrived in unsanitary and poorly drained work sites. As canallers could be compelled to drink (as well as cook and wash with) *"swamp waters,"* home to vegetable matter, not to mention human and animal waste, the presence of typhoid and dysentery is easily explained. Malaria and yellow fever were spread by the anopheles mosquito, then common in the swampy or bushy land that bordered canals.[56] Moving from an infected individual to his mates, the blood-sucking insect was more sinister than people realized at the time, as it was believed that fevers resulted from standing water, rotting vegetation and the resulting effluvia. Maturing mosquitoes began their depredations in late spring; with a period of incubation the diseases manifested themselves in mid-summer. As a result, July to October was known as the sickly season, and the onset of summer fevers often precipitated an evacuation of the line. The labourers may not have been certain of the illness's root cause, but were convinced of its identification with the conditions of their work.

John Mactaggart gave a graphic account from experience of a malarial attack of the *"Fever and Ague"*:

They generally come on with an attack of bilious fever, dreadful vomiting, pains in the back and loins, general debility, loss of appetite. . . . After being in this state for eight or ten days, the yellow jaundice is likely to ensue, and then *fits* of trembling. . . . For two or three hours before they arrive, we feel so cold that nothing will warm us; the greatest heat that can be applied is perfectly unfelt; the skin gets dry, and then the *shaking begins*. Our very bones ache, teeth chatter, and the ribs are sore, continuing thus in great agony for about an hour and a half; we then commonly have a vomit, the trembling ends, and a profuse sweat ensues, which lasts for two hours longer. This over, we find the malady has run one of its

55 Frances Trollope, *Domestic Manners of the Americans* (orig. ed. 1832; New York: Vintage Press, 1949), 290–91.
56 Mactaggart, *Three Years in Canada* (see Ch. 3, n. 55 above), v. 2, 244; Wylie, "Poverty, Distress, Disease" (see Introduction, n. 11 above), 23.

rounds, and start out of the bed in a feeble state, sometimes unable to stand, and entirely dependent on our friends (if we have any) to lift us on to some seat or other.[57]

Such symptoms laid low 1,000 Erie navvies and forced work to a halt in the Montezuma marshes near Syracuse during 1819. The men took to wearing "Montezuma necklaces" around their necks, smudge pots containing a small fire covered with green leaves, in an effort to keep off the mosquitoes. A doctor bled the sick, then dosed them with feverwort, snakeroot, green pigweed, Seneca Oil and "Jesuit's Bark" (which fortuitously contained quinine), but could not halt the advance of the illness. Similarly, three in five were infected and fifty-five died from malaria on the Rideau during the peak season of 1830 (a mortality rate William Wylie calculated at 4.1%). Illness recurred the next summer, causing the Inspector of Hospitals to report that "nothing could exceed in wretchedness, & apathy, the poisoned, & exhausted objects . . . wandering about the gloomy and deserted log-huts at the principal working stations and many most unfortunate sufferers are still to be met within various quarters, too thoroughly broken up, that, with their means, they are not likely to recover." On Indiana's Whitewater Canal in 1838 nearly everyone was laid low by "Billious complaints & Chills & Fever Ague." "Deaths occur frequently among the workmen on the canal, and some of the work has wholly ceased on account of sickness." The same year, at least a hundred men were still confined to their shanties on the Western Division of the Illinois & Michigan as late as December, and this was just the residue of those laid low by the late summer sickly season. During 1846, there was extreme sickness on the canal, with only one in five hands able to work for one contractor. The company was particularly worried that these conditions drove wages up and productivity down.[58]

If they escaped malaria, canallers had to contend with a host of other diseases. A number of workers and several of their children, living in tents on the Grenville Canal, died of dysentery during the work season of 1820. In New Orleans where the New Basin Canal was dug in the 1830s, the English traveller, Captain E. J. Alexander, reported that six hundred Irish labourers died annually of yellow fever, an exaggerated figure.[59] In the summer of 1825, typhoid broke out among Ohio Canal labourers digging

57 Mactaggart, *Three Years in Canada* (see Ch. 3, n. 55 above), v. 2, 17–18.
58 *Annual Report of the Canal Commissioners, Communicated to the Legislature* (Albany, 1820), 13–14; Harlow, *Old Towpaths* (see Ch. 1, n. 54 above), 54; Andrist, *Erie Canal* (see n. 5 above), 45–46; Wylie, "Poverty, Distress, and Disease" (see Introduction, n. 11 above), 23–24; Inspector quoted in McKenna, "Working Life at the Isthmus" (see Ch. 4, n. 26 above), 39; M. Webb to William Webb, 22 Sept. 1838, Whitewater Canal Correspondence, IN/II; *Report of the Illinois and Michigan Canal* (Vandalia, 1838), 52; "Report of the Board of Trustees of the Illinois and Michigan Canal" (House of Representatives, Illinois Legislature, Fifteenth Assembly, First Session, Jan. 1847), 93; *Report of a Majority of the Board of Trustees of the Illinois and Michigan Canal* (Washington, 1847), 9.
59 DuVernet's Memorandum respecting the Tents, n.d. [Nov. 1820], v. 40, Canal Papers, PAC/RG8; Niehaus, *The Irish in New Orleans* (see Ch. 3, n. 29 above), 31–32.

the basin at Cleveland, raged up the Cuyahoga Valley and resulted in seventeen deaths among the local population. Two years later, sickness infected canallers in the Tuscarawas Valley, causing work to be suspended for two months, and in 1829 a smallpox epidemic broke out at Licking Narrows. Folk memory maintains that a worker died for every six feet of completed canal on the Maumee extension joining Ohio's Miami & Erie and Indiana's Wabash & Erie.[60]

The human and monetary costs of illness on canals is underlined by the experience on the C&O. From the opening of construction in 1828, the ranks of workers were decimated, causing a labour shortage and driving up wages.[61] Wracked with fevers and unable to work, the hands turned up destitute on the streets of Frederick, Maryland, Georgetown and Washington, where they were taken in and cared for in the cities' poorhouses. Dr. John Little, in his role as a Trustee of the Poor for Georgetown, received "daily, almost hourly calls to relieve the labourers coming into town, from the line of the canal, sick and destitute of the means to procure medical aid or the common necessaries of life." Little avowed: "I have frequently had three poor men sent to me in carts, and at unnameable hours when they have been taken up in the Streets perishing and several have died more from a want of food than as a consequence of disease." In the year prior to October 1829, 126 sick canallers were admitted to the Georgetown asylum, of whom 7 died (5.5% mortality to date), 68 were cured and discharged and 51 remained.[62] Similarly, the Washington Poorhouse treated 53 canallers between October 1828 and February 1829, and the trustees conveniently left a record of patients and their illnesses. Of the 4 mortalities (7.5%), 3 died of ague and fever and 1 of consumption. Twenty were treated successfully for ague and fever, 15 for debility, 9 were just plain sickly, 8 had sore or fractured legs and 1 suffered from consumption. In all, the canallers accounted for 1,703 patient days (with an average stay of 32 days), for which the trustees made a claim of $267.45. The C&O Board reluctantly reimbursed these institutions for

---

60   Ohio Board of Canal Commissioners, "Fourth Annual Report, 1825," in *Public Documents Concerning the Ohio Canals*, ed. Kilbourne (see Ch. 2, n. 64 above), 184; Teagarden, "Builders of the Ohio Canal" (see Ch. 3, n. 10 above), 102–03; Kelley to Brown, 14 Oct. 1827, Ethan Allen Brown Papers, Ohio Historical Society; Micajah Williams to Benjamin Tappan, 8 Sept. 1827, Benjamin Tappan Papers (MS. 326), Ohio Historical Society; Scheiber, *Ohio Canal Era* (see Ch. 3, n. 66 above), 50–52; Andrist, *Erie Canal* (see n. 5 above), 115–16.

61   E. L. Lanham to President and Directors, 22 July 1829, C&O/LR; Henry Smith to Board of Directors, 12 Aug. [1829], ibid.; Benjamin Wright, 21 July 1830, ibid.; T. B. Tripp, 22 July 1830, ibid.; Jared Darrow & Co., 28 July 1830, ibid.; Thomas Beer and James Hyde, 21 July 1831, ibid.; O. H. Dibble to Purcell, 14 July 1831, ibid.; Diaries and Papers of Father John McElroy, 10 Oct. 1830, 19 Jan. 1831, Archives of the Woodstock Jesuit Community, Maryland Hall of Records, Annapolis.

62   John Little to President and Directors, 13 Oct. 1829 (enclosure: Jos. Brigum? to Dr. John Little, 10 Oct. 1829), C&O/LR. The majority of these sick canallers had recently been brought to work on the C&O from the Erie Canal.

expenses incurred in caring for the workers, although disavowing any legal responsibility.[63]

Serious illnesses were thus a very real threat to canallers. In an industry that recognized no liability, labourers were forced to rely on their own meagre resources. Local charities, some of which were partially funded by canal agencies in times of severe outbreaks, could help canallers in a pinch but groaned under the strain when inundated by an epidemic of distress.

The unhealthfulness of canal construction and the fragility of available medical aid was brought home with a vengeance by the dreaded scourge of cholera, which several times between the 1830s and 1870s reached epidemic proportions in North America. Cholera, caused by a microorganism that entered the body through the mouth, could cause either minor symptoms or severe illness and was fatal in over half of those affected. A toxin was produced that affected the walls of the stomach and intestines and led to vomiting, diarrhea and severe dehydration. Symptoms included spasms and cramps, bluish-black skin discolouration, a sunken face and raspy voice, and, ultimately, kidney failure and shutdown of bodily processes. The disease attacked suddenly, often killing within twenty-four hours or several days at most. The cause of cholera was not known at this time, so there was no cure. Originating in Bengal, cholera began spreading through Asia and Europe in 1817, reaching Britain in 1831 and Canada the following year.[64] Brought over by immigrants, especially the Irish, the disease took hold in Quebec and spread throughout eastern North America. Rivers and canals provided a venous system carrying the infection, with canallers acting as carriers in this epidemiological drama.

Cholera several times swept canals, scattering men and their families, and leaving a trail of bodies in their wake. The mere report of approaching disease, followed closely in the local press, was enough to create a panic. The first epidemic occurred in 1832, the disease having insidiously worked its way throughout the Northeast within months of its arrival, forcing company officials to deal with the mysterious killer. The directors of the Welland Canal reported that as "soon as the cholera made its appearance, the affrighted workmen fled the scene of death . . . upwards of seventy labourers, who a few weeks before were in perfect health, fell victims to this sweeping scourge."[65] This pattern of reported cases, panic and flight was repeated all along canals. A song sung by workers digging New Orleans's New Basin Canal (presumably those same men that caused Power's fulminations) captures the respect the disease commanded:

---

63 J. George Whitewell to Mercer, 9 March 1830, C&O/LR; Chas. H. Lamb, M.D., to Mercer, 31 July 1830 (enclosure: Lamb to Dr. Frederick May, 7 July 1830), ibid.; C&O/PRO, 21 Oct. 1829 (A 380–81), 28 April 1830 (B 65).

64 Geoffrey Bilson, *A Darkened House: Cholera in Nineteenth-Century Canada* (Toronto: University of Toronto Press, 1980), 3–4.

65 *The Annual Report of the Board of Directors of the Welland Canal Company, 1832* (St. Catharines, Ont., 1833), 3.

Ten thousand Micks, they swung their picks,
To dig the New Canal
But the choleray was stronger 'n they.
An' twice it killed them awl.[66]

The experience on the C&O captures the tragedy caused by cholera. The disease first made its appearance on the canal near Williamsport in June 1832. Seven cases appeared in three days, five of them proving fatal, and the resident engineer feared the line would soon be deserted. In September, a contractor near Williamsport again reported that "the collery is on our work . . . we had one case last night how it will determan is doubt full but shold it be fatle nearly all of our hand will liev the work." He warned that "a grate dale of excitement provales a mongst the people thay are flying to and frow." Thirty deaths occurred within the space of a few days opposite Shepherdstown, Virginia, and, as a result, "the poor Exiles of Erin are flying in every direction," leaving the line virtually deserted. The fear engendered by this merciless predator effectively broke down what tenuous community existed among the canallers. "Humanity is outraged by some of the scenes presented," wrote Thomas Purcell, the resident engineer. He described a nightmare landscape where "men deserted by their friends or comrades, have been left to die in the fields, the highways, or in the neighbouring barns & stables: in some instances . . . when the disease has attacked them the invalid has been enticed from the shandee & left to die under the shade of some tree." "The poor creatures, after seeing a few sudden & awful deaths amongst their friends, straggled off in all directions through the county; but for many of them the panic came too late," wrote another company official. "They are dying in all parts of Washington County at the distance of 5 to 15 miles from the river." It is no wonder that panic, selfishness and flight were common responses. Charles Mercer, president of the C&O, gave graphic detail on how the disease sowed such seeds when making an appeal for a hospital. "If the Board but imagine the panic produced by a mans turning black and dying in twenty four hours in the very room where his comrades are to sleep or to dine," he urged, "they will readily conceive the utility of separating the sick, dying and dead from the living."[67]

The scourge returned in somewhat milder form the next two years. In 1834, twenty cases broke out near Newark, Ohio, nearly all proving fatal. As a result, it was virtually impossible to get hands to work, the men being "scared to death by the Cholera." Another serious outbreak occurred in 1849, when hundreds of Irish canallers on Indiana's Wabash & Erie

66 From *New Orleans Times-Picayune*, 18 July 1837, quoted in Niehaus, *Irish in New Orleans* (see Ch. 3, n. 29 above), 45–46.
67 Purcell, 24 June 1832, C&O/LR; Joseph Hollman to Ingle, 4 Sept. 1832, ibid.; Boteler to Ingle, 4 Sept. 1832, ibid.; Purcell, 11 Sept. 1832, ibid.; Benjamin Price to Ingle, 5 Sept. 1832, ibid.; Mercer to Ingle, 3 Sept. 1832, ibid.

died. One hundred and fifty more died when the disease returned the next year. "The terror produced by this disease scattered the forces on the line, suspending most of the contracts under contract, and retarding the work very seriously," reported the state's canal trustees. There were 200 victims when cholera struck the St. Mary's Canal five years later, leading workers to riot over health and sanitation conditions.[68] For navvies nothing brought home the tenuous thread of existence in canal construction like the outbreak of cholera, when death stalked in human form; people ran in terror from hollow-eyed skeletons, former mates, now jerking with skin of bluish tint a convulsive St. Vitus's dance.

Cholera and other recurrent sickness posed a different type of horror for canal companies. Summer often meant a deserted line and disrupted construction, prompting officials to take various initiatives to keep men at work. Their primary concern was not for the well-being of labourers but for the financial health of the canal. For an industry operating in an extended network of credit, work interruptions stretched capital resources to the breaking point. Epidemics meant loss of construction time, a drain on labour supply and lost revenue on completed sections. Reports of illness thus sent shock waves through headquarters as well as through the work-force, and measures were taken to avert its consequences. When a smallpox epidemic chased labourers from Ohio's Tuscarawas Valley and several cases were reported between Chillicothe and Circleville, officials were worried that this would further shrink an already tight labour market. It was reported that "everything is being done to prevent its [the smallpox] spreading & to stifle the report." Ohio's canal commissioners clearly drew the bottom line when they tallied the cost of the 1832 cholera epidemic at $20,000 in lost business. Such economism trickled down to contractors who had to watch the profit margin even more closely. During the cholera outbreak of 1849, a builder on the Wabash & Erie Canal complained of having to pay "extravigant wages" to draw men to the line.[69] The news and financial consequences of illness were as dangerous as the disease itself in employers' eyes.

The sheer magnitude of an epidemic or the need to preserve an evaporating labour force at times pushed canal boards to more than stopgap

---

68 Leander Ransom to Kelley, 25 Aug. 1834, OH/CC; Fatout, *Indiana Canals* (see Ch. 2, n. 10 above), 141, 147; Franklin F. Sawyer to Board of Trustees of Wabash & Erie Canal, 11 July 1849, W&E/COR; "Annual Report of the Trustees," *Documents of the General Assembly*, Part Second (Indianapolis, 1851), 146–47; Harlow, *Old Towpaths* (see Ch. 2, n. 10 above), 276–77; *Lake Superior Journal*, 8 July 1854; Irene D. Neu, "The Building of the Sault Canal, 1852–55," *Mississippi Valley Historical Review*, v. 40 (June 1953), 41; Dickinson, *To Build a Canal* (see Ch. 2, n. 14 above), 79–80.
69 Francis Cleveland to Williams, 27 July 1829, Micajah T. Williams Papers, Ohio Historical Society; Ohio Board of Canal Commissioners, "Sixth Annual Report, 1827," in *Public Documents Concerning the Ohio Canals*, ed. Kilbourne (see Ch. 2, n. 64 above), 382–83; Board of Canal Commissioners, "Annual Report, 1832," in Ohio Canal Commission Minute Books (see Ch. 2, n. 46 above), v. 1, 148; A. J. Mosely to Thomas H. Blake, 15 Aug. 1849, W&E/COR.

efforts, and doctors were hired or hospitals established to address the problem. Workers on the Western Canal Company of New York were so ravaged during the sickly season in the 1790s that a blockhouse of Fort Schuyler was turned into a hospital. At the same time, the Santee Canal provided medical aid to its slave and free labourers. In 1823, the Virginia Board of Public Works issued $50 for a temporary hospital at Goochland for "that class of the community who are entirely dependent on their daily exertions for their daily support, who . . . must perish unless they obtain that kind of relief . . . and who must also be necessarily employed in water, in marshes, & in every way calculated to generate the most fatal diseases." Similarly, the Cape Fear & Deep River Company hired a doctor to care for its slave hands through the summer of 1855.[70]

While these initiatives served the workforce at the same time as they soothed the labour supply problem, they could prove an expensive gratuity, and some companies sought to make them pay their own way. In 1824, the Chesapeake & Delaware Canal adopted a scheme to provide health care that became popular on many public works. The C&D planned to erect a hospital, but have contractors and workers pay for both the building and its services; a levy was made on them in what amounted to a crude form of insurance. Similarly, civilian labourers on the Grenville Canal had 6d. per month deducted from their wages to cover the expenses of medicine and medical services, and a hospital was erected at the Isthmus on the Rideau and stoppages made on the pay of military personnel. On the Western Division of the Illinois & Michigan it was decided to provide a hospital for workers, as "their utility in the construction of public works" had been proven. And on the Beauharnois and Lachine canals in 1843, labourers were charged $\frac{1}{2}$d. for each day worked for doctoring, a not-insignificant deduction given their limited resources.[71] As a rule, these medical schemes were imposed on canallers without consultation, and were tolerated or resented in relation to need or cost.

In the C&O's response to the cholera epidemic of 1832, we can see how a modicum of concern for the well-being of workers mixed with larger worries over continuing labour supply, lost revenue, public image and expense cutting to produce an apparent act of corporate philanthropy. The

70 Shaw, *Erie Water West* (see Ch. 1, n. 21 above), 19; South Carolina Public Service Authority, *History of the Old Santee Canal* (see n. 17 above); J. Brown to John Robertson, 21 Oct. 1823, Correspondence, Reports, etc., box 192, JRCR; M. Swain and McDuffie to London, 6 Oct. 1855, London Family Papers (No. 2442), SHC.

71 *Fifth General Report of the President and Directors of the Chesapeake and Delaware Canal Company* (Philadelphia, 1824), 13–14; David [Jearrad?] to Captain King, 20 April 1826, v. 42, Canal Papers, PAC/RG8; Wylie, "Poverty, Distress, and Disease" (see Introduction, n. 11 above), 23–25; McKenna, "Working Life at the Isthmus" (see Ch. 4, n. 26 above), 37–38; Valentine, "Supplying the Rideau" (see Ch. 2, n. 50 above), 60–62; *Report of the Illinois and Michigan Canal* (Vandalia, 1838), 52; Deposition of Martin Donnelly (No. 3), "Beauharnois Report" (see Introduction, n. 3 above); Scott & Shaw to Maj. Gen. Sir James Hope, 31 March 1843, Lachine Riots (see Ch. 3, n. 53 above).

first reported cases of cholera on the canal in late spring resulted in five deaths and panicked the workers, who threatened to leave. Charles Mercer, the company president, sought to calm their fears by promising a hospital would be built to care for them. A physician was first hired to inspect the shanties, care for the contractors and men and provide medicine. In September, the company decided to set up two "hospitals" – in rented cabins near Harpers Ferry and in a large shanty on a section west of town – but set a $500 ceiling on company financial expenditure.[72] Mercer was committed to low investment, and high return on the hospital venture: "I shall buy some hundred feet of planks for bunks and some blankets and sacks for straw and as few and as cheap articles for the Hospital as possible." A doctor and one or two nurses would be hired, sick hands placed in their shanty asylum and cholera would be vanquished. "The whole cost will be but little," affirmed Mercer, "and the moral effect, I am persuaded, invaluable." To ease expenses further, canallers were to shoulder most of the costs. At Mercer's suggestion, each labourer was to give 25¢ per month into the hospital fund, leaving the company to pay only for rent and outfitting. The hospital was open from October to December, when workers refused to pay the surcharge, the cholera threat having passed for the time being. One canaller, resenting the imposition of the system, had even brought suit against his contractor and won his case in court.[73]

Essentially, the company policy of the C&O and other canals was to create a low-cost antidote to infectious disease to maintain a force on the line. There was a degree of genuine concern for the canallers, but economics drew the bottom line. Work had to go on or the company faced financial failure; sick workers had to be treated to restore confidence and keep the still-healthy at their labours. Cheap health care sought to solve these linked problems. But given the fact that these diseases concentrated on canals, this policy of providing hospitals paradoxically lured workers to their death. And, if this was not enough, the company expected hands to pay their way.

Injury or death was part of the job, ordinary, unavoidable, indiscriminate, a danger assumed when one picked up a shovel.[74] Employers maintained that canallers chose to risk their well-being and were thus responsible for any consequences, but there really was no choice involved. The vast majority of canal workers did not have the power to choose to be a

---

72 Mercer, n.d. (in file for May 1832), C&O/LR; Mercer to Walter Smith, 24 Sept. 1832, ibid.; C&O/PRO, 23 June 1832 (C 174–75), 31 Aug. 1832 (C 212), 8 Sept. 1832 (C 214–15), 7 Sept. 1834 (D 47–48).
73 Mercer to Ingle, 27 Aug., 3 Sept. 1832, C&O/LR; Engineer, Department of 4th Residency to Contractors, 10 Sept. 1832 (enclosure: Purcell, 11 Sept. 1832), ibid.; C. Rush, 5 Aug. 1833, ibid.
74 Between 1827 and 1831, for instance, the detachment of Royal Sappers and Miners engaged in the construction of the Rideau Canal experienced 21 fatalities: 7 were killed when blasting, 5 died of fever, 4 of apoplexy, 3 of consumption, and 2 by drowning. Extracts from War Office Records, 25, v. 2972, Registry of Deceased Soldiers, Corps of Royal Sappers and Miners, Ford McCullough Goodfellow Papers, Queens' University Archives, Kingston, Ontario.

nonmanual worker, say a merchant, clerk, lawyer or even a farmer, where the risk would truly be the worker's. They did not make a choice to be canallers after some objective evaluation of a multitude of alternatives nor of the dangers of accidental injury or exposure to all manner of ailments and infectious diseases. Most moved into canalling by accident and as a result of having precious few options. Once there, they had to pay the price.

Canallers were "worse lodged than the cattle of the field," wrote Power, and "the only thought bestowed upon them appears to be, by what expedient the greatest quantity of labour may be extracted from them at the cheapest rate to the contractor." Despite his condemnation of the industry, in particular its treatment of his Irish countrymen, Power chose to look on the bright side. "I think, however, that a better spirit is in progress amongst the companies requiring this class of labourers." In fact, "it becomes necessary this should be so, since, prolific as is the country from whence they are drawn, the supply would in a little time cease to keep pace with demand." "Independent of interest," continued Power, "Christian charity and justice should alike suggest that the labourers ought to be provided with decent quarters, that sufficient medical aid should always be at hand, and above all, that the brutalizing, accursed practice of extorting extra labour by the stimulus of corn spirit should be wholly forbidden."[75]

Despite building his hopes on the twin pillars of emerging bourgeois culture – economic rationality and Christian piety – Power had a vision of an improved working environment on canals that was to crumble as readily as a weakened bank under the force of a spring freshet. The expectation of an exhausted labour supply was grossly misplaced. Continued immigration, culminating in the Irish Famine, combined with a severe scaling back of construction during the depression to flood the labour pool and strip workers of the advantage shortages had heretofore afforded them. Christian morality failed to melt the hearts of contractors or canal officials, who nonetheless solemnly demanded of the workers sobriety and acquiescence to their lot in life. In fact, conditions worsened for canallers, as growing job competition and dwindling employment opportunities drove down wages and stripped employers of the need to provide room and board. For many canallers, not just the Irish, life became a vicious round of work, drink and illness, with death ever lurking nearby, a common scenario for those at the bottom of society.

The labourers who dug the canals were a sweating, drinking, brawling, hurting, dying mass that seemed to well up from the muck in which they worked, scorched by the sun, choked by rain, bitten by chill frost. Their

75 Power, *Impressions of America* (see n. 4 above), v. 2, 242–43.

days were measured out by the dull thud of shovel in dirt, by the chink of mallet on rock, by the muffled explosion of a powder blast; their nights were marked by the pool of light spilling from shanty windows, by fumes of bubbling stew and acrid rotgut hanging in the air. From this world they extracted what they could – a degree of family life, worker and ethnic camaraderie, the playfulness of roughhousing, shared religious faith, and the conviviality of the bottle – in effect, a community of sorts. But, for all its strengths, canaller culture was not a healthy one. It was built upon swamp land, a bog of harmful social and economic forces, and was in everpresent danger of sinking into the mire. The "ditch" was the demarkation point of their lives, a figurative barricade between them and broader society. They could cross this line seemingly at will, but they usually were drawn back to a life of hard work, rough conditions and few choices, whether on canals, railroads, mines or elsewhere.

CHAPTER 6

"Canawlers and citizens"

For three hundred and sixty miles, gentlemen, through the entire breadth of the state of New York; through numerous populous cities and most thriving villages; through long, dismal, uninhabited swamps, and affluent, cultivated fields, un-rivalled for fertility; by billiard-room and bar-room; through the holy-of-holies of great forests; on Roman arches over Indian rivers; through sun and shade; by happy hearts or broken; through all the wide contrasting scenery of those noble Mohawk counties; and especially, by rows of snow-white chapels, whose spires stand almost like milestones, flows one continual stream of Venetianly corrupt and often lawless life. There's your true Ashantee, gentlemen; there howl your pagans.[1]

> When at night we all rest from our labor, be sure but our rent is all paid
> We laid down our pick and our shovel, likewise our axe and our spade.
> We all set a joking together, there was nothing our minds to enthral,
> If happiness be in this wide world, I am sure it is on the canal.[2]

While trekking along the line of the Pennsylvania Mainline Canal in 1827, a correspondent for the *Harrisburg Chronicle* was struck by the pastoral beauty around Second Kittitanny mountain, "truly a scene for a painter." The "rugged mountain scenery on either side the Susquehanna, and the river dashing through the rocks of Hunter's Falls, are of themselves grand," he reported, "but when to these are added the labourers, some perched upon the cliff, plying their hammers to perforate the rocks, others below at their barrows or carts, further south on the river bank, the shantees, with women washing and cooking, the children gamboling on the green, the white linen hanging on the lines, &c. it was exceedingly lively and interesting." In 1838 the editor of the *Maumee Express* stumbled upon a similar scene while travelling along the line of the Wabash & Erie. "Little

1 Herman Melville's description of the Erie Canal in *Moby-Dick: or the Whale* (orig. ed. 1851; Harmondsworth, England: Penguin, 1972), 353.
2 From "Paddy on the Canal," in *Irish Emigrants Ballads and Songs*, ed. Wright (see Ch. 2, n. 2 above), 533.

villages of shantees, filled with laborers and their families nestle in the edge of the woods, while scores of half naked, tow headed urchins play all sorts of antics by the way-side." Work seemed to merge seamlessly with nature, yet these pastoral idylls faded upon closer inspection. The *Chronicle* recounted that the workmen at Hunter's Falls, having been left unpaid, burnt a shanty and stable belonging to their employers, then clashed with the law, while the *Express* bemoaned: "The everlasting 'grocery' forms a conspicuous object in these villages, and bands of squalid, blear-eyed Irish rowdies, with here and there a solitary Indian luxuriating in all the grandeur and pomposity of Indian drunkenness cluster around the doors."[3] Violence and vice had entered Eden.

This latter reading of canal life was apparently corroborated by reports of intemperance, assualts and murders among navvies. One such case was that of John Brady, a cook in the shanty of C&O contractor Patrick Ryan. Brady fell under the supervision of Ryan's wife Mary, a woman known to be quarrelsome with the hands. After he had been with the Ryans for several weeks, he became ill and was unable to work for several days, a situation that aroused Mrs. Ryan's ire. On the evening of 8 November 1834, a number of people were gambling and drinking in the Ryan shanty. Brady, who by reports "was not very sober that night," got into an argument with Mary Ryan in the kitchen and struck her. Invoking the old animosities, she exclaimed that "if any county of Clare man or Fardoun, or any other man would strike her or offend her in her own shantee, she would hammer the life out of him," upon which she bludgeoned Brady with a candlestick until her husband intervened. Patrick Ryan put the gore-spattered canaller out of the shanty as a precaution against further violence. The hapless victim wandered about the darkened camp crying murder and pleading for help, but his cries fell on deaf ears. Later Brady was let back in the shanty and went to his bed in the loft. In the morning, he was "very dead," as one witness put it. Patrick and Mary Ryan were tried for the murder of John Brady, but their record of service to the canal led to an acquittal.[4]

From the door of the Ryans' shanty we catch a glimpse of canaller community. A temporary settlement of ramshackle huts was set off in the woods right at the work site, dependent and focused on the contractor, by all reports a fair man. His wife was responsible for maintaining the semblance of family life, catering to a gang of men in an environment geared to production. Finally, workers and boss were joined together by shared Irish ties as well as economic needs. Yet, the Ryan encampment was more a collection of people than a real community, the housing, camaraderie, domesticity and ethnic solidarity masking the real purpose of the arrangement, the exploitation of labour for profit. This was made clear by Brady's

3 *Bedford Gazette*, 5 Oct. 1827; *Maumee* [Ohio] *Express*, 25 Aug. 1838.
4 Hagerstown *Torchlight*, 11 Dec. 1834. Also *Hagerstown Mail*, 14 Nov. 1834.

experience, an employee living within the bosom of his boss's house but not of it, and clearly tolerated only because of his labour power. At the same time, canaller society was intersected by lines of tension – personal, gender, class, ethnic – the whole maintaining a fragile balance that one night, in part owing to alcohol, was knocked horribly awry. The shanty rocked with the tumult, John Brady's plaintive cries echoed across the Potomac, and in the morning he was "very dead," one more casualty. As one witness swore in a revealing defense of the Ryans, "such disturbances are common in shantees."[5] Sadly, this was too often the case, and, although much lies shrouded by time and the rough shanty walls, it is evident that the canaller community struggled to contain simmering pressures that periodically erupted into violence.

This ferment proved a continuing source of unease to contemporary observers. Canals were viewed as opening rich, unspoilt territories, but the work sites with their collection of shanties were often seen as dens of iniquity, and those who worked on them as debauched, depraved inebriates. The accounts of this world painted a pathological portrait of individuals, who, partly by condition, partly by choice, were drawn down in a spiral of intemperance, bad hygiene, vice and violence. James Buckingham was struck by the squalor of a work camp on the Illinois & Michigan Canal. "I never saw anything approaching to the scene before us, in dirtiness and disorder . . . whisky [*sic*] and tobacco seemed the chief delights of the men; and of the women and children, no language could give an adequate idea of their filthy condition, in garments and person." Buckingham considered that the Irish "are not merely ignorant and poor – which might be their misfortune rather than their fault – but they are drunken, dirty, indolent, and riotous, so as to be the objects of dislike and fear to all in whose neighbourhood they congregrate in large numbers." John Mactaggart, an official of the Rideau Canal, had a similar view of the canallers, some of whom lived in caves along the Ottawa River where "families contrive to *pig* together worse even than in Ireland." Despite the construction of "large and comfortable" houses for them "so that they might become useful labourers on the public works," they still chose to live in such mean conditions. "You cannot get the *low Irish* to wash their faces, even were you to lay before them ewers of crystal water and scented soap: you cannot get them to dress decently, although you supply them with ready-made clothes." Totally exasperated, Mactaggart complained "they will smoke, drink, eat murphies, brawl, box, and set the house on fire about their ears, even though you had a sentinel standing over with fixed gun and bayonet to prevent them." In like vein, the irascible Anne Royall vented her spleen over the Irish she encountered while travelling near canals by stagecoach. The canallers were

5 Hagerstown *Torchlight*, 11 Dec. 1834.

eternally getting in and getting out, and suffocating you with the stench of drunkenness. They are, for the most part, covered with mud, where they have rolled when drunk, and never think of buying a little trunk, or light valisse, to carry their clothes from place to place, but always have a wad of something tied up in an black greasy old pocket hand-kerchief, and crowd you, and grease you, and stench you to death.[6]

On one level, such characterizations grew out of existing ethnic stereo-types. On another, reports of the vicious nature of canal labourers and the lives they lived emerged directly out of class. Concerns expressed regarding moral conduct – drunkenness, uncleanliness and indolence – were those of an employing class concerned ultimately with the productivity and mal-leability of a working class; disdain for criminality and violence were the inevitable upwellings of fear that those at the top of society have felt throughout history toward those at the bottom.

Labour historians have rejected such crude images of working-class life because of these biases, instead choosing to focus on the community networks that such people were able to construct. But were contemporary observations mere figments of overheated bourgeois imaginations, or were they also reflections, admittedly distorted, of the reality of existence for common labourers? While there is danger in taking such sources at face value, there is equal peril in dismissing them out of hand. In the relative absence of first-person accounts of working life on canals, the historian must resort to documents that admittedly promote an authoritarian reading of the canaller story. Slavery studies provide a fitting example of how to contend with such a problem. Plantation records, when supplemented by scattered accounts by African-Americans themselves, have been decoded of their class and racial biases to help construct a model of slave existence that takes in both the restrictive and self-affirmative realms of their lives. In this way, the recurring image of Sambo has been transformed into a "prepolitical" rebel conniving at the amelioration of his chattel status. The observations of casual commentators, canal officials and contractors can be used in a similar fashion to portray canallers not as drunken brutes, but as human beings caught in a pathological environment of narrowed economic resources where vice and violence resided alongside more positive expressions of their culture, such as family life and social cooperation. To see this aspect of their existence is to accept the negative effects of industrial capitalism, which bred accommodation and internal squabbling among workers as much as class consciousness and labour militance. By looking more closely at the experiences of canal labourers and placing them in their economic and social context, this dimension of working-class culture, powered by exploitation and the stresses this engendered and as divisive as it was cohesive, can be illuminated.

6 Buckingham, *Eastern and Western States of America* (see Ch. 5, n. 35 above), v. 3, 223–24; Mactaggart, *Three Years in Canada* (see Ch. 3, n. 55 above), v. 3, 243–44; Royall, *Mrs. Royall's Pennsylvania* (see Ch. 5, n. 44 above), v. 1, 126.

Worker culture on canals had important social props that sustained a certain commonality of experience. Canallers lived in shanty towns that, while moulded by work and contractor paternalism, were largely held together by ethnic ties. Here, they were able to enjoy family life and religious worship. Workers developed a rough culture shot through with concepts of maleness that promoted group unity; this culture was inevitably marked by the dangerous and physically taxing nature of the work, as well as by the social exclusion the canallers as manual labourers and/or as members of disliked ethnic or racial groups. To stress cohesion and idealize the rough life of the canallers would be to do them an injustice by minimizing the difficulty of their existence. The culture was riddled with weaknesses. Religion, although weakened by the impermanence of canal life, was a tie that both bound workers together and tied them to a conservative social message. Ethnicity, a central organizing principle in these people's lives and a key means for them to absorb and resist their exploitation as workers, also created divisions among and within the different groups that inhibited the development of a truly collective consciousness and often ended in bloody conflict. Finally, there is no question that the attributes isolated by contemporary observers – vice, violence and criminality – were not mere manifestations of stereotypes but real problems that pulled at the seams of group unity. Drinking and brawling from one angle can be seen as a rejection of authority, but were also potentially self-destructive or antisocial. Similarly, personal and collective violence pulled at the fragile bonds of canaller culture, leading to physical harm and often making shanty communities warring camps. Still, canaller society was not some sort of freak. The social tensions at its heart, the disturbances that seethed on the surface, and the impermanence that undermined its foundations were but exaggerations of forces at work within North America's developing working class.

Community life

Social history's focus on community is understandable, as permanent settlements provide a manageable evidenciary base that allows the researcher to attempt to reconstruct the lives of the masses who left few literary clues. However, this focus inevitably has a bias toward rootedness, toward those people who remained to construct a culture and those communities that survived. The concept becomes problematic when dealing with people on the move such as canal workers, who spilled in and out of towns or lived in temporary work camps, and left few marks of their passing. Most navvies did not have a real chance to develop community, at least not in the way the term is usually applied. Canal settlements by their very nature were evanescent, a fabrication of a particular alignment of capital and labour that inevitably shifted from place to place. Transiency was high, residence along the canals temporary and pitched to the rhythms of work, with families commonly distant. Theirs was a fluid existence, swept along in a current, catching on a bank here, held in an eddy there, only to break away and continue bobbing downstream. Social arrangements were by necessity makeshift and temporary. In light of this, the real issue is not what the parameters of their community were, but to what extent they were able to construct their own social reality and at what cost. Community connotes some sense of permanence. This does not have to mean that the same people remain, or that families persist from generation to generation, but it does imply continuity of place and of institutions, something militated against by the nature of canal work. Workers' associational life was continually breaking up and reassembling, their sense of place stuck in the shifting mud of the "ditch." It is hard to see such flux as canallers experienced as having other than a disintegrative impact.

First and foremost, the nature of canal construction – a shifting work site requiring large numbers of mobile men – made for male-dominated, temporary communities, which limited the scope for stable family life. While lying at the heart of many shanties, the worker family served the needs of the industry as much as those of its members, providing, as it did, the domestic core to the productive unit of the bunkhouse. The male-centredness of the industry also necessarily influenced gender relations among canallers, slotting their women into dependent and subordinate positions both in the work camps and the removed shanty towns by making them appendages to male breadwinners.

The greatest hurdle to constructing a balanced family environment was the uneven sexual composition of most shanty camps. Canal work attracted young single men; 62 percent (268 of 430) of those labourers working at a C&O camp in 1850 were aged seventeen through twenty-nine, and 82 percent of the workforce was single.[7] As a result, work camps were largely male bastions with a lopsided male–female ratio. Men outnumbered women by more than five to one in the C&O camp, 430 against 81 respectively. By comparison, there were twice as many men as women at Broad Creek on the Welland in 1842, and the ratio was just under that figure on a division of the same canal two years later. Even destitute German workers on the Williamsburg canals in 1854, who had an unusual representation of families, outnumbered their women by 32 to 22 (Table 9). Single men thus had little chance of meeting a woman of marrying age while working on the canal unless they were near a shanty town.

Even those men who married did not always live in a family setting year round. Many left their wives and children in a town or city while they

---

7   This and ensuing statistical conclusions on the 1850 C&O work camp derive from an analysis of the 1850 U.S. Manuscript Census, Glade District, Allegany County, Maryland, households 629–98, 721–31.

laboured from spring through fall on a canal, only to return to their family during winter when construction froze up. This "split" family pattern was more the case into the 1830s, and it was the model Mathew Carey used when he constructed his labourers' budget in 1832.[8] It was also an arrangement that served the needs of an industry that wanted a flexible and cheap labour source; married men worked where and when capital dictated while the rest of the family laboured in urban centres where equally unrewarding employment was available, all scrimping to survive the year. Necessarily, this pattern undercut stable, contained family life.

Still, quite a few men managed to make families and canals mix. While working as a blacksmith at the Fulton shanty camp on the Wabash & Erie, Hugh Martin from County Cork met Ann Crouch, native of Killarney and a cook at the Maysville camp. As luck would have it, the two fell in love and wed, spending the rest of their lives in the area.[9] The hands on the eastern section of the Chesapeake & Delaware in 1827 were reported to be living with their dependents in temporary buildings near the canal. Fifty labourers were encamped with their families at North Bend on Ohio's White Water Canal in 1840. And it was reported that in 1838 many of the 1,902 labourers on the C&O were accompanied by wives and children.[10] These are impressionistic reports that do not give a solid sense of the family presence, but the C&O camp does hint at its importance. Although only 18 percent of men were married, the proportion of women at the camp (roughly one-fifth of the population) appears to indicate that most of those who were married had their wives with them. This pattern of families living on the public works was more common in the 1840s. Yet this was as much a bad sign as a positive one. The facts that more married men felt compelled to work at a gruelling job previously the preserve of young single men and that their families found it difficult to get work off canals indicated a decline in family fortunes that vitiated the benefits of living together.

The increased domestic presence in these years did not mean that shanty camps became worker suburbs dotted with family cottages. There were 76 labourers' households and 76 families enumerated at the C&O work camp, but only a minority of dwellings were occupied by single families (see Table 10).[11] There were nine nonfamily barracks occupied by single males

8 Carey, *Address to the Wealthy of the Land* (see Ch. 4, n. 18 above), 5–6.
9 Wesley J. Whicker, "Historical Lore of the Wabash Valley," from *Waynetown Dispatch*, 15 May 1916, in Wabash Valley File, Indiana Division, Indiana State Library.
10 *Eighth General Report of the Chesapeake and Delaware Canal Company* (Philadelphia, 1827), 14; *Report of the President to the Stockholders in the Cincinnati and White-Water Canal Company* (Cincinnati, 1840), 12; "Report of the Sub Committee to whom were referred the books and accounts of the Company during the year ending 31 May 1838," n.d. [July 1838?], rough draft, 9–11, C&O/LR.
11 By family I mean a couple, a couple with children, or single parents with children (of which there were five examples). All may include grandparents, but I do not count brothers by themselves, of which there were sixteen pairs.

(in numbers as high as seventeen to twenty-two per unit), usually with one woman who acted as cook and cleaner. There were nine two-family dwellings, and, while there were fifty-eight single-family units, thirty-three of these housed boarders. In all, fifty of seventy-six shanties had boarders. This was not unusual for working-class households elsewhere at this time, but the number of nonfamily residents per shanty was greater. Sixteen had four or fewer boarders, and thirty-four were home to five or more. Only twenty-five of the seventy-six were single-family dwellings without lodgers. All told, 80 percent of the male workforce lived in some form of familial situations, even if it was just boarding with a married couple. This fact meant that, for shanty camps like that on the C&O in 1850 at least, the family provided an important anchor for canaller culture.

Nor was reproduction inhibited. Fragmentary evidence indicates that married canallers bore and raised children without hindrance. Roughly one in five residents of the C&O work camp (124 of 634) were children; as fifty-four families had offspring, this meant an average of almost three children per family. Similarly, along with the 1,303 men and 666 women on the Welland in 1844 went 1,209 children (38% of population), and the twenty-two German families on the Williamsburg had ninety-seven offspring.[12]

It is clear that families continued to play an important role in the shanty camps. Mating and procreating are fundamental urges that tend to overcome all but the worst conditions. The prospect of marriage and childbearing or, at the least, boarding in a domestic household offered a human context to offset the harshness of the environment and alternative mores to those of work and wages. At the same time, families were hardly immune to economic forces. The shape that families took and the roles they played were reflections of the productive needs of the industry.

The conclusion that emerges from this analysis of the C&O work camp is that the majority did not lead a conventional family life – that is, a life centred on a nuclear or extended kinship group living under one roof with some permanence to it. Over eight people lived in the average dwelling. Almost half had more than five nonfamily members sharing accommodations, and less than a third were actual single-family dwellings. The norm appears to have been families hosting labourers, a pattern not too dissimilar from that in other labouring families at this time. But the marked imbalance of the sexes and the unusual number of boarders in over a quarter of the homes, when added to the temporary nature of residential patterns, made this a more unstable arrangement. Thus, some of these "households" became male barracks with a family at its core to provide essential domestic

12 St. Catharines Journal, 16 Feb. 1844; List of Unemployed German Labourers, 4–5 Dec. 1854, Williamsburg Canals – Estimates, Paylists, Accounts, file 22, v. 59 (hereafter Williamsburg Estimates), PAC/RG11.

services. And working families on public works often were reliant on the contractor for housing and provisions as well as employment, an arrangement that, while serving family subsistence interests, made them dependent on and vulnerable to employers. In times of labour scarcity, the industry provided an opportunity for family life to attract labourers and to make them more likely to stay in place. The fact that familial existence usually makes subordinates less likely to cause trouble was a fringe benefit. In difficult economic times, particularly during depression years, the degree of family life in shanty camps was more a reflection of lack of opportunity off canals. In either case, the social desires of workers confronted the business needs of the industry and a compromise was struck.

Women paid a higher price in this bargain. Their numbers in canal settlements (anywhere up to a third or more of the population) attested to their importance, but their position within this community as wives, daughters and workers was set below that of their male counterparts. Thus they experienced the inequality of the social setting more profoundly. In shanty town or work camp, women were slotted into the domestic sphere and the least rewarding work. As canallers were not paid enough to support a family, wives and children had to work to survive. Their labour thus allowed the industry to pay lower wages. Women were drawn into jobs even less well paid, and thus they helped prop up other industries as well.[13] Those who lived at the camps made what money they could as laundresses, cleaners and cooks for the men, or sold liquor, and presumably a few sold their bodies.[14] Wives and daughters back in the city worked as domestic servants and seamstresses to provide subsistence for the family, functioning thus as an extension of the canal economy. As a result, women, although rarely involved in construction, were ensnared in the industry's mode of production and proletarianized simultaneously with their husbands and fathers.

At the same time, women's marginality served the interests of men of their class. They performed the traditional domestic functions of cooking, cleaning and child rearing, which freed men, single and married, to relax during their spare time. Their exploitation as workers was compounded by their oppression as women, the husband-father controlling their wages and whatever property the family owned. Further, women's position within canalling society helped solidify sexual relations in a potentially unstable situation, and to the benefit of the opposite sex. With the economic margin

13 Christine Stansell's study of sweating in New York showed how domestic ideals were manipulated by an industry to create a cheaper labour source that fed its process of capital accumulation. "The Origins of the Sweatshop" (see Ch. 3, n. 15 above).

14 There is virtually no surviving evidence of prostitution, but an official on the Wabash & Erie at Fort Wayne hinted at its presence on the canal. "I am very anxious to get out of the House we at Present occupy Henderson keeps a Rough House it is a Real Brothel or Grog Shop." Henry Rudisill to John Barr, 16 Jan. 1830, Rudisill Letterbook, Indiana Division, Indiana State Library.

between the sexes so narrow, men had to look elsewhere for a power source. Clearly defined gender roles, with hard-working and hard-playing males opposed to family-oriented and submissive females, offered them the edge they needed. This ideal was obviously at odds with reality. Nonetheless, women's subordination as inferior worker and domestic servant served the psychic needs of men who were themselves held down within society; however low a man was he could draw some status from his superiority to women. As props both to the economy of the industry and the male ego, and as the key to family life, women were a crucial link to canal society, however distant they may have been from actual construction. Their "domestication" was a necessary ingredient to production.

Canal work thus appropriated family life, rendering it difficult demographically, fragmenting it, or grafting a male workforce onto it as a productive strategy. This did not mean that the family lost its social or economic functions, only that the choices made within the family – whether to marry, where and with whom to live, what work to follow – were necessarily constrained by the nature of canal work. Production's infiltration and manipulation of the family were ironically reflections of the institution's continuing importance.

Rough culture

In his examination of artisan festivals in New York City, Sean Wilentz turned his attention to the celebration of the Erie Canal's completion in 1825, when the city's craft associations marched in mammoth procession. Wilentz saw in this pageantry a continuation of a tradition of artisanal republicanism emphasizing independence, commonwealth and craft pride, as expressed by the unity displayed among masters, journeymen and apprentices. For Wilentz, this "festival" rested on the cusp of a new world in which craft values would be fragmented by the rise of wage labour.[15] This is a revealing rendition on two levels. First, the marked absence in this procession of the labourers who dug the Erie sheds light on the attitudes of canal promoters and the general populace, who saw the Erie as a public work that somehow magically appeared. Those responsible for its construction were already a dim memory. Wilentz demonstrates a similar amnesia; the canallers are of no account to him, primarily common labourers and unlikely exponents of republicanism. Wilentz's focus on artisanal culture and resulting blindness to the trunk of the working class is symptomatic of the limitations in prevailing labour history. If he had turned his eye to the "festivals" of canal diggers perhaps he would have come away with a different formula for working-class culture than craft pride, republicanism and the regrettable decline of artisanal skill.

15 Sean Wilentz, "Artisan Republican Festivals and the Rise of Class Conflict in New York City, 1788–1837," in *Working-Class America*, ed. Frisch and Walkowitz (see Ch. 3, n. 15 above), 47–53.

A more revealing civic celebration for our purposes was held to mark the groundbreaking of the Illinois & Michigan Canal on the Fourth of July, 1836. The steamboat *Chicago* brought dignitaries and pleasure seekers up the Chicago River from Lake Michigan to the scene of the event, where the Declaration of Independence was read, speeches were made, the sod was turned and numerous toasts were drunk. On its return to Chicago, the city's namesake steamboat was assaulted by a group of Irish stationed in the quarry on the bank overlooking the river. Rocks rained down among the gentlemen and ladies on board, the boat landed and fifty of the frontier gentry rushed ashore with bludgeons, where they reportedly bloodied "the heroes of the Emerald Isle," twelve of whom were jailed. The motivation of the labourers was not made clear. Rather than from any discontent with the patriotic celebration, the assault more likely resulted from mischievousness and a sense of pique at their exclusion from festivities initiating a project they would complete by sweat of brow and strain of muscle.[16]

This affray hints at the public presence of canallers. First, it was generally roughhewn: no orderly processions harking back to a shared political past, but intrusion with rock and fist rather than inclusion with banners. Second, the message was not one of harmony with employers, but more often a physical expression of conflicting interests. Feeling their exclusion from society, canallers reinforced the barrier by assaulting it: hurling rocks from quarry to steamboat to describe the social divide. In the process, a culture with an oppositional quality to it developed. At work, in their shanties, and particularly while drinking, they created a distinctive lifestyle that set them apart from most of society. But components of this labour culture – drinking, brawling, ethnic fraternity – had a paradoxical disintegrative effect, etching a spiderweb of social and personal divisions that threatened to fragment and blow apart the same solidarity they promoted.

A mix of pride in their work and a strong masculine identity increasingly set canallers apart from contractors, canal officials and citizens in general. Most important was the demography of the workforce, which was over-whelmingly made up of young males. Thrown together in often quite large numbers, experiencing the same conditions, braving the same dangers and usually sharing a similar ethnic background, these men developed a rough camaraderie founded on male bonding. A jaunty spirit and acceptance of the difficult and often dangerous work was one form this masculine culture took. As is normal with young men, such bonding also manifested itself in drinking and roughhousing. At the centre of this milieu lay the grog store, where liquor flowed within and brawling often welled up to spill outdoors. Alcohol was the lubricant that sped the backslapping and knucklebusting. The fraternity of canallers provided workers with a social world of their

16 *Chicago American*, 9 July 1836.

own, a place where they could make decisions and pursue interests, in effect a refuge from the world of work, but one with real limitations.

For navvies, the manual, sometimes dangerous nature of their profession helped shape an identity that espoused the values of physical prowess, virility, a certain nonchalance regarding risks and an equal willingness to live hard outside of work, with drinking and fighting two main measures of a man's worth. Their exclusion from the rest of American culture also contributed to a clubbishness, a sense that they were outside the pale, a social threat, which gave them a status that swelled their male pride. An idea of this image of the proletarian bon vivant is conveyed by Herman Melville's description of canal boatmen, which was equally applicable to navvies:

Freely depicted in his own vocation . . . the Canaller would make a fine dramatic hero, so abundantly and picturesquely wicked is he. . . . The brigandish guise which the Canaller so proudly sports; his slouched and gaily-ribboned hat betoken his grand features. A terror to the smiling innocence of the villages through which he floats; his swart visage and bold swagger are not unshunned in cities.[17]

Canallers derived certain benefits from the social role they played, such as pride in their skill and the feeling that they were men of action. As early as the 1780s, blasters on the Potomac Company works were sporting such names as "Hercules," "Bob the Blaster," and "Monster Manley." An Irish blaster named Patten deserved such a moniker for making a spectacular explosion on the Delaware & Hudson near Marbletown, New York. With seventy pounds of powder he blew a rock measuring forty by twenty-five feet from its bed so that it landed exactly on the canal bank, a feat of skill that saved his contractor the need for building an embankment and earned himself a $100 bonus. Like spirits welcomed the Revolutionary War hero General Lafayette to Lockport on the Erie Canal, where he was saluted "by a very extraordinary kind of artillery. Hundreds of little blasts, loaded by the workmen employed in excavating the rock to form the bed of a part of the canal exploded almost at the same moment, and threw into the air fragments of rock, amidst the acclamations of a crowd of people." The Frenchman, suitably impressed, was moved to exclaim, "The very rocks rend to welcome me." Professional bravado could run to needless risk, however, as Thomas Nichols found at the same Erie rock cut, "where tons of gunpowder were burnt, and the Irish labourers grew so reckless of life that at the signal for blasting, instead of running to the shelter provided for them, they would just hold their shovels over their heads to keep off the shower of small stones, and be crushed every now and then by a big one."[18]

17 Melville, *Moby-Dick* (see n. 1 above), 354.
18 Garrett, "Washington's Patowmack Canal" (see Ch. 1, n. 65 above), 751; *Niles' Register*, v. 30, 143; A. Levasseur, *Lafayette in America* (New York, 1829), v. 2, 213; Condon, *Stars in the Water* (see Ch. 3 n. 43 above), 88–90; Thomas L. Nichols, *Forty Years of American Life* (London, 1864), v. 2, 120.

Emphasizing his strength, endurance and ability to both defend himself and drink to excess – typically male values – was a means of self-definition and a way to reclaim masculinity within a capitalist society that threatened to emasculate him. Whatever its positive functions, the male gender role was based upon the canallers' own alienation. By working hard and laughing in the face of danger, they were actually engaged in self-exploitation, simultaneously pushing themselves to prove their own worth and enriching the contractor. In the same vein, by wantonly brawling and imbibing, navvies might be inching up the pecking order within the male community, but they were also dragging themselves down. Beneath the cockiness and colourfulness of canallers ran a thread of social and sexual anxiety that emerged from the weakness of the cultural fabric on public works sites.

Sport and gambling went hand in hand with the male domain of the workplace, and horse racing was a particular favourite. John Campbell, who worked on the Wabash & Erie as a boy, remembered a race held in the summer of 1847 at Cook's Lane, Indiana, when easily two thousand attended and the "fence along the lane was as black with men as of a flock of blackbirds." The crowd was about equally split between "Hoosiers" and Irish, and betting was fierce. A brawl broke out when the Irish horse lost the race; a more serious riot occurred at another event two weeks later. Similarly, canallers from the Chesapeake & Delaware Canal had rioted with jockeys and gamblers at a race in Elkton, Maryland, in 1804.[19] Boxing was another crowd pleaser. A match held outside of New Orleans in 1837 between Deaf Burke, an Englishman, and O'Rourke, the Irish champion, attracted a large crowd. Only three rounds had elapsed when a brawl broke out, and Burke was chased from the field and back to the city by O'Rourke's followers, causing the militia to be called out.[20] These two examples give some sense of the attraction of sport to canallers. A festive spirit prevailed and ample opportunity existed for friends to get together, share a drink, gamble and cheer on a favourite. Such camaraderie and its raucous public nature constituted a release from the pressures of work. From the perspective of their employers and surrounding citizenry, however, it seemed that wherever canallers went disorder followed. Josiah White, proprietor of Pennsylvania's Lehigh River Improvement, noted: 'While we boarded at Laussane, the hands on the first day (being a day of leisure) as usual must needs kill time with sport, as usual, a number of them got drunk and then quarrelled; they drove the landlord out of his house, broke his windows, etc."[21] By drawing together people with similar work experience and ethnic background, or by scaring off those who did not belong, sport acted as a means of group definition for canallers.

19 *Indianapolis Star*, 26 July 1907, in John T. Campbell Scrapbook (see Ch. 3, n. 20 above); Latrobe to Joshua Gilpin, 7 Oct. 1804, Latrobe Collection, MHS.
20 New Orleans *Picayune*, 6, 7 May 1837.
21 "Josiah White's History" (see Ch. 2, n. 43 above), 13.

Equally important to canaller social life were days off and holidays, times when they carved out their own existence separate from yet embedded in their work environment. The weekend, Saturday evening and Sunday, was canallers' own time, spent the way they wished and largely outside the control of contractors. Maybe they would enjoy time with their families, wash and mend clothes, visit nearby towns, make purchases at stores – in effect, relax and try to diffuse the accumulated tensions, aches and pains of a long work week. For many drinking was a prominent feature of this leisure time. In addition to the weekly day of rest, special occasions and holidays interrupted the grind of work. Navvies on the Schuylkill Navigation, for example, refused to work the day of a militia muster no matter what wages were offered. But Christmas was the big holiday of the year. A break of from several days to more than a week during Yuletide was deemed a right by those lucky enough to have work at this time of year. Hands with family at a distance would return to them, and shanty camps took on a festive air all their own. It was also the central social event on the calender for slaves who worked on canals. Hired slaves working at Lock 13 on the James River & Kanawha Canal had six days off during the Christmas season of 1837, presumably to return to their families on their master's plantation, and those at Gwynn Dam and Lock received an eight-day break in 1855. Similarly, both slave and free labourers on Lock 19 were off five to eight days during Christmas 1850; most slaves had left for home by 20 December the following year. Special pay had to be given for work done during this festive time.[22]

Canaller culture had its darker side, where pranks and roughhousing could quickly become criminality and violence, which was turned within as much as without. Workers often stole from local residents, usually petty thefts to make life a little easier. Most commonly they took wood for fuel, either by chopping down trees or pulling apart fences. One farmer living near the Williamsburg Canal lost 300 rails in this fashion. When caught in the act, labourers were likely to threaten with sticks and axes, "saying they cannot do without it and they will take it." To supplement their diet, navvies also took poultry and pigs from farms or fruit from orchards.[23] As conditions worsened in the late 1830s and many labourers became unemployed, stealing grew out of necessity, assuming epidemic proportions on Canada's

22 *Report of the Schuylkill Navigation Company to the Stockholders* (Philadelphia, 1831), 9; Peter Owens, 23 Dec. 1829, C&O/LR; Richard Howe to Kelley, 9 Jan. 1832, OH/CC; William Paxton to William J. Brown, 22 Dec. 1833, Blue Ridge Canal Turnpike Correspondence, in Kanawha River Improvement Letters, JRCR; Time Charts for Workers on James River and Kanawha Canal, 1837, Time Book for the Gwynn Dam and Lock, 1855, Time Charts for Workers on James River and Kanawha Canal, 1850–51, Austin-Twyman Papers (see Ch. 3, n. 25 above).
23 J. Hill to Begly, 6 Feb. 1847, Williamsburg Canals – Police Protection on Canals 1844–1852, file 23, v. 59, PAC/RG11 (hereafter Williamsburg Police); Laviolette to Killaly, 15 Dec. 1842, Beauharnois Riots (see Ch. 5, n. 18 above); Hagerstown *Torchlight*, 8 Nov. 1838.

canals. Management sympathized with the citizenry, but it in no way admitted culpability for the criminal activity of erstwhile canallers. At the opening of construction on the Williamsburg canals, Canada's Board of Works warned: "From the number of strange labourers who may be naturally expected to congregate, the attempts at pilfering or trespassing, usual in similar cases, may be anticipated," but "the Board of Works do not in any manner hold themselves accountable." Instead a police force was established on the line, but the head of Lachine's canal police admitted his force's inability to head off transgressions given "the utterly destitute situation of the labourers."[24]

Such conditions also drove canallers to commit assaults and outright robbery. It was reported that in the vicinity of Canada's Edwardsburg Canal "felonies and other outrages have been committed. The peaceable inhabitants have been stopped by gangs of men in the public High way and the most unprovoked assaults have been committed upon travellers and total strangers to the Laborers."[25] Frances Trollope recorded a notorious case. James Porter was an Irishman who as a young thief had fled to Liverpool. He later moved to North America, finding work as a day labourer on the Erie Canal, where he gained a reputation for violence and was reportedly involved in a number of riots. Eventually sentenced to the Maryland Penitentiary, Porter hooked up with two other men and, upon their discharge, these three robbed a mail coach near Reading, Pennsylvania. All three were captured, but Porter, the Irish canaller, was the only one to hang for the crime.[26]

Canallers were also a threat to their employers' possessions, stealing provisions or tools when they had the chance. More seriously, employers feared their hands would rob them of the payroll. Josiah White and his partner in the Lehigh Company paid their men in signed checks "so that if any of our wild hands caught either of us alone in the wilds he had no inducements to waylay us, for money." One enterprising thief managed to hit the big time, however, when he relieved the Morris Canal Company of $3,000, but was struck by his conscience "at the confessional" and was persuaded by his priest to return the money.[27]

Whether poaching firewood, practicing highway robbery or thieving from the boss, criminality had the effect of isolating workers, marking them off from the general population by a wall of fear and mistrust. At the same time, it did have some positive social benefits for them. Theft –

24 Notice of T. A. Begly, Secretary, Board of Works, 26 Feb. 1844, Williamsburg Police (see n. 23 above); Wetherall to D. Daly, 2 Sept. 1844, Lachine Riots (see Ch. 3, n. 53 above).

25 Petition of the Undersigned Freeholders, Merchants, Traders and other inhabitants of the Township of Edwardsburg to Governor General Elgin, 26 Feb. 1852, enclosed in A. Keefer to A. Morin, 28 Feb. 1852, Williamsburg Police (see n. 23 above). See also "Reports And other Papers connected with Outrages that have been committed in the vicinity of certain Public Works in progress," *Journals of the Legislative Assembly of the Province of Canada.* 1844–45, Appendix Y.

26 Trollope, *Domestic Manners of the Americans* (see Ch. 5, n. 55 above), 285–87.

27 "Josiah White's History" (see Ch. 2, n. 43 above), 13; *Niles Register,* v. 46, 173 (10 May 1834).

growing out of common conditions and serving common needs – could reinforce social bonds among labourers and add to their self-image as romantic ne'er-do-wells.

When worker stole from worker such bonds were threatened. Missing tobacco, tea, clothing or a watch would start people looking around at their shanty mates, sparking suspicion, accusations and perhaps violence. Pádraig Cúndún, farmer, poet and temporary worker on a New York canal in the mid-1820s, had a number of Irish-language books stolen from him while staying at a lodginghouse with fellow workers. Cúndún confided, "I mostly suspect those from Cork of stealing them – people from the west of the county!"[28] Although evidence is scanty, it is not hard to imagine how theft in the shanty camps would pry open existing tensions. Criminality thus had a dual effect, defining and separating canallers from citizens, but, when turned inward, corroding the social bonds of shanty life.

Violence had a less ambiguous impact. Given navvies' penchant for contests of strength and friendly brawling, it was not surprising that fights regularly became serious, with fists flying, knives slicing and blood flowing. There was a thin line between the canalling fraternity's male competition and actual combat. People struck others, sometimes killing them, gangs attacked individuals, group clashed with group. This did not mean that the situation on public works was unique, as there was no shortage of violence in North American society at this time. But on canals the hardships of class were exacerbated by ethnic and racial cultural differences and liquor weakened inhibitions. As a result, violence was a prominent feature of masculine culture on canals.

By far the most common form was assault, such as the case of Thomas Lyon, for whom a warrant was issued for striking another labourer on the Beauharnois. In Cornwall, Ontario, there was a report of a fight with one canaller chewing off another's lips and ears, and the other biting off his opponent's nose. It was no great distance from such brutal violence to murder. James Porter, the future mail robber, had been suspected of killing a mate. Henry Grady, a labourer on the Ohio Canal, was allegedly killed by his wife and a workmate. Violence also often erupted between employer and employed. Richard Hall, who worked on the canal near Zoar, Ohio, was shot dead by an overseer after an argument over the latter's refusal to hire the drink-prone worker. In the midst of a labour dispute on the Illinois & Michigan, a contractor's brother shot and killed a canaller who was destroying one of their pumps. An overseer on the Wabash & Erie, annoyed when Irish hands came to work late, knocked one from a scaffold to the ground, breaking his neck. Such cases rarely received more than a passing mention in the press. Violence and murder, it was believed,

---

28 Cúndún to Tomás Stac, 18 Oct. 1851, in *Pádraig Phiarais Cúndún*, ed. Risteárd Ó Foghludha (see Introduction, n. 1 above), as translated by Bruce D. Boling.

were natural to canal work sites, and as long as these evils did not touch citizens it sparked little concern, a point brought home by Frances Trollope. Bodies twice turned up in the vicinity of the C&O Canal during her stay in the area. One was thought to be a case of murder, as the victim "had marks of being throttled," yet no "inquest was summoned; and certainly no more sensation was produced by the occurrence than if a sheep had been found in the same predicament."[29]

The story was different when mayhem inevitably spilled over canal banks and flooded surrounding areas. On the Wabash & Erie, a number of labourers beat a man for telling them to be quiet, prompting his brother to shoot one of them dead. John Burbridge, who lived on the C&O below Cumberland, was beaten for sending his slaves to the canallers' shanties to recover stolen turkeys. A constable in Dublin, Ohio, who fired his pistol at a threatening canal hand, was severely beaten by his friends. In February 1836, Colonel Albert French, commanding officer of a regiment of the Stormont militia, was met on the road outside Cornwall, Ontario, by two Irish labourers and a woman who demanded a ride in his sleigh. When he refused he was pulled to the frozen ground and his head was bashed in. Three men were arrested and one was sentenced to death.[30]

Clashes between canallers and local residents occasionally led to full-scale riots. The first trial held in Lockport, New York, resulted from such a battle on Christmas Eve, 1822, when a group of Irish labourers fought the town's male population, leaving one worker dead. In March 1829, canallers attacking a house in Waynesburg, Pennsylvania, clashed with armed citizens, and one of the assailants was shot in the cheek and another through his hat, "taking a little of the *fur* off his head." The following year, at Dunnstown on the West Branch of the Pennsylvania Canal, German residents clashed with Irish workers thieving apples from their orchards, leading to one man's death and the deploying of the militia. Similarly, an 1833 riot between canallers and citizens on the Delaware & Hudson near New Brunswick, New Jersey, caused several deaths, and the "rows and riotous conduct" of labourers on the St. Mary's Canal led the citizens of Sault Ste. Marie, Michigan, to jail several and organize a police force.[31]

Canallers also fought with other labourers, as happened in 1828 near

---

29 André Robillard to Chief Constable Miller, 9 Sept. 1844, Beauharnois Riots (see Ch. 5, n. 18 above); Ellis, "Labourers, Contractors and Townspeople" (see Ch. 4, n. 5 above), 21; *Canton Ohio Repository*, 27 July 1826, 15 Feb. 1828; *Chicago American*, 15 July 1837; Whicker, "Historical Lore of the Wabash Valley" (see n. 9 above); Trollope, *Domestic Manners of the Americans* (see Ch. 5, n. 55 above), 163.

30 *Dayton* [Ohio] *Democratic Herald*, 29 Nov. 1834; Hagerstown *Torchlight*, 8 Nov. 1838; *Canton Ohio Repository* 31 Aug. 1826; *Montreal Gazette*, 9 Feb., 11, 13 Aug. 1836; Ellis, "Labourers, Contractors and Townspeople" (see Ch. 4, n. 5 above), 23–24.

31 Condon, *Stars in the Water* (see Ch. 3, n. 43 above), 91–92; *Bedford Gazette*, 6 March 1829; Borgeson, "Irish Canal Laborers" (see Ch. 3, n. 31 above), 74; *Niles' Register*, v. 45, 66 (28 Sept. 1833); *Lake Superior Journal*, 26 Aug. 1854.

Hawley, Pennsylvania, when they had a series of skirmishes with the raftsmen and lumbermen of the Delaware and Lackawaxen rivers, who did not like the canal dam built across the Delaware as it interfered with timber rafts. Likewise, labourers on the New Basin Canal at New Orleans quarreled with sailors on the schooner *Napoleon*, drew the ship into shore and beat the crew.[32]

Canallers' participation in the political process was often indistinguishable from such affrays. As transients and immigrants, few satisfied the residency requirements to vote and were rarely courted as valued constituents when they did remain in place. Labourers tended to participate in politics indirectly. In many cases they were manipulated to party ends by employers and canal officials, used as goons or counted as so many votes at election time, for which they received small favours. One particular crew of maintenance workers on the Wabash & Erie Canal, for instance, were given lighter duties by their superintendent in return for acting as bodyguards at political meetings. Coercion of canallers occurred during political campaigns, as well. In Pennsylvania during the 1838 gubernatorial election, canal commissioners backed the Anti-Mason candidate and made it known that only those workers promising to support their man would be hired. And navvies on the Wabash & Erie above Lafayette refused to work under James Johnson because in the 1840 election "he only had to point his level at an Irishman and he was dismissed from the work," unless the labourer agreed to vote Whig.[33]

Canallers most visibly entered the political arena at the rough-and-tumble polling process. They were often used by a political candidate to cut paths through the crowd for supporters and beat off opponents, with liquor, cash and work exchanged for their strong arms. Too often such tactics deteriorated into riots in which lives were lost. In Montreal canallers became a staple feature of elections in the mid-1840s. In 1844, it was reported that one thousand workers from the Lachine Canal were brought in by candidate Lewis Drummond to carry the election. Soon after the polls opened, "they were taken possession of by large bodies of canalmen, who drove back every elector who came forward to tender his vote in favour of Mr. Molson," so that "the city was throughout the day in the possession of, and at the mercy of, a body of canal men."[34] The troops were called out and, during the attempt to put down the riot, a master bargeman was

32 Borgeson, "Irish Canal Laborers" (see Ch. 3, n. 31 above), 76–77; *Niles' Register*, v. 50, 75 (2 April 1836).
33 Petition of Citizens of Paulding County, 20 Jan. 1844, Board of Public Works Correspondence, Board of Public Works Papers, Ohio State Archives; Wallner, "Politics and Public Works" (see Ch. 3, n. 10 above), 163–64, 175–79 (Stevens quoted on pp. 175–76); R. S. Ford to E. F. Lucas, 9 Feb. 1844, Aborn Collection, Indiana State Library.
34 *Montreal Gazette*, 18 April 1844; Chief Constable Lachine Police to H. H. Killaly, 15 March 1844, Lachine Riots (see Ch. 3, n. 53 above); Wetherall to Killaly, 1, 2, 3, 4, 8, 11, 12, 16, 17, 18 April 1844, ibid.; Wetherall to Daly, 7 Feb. 1844, ibid.

killed by a bayonet thrust. Canallers had little stake in the contest other than the pittance they received for their participation, as few had the vote. The *Montreal Gazette* traced the conflict back to the canal where unemployment and privation prevailed, and a strike for higher wages had just been held. These "navigators" had no means to move on and it was "little likely that a thousand families will starve in peace."[35] The feelings of hopelessness bred by this situation were easily exploitable by politicians making promises and catering to the workers' ethnic sensibilities. Political involvement thus cut both ways, offering canallers limited access to the power structure but harnessing them to politicians and programs that had little to do with their daily lives.

Canallers' fraternal society buffered them from and created a potential source of conflict with work discipline. To this extent, the culture was separate and largely autonomous. But it was a distinction that was founded as much on the workers' exclusion from society and the negativity of their lives as on the integrity and soundness of their world. And the culture divided workers as much as united them. Alcohol helped pry open the cracks.

The bottle

Until the advent of industrial work discipline liquor was firmly ensconced in the workplace, and afterwards remained a key feature of working-class culture. As a result, labour historians have portrayed drink as an important and largely positive prop of worker identity. As Roy Rosenzweig has argued, the drinking establishment was "a distinctive ethnic working-class leisure institution – a separate and largely autonomous cultural sphere."[36] Alcohol also played an important role in Irish culture. It acted as a food substitute, was used to keep out the chill and was distilled illegally as a source of income; it also served many social functions. The "shebeen" was a place where Irish males could retreat from their harsh existence.[37] For both class and ethnic reasons, liquor was a fixture on canals and a main indicator of masculinity among canallers. But while drink was fun, relaxing, socially affirmative and no doubt liked by workers, to emphasize only its benefits masks its tendency to fragment and isolate individuals. Alcohol and its abuse created many problems that ate away at working-class community. The question that should be explored is not just what social role drink

35 *Montreal Gazette*, 23 April 1844. Drummond again brought workers to the hustings in 1845, although not with the same extreme results. Wetherall, 13 April [1845], Lachine Riots (see Ch. 3, n. 53 above).
36 Roy Rosenzweig, *Eight Hours for What We Will: Workers and Leisure in an Industrial City, 1880–1920* (New York: Cambridge University Press, 1983), 4, 61–64.
37 David A. Gerber, *The Making of an American Pluralism: Buffalo, New York, 1825–1860* (Urbana: University of Illinois Press, 1989), 133–34.

played among workers, but why a drug assumed such prominence within this class. The answer is found in the material forces breaking down and reformulating their existence. For canallers, alcohol was situated in an economic relationship that exposed its use to exploitation and a social environment that promoted abuse.

William Rorabaugh argued that American society in the early nineteenth century was riddled with excessive drinking caused by rapid social change, with canallers a particularly rootless lot. "This anomic existence, lawless and alienated from society, gave rise to acute drinking." Canal workers "lacked traditions and stability," their "alienation from society" compounded because they were Irish immigrants. "Bewildered by separation from native church and tavern, ancestral hearths, and the fabric of Irish culture, they found life in an alien and sometimes hostile land difficult and confusing."[38] Yet this condition was not due to "alienation from society," but was a product of a particular environment, existing for specific reasons and serving certain purposes. More accurately, alienation from control of their labour fuelled canallers' excessive drinking. As a prop to increased performance, as a narcotic to a spent body but still active head, as a frenetic release from a world consumed by toil, liquor primed the pump of the canal industry.

Anne Royall claimed Irish canallers were "strung along the canal, scarcely alive, stupid from drink. . . . They care little about eating, provided they get whiskey." Royall's ethnocentrism was blatant, but the essence of her portrayal was borne out by a more sympathetic observer. Andrew Leary O'Brien was an Irishman trained for the priesthood who by necessity found himself working on the Pennsylvania Canal, where his more refined sensibilities were affronted by the alcohol abuse he witnessed. "There was plenty of liquor on the works kept by the contractor, and also by some of the workmen, who had families, & kept it for sale. . . . At night you could hear these wild Irish in their Bacchanalian revels fighting, singing, dancing, &c., all hours of the night." While laced with bourgeois morality, these accounts suggest the volume of the problem on canals. The presence on the Welland Canal in 1845 of 124 unlicensed grog shops (or five per mile) gives an indication of drink's pervasiveness.[39]

There were two types of drinking among canal diggers. The first occurred at work where the men consumed their daily ration of liquor, usually three

38 W. J. Rorabaugh, *The Alcoholic Republic: An American Tradition* (New York: Oxford University Press, 1979), 8–11, 140, 143–44.
39 Royall, *Mrs. Royall's Pennsylvania* (see Ch. 5, n. 44 above), v. 1, 126; *The Journal of Andrew Leary O'Brien, Including an Account of the Origin of Andrew College, Cuthbert, Georgia*, ed. Annette McDonald Suarez (Athens, Ga.: University of Georgia Press, 1946), 31; Samuel Power to Begly, 2 May 1845, General and Departmental Correspondence Sent, Welland Canal, v. 2248, PAC/RG43. Similarly, Irene Neu found fifty grogshops for the nearly 1,600 workers on the St. Mary's Canal. "The Building of the Sault Canal" (see Ch. 5, n. 60 above), 41.

to four gills a day for a total of twelve to twenty ounces. This pattern was rooted in the workplace, serving economic as well as social needs, and fell more directly under the control of the contractor. The second type occurred after hours back at the shanties or in local grog shops, where the shared mug or pipe reinforced canaller solidarity. It is this aspect of alcohol consumption that is usually examined by labour historians. But social drinking could soon become bingeing, or the consumption of inordinate amounts of liquor, which often led to squabbling and fights. Alcohol consumption thus had rhythms that mirrored the work itself: repetitious and steady from Monday through Saturday, loose and unregimented evenings and weekends.

Drinking on the job had historical roots in work culture and was a prerogative demanded by labour. Most hands liked to drink and refused to work without it, leading contractors to integrate alcohol into their system of production, but builders' embrace of "ardent spirits" was not all paternalistic benevolence. Alcohol performed a number of economic roles that ultimately bound canallers a little more firmly to their profession. First, it was often a component of real wages, implicitly figured into labour costs, directly exchanged for work in lieu of cash, or sold on credit from a company store.[40] Second, drink acted as a pacifier of labour. Three or four jiggers of whiskey a day, consumed during sustained manual exertion, bled canallers not only of body fluids but of the will to do anything other than the dull, physical spadework required to put bread and more whiskey in their bellies. Third, potential existed as well for the denial of liquor rations as punishment for laziness or haphazard work. Finally, drink could be used as an incentive, the jigger measuring out the day with hands lured on by the whiskey pail. The promise of extra rations also proved a spark to heightened exertions, as when the Erie Canal was nearing its terminus in Buffalo and the contractor placed whiskey barrels at intervals along the line of construction, the contents of which would be consumed by the men once the work reached each barrel.[41]

Alcohol was thus a potential means of exploitation, and, wittingly or unwittingly, alcohol abuse was promoted by contractors, with the net effect of depressing workers while addicting them to a work setting where whiskey flowed. Frances Trollope recognized the role of drink in labour relations on canals when she was exposed to C&O navvies. "It is by means of this hateful poison that they are tempted, and indeed enabled for a time, to stand the broiling heat of the sun in a most noxious climate." Similarly, Tyrone Power inveighed against "the weary frame stimulated by the worst

40 See Chesapeake and Ohio Canal Company to John Reilly, Voucher No. 8, Account No. 1, n.d. [received 5 March 1839], C&O/LR; Whitacre and Avery Ledger, 1827–28, Ohio Historical Society; Hugh Beale Ledger (v. 2), Ohio Historical Society.
41 Condon Stars in the Water (see Ch. 3, n. 43 above), 92.

alcohol, supplied by the contractor, at a cheap rate for the purpose of exciting a rivalry of exertion among these simple men."[42]

Canallers were not oblivious to drink's economic underpinnings. Williamsport, Maryland, had developed a reputation as a town of drunkards during the construction of the C&O, but a local citizen jumped to its defense. "Barney" admitted "that among a certain class of our population, tipling and drunkenness are practised morning, noon and night, and that the disgusting form of the drunkard can be seen too often in our streets," yet warned that a distinction must be made between "*Canawlers* and *Citizens*." Annoyed at Barney's identification of drunkenness with the C&O's Irish workers, "A Canaler" responded "that if the same number of the laboring class of any other country on the face of the globe, were collected on the line of the Canal, at least as many excesses would be committed by them, as by my hard working generous countrymen." Out of ethnic pride, Canaler grasped the essence of alcohol abuse on canals: that it was rooted in the workplace, as well as in the very nature of labouring culture. More pithily, a former jigger boss on the Wabash & Erie, remembering back over fifty years, put the use of alcohol in context. When someone commented to him, "Why those workmen must have been drunk all the time," he replied gruffly, "You wouldn't expect them to work on the canal if they were sober, would you?"[43]

While liquor had a certain role to play in labour relations, it also posed problems that (in the eyes of canal officials at least) were increasingly seen to outweigh its economic benefits. Employers in mid-nineteenth-century America were becoming obsessed with the seeming truism that alcohol and industry do not mix. This revelation was transformed into a moral evaluation identifying intoxication with individual failing, which was apparently proven by the profusion of vice and violence that seethed and occasionally welled up on canals. Thus, a concern for order in production as well as in the sphere of morality increasingly infused company attitudes to the drink problem. Directors of the Chesapeake & Delaware Canal made clear the evil effect of tippling houses in 1826. "These nuisances, by furnishing the pestiferous draught by day and by night, rendered the workmen not only unfit for labour, but the ready instruments of riot and disorder." Similarly, Indiana's Board of Internal Improvements warned that liquor retailers "will be a source of endless quarrels and riots, attended in some instances with the risk of life to citizens, as well as the means of weakening the physical force of the laborers employed."[44]

---

42 Trollope, *Domestic Manners of the Americans* (see Ch. 5, n. 55 above), 290; Power, *Impressions of America* (see Ch. 5, n. 3 above), 2, 241.
43 *Williamsport Banner*, 21 Dec. 1833, 18 Jan. 1834; *Lafayette Journal*, 10 Sept. 1899, in George A. Cottman Scrapbook, Indiana Division, Indiana State Library.
44 *Report on the Chesapeake and Delaware Canal* (n.p., 1826), 15–16; "Report of the State Board of Internal Improvements," in *Documentary Journal of Indiana Reports* (n.p., 1836), 11.

Canal companies looked to three sources to combat the alcohol problem. First, they sought to sever the traditional bond of booze between employer and employee by making contractors disavow the use of ardent spirits on the line. For example, contracts on the Wabash & Erie Canal stipulated that contractors "shall not permit any of the workmen employed in the construction of the work . . . to drink distilled spirits of any kind, under liability of forfeiting this contract." And builders on the Illinois & Michigan faced loss of their contracts if they sold drink to their hands. Second, punitive action could be taken directly against an offender. Men found drunk on the Beauharnois Canal were to be first punished and then discharged, and foremen were exhorted to watch their men closely, even to the point of entering their homes to ensure they were not being used as grog shops. Finally, canal officials turned to government to solve the problem that their first two initiatives had left unresolved. Indiana's Canal Board thus petitioned the state legislature to pass a law restricting the sale of alcohol within three miles of any public works, a tactic that was followed by several other canals but with little success.[45]

The C&O's decade-long fight to get alcohol off the canal demonstrates just how firmly planted drink was in the workplace and labour culture. Complaints about grog sellers disturbing the line began not too long after the opening of construction, and by 1832 the problem had grown to the extent that the company moved to put an end to it. A regulation prohibiting liquor from the line was included in all contracts and the state assembly was petitioned unsuccessfully to restrict licensed retailers from within two to three miles of the canal. Dram shops continued to proliferate in the area and the proscription of drink from the line proved worse than the original malady. The men, held to water all day, would get drunk every night. This reportedly not only led to much disorder, but made them unfit for work the next day. As a result, the company decided not to enforce prohibition. In 1835, there were again reports of disturbances resulting from grog sellers operating on company lands. Contractors were warned that their contracts would be declared abandoned if they gave their hands liquor or knowingly hired someone who brought spirits on the line. But drink did not disappear from the line and was a continuing irritant to the company. "An undoubted source of much of the riot and outrage on the Canal, has been the unlimited access of the workmen to ardent spirits furnished on the work," reported Charles Fisk, the chief engineer, "and this, too, has certainly greatly enhanced the cost of the work, alike to the

45 *Report of the Commissioners of the Wabash and Erie Canal* (Indianapolis, 1833), 21; William Gooding to Gen. J. Fry, 27 July 1846, Swift Papers, Chicago Historical Society; Gooding to Board of Trustees, 30 Aug. 1847, ibid.; I. B. Laviolette to H. H. Killaly, 10 Oct., 15 Dec. 1842, Beauharnois Riots (see Ch. 5, n. 18 above); "Report of the State Board of Internal Improvements," in *Documentary Journal of Indiana Reports* (n.p., 1836), 11.

contractor and company."[46] The parallel concerns for moral and economic order are here clearly expressed. But to place all the blame for the alcohol problem on the men was to turn a blind eye to the conditions they worked and lived under, and to attribute labour disputes to the bottle – the common explanation in this period – was but another manifestation of this purblindness.

One ingredient was conspicuous by its absence, despite all the hand-wringing over alcohol use: real concern for the effects of drinking on the workers. This issue is of primary importance to any study of worker culture on canals. The environment on public works promoted excessive consumption of alcohol, and this exacted significant personal costs. Addiction was the most imminent threat. Canallers were provided with an average of twelve to twenty ounces a day, six days a week, for perhaps two hundred working days a year, exclusive of what they drank after work.[47] This was consumed during the performance of strenuous labour under taxing conditions. Anyone who partook of their full ration would have been working drunk much of the day, a combination of the sun and the alcohol dehydrating the body, creating a thirst that could not be slaked, at least not until the next visit of the jiggerman. Many must have been drawn into chemical dependency. Harry McGowan routinely missed work on the James River Canal in 1851 through being "in bad conditions" as a result of drink, as did Jack Kinness, who was dismissed for his drinking problem. McGowan and Kinness seemed to prove what a C&O engineer had claimed about canallers some twenty years earlier. "These men have always been accustomed to a stimulus of this nature, require it, and it has become an absolute necessary."[48]

Alcohol abuse meant more than lost work and wages; it could also wear down the canaller's body. "Many indulge in drinking liquor to such an excess," claimed the *Lake Superior Journal*, "that they become enervated to that degree that, when attacked by even some trifling disease, it proves fatal." Even for the casual tippler, inebriation could lead to mishaps, such as those described on the Chesapeake & Delaware Canal: "When drunk, they frequently fell, exposed for hours, unsheltered, to the rays of the sun, and the evening dews – fever, and death, were but too often the melancholy consequences."[49] Drink was undoubtedly an important factor in workplace

---

46 Edward Watts, 9 Dec. 1829, C&O/LR; Mercer to Ingle, 23 Jan. 1832, ibid.; Alfred Cruger, 7 July 1832, ibid.; C&O/PRO, 11 July 1832 (C 185–86); Extract of a letter from Jno. McP. Brien, 3 Feb. 1835, C&O/LR; Ingle to Fisk, 20 Feb. 1835, ibid.; Fisk, 2 March 1835, ibid.; George Bender to Ingle, 27 Aug. 1835, ibid.; Ingle to Fisk, 20 Feb. 1835 (B 415), C&O/LS; Proceedings of Stockholders of the Chesapeake and Ohio Canal, 21 July 1840 (Letterbook B, 372–73), series 180 NA/RG79.
47 Workers at Burrit's Rapids on the Rideau were supplied on the average with more than a gallon of whiskey a week by their contractor. Valentine, "Supplying the Rideau" (see Ch. 2, n. 50 above), 52.
48 Time Charts for James River and Kanawha Canal, 1851, Austin-Twyman Papers (see Ch. 3, n. 25 above); Alfred Cruger, 7 July 1832, C&O/LR.
49 *Lake Superior Journal*, 8 July 1854; *Report on the Chesapeake and Delaware Canal* (n.p., 1826), 15–16.

accidents as well, rendering inherently dangerous jobs life-threatening; knowing that the man who packed the charge and lit the fuse probably had his nose in the whiskey pail not too long before helps explain the incidence of work-related injury and death on canals.

Alcohol could have a corrosive impact on worker community. Not only did drink weaken relationships by worming its way to the front of a person's commitments, it led to violence – among comrades, within the household and between broader groups of workers – as the murder of John Brady in the Ryan shanty suggests. Ultimately, excessive drinking had the potential effect of fragmenting canallers as a group and promoting internecine violence.

The masses

Religion has rightly been seen as a bulwark to the social life of dependent classes, particularly among immigrant workers. Largely focusing on Catholic immigrants, studies of the church have shown how it remained a constant in the destabilizing experience of immigration. Catholics in nineteenth-century Protestant America not only worshiped together, but commonly lived, married, learned, worked, played and were buried next to other Catholics.[50] Yet the church was not a wholly benign influence, as it absorbed change by accommodating itself to the emerging order, at times against the interests of parishioners. While religion taught the message of self-worth and sought to instill a moral code, it also preached acceptance of existing conditions, a necessarily conservative message. This dualism, a tension between resistance and accommodation, emerges from the heart of Christian theology.[51] When looking at religion's role on canals, then, attention must be paid not only to its constructive impact but also to the way it siphoned off tension, actively preached acceptance of the social system, and, in effect, promoted the breakdown of cultural norms.

The community focus of most studies of the immigrant church poses problems for applying their findings to public works. They study urban areas with some permanence about them and emphasize the parish, a set jurisdiction with a church building at its centre.[52] But too often on canals there was no parish or only one in name, the clergy were missionary circuit riders who saw their parishioners only infrequently, and the "church" was an improvised shanty or forest glen. Despite canallers' demonstrated craving

50 Jay P. Dolan, *The Immigrant Church: New York's Irish and German Catholics, 1815–1865* (Baltimore: Johns Hopkins University Press, 1975); Gerber, *Making of an American Pluralism* (see n. 37 above), 145–54; Lynn Hollen Lees, *Exiles of Erin: Irish Migrants Victorian London* (Ithaca, N.Y.: Cornell University Press, 1979), ch. 7.

51 Genovese made this point in his section on slave religion in *Roll, Jordan, Roll: The World the Slaves Made* (New York: Vintage, 1974), Book 2, Part 1.

52 Dolan, *Immigrant Church* (see n. 50 above), 2–5.

for spiritual guidance, such conditions necessarily diminished the impact of religion on their lives. Continuity was difficult to maintain among a flock when the shepherd had hundreds of square miles to patrol.

Admitting the institutional inadequacies of religious life, it could still be argued that faith, the spiritual message of Christianity, infused canallers' lives on a daily basis. Yet (as Jay Dolan points out), many of the Irish immigrants at this time were ignorant of Catholicism and were Catholic in name only. Kerby Miller has argued that Irish Catholicism in the nineteenth century saw its Celtic mysticism stripped away to be replaced by a formalized, Roman-directed, essentially conservative faith as part of an Anglicization process. It was this latter variant, denuded of the original ethnic culture, that was cultivated in North America and became the bedrock of American Catholicism.[53] The upshot of this process for canal workers was that often the religion they embraced, an amalgam of folk beliefs, was not the doctrine being preached to them by the Catholic clergy. Thus ministration on public works, at least from the perspective of Irish Catholics, involved a weaning away from old ways in an attempt to make respectable an alien faith for a Protestant society; in effect it was as much a force to destroy established beliefs as to promote cultural persistence.

Two works by Catholic priests provide helpful insights into the practice of religion among canallers. In his 1853 novel *The Cross and the Shamrock*, Hugh Quigley offered a revealing fictional look inside the devotional life of public works labourers. Quigley, a Catholic priest who came to America after the failed Young Ireland rising in 1848, took up a parish near Troy, New York, and counted navvies among his flock. His book was based on his own experiences. Our second cleric, Father John McElroy, was a Jesuit priest in Maryland who sometimes ministered to labourers on the C&O. He left a handy diary that recorded his missionary work along the canal.[54]

Arrangements for worship on canals were decidedly makeshift. Father McElroy regularly said mass in the woods, as well as in shanty chapels.[55] Similarly, the priest in Quigley's novel travels from flock to flock and has to make do with whatever accommodation is available. The mass that Quigley recounts takes place in a shanty, yet measures are taken to spruce up the rough altar:

The largest shanty in the "patch" was cleared of all sorts of lumber. Forms, chairs, tables, pots, flour and beef barrels, molasses casks, and other necessary stores were all put outside doors. The walls, if so we can call them, of the shanty, were then hung round with newspapers, white linen tablecloths, and other choice tapestry, while a good large shawl,

53 Ibid., 55–57; Miller, *Emigrants and Exiles* (see Ch. 3, n. 33 above), 75–78, 124–27, 526–34.
54 An excerpt from *The Cross and the Shamrock: or How to Defend the Faith. An Irish-American Catholic Tale of Real Life* is contained in *The Exiles of Erin: Nineteenth-Century Irish American Fiction*, ed. Charles Fanning (South Bend, Ind.: University of Notre Dame Press, 1987), 121–27, reprinted by permission; McElroy Diaries (see Ch. 5, n. 61 above).
55 McElroy Diaries (see Ch. 5, n. 61 above), 27, 28 June, 10 Nov. 1830, 28 June–18 July 1837.

spread in front of the altar, served as a carpet on which his reverence was to kneel and stand while officiating. Green boughs were cut in a neighboring wood lot and planted around the entrance by the men, while around the altar and over it were wreaths of wild flowers and blossoms, gathered by the little girls of the "patch" in the adjacent meadows.[56]

The festive air clearly indicates that the mass means a lot to the labourers and their families. Much effort goes into making their rude surroundings "a decent place for the holy mass," but at the same time the presence of boughs and wild flowers harks back to Celtic, pre-Christian religious beliefs. Here, in a most unlikely place, we have a meeting of old and new Irish faiths, seemingly in balance but perhaps masking a tension lost on the Roman-trained Quigley.

Not only were churches few and far between, but a frequent complaint from the priesthood was that there were too few clergymen to meet the needs of the thousands of labourers on public works. Father St. Cyr, the pastor in newly chartered Chicago, was the only priest on the line of the Illinois & Michigan Canal when it first got under way, and the paucity of clergy on the Indiana frontier meant canallers were lucky to see one once every few months. An examination of McElroy's diaries shows that between June 1830 and December 1831 he preached nine times on the C&O, or about once every two months, although he made visits for other purposes (Table 11). The relative scarcity of both clergy and churches was compounded by their parishioners' transience. Often, as soon as plans were under way to erect a chapel, the people it was meant for were miles away following the ever-advancing line of construction. Father Badin urged the immediate building of chapels at Fort Wayne and along the Wabash & Erie "because as soon as the work is done in one section of the country the Catholic hands move to another section." In Snelingsgrove, Pennsylvania, canal labourers made donations of money and labour to aid Father John Fitzpatrick build a church but moved on before it was completed.[57]

The clergy still provided many important services: preaching or saying mass, performing baptisms, marriages and funerals, hearing confessions, teaching catechism, administering last rites, and making sick calls. Father McElroy performed all of these duties over miles of canal, often through snow and intense cold. Moreover, certain priests indirectly became working-class advocates by trying to correct conditions on canals. Contractors who treated labourers cruelly or failed to pay them on time often had to deal with an irate clergyman. When work conditions deteriorated on the Beauharnois in 1843, for instance, Father John Falvey made their case against long hours, low wages and store pay to the extent that a local magistrate judged

56 *Exiles of Erin*, ed. Fanning (see n. 54 above), 124–25.
57 George J. Fleming, *Canal at Chicago* (Washington: Catholic University of America, 1950), 131–32; Newcomer, "Construction of the Wabash and Erie Canal" (see Ch. 4, n. 26 above), 206–07; Father Badin quoted in Poinsatte, *Fort Wayne During the Canal Era* (see Ch. 3, n. 64 above), 63; Borgeson, "Irish Canal Laborers" (see Ch. 3, n. 31 above), 82–86.

him overly meddlesome. Likewise, John McDermott, a Catholic clergyman on the Wabash & Erie, complained to the canal trustees about a contractor who absconded "without paying his just debts, and often defrauding the poor men, who earned hard, what was coming to them on his work." As a result, they had been reduced to a "wretched and miserable condition . . . without food, without raiment, without shelter, without those common necessaries, the absence of which will press heavily upon them during this cold and inclement season." The men, McDermott concluded, depended upon the trustees "to see that they will be treated with kindness and I will add from myself, with justice."[58]

The labourers and their families were truly grateful for these services, as was shown by their performance of odd jobs for the church. Irish canallers for the C&O cut wheat for McElroy's Society of Jesus, and helped dig the foundations of its Orphans' Asylum.[59] The hands also made what contributions they could from their hard-earned wages to support the church. On 16 September 1830, they presented McElroy with $47, and during a preaching tour in 1837 he collected $1,960 from labourers and contractors toward a new church. McElroy reported after this successful drive that "all gave with a very good will, vieing in some instances with each other, even Protestant contractors contributed liberally."[60]

This final point leads away from the constructive contributions of the church and toward an assessment of its conservative dimension. The fact that contractors in general, and Protestant ones in particular, contributed to the establishment of a Jesuit church is certainly suggestive. The late 1830s were years of recurrent labour unrest on the C&O. The year before McElroy's collection tour, a worker turnout for higher wages had been broken by the use of blackleg labour, which resulted in threats and vandalism against contractors and their picked men. Builders probably saw the church as a means of promoting order on the line, and thus contributed as an investment in their future financial well-being. McElroy cemented his bonds to contractors by regularly dining with them and staying overnight at their homes while visiting parishioners along the canal.[61] Builders rested atop shanty society, and it is the rock of the elite, however rough-hewn, upon which the church inevitably is founded. As a result, an informal partnership born of a mutual desire for order grew up along public works between the clergy and contractors and canal officials. At the same time, labourers were closely linked to all three groups, and the church was a chain that bound all together.

---

58 Depositions of John Falvey (No. 9), J. B. Laviolette (No. 32), "Beauharnois Report" (see Introduction, n. 3 above), Father John McDermott to the Trustees of the Wabash and Erie Canal, 13 Dec. 1849, W&E/COR.
59 McElroy Diaries (see Ch. 5, n. 61 above), 4 July, 1 Dec. 1830.
60 Ibid., 13 July 1837.
61 Ibid., 19 Sept. 1830, 28 June–18 July 1837.

The sermon preached in Quigley's *The Cross and the Shamrock* illuminates the spiritually liberating but socially conservative message of religion. After warning his navvy fold against "drunkenness and faction fights, for these crimes brought their proper punishment both here and hereafter," the priest addresses the moral state of the modern industrial world. In the past when population was small and work but little, God had appointed a day for rest, intones the priest, but now "when the cares, distractions, and labors of life had increased a thousand fold," more than one day for rest and worship was required. "And if the Church had her way unrestricted, she, by her festivals and holydays, would do a great deal towards alleviating the present hardships of labor, and men would be taught to be content with a competency, and employers would treat their men with kindness and justice combined." Having summoning up this heaven, the priest returns to earth. "You are exposed to dangers from accidents, and frequently from the influence of evil-advising men. In Religion and her resources alone you can find the only safeguard against the effects of the former, and the best security against the wiles of your enemies: keep the commandments, and hear the church."[62] This sermon highlights the ambiguities of the religious message for workers. It deplores the excesses of modern work discipline but counsels patience, as a better world may be obtained under the direction of the church. It concedes the dangers of the work but cautions against listening to those who would cause trouble. In effect, it encapsulates the message of religion – the only way to harmonize the competing evils of the world is to have faith, "to keep the commandments, and hear the church" – that promotes acceptance of the staus quo.

Religion's benefits to labour discipline were recognized by canal management, which encouraged the clergy's presence along canal lines as the best guardian of peace. Initially at least, priests' role in preserving order among canallers was an informal one, part of their larger duties of tending to their flocks. Hence, when Father O'Reilly heard of Irish labourers near Towanda, Pennsylvania, brawling and drinking heavily, he rode to the line, rebuked the men, and broke a whiskey barrel with an axe to make his point. More importantly, bringing in a priest was often the only way to head off bloodshed and get the men back to work at times of labour unrest. Father Curran was instrumental in settling the 1829 strike at Clark's Ferry, Pennsylvania, and Reverend McElroy calmed workers on the troubled C&O Canal during the mid-1830s.[63] While Father Falvey rose to the defense of his Beauharnois parishioners, he also preached obedience to their wordly masters, the contractors, and worked to keep them from going on strike. A government commission investigating the 1843 Beauharnois strike noted

---

62 *Exiles of Erin*, ed. Fanning (see n. 54 above), 126.
63 Borgeson, "Irish Canal Laborers" (see Ch. 3, n. 31 above), 48–51, 82; *Baltimore American and Commercial Advertiser*, 9 April 1829; McElroy Diaries (see Ch. 5, n. 61 above), passim.

"he has endeavored to impress them [the labourers] with the necessity of obeying their employers[,] of respecting the law, and of acting with forbearance and charity towards each other."[64] Spreading this gospel was obviously in the interest of the industry. It is not surprising, then, that strong ties developed between the clergy and canal officials, a bond formalized during the 1840s in Canada when priests were put on the company payroll, as will be discussed in Chapter 8.

Clergymen performed many valuable services on canals. They spoke out against poor conditions, made claims for prompt and fair payment of wages, and cultivated in the canallers a sense of self-worth as Christians and honest labourers, values that would be rewarded in the hereafter if not the here and now. When it came to incidents of labour organization and protest, however, the church was firmly behind employers, being unable to accept the only tactics of protest open to the men, combination and violence, or the undermining of authority it entailed. Moreover, provisions of services and cash by canal officials to the church carried with them the implicit assumption that clergymen would be soldiers of capital as well as of Christ. This dual effect of religion naturally grew out of the competing tendencies of Christianity to spiritually liberate the individual but socially constrict the group. If not quite an opiate, religion was a pacifier that both nourished and sapped the vital energy of canallers.

"Burn & Butcher"

The various streams of working people that flowed into canals came from very different cultural backgrounds. Naturally, they interpreted their time as canallers according to their particular traditions. In this way, ethnicity acted as a common bond, but it also pitted labourer against labourer both within and across ethnic lines in ways that undercut community.

Canallers of different ethnic backgrounds did not mix freely. Instead, the norm was socially exclusive enclaves in which each group tended to work and live with their own kind. French-Canadians accounted for 88 percent of Philemon Wright's labourers at Dow's Swamp on the Rideau and at least two-thirds of John Redpath's Jones Falls crew, but other contractors on the same line did not employ a single *Canadien*, instead relying on Irish immigrants. Similarly, Germans clustered together on Ohio's Miami Canal between Dayton and Picqua in 1837. Slaves worked together with little turnover on one James River contractor's sections in the 1840s–50s, whereas his hired white hands came and went quickly and seemed to dwell off the line. And of the 511 men and women recorded at the C&O work camp in 1850, 459 (or 90%) were of Irish origin (Table 12).[65] The net

64 "Beauharnois Report" (see Introduction, n. 3 above).
65 Valentine, "Supplying the Rideau" (see Ch. 2, n. 50 above), 10–12; *First Annual Report of the Board of Public Works of the State of Ohio* (Columbus, 1837), 8–9; Time Charts for Workers on James

result was a settlement pattern of different groups collecting in tribal villages dotted along extended lines of public works. Shanty camps thus became fragments of other cultures. It can be presumed that such insularity not only built up community *within* groups but at the same time erected barriers *between* them. For it was community erected on exclusion – both of workers from society and of canaller from canaller – that reflected the powerlessness of these groups. As in the rest of society, ethnicity and race were used as justifications of exploitation within wage labour and slavery. Pushed off to the wilderness or margins of towns, dependent on an occupation increasingly looked down upon by those with options, canallers were both physically and psychologically marginalized. In this sense, the relative homogeneity of their settlements and ability to live as Irish or blacks were measures of their subordination.

One negative effect of this social particularism was the presence of interethnic hostility that regularly resulted in violence. Irish canallers often fought with local native-born citizens, as has been shown. They brawled with blacks at Elkton, Maryland, in 1804, and with German residents of Dunnstown, Pennsylvania, in 1829.[66] Canallers also turned on fellow workers of other ethnic groups. In August of 1839, Irish navvies on the C&O viciously attacked German labourers, leaving one man dead, and fellow countrymen threatened and beat Scottish stonecutters on the Welland in 1844. A year earlier on the Lachine, unemployed Irish attacked French-Canadian strikebreakers.[67] This last example points to a common feature of interethnic violence: that often it was not just a matter of simple national bigotry, but of competition for the limited jobs available in the industry.

More importantly, deadly violence also frequently occurred amongst the Irish themselves, with regional rather than national affiliation the dynamic. This fact underlines the problem of using ethnicity as a surrogate for nationality, as is too often the case in ethnic studies, for most European countries in the nineteenth century were more aggregations of cultural or ethnic groups than unified wholes. In Ireland a tradition of county rivalries was wedded to a long-term experience with violent social conflict to produce severe internal squabbling. The Cork–Connaught distinction, more than pure and simple Irishness, was the axis around which existence was ordered. As with ethnicity, these subsets created social solidarity, but more profoundly led to dissonance in the canaller community.

The origins of county feuds are unclear, but they may have resulted from

---

River and Kanawha Canal, 1850–51, Time Book for the Gwynn Dam and Lock, 1855, Austin-Twyman Papers (see Ch. 3, n. 25 above); 1850 U.S. Manuscript Census, Glade District, Allegany County, Maryland, households 629–98, 721–31.
66 Latrobe to Gilpin, 7 Oct. 1804, Latrobe Collection, MHS; Borgeson, "Irish Canal Laborers" (see Ch. 2, n. 31 above), 74.
67 M. Guth to Fisk, 13 Aug. 1839, Peter Pitchlynn Papers, T. Thomas Gilcrease Museum, Tulsa, Okla.; John R. Brook to O. H. Williams, 15 Aug. 1839, ibid.; *Washington National Intelligencer*, 24 Aug. 1839; David Thorburn to Daly, 17 Jan. 1844, Welland Canal – Riots on the Canal, file 5, v.

conflict between agricultural workers of one county and transient blackleg labourers from another who competed for limited harvest jobs. Despite the uncertain historical roots, the Irish tradition of faction fighting and clandestine agrarian violence crystallized on British and North American public works.[68] Faction fights characteristically took the form of feuds between groups identified as Corkonians (from County Cork in the south-western province of Munster) and Connaughtmen, also known as Fardowners (from the province of Connaught on the west coast). This particular feud had not been heard of in Ireland, however, but was something new, bred on canals where workers, the majority of whom came from these two regions, were placed in direct competition for jobs.[69] Latent county-based allegiances came to the fore as a result, gaining credence as terms of group identification and providing a context of social and economic organization. Corkonians typically worked and lived in shanty communities together, and Connaughtmen cleaved unto Connaughtmen. Contractors often came from or led the same faction, and work decisions – who was hired, who got which contract – would take into account these allegiances. Public works sites thus were fractionalized by worker enclaves, tribal villages united and divided by particularistic bonds of undoubted force that were dimly under-stood by canal officials.[70]

Andrew O'Brien's journal gives the best sense of how factions shaped social life. When forced to take up wage labour, O'Brien made his way to Muddy Creek on the Pennsylvania Canal. Here he was surprised to find several acquaintances from his home parish, an indication of how ethnic and personal ties could blunt the strangeness of a new land. O'Brien found solace among his fellow Corkonians, but was dismayed by the intensity of regional discord among the workers. "The Irish on the public works in this country, are divided into two great parties, viz., Fardowns & Corconians, & bear a deadly hatred towards each other," he observed. "One of an opposite party dare not seek employment on a contract where the other party were in employ." At Muddy Creek one contract was worked by one group and a second by the other, "and so deadly was the character of their enmity towards each other, that one of a different party even passing by the

---

68, PAC/RG11 (hereafter Welland Riots); Charles Atherton to Begly, 30 March, 5 April 1843, Lachine Riots (see Ch. 3, n. 53 above); Joseph McDonald to H. H. Killaly, 3 April 1843, ibid.

68 Lees, *Exiles of Erin* (see n. 50 above), ch. 8; Powers, "Invisible Immigrants" (see Ch. 2, n. 37 above), 84–86; Brian C. Mitchell, *The Paddy Camps: The Irish of Lowell 1821–61* (Urbana: University of Illinois Press, 1988), 23–27.

69 Andrew O'Brien, a native of Cork, claimed he had never heard of the feud before he found himself on the canal, but speculated it had its roots in the Irish Rebellion of 1798. *Journal of Andrew Leary O'Brien*, ed. Suarez (see n. 39 above), 30–32.

70 On the Illinois & Michigan Canal, the "Connaught Rangers" settled along the main and north branches of the river while those from Munster lived at "Limerick" or "Cork" upriver. Similarly, Lowell's canal diggers were separated into two camps, with those from southwest Ireland living in the "Acre" and Connaughtmen in the "Half-Acre" to the north. *Chicago Tribune*, 19 April 1874; Mitchell, *Paddy Camps* (see n. 68 above), 23–27.

other party would be run down like a rabbit by a pack of bloodhounds, & murdered on the spot he was overtaken on." O'Brien spoke from experience. "I have seen a number of these men leave their work & run down a man from the next job who was the different party, & beat him with pick and grub hoe handles, till he was so dead that he was not worth another blow." Assault led to assault and full-scale warfare always seemed imminent. Suspicion of attack from the opposing side bred paranoia and a watch was kept over the shanties, "fearing the next party would attack them of nights, & burn & butcher them up while asleep."[71] Any rumour of the approaching enemy created a panic, sending all rushing for their weapons. O'Brien grew disgusted with these factions during his five months on the canal. "On these works I got so, that I felt mean at the thought that I was an Irishman, & had it not been, that by reasoning with myself, & knowing that these were generally the dregs of the Irish, I could never more respect the Irish character."[72] No doubt salving his own pretensions to respectability despite his diminished condition, O'Brien attributed faction fighting to class more than ethnicity, with the great passion of the "lower classes" – alcohol – being largely at fault. Violence was not the result of depravity as O'Brien would have it, but he was right to refer it to the work environment.

Physical and social divisions separating worker from worker, Irishman from Irishman, easily translated into conflict, and battles between these groups were notoriously vicious. The paradox here that sometimes eludes ethnic historians was that ethnicity not only formed a basis for community but also promoted sectarian warfare. At the same time, ethnic feuding was never divorced from the conditions of life and labour on the canals, which explains why the feuds were virtually unknown away from public works construction sites.

As the situation deteriorated on canals in the late 1830s and early 1840s, faction fighting acquired more of an economic basis; class interests often were at stake, even as worker fought worker. Ethnicity acted as the central organizing principle of class, with the culture of the overwhelmingly Irish workforce fusing with their exploitation as workers to produce a particularly dangerous and volatile force.

The experience of the Welland canallers illuminates this dark passage. In the spring of 1843 there were reports of nonpayment of wages, and, with

---

71 *Journal of Andrew Leary O'Brien*, ed. Suarez (see n. 39 above), 30–31. Such fears were not wholly unreal. For instance, one night in March 1834, an armed gang of Corkonians led by a contractor named Allaher attacked a company of United Irishmen in their shanties on a New Orleans canal, killing several and wounding more. Allaher had been underbid for a contract and chose this way to repay the successful bidders. This particularly brutal assault led to the calling out of the City Guards and the arrest of twenty-five Corkonians, although Allaher escaped. *Hagerstown Mail*, 21 March 1834; *Niles' Register*, v. 46, 35 (15 March 1834).

72 *Journal of Andrew Leary O'Brien*, ed. Suarez (see n. 39 above), 32–33. O'Brien did not escape factions by leaving the canal. Two years later he again worked among them on the Croton Water Works in New York, but he left as soon as he could.

work on the Feeder and Broad Creek Branch drawing to a close in April, it was feared that the discharged workers ("a more disorderly & riotous multitude could not be assembled") would cause problems, most being too destitute to move on. That summer, 3,000 canallers were "on the verge of starvation, and cannot possibly be kept quiet much longer." By winter it was reported that 5,000 men were on the line and the same number of women and children, yet only 3,000 people were employed and these but part-time. Wages had been rolled back in November to 2s. 6d. as the costs of provisions rose. With the Connaughtmen settled at Slabtown near Thorold on the northern section of the canal and the Corkonians below Port Robinson in the south, the scene was set.[73]

The chain of events started innocently enough. On Christmas Day two men got into a fight in a shanty at Stone Bridge near Lake Erie, and "like wild fire the evil spirit run throughout every work on the whole line," reigniting the Cork–Connaught feud. Bodies of armed men, 500–600 in number, clashed as "their women and children flew from their Shanties for safety and took refuge where ever they found a door." The canal police, contractors, foremen and local citizens eventually managed to quell the riot. A troop of the Coloured Incorporated Militia arrived the next day and by 27 December seventy labourers had been arrested. Meanwhile, conflict raged up and down the line. The rest of the coloured militia met a group of Connaughtmen and would have become engaged in fatal conflict if Father McDonagh had not intervened to check the workers, using "the whip upon them with his priestly authority." An interval of quiet was broken early in January when the Connaughtmen determined to seek revenge for their defeat at the battle of Stone Bridge. They took possession of blacksmiths' shops to make weapons and, 200 strong, marched on their foes. Again Father McDonagh and the coloured militia managed to keep the two groups apart.[74]

McDonagh attributed this feuding on the Welland to "Secret Societies" that existed among the Irish "binding them by oaths to be faithful to each other. One is called the Hibernian and another the Shamerick Society." Despite his best efforts, he was unable to break up these groups. The local magistrate, David Thorburn, reported that "an organized system exists amongst the labourers, they are armed with all and every kind of weapon consisting of Guns Pistols Swords Pikes or poles pitch Forks, Scythes." When wages did not suit them they stopped work, and a patrol of canallers armed with bludgeons drove off those willing to work.[75] The economic underpinnings of secret societies nonetheless eluded the authorities, and it

73 Begly to Power, 6 March 1843, Welland Canal Letterbook, PAC/RG43; Power to Begly, 14 Feb., 20 March, 8 April, 17 July, 6, 18, 25 Aug. 1843, ibid.; Father McDonagh to Killaly, 2 May 1843, Welland Riots (see n. 67 above); Thorburn to Daly, 10 Jan. 1844, ibid.
74 Thorburn to Daly, 10 Jan., 17 Jan. 1844, Welland Riots (see n. 67 above).
75 Thorburn to Daly, 10 Jan. 1844, ibid.

was felt that if somehow the warring factions could be brought together they would see the light, put all their differences behind them and the problem with social disorder on canals would disappear. It was toward this end that a new tactic was adopted to return calm to the Welland.

Father McDonagh brought in James Buchanan – Irishman, British Consul at New York for twenty-six years, and reputedly an influential man among the immigrants – to speak to the workers in an attempt to get the warring sides to draw up a peace treaty. Only the Connaught leaders showed up at the meeting. Buchanan, McDonagh and Thorburn took turns haranguing them on their duty to keep the peace and give up their weapons. The canallers cut through the rhetoric, crying "give us work to earn a living, we cannot starve, the Corkmen now have all the work, give us a share of it." They threatened that if they were not given jobs they would take them by force.[76]

Clearly the two groups were talking at cross-purposes. The authorities would concede that want of work was the first cause of problems, but they were only concerned with restoring order and saw canallers as squabbling Irish, who should give up their traditional feud. The Connaughtmen, on the other hand, undoubtedly hated their enemies and were quite willing to victimize them to survive, but would be more than satisfied with work for all. This was something the industry could not provide, and thus the fires of factionalism were stoked to white-hot intensity. Ethnicity and class were forged into a brittle alloy on canals, and each shutting down of work, drop in wages, or even personal quarrel threatened to fracture it into pieces. Thus faction fighting directed by secret societies persisted throughout this period, intermingled with acts of collective protest, both pulling the canaller community apart and welding it together once more. The fit was never strong and violence of one sort or another was a recurring reality.

While on the surface faction fights appeared to be ethnic brawls writ large, they were often fed by job concerns over issues of employment, wages and hours. In the best of times for canal labour, as in the 1820s and 1830s, driving off the opposing faction created an artifical labour shortage, thereby forcing up wages and increasing the bargaining power of those who remained. This was the case on the Chesapeake & Ohio Canal, as we shall see in Chapter 7. In the worst of times when jobs were scarce and labourers a dime a dozen, as on Canada's canals during the early 1840s, chasing the other group from the line was the key to keeping or acquiring employment. In either context, faction fights were rational labour strategies that both recapitulated traditional social conflict and undermined a broader understanding of labour's collective interests.

Employers both acknowledged and exploited factional divisions among

76 Notice to the Sons of Erin, from James Buchanan, 12 Jan. 1844, Broadside, ibid.; Thorburn to Daly, 17, 19 Jan. 1844, ibid.

canallers. Workers settled in cliques by choice, and the arrangement was also promoted by contractors, partly because the enmity between various groups led to violence. This need for buffer zones necessarily influenced the awarding of contracts and appointing of overseers to direct the work.[77] The inevitable violence that resulted from factions was against the interests of public works, as it interrupted construction, scattered workers, hurt the public image of canals and drove up costs. Moreover, lessons learned in faction fighting were also increasingly turned to labour's interests, organization and selective violence being used to create jobs by scaring off other workers, and to drive up wages or secure delayed payments.

At the same time, the mere fact that their labour force was divided among groups with little empathy for each other worked to the advantage of employers and owners. Hands could be kept in the tribal villages they preferred, and divisions played up to submerge fundamental issues of wages and conditions. More perniciously, preexisting conflict could be used by unscrupulous contractors to avoid paying their men. Michael McQuade, a labourer from Utica, maintained that a "great many of the contractors have themselves confessed to me that they got up those fights on purpose, in order to evade the payment of the men, and said all they had to do coming on pay-day, was to employ some persons to kick up a row, and that they would be sure to get off from paying at all." McQuade recounted meeting one contractor bringing six whiskey barrels to the line, who admitted that, in lieu of the cash he did not have, he hoped to get up a fight. The battle ensued, many of the workmen ran away as planned, and only 30 of 150 men remained to demand payment.[78]

The segmented nature of the workforce and the disadvantaged condition of most canallers bred a fragile mosaic riven with tensions that militated against the creation of a healthy social life and inhibited the development of a unified class consciousness. Divided workers were good for the industry, at least when not literally at each others' throats. Quarreling over the respective virtues of Cork or Connaught distracted from the real issues of the workplace, like wages, harsh conditions and unsteady employment. By arraying worker against worker, the ultimate effect of ethnic and racial divisions was a blurring of the lines of class conflict.

Ethnicity thus had an ambiguous impact on canals. It provided a social context and contributed to worker organization, which ultimately was turned to the fundamental economic issue of control of the labour process. But it also perpetuated and elaborated on ritualized cultural conflict that led directly to the most brutal kind of violence. Ethnic culture made sense of the material *here and now* by applying the traditional *then*. Necessarily,

---

77 See Jacob Blickensdeefer to Kelley, 8 Aug. 1827, OH/CC; D. Kenyon Cahoon & Co., 16 Nov. 1835, C&O/LR; C. Carter to E. F. Lucas, 27 March 1844, Aborn Collection, Indiana State Library.
78 *Irish American*, 31 July 1852, quoted in Ernst, *Immigrant Life in New York City* (see Ch. 3, n. 43 above), 105.

confusion and conflict emerged as much as comfort and consensus. This dual aspect to tribal identification, both pulling workers apart and binding them together, was typical of the competing social allegiances that tugged at working people in the transition to industrial capitalism, a transition marked by the breaking down of an old world as much as the building of a new.

Life was hard on canals. The material conditions, the fragmentation of cultural norms fostered by the impermanence of shanty life, and the social tensions percolating within camps that led to vice and violence made mere existence a trial. This did not mean canallers were battered down and bludgeoned of hope; they lived on, working, eating, drinking, procreating, but within the closed confines of canals. The choices they made were drawn from options circumscribed by the ditch, by their status as relatively powerless labourers. To overstate the integrity and dynamism of working-class culture is to downplay the difficulty of workers' lives and the strength of forces changing them. From their experiences, good and bad, integrative and fragmenting, canallers made sense of their world and developed strategies to ameliorate its worst consequences; in effect, they sought to absorb those things they could not change. Thus, from their history of ethnic squabbling, their shared religious beliefs, their rough culture of drinking, brawling and dangerous living, was crafted a sensibility solid enough to mount coordinated but ultimately unsuccessful resistance to the worst excesses perpetrated against them. Here is the true wonder: weighed down by their burden, they still periodically rose up with Sisyphean resolve in an attempt to ease their load, perhaps anticipating a world in which gravity was revoked and the masses rode on high.

CHAPTER 7

"Guerilla war": labour conflict in the 1830s

I learned for to be very handy, to use both the shovel and spade,
I learnt the whole art of canalling, I think it an excellent trade.
I learnt to be very handy, although I was not very tall,
I could handle the sprig of shallelah, with the best man on the canal.[1]

A "kind of guerilla war" raged along the line of the C&O Canal near the little town of Williamsport, Maryland, in late January 1834.[2] "Armies" of Irish labourers numbering in the hundreds marched, made sorties against each other, and finally engaged in open battle. In the aftermath, witnesses "observed five men in the agonies of death, who had been shot through the head; several dead bodies were seen in the woods, and a number wounded in every direction. Those who observed the battle described it as one of great rage and most deadly violence." Two factions were involved: the Fardowns, or Longfords, and the Corkonians, "composed respectively of those from the North and those from the South of Ireland." Trouble had flared on Thursday the 16th when Corkonians assaulted Longford labourers, one of whom was beaten to death. His friends prepared for war, and the following Monday 200 attacked their opponents working six miles south of Williamsport. On the Friday, from 600 to 700 Fardowners armed with guns, clubs and helves marched to a hill at Middlekauff's Dam, where 300 Corkonians, "armed, in part, with military weapons," had assembled. Volleys of gunfire were exchanged and a pitched battle ensued. The outnumbered Corkonians were routed and hunted through the surrounding woods. That night, the victorious Longford men passed quietly through the streets of Williamsport and returned to their shanties.[3]

1 From "Paddy on the Canal," in *Irish Emigrant Ballads and Songs*, ed. Wright (see Ch. 2, n. 2 above), 533.
2 *Frederick* [Maryland] *Herald*, 1 Feb. 1834.
3 *Williamsport Banner*, 25 Jan. 1834. See also *Hagerstown Mail*, 31 Jan. 1834; Purcell to Ingle, 23 Jan. 1834, C&O/LR; Thomas J. C. Williams, *A History of Washington County Maryland* (orig. ed. 1906; Baltimore: Regional Publishing Co., 1968), 223–24; Sanderlin, *Great National Project* (see Ch. 1, n. 69 above), 117–18.

The scope of the conflict stunned the people of Maryland. The state militia was called out and thirty-five rioters were arrested, and, for the first time, federal troops were called into a labour dispute. Two companies arrived from Baltimore and remained for the rest of the winter. Eventually, a peace conference was arranged between the two factions: the workers' delegates signed a treaty promising not to interfere with anyone working on the line and to inform on those breaking this pledge or inciting riot. Each delegate posted a $20 bond to keep the peace.[4] For the time being calm returned to the canal.[5]

To contemporaries (and later historians) this riot appeared to have been simply an ethnic conflict, rival factions of Irish brawling yet again for reasons long lost in the haze of history. It did not involve job concerns and was an incident of labour violence only to the extent that labourers were involved.[6] The same was said of other canaller mass disturbances. But sundering ethnic from workplace issues on canals is problematic.

In reality, the 1834 riot grew out of the C&O's worsening financial situation. Throughout that winter and spring, the company tottered on the brink of insolvency, and frantic efforts were made to secure loans from local banks so that contractors could be paid.[7] Labourers feared that work would be abruptly halted and wages lost. Such doubts seemed to be confirmed when a contractor, owed money by the company, discharged his unpaid men upon the completion of the job. These disgruntled labourers later formed the core of the rioters. "The cause of the difficulty," reported the Hagerstown *Torchlight*, "is said to have been, either the suspension of work, or of payment, on one or more sections of the canal."[8]

4 *Washington National Intelligencer*, 29 Jan. 1834; *Hagerstown Mail*, 31 Jan., 1, 7 Feb. 1834; *Williamsport Banner*, 1 Feb. 1834; Morris, "Andrew Jackson, Strikebreaker" (see Introduction, n. 11 above), 57–61.

5 This feud was carried by migrating workers to Indiana's Wabash & Erie, where they settled along a fifty-mile stretch of the canal, Corkonians on the upper end and Fardowners on the lower. As a canal commissioner reported, they immediately "manifested their ill will to each other by merciless beatings on such of each party as chanced to fall in the power of the other." Hostilities mounted until July 1835, when both sides marched on each other and a battle was averted only by the militia's intervention. D. Burr to Noah Noble, Governor of Indiana, 30 Dec. 1835, State of Indiana, *Journals of the House of Representatives* (Columbus, 1835); *Niles' Register*, v. 48, 439 (22 Aug. 1835).

6 David Grimsted makes this distinction, leading him to class the 1834 riot as "purely ethnic," whereas Richard Morris saw the riot primarily as a labour dispute, a strike broken with military force. Grimsted, "Ante-bellum Labor: Violence, Strike, and Communal Arbitration," *Journal of Social History*, v. 19 (Fall 1985), 9; Morris, "Andrew Jackson, Strikebreaker" (see Introduction, n. 11 above).

7 Ingle to William Price, 16, 20 Dec. 1833 (B 175–76), C&O/LS; Ingle to Purcell, 20 Dec. 1833 (B 177–78), ibid.; Ingle to R. H. Henderson, 21 Dec. 1833 (B 178), 20 Jan. 1834 (B 187), ibid.; John H. Eaton to Price, 27 Dec. 1833 (B 180), ibid.; Ingle to Horatio McPherson, 13 Jan. 1834 (B 185–86), ibid.; C&O/PRO, 6, 13 Jan. 1834 (D 39, 41–42); Byrne & Co. to Ingle, 3, 24 March, 2 May 1834, C&O/LS.

8 A. B. McFarlan to Ingle, 20 Jan. 1834, C&O/LR; Hagerstown *Torchlight* report reprinted in *Hagerstown Herald*, 1 Feb. 1834. The company, recognizing the root of disorder, moved to placate these men in the riot's wake. It paid the contractor the $3,000 owed him, and ordered him to place notices in local papers calling his men together to be paid. It is not clear whether this meeting took place. R. B. to Purcell, 25, 28 Jan. 1834 (B 190–91), C&O/LS.

Growing tensions fissured the workforce along preexisting fault lines. Labourers split into their traditional factions, and banded together in an attempts to lay claim to remaining jobs. According to the resident engineer, Thomas Purcell, the disturbances were "the result of a regular organization for that purpose, the ultimate object being to expel from the canal all except those that belong to the strongest party and thus secure for the remainder higher wages." Such attempts to manipulate the labour market and establish what amounted to a closed shop were reasonable strategies for workers given prevailing conditions on the canal and their limited options. These initiatives were eventually lost in mushrooming factional conflict and ultimately squelched by military intervention, and the state of Maryland's additional subscription of company stock in March 1834 financially revitalized the C&O, temporarily obviating the need for workers to fight over employment.[9] But the events on the C&O formed a pattern evident on most canals during this period. Canal companies' continuing financial woes undermined the contracting system and threatened the labourers' livelihood. In response, Irish workers joined together along factional lines and used violence to establish control over jobs and wages, usually at the expense of fellow canallers.

Much of the squabbling on canals used traditional Irish forms of organization and tactics of conflict. But even in their seemingly most parochial form, faction fights were generally precipitated and conditioned by the nature of the work environment – the exploitative character of the labour relationship and the fragility of community life. In this way, ethnic bonds mediated canallers' experience as wage earners. The result was a high degree of social and economic conflict on public works, which peaked in the 1830s–40s when a number of forces – the depression chief among them – combined to bring about a reorganization of production within the industry that eroded canallers' tenuous purchase on subsistence. Conflict on the C&O during the 1830s highlights the workers' dwindling fortunes in the initial stages of this shift; an examination of the changed productive environment and even more virulent labour unrest of the 1840s in the next chapter completes the picture.

The dimensions of the conflict

Social conflict was common among canallers, arising from the many tensions within the industry: the demanding nature of the work, the rudimentary and often deleterious living environment, and the diverse workforce. But for all the weaknesses of canaller culture and its internecine violence, there was also a significant amount of collective labour action, riots and strikes

9 Purcell to Ingle, 23 Jan. 1834, C&O/LR; Ingle to Philip E. Thomas, 15 March 1834 (B 200–01), C&O/LS.

directed at bettering work and living conditions. An inchoate working-class consciousness developed that was never too divorced from navvies' ethnic identities, a pattern common in the early industrial era. Before there was a conscious labour movement, organization existed among workers, and before unions and strikes dominated labour protests, occupational and ethnic groupings adopted riots and demonstrations as strategies of collective action. Of course, riots were only partly expressions of working-class organization. Ethnic and political allegiances intertwined with class, often promoting harmony between employers and employed. But slowly, driven on by the narrowing of economic life, labourers came to identify with one another as fellow workers as often as fight over jobs or cultural differences.[10]

Riots and strikes on canals thus point to competing pulls on canallers, drawn simultaneously by particularist loyalties and emerging class solidarity. What joined the two strains of violence and sparked social conflict as a whole was the exploitation of canallers both as workers and as members of proscribed groups within society. Economic and social oppression fused to produce a high degree of labour unrest, a process galvanized by depression in the late 1830s. Conflict antedated this economic downturn, but was multiplied and intensified by its attendant sufferings and the organizational changes it precipitated; unrest persisted afterwards because of the changed productive terrain.

Workers rioted and struck virtually everywhere canals were dug, from New Orleans to Sault Ste. Marie, Fort Wayne to Montreal, and with a regularity that made the industry perhaps the most significant source of collective action among labourers in this period.[11] A preliminary compilation of riots and strikes along canals between 1780 and 1860 yields a total of 160 incidents, with riots outnumbering strikes roughly two to one (Tables 17 and 18). Incidents were fairly evenly distributed among the canal-building regions, with two big exceptions (Table 13). The South (exluding Maryland) was virtually unscathed by labour protest because of less construction and, especially, greater use of slave labour. More startling was the degree of violence north of the border, with Canadian strikes and riots accounting for almost two-thirds of the total, all the more surprising given canals there only amounted to a few hundred miles.

Labour conflict was not distributed evenly over time (Table 14). It was concentrated, not surprisingly, in the decades between 1820 and 1850. Only five incidents have been recorded for the period 1780–1820, after which disorder on canals mushroomed before tailing off again at mid-

10   Bryan D. Palmer, "Labour Protest and Organization in Nineteenth-Century Canada, 1820–1890," *Labour/Le Travail*, v. 20 (Fall 1987), 61–83.
11   Bryan Palmer found that canallers led 20% of the riots in Canada for the years 1820–75 in which the participants' occupation was identified; they were responsible for 15% of the strikes in the period 1815–49. "Labour Protest and Organization" (see n. 10 above), 63–69.

century. This pattern is to be expected given the contours of construction: fewer projects and a smaller labour force in the early years, the industry reaching its peak in the middle decades only to wind down in the 1850s. Yet there were a surprising number of smaller projects before the War of 1812, with three thousand to four thousand hands needed during the mid-1790s alone, and almost as many canals were under construction and as many men employed in the mid-1820s as in the more disturbed 1830s. And the peak of labour unrest came at a time when work had dropped off and the workforce had shrunk (from about 30,000–35,000 jobs in the 1830s to 7,000–10,000 in the following decade). Labour conflict was not just a function of the extent of ongoing work. Factors both internal and external to canal construction were fuelling the disorder. A closer look at its timing provides clues to its origins.

There were two principal waves of labour conflict. One surged from 1834 to 1838, when forty-two incidents – approximately one-quarter of the total – occurred, and the other swelled between 1842 and 1845, when 43 percent of the incidents took place (Table 15). Strikes and riots in these two periods were distinguished by one feature, their location. Conflict in the first wave overwhelmingly occurred on U.S. canals, while the latter series was wholly Canadian. The timing of labour unrest, years of relative calm punctuated with violent explosions, seems to indicate a crisis in the industry, and the shift from an American to a Canadian arena constitutes another clue to the material basis of canaller discontent. Something peculiar to canal construction was at work, altering the very structure of the industry and lashing labourers to new heights of excitement and organization.

The nature of the conflict was also changing at this time. Although workers continued to war with each other more often than joining together, incidents of collective action by labourers against employers became more common. Faction fights and riots, while following traditional paths of social conflict were increasingly sparked by concerns of employment, wages and working conditions. Such economically instrumental incidents reflected worsening conditions within the industry. Similarly, the rise in the number of strikes is an important indicator of growing solidarity among broader groups of workers and of a dawning perception of class relations, although too much stress should not be placed on this aspect. Fifty-seven strikes have been identified, by no means a complete figure, but it does indicate a sharpening of tensions attending the transformation of canal work.

Early strikes in canal construction were small in scale and conservative in nature, born of specific grievances and aimed at protecting established labour relations. Most commonly, they were waged in defense of the labour contract and resulted from the nonpayment of wages or unacceptable work and living conditions. As the situation worsened in the 1830s, canallers periodically left off their faction fighting and nightriding assaults to confront head on the sources of their exploitation. It was at these times they exhibited a form of class consciousness, protean, ephemeral, but clear about the bases of power in their world. In identifying contractors and canal officials as the common enemy, and by making demands for the right to work, a fair wage and an honest workday, they sought to build a world in which workers could live in relative comfort free of the spectre of starvation. Still, the state could not tolerate this vision, which, by conferring labour rights other than freedom to move, questioned the ultimate authority of the employer and the omnipotence of the market. The backlash from employers grew proportionately. Whereas faction fights were merely refereed and vandalism was policed, serious strikes were met with the iron fist of the state.

Military intervention is the best indicator of the increasing intensity of canaller disputes, as well as of the state's burgeoning role in shaping labour relations. From 1829 to 1849, soldiers were called upon thirty-two times to put down a riot or break a potentially violent strike (Table 16). Military actions naturally mirrored the two peaks of labour conflict; cases were roughly split between the two countries, with U.S. examples concentrated in the 1830s and Canadian ones in the following decade. Public works promoters in British North America were blessed with highly trained British regulars close at hand, and they repeatedly took advantage of these forces to suppress labour conflict. Though less organized and more likely to be local militias, the military was also a recurring force on American canals. Compared to other industries, canal construction suffered the most military intervention in labour disputes during this period. Reluctantly, the state was repeatedly drawn in to maintain order and defend property rights, in the process gaining experience for the height of industrial conflict later in the century.

The marked increase in conflict during the 1830s–40s, the emergence of strikes as a prominent form of protest and the growing use of the military to maintain order on the canals indicated mounting strains in labour relations, paralleling changes within the canal-building industry. Most projects had always experienced periodic financial problems, and contractors and workers alike lived with the imminent threat of not being paid. But the panic of 1837 and ensuing depression caused an economic crisis throughout the industry that forced most projects either to curtail or suspend construction. Contractors were strung along with promises and paper pledges for as long as possible. Canallers inevitably suffered, being thrown out of work or paid in depreciated canal scrip. They fought with each other for what work there was, or organized to resist their worsening condition. This conflict was manifested in the rash of riots and strikes of the late 1830s. The financial constriction of the industry and the labour unrest it sparked will be the subject of this chapter. As canal after canal closed and labourers drifted away, a period of quiet ensued. In 1842, however, the government of Canada initiated a number of projects and thousands of unemployed workers flooded across the border hungry for work. There they were joined by an increasing flow of immigrants from Ireland. The result was a grossly overstocked labour pool, vicious competition for jobs, hunger and privation for the majority and, periodically, coordinated efforts among workers to secure employment and a living wage from the Board of Works. From the detritus of the old system of personal bonds between contractor and labourer emerged a fully formed capitalist–labour relationship, with wages set by the market and workers unprotected from slow times and unemployment, a transformation that will be examined in Chapter 8. The explosion of labour strife in 1842–45 punctuated this alteration in productive relationships. This two-staged process – the first wrenching apart the industry and the second piecing it together into a more productive whole – completed the metamorphosis of canaller into worker.

Nationally, organized labour had also waged a series of strikes in urban centres in the mid-1830s, but these actions were beaten down by an employer backlash and the general depression beginning in 1837, and the 1840s were a decade of relative calm.[12] Industrial workers and public works laborers thus experienced opposed trajectories of labour militancy: the former falling while the latter rose. This situation perhaps indicated that different causes and goals lay behind the mobilization of these groups. With fewer alternatives open to them, and with the essential question of subsistence underlying organization, the depression did not breed retrenchment among canallers, but instead fanned the flames of labour unrest. In this way, their concerns were more "materialist" and less "political" than skilled manufacturing workers. Both were driven by exploitation, but canallers' relative deprivation made for a different configuration of class conflict.

Depression within the industry

For all its economic and labour problems, the canal industry had been quite successful. Companies ran short of money, contractors went broke and fled the line, workers barely scraped enough together to make a living, but massive arteries of commerce had been carved throughout the land, most builders made a profit, and labour shortages meant relatively high wages for canallers. This system increasingly broke down in the 1830s, however, just as a new wave of canal construction was surging ahead, and the whole structure came apart in the depression with grave consequences for all involved in the industry.

Canal promotion was an exercise in speculation. Investors, be they private individuals, financial houses or states, banked on the hope that their

12 Wilentz, *Chants Democratic* (see Introduction, n. 8 above), chs. 7–8.

particular canal would be the one to replicate the Erie's success. Overly ambitious projects were initiated, massive public works schemes that would penetrate every corner of a state. Hundreds of miles of line got under way in the mid-1830s. Work began on enlarging the Erie Canal in 1834. The State of Virginia invested more money in the James River & Kanawha Company the following year, initiating a two-decade cycle in which almost 200 miles of canal would be constructed. In 1836, Pennsylvania put another 225 miles of canals under contract, and Ohio initiated the construction of 194 miles of lateral lines. Not to be outdone, Indiana authorized $13 million in loans for internal improvements in what became known as the "Mammoth Internal Improvements Bill."[13]

All this development required unprecedented investment. As many of the new ventures were run by public agencies, state governments footed much of the bill. Even private companies found it relatively easy to prime the public pump. States could not assume the entire burden, however, and canals became increasingly dependent on domestic and, especially, foreign money markets. Most of the capital financing this expansion came from the sale of state bonds, which were bought by large financial institutions, domestic and foreign, for resale to smaller investors. For the period 1835 to 1840, foreign loans provided 90 percent of the funds invested in U.S. canals, which prompted domestic financial institutions to purchase canal bonds for resale abroad. When these markets tightened in the late 1830s, however, domestic banks recoiled from investments in long-term canal bonds.[14]

Unfortunately, burgeoning construction with its associated financial commitment was soon followed by the panic of 1837 and the ensuing depression, a prolonged crisis that spanned the Atlantic and froze the flow of capital into public works. Canal bonds survived the tightening of the London money market in 1836–37, but the collapse of 1839 undercut their value. A number of states defaulted on their foreign-held canal debts and it became virtually impossible to get further loans. With the financial tap turned off, most states resorted to issuing scrip or notes in an effort to keep construction flowing, but this only prolonged the agony. Construction ground to a halt, and there was a general suspension of works by 1842, with contractors and labourers left high and dry.[15]

The depression staggered, then stopped canal building. The effects were a little more muted on Eastern public works, as construction was usually more advanced and state governments had more financial resources and better credit. Still, virtually all work was eventually suspended. The Erie Canal enlargement slowed in 1839 and was suspended in 1842, not

13 Segal, "Cycles of Canal Construction" (see Ch 2, n. 9 above), 192–94.
14 Ibid., 180.
15 Taylor, *Transportaion Revolution* (see Introduction, n. 12 above), 344–45; Segal, "Cycles of Canal Construction"(see Ch 2, n. 9 above), 194–201.

to be resumed until five years later. In order to continue construction, Pennsylvania issued "relief notes" in 1841, which by the following year were circulating at an extreme discount. In 1842, the legislature ordered all work on the Erie and North Branch extension stopped immediately, causing much hardship among the contractors and their men. The James River & Kanawha Canal Company was forced to issue $730,000 in post notes in 1839. Three years later, the state authorized a loan so the company could pay off its short-term debts and redeem the notes. In return, the company had to mortgage all its property to the state Board of Public Works, which ruined the canal's credit and interrupted work. In Canada, the Cornwall Canal began experiencing problems in 1837, but the commissioners kept work going by paying with scrip. Regardless, construction slowed and the labour force shrank, with work finally halting in 1839. The Chambly Canal in Quebec and the Trent in Ontario also stopped in their tracks. Unlike the situation on U.S. canals, work would resume on Canadian public works, as the Imperial government gave the colony a £1.5 million loan guarantee, a Board of Works was established in 1841 and a five-year plan adopted.[16]

The impact of the depression was more resounding in the Midwest where states were dangerously overextended with their grandiose public works schemes. Ohio began having problems selling its bonds in 1837, and the canal board stopped payments to contractors on all public works except the Wabash & Erie extension.[17] By April 1838, it had been four months since payments had been made to the contractors on the extension, and they were forced to take loans in useless notes from Michigan banks. It was reported that "a state of unparalleled distress to the businessman and to the labourer, has come upon us. The poor can purchase no provisions with the trash that their necessities have compelled them to receive, and the men of business have been obliged to suspend operations entirely."[18] Some contractors were forced to declare bankruptcy and adandon their sections, which then had to be re-let at higher prices. "The embarrassments to the contractors, resulting from a failure to make any regular payments, are peculiarly severe," reported the canal commission. "Their operations are always necessarily

---

16 Whitford, *History of the Canal System* (see Ch. 3, n. 57 above), v. 1, 159–69, 181; [Harrisburg] *Pennsylvania Telegraph*, 27 July 1842; Wallner, "Politics and Public Works" (see Ch. 3, n. 10 above), 214–15; Dunaway, *James River and Kanawha Company* (see Ch. 1, n. 38 above), 134–42; Ellis, "Labourers, Contractors, and Townspeople" (see Ch. 4, n. 5 above), 2–3; Passfield, "Waterways" (see Ch. 2, n. 7 above), 117–19.

17 William Wall to Alexander McConnell, 24 March 1837, OH/CC; Ohio Board of Public Works, Minute Books, v. 2, 199 (13 May 1837), Board of Public Works Papers, Ohio State Archives; Sam Maccracken to J. G. Bates, 13 May 1837, Canal Fund Commission, Letterbooks, Board of Canal Fund Commissioners Papers, Ohio State Archives; Maccracken to L. Ranson, 15 May, 1837, ibid.; Scheiber, *Ohio Canal Era* (see Ch. 2, n. 67 above), 124–26, 144.

18 *Maumee* [City, Ohio] *Express*, 7 April 1838.

based upon the expectation of prompt payment, and they are compelled to use their credit from estimate to estimate, for their ordinary expenditures for labour and provisions." Nor did the future look very bright. "Few, if any, have capital of their own sufficient to carry on their contracts any great length of time, and any failure to supply them with means, destroys their credit with the capitalist, the farmer, the merchant, and the daily labourer. These in their turn suffer under the same evil." This report seemed to have little effect, as regular payments were still not being made as late as 1841, and only two payments were made on time the following year.[19] Contractors were owed nearly $1.4 million in 1842. From March of that year, payments for both past and future work were made in treasury checks redeemable in "Domestic Bonds" of the state, but these checks rarely were redeemed because they were discounted 30 to 50 percent. In 1843, it was reported of the Wabash & Erie extension that for "the last fifteen months there has not been one dollar, in money, paid to contractors on this canal," and that as a result the state was indebted to "all classes of its citizens – the labourer, the farmer, the mechanic, and the merchant." Nonetheless, many contractors persisted because their investment in the completed portions would have have lost if they had abandoned the work. In 1844, the state issued an additional $210,000 in bonds, enough to pay contractors' last arrears and stabilize the canal debt.[20] Ohio weathered the storm without defaulting on its loans, thus upholding its fiscal responsibility to its corporate debtors, but not to its builders, who were paid late, if at all, and in devalued scrip. In turn, contractors were forced to pass this paper on to their workers. The situation was actually worse in other Midwestern canal-building states.

There were capital shortages on Indiana canals almost from their inception. In 1834, it was noted of the Wabash & Erie that there was "much distress on the line for cash, and it was so much needed to lay in provisions and pay hands."[21] Work was hit by the panic but struggled on into the summer of 1839 until the crash of the Morris Canal and Banking Company, the chief source of funds for Indiana's canals. The Board of Internal Improvements ordered a halt to all construction except a stretch of the Wabash & Erie. Indiana bonds were being sold at 50 percent and the distressed contractors were owed over $700,000. The state assembly authorized an issue of $1.5 million in treasury notes to pay off contractors,

19 *Second Annual Report of the Board of Public Works of the State of Ohio* (Columbus, 1839), 11–12; *Fourth Annual Report of the Board of Public Works of the State of Ohio* (Columbus, 1841), 12; *Fifth Annual Report of the Board of Public Works of the State of Ohio* (Columbus, 1842), 14.
20 *Annual Report of the Auditor of the State* (Columbus, 1842), 32–33; *Sixth Annual Report of the Board of Public Works of the State of Ohio* (Columbus, 1843), 13–14, 19 (quotation), 24–26; Scheiber, *Ohio Canal Era* (see Ch. 2, n. 67 above), 153–58; Robert Lanimore to William Spencer, 23 Jan. 1843, Ohio Board of Public Works Correspondence, Ohio State Archives.
21 D. Burr, Samuel Lewis, J. B. Johnston to Messrs. Linton, Sullivan and McCarty, 28 Feb. 1834, Canal Fund Commissioners Letter Book, 1832–1834, Wabash & Erie Canal, IN/II.

but these notes eventually circulated at discounts of 10 to 60 percent and some merchants refused to accept them.[22] The chief engineer, without authorization, issued printed notes, so-called White Dog scrip based on the security of the federal lands granted to the canal. In 1842, "Dog" was initially selling at only 10 to 12 percent below par, and was "the best & safest funds we have except in bank paper," but soon was worth only half its face value.[23] "We have a very gloomy prospect before us now for canaling," wrote an official in 1843. "Our script is down to $\frac{1}{2}$ the face or less, and I do not know what will be the result. The farmers and millers are refusing it for provisions, etc." By 1849, the Canal Land Office would not take White Dog.[24] Quite clearly, builders and canallers were left with considerably less than they had earned. This caused contractor failures and much privation among the hands. Speculators came in offering hard cash to labourers for the notes at such depreciated values that the real value of some workers' wages fell to $3 a month. Yet Indiana's attempt to pay for public works with promises was all for naught, as the state defaulted on its bond payments in 1841 and the next five years. The 1841–42 assembly disbanded the Board of Internal Improvements and invited private companies to complete the abandoned projects. In 1846, the Wabash & Erie was placed under the control of a board of trustees operating in the interests on investors.[25]

A similar fate befell the Illinois & Michigan Canal, which suffered financial problems almost from the opening of construction in 1836. The Illinois state bank suspended specie payment in May 1837, soon followed by all other financial institutions. The Board of Works was late in its payments to contractors, who rolled back wages from $26 to $22 in June 1837 (sparking a stoppage of work and attacks on contractors' property and tools, during which one worker was fatally shot). The payment of the March 1839 estimate virtually exhausted the treasury, and the state was unable to pay either in April or May. Contractors were alarmed and the labourers, "apprehensive of losing their wages, if they continued to work without security, grew restive and threatened to leave the country." The contractor was paid by certificates of indebtedness, but "could not divide it among his many creditors embracing his labourers, mechanics, farmers, drovers and merchants." A "rapid decline of confidence" was the natural

22 *General Laws of the State of Indiana* (Indianapolis, 1841), 199–200; *General Laws of the State of Indiana* (Indianapolis, 1842), 33, 41; *General Laws of the State of Indiana* (Indianapolis, 1843), 33.
23 Lewis G. Thompson to W. L. Thompson, 15 March 1842, Lewis G. Thompson Letters, Indiana Division, Indiana State Library; C. Carter to E. F. Lucas [26 July 1844], Aborn Collection, Indiana State Library; Memo of 8 April 1845, Ewing Papers, Indiana Division, Indiana State Library; Nathan Ross to W. G. Ewing, 10 Feb. 1845, ibid.
24 J. W. Wines to Elizabeth Wines, [c. 1843?], Charles James Worden Family Papers, Indiana Division, Indiana State Library; J. L. Williams to Col. T. W. Blake, 9 Jan. 1849, W&E/COR.
25 Fatout, *Indiana Canals* (see Ch. 2, n. 10 above), 98–106; Poinsatte, *Fort Wayne During the Canal Era* (see Ch. 3, n. 64 above), 71; Shaw, *Canals for a Nation* (see Ch. 1, n. 12 above), 140.

result. Subsequently, the Canal Commission issued scrip in denominations of $1 to $100 due on the state bank in ninety days. Workers were paid in part with this scrip, which was accepted at par for some time but inevitably depreciated.[26] The canal fund was exhausted by early 1840, but contractors agreed to take $1 million in canal bonds at face value and bear the discount. The bonds were disposed of at 83 percent and work straggled on, but labourers' suffering became acute. Many had been thrown out of work, and those with employment were paid in scrip selling at 50 percent by June 1841 and depreciating. Workmen were disappearing, many to Chicago where they became a burden on relief agencies, but some used their scrip to purchase canal lands and set up as farmers along the line.

In 1842, the state bank failed and all work was suspended. The next year, the governor arranged a $1.6 million loan with canal property, its tolls and revenues being used as security. Construction of the canal was to be overseen by three trustees, two representing bondholders and one the state, to remain in control until debts were paid.[27] Construction resumed two years later, with many of the old contractors taking up their sections. All was not right, however. Builders were still being paid with scrip and were grumbling. "Although the drafts which they have rec.ᵈ at the last payment are *nominally* above par, they have been compelled to sell them for any kind of trash that the merchants or brokers chose to give them," reported the chief engineer. "They cannot pay their debts to the labourers and farmers in drafts, and an advantage is, of course, taken of their necessities. . . . Contractors will take *any thing* that they can pay out, but the community is suffering by the present system."[28] Thus the financial problems of the canal were not mere business concerns, but had social effects; shock waves rippled out from the epicentre, staggering the state, undermining contractors, jarring local merchants and farmers, and fissuring the land beneath labourers' feet.

This brief synopsis of the depression's impact on the main canal-building states underlines the fundamental problems within the industry. But, while governments could worm their way out relatively unscathed, individuals were less lucky. Contractors went broke, lost their livelihood and fled the line. Labourers went hungry, lost their jobs and turned on each other or turned out against contractors and canals, as the experience of workers on the C&O will show.[29]

26 *Fourth Annual Report of the Board of Commissioners of the Illinois and Michigan Canal, 1839* (Springfield, 1840), 6–10; Fleming, *Canal at Chicago* (see Ch. 6, n. 57 above), 128, 140–47.
27 *A Law to Provide for the Completion of the Illinois and Michigan Canal . . . Passed February 20th, 1843* (New York, n.d.); Fleming, *Canal at Chicago* (see Ch. 6, n. 57 above), 163–67, 180–83.
28 William Gooding to William Henry Swift, 20 Feb. 1846, Swift Papers, Chicago Historical Society; Fleming, *Canal at Chicago* (see Ch. 6, n. 57 above), 212–14.
29 Of course, the experience on public works was not unusual, as the depression struck all sectors of the economy. Samuel Rezneck many years ago documented its crushing impact on business and labour; Alexander Keyssar noted that unemployment was pervasive in Massachusetts during these years, but

Crisis on the C&O

Construction of the Chesapeake & Ohio Canal was officially opened on the Fourth of July, 1828, with John Quincy Adams presiding. Before turning the first spadeful of soil the President prayed that God "would have in his holy keeping all the workmen by whose labours [the canal] is to be completed. That their lives & their health may be precious in his sight, and that they may live to see the work of their hands contribute to the comforts and enjoyments of millions of their countrymen."[30] Unfortunately for the object of this benediction, neither the words of so eminent a supplicant nor the intervention of God proved adequate to the task of keeping them from harm's way. Most failed to see the culmination of their labours more than twenty years later, having moved on or succumbed to the dangers of their profession. The intervening years were eventful.

The C&O experienced at least ten significant disturbances and virtually continuous labour unrest between 1834 and 1840, necessitating the state militia to be called out five times and federal troops once. Such sustained militancy and swift state suppression, unique at this time of American economic development, was indicative of something more than mere ethnic hostility, although usually involving Irish workers. The struggle was rooted in the organization of work common to canal building – its methods of financing, work management, labour recruitment and discipline, and the nature of work and consequent living conditions. This organization was unhinged on the C&O by economic problems that emerged virtually from the beginning of construction. The struggle was expressed in tried-and-true cultural forms, however, with workers often warring among themselves. But increasingly the conflict was turned to class ends, ultimately pitting workers against the interests of contractors and company. Management's response was hinted at early on when the directors petitioned the Maryland General Assembly in 1830 for a police force to be established on the line to protect the canal's rights and property from injury by an unruly workforce.[31] While unsuccessful in this case, a dialectic of protest and repression was repeated throughout the 1830s. Played out in the workplace, labourers' shanties and villages that dotted the canal, this conflict periodically burst out in violence. Nascent labour organizations directed riots and strikes, while the capital responded with military intervention and legal prosecution. The C&O was the inheritor of the Potomac Company, which had built a series of locks and short artificial waterways in the early Canal Era

was ameliorated by the survival of other economic options within the "precapitalist social order," such as access to a family farm. The experience of canallers, however, suggests that they had few alternatives, and consequently their suffering was magnified. Rezneck, "The Social History of an American Depression, 1837–1843," *American Historical Review*, v. 40 (July 1935); Keyssar, *Out of Work* (see Ch. 4, n. 29 above), 32–35.

30 *Bedford Gazette*, 25 July 1828.
31 C&O/PRO, 19 Oct. 1830 (B 206).

(1785–1802), but had been all but dormant for the previous two decades. The new company's plans were on a much grander scale: following the Potomac into the heart of the Appalachians, crossing the mountains to join the Ohio River system at Pittsburgh and thereafter the Mississippi. Like other large interregional projects, the C&O was a massive business concern for its day and was dogged by chronic shortages of capital and labor. Although it relied heavily on the sale of bonds in the domestic and foreign money markets, the bulk of financing came from the Maryland state government, which the company had to repeatedly beg for infusions of money as original investors dropped out and increased contract prices drove up costs. The company repeatedly hit the jackpot in this period, receiving a $2 million loan in 1835, a $3 million stock subscription the next year and another $1.65 million loan in 1839. Nonetheless, the company hovered on the brink of insolvency throughout the 1830s, as it continually fell behind in payments to contractors and was often forced to issue scrip to keep going.[32]

The proposed canal route was divided into sections and opened to tender. Company policy was to accept the lowest responsible bid, which placed great pressure on contractors to cut their estimates to a minimum as keen competition for contracts prevailed; the first letting of thirty-four sections in 1828 received almost five hundred proposals.[33] This system forced bids down and created a situation in which luck as much as skill was required for contractors to complete their sections at a profit. They were never far from insolvency as a result, a situation exacerbated by the mode of payment common to public works contracting. Builders were paid on a month-to-month basis according to their established scale of prices, minus 20 percent which was retained by the company to ensure good faith and completion of work. In continual crisis throughout the 1830s, this system broke down during the depression. As the company's financial problems increased, their ability to pay on schedule declined. Lee Montgomery, Methodist preacher and contractor at the Paw Paw tunnel, complained that a man "in the Imploy of the company is doomed to distress and distruction and when Ever there is a pressure in the money market it is to fall with all Its sad consequences on the contractors."[34] When debts grew too large to be redeemed by future construction, contractors often fled the line, abandoning their contracts and leaving their creditors and unpaid workers to scramble for whatever property and outstanding money was left behind.

32 Segal, "Cycles of Canal Construction" (see Ch. 2, n. 9 above), 192–94. The company first issued scrip in April–May 1834 ($128,705 worth of 4% interest-bearing notes payable in one year). Again, during the specie suspension crisis of 1837, it issued $436,513.50 of notes in denominations of 25¢ upwards. *Report of the General Committee of the Stockholders of the Chesapeake and Ohio Canal Company* (Washington, 1839), 34–35.
33 C&O/PRO, Report, 10 Sept. 1828 (A 68–69).
34 Lee Montgomery to George C. Washington, 21 Jan. 1839, C&O/LR.

During the 1830s, the workforce fluctuated between two and five thousand. Some German workers found their way onto the canal in the 1830s, and natives worked there as well, but for the most part canallers were Irish. Riots and strikes waged by these navvies, while fuelled by ethnic tensions, usually derived from the wage relationship and what it represented: a means of subsistence. For these labourers, relatively steady work and prompt payment of wages were keys to survival. Organization among workers was aimed at establishing and protecting these principles. When they were violated, labourers organized to restore the tenuous balance of subsistence. It is not surprising, then, that most labour unrest of this period was sparked by nonpayment of wages, and was directly attributable to the system's shifting of the company's financial problems through contractors onto the shoulders of those least able to sustain the burden.

Labourers on the C&O lived a hand-to-mouth existence, adequate in normal times but with a too-thin margin of subsistence to withstand shocks to the industry's unstable payment structure. To protect themselves and their own in such crises, to assert their right to subsist, they banded together and sought to establish a certain amount of control over the workplace and relations with their bosses. The Irish secret society acted as their model for mobilization. Such organizations, first appearing in Ireland during the late eighteenth century, were rooted in the breakdown of traditional social and economic relations and governed by a traditional code, the basic premise of which was the right to subsistence. Communally based, loosely organized, bound by oaths, with a leadership drawn from within the peasant community, secret societies used terror to achieve their ends. These organizations were, in effect, primitive syndicalist organizations, which, while not class-conscious, were keenly aware that their interests differed from those of the expropriating gentry and middle classes and their agents.

Clandestine organization among workers was a continuing phenomenon on the C&O during the late 1830s. Neither formally structured nor unchanging, organizations lay dormant, then mobilized for specific grievances. Their ephemeral character reflected the rhythms of class struggle, periods of dynamic tension punctuated by explosive conflict. On one level, the secret society's presence was continuous, if elusive, and marked by highly personal conflict with contractors and other labourers. This violence entailed an effort to dominate allocation of contracts and jobs, the basis of subsistence, and in effect constituted a claim of control over the labour process. On another level, these organizations fought directly with the C&O and, beyond, the state. Conflict took the form of mass protests against nonpayment of wages, and entailed an assertion that the company was ultimately responsible for labourers on the canal. Organization among the workers proved a thorn in the side of the company, undermining its authority, interfering with construction and damaging its property.

Resident engineer Thomas Purcell maintained that "a regular organization" lay behind the January 1834 faction fight near Williamsport. Another engineer, George Bender, reported in 1836 that the area around Hancock was "the seat of a regularly organized society of these desperadoes." "The Society," he continued "is believed to be but a branch of one in the City of New York, and that it has branches in all the States where internal improvements are in progress." In 1838, Charles Fisk, the C&O's chief engineer, complained of "a tyranical, secret, party organization, which for the last two years has been entirely beyond the reach of all law, all authority." And a secret society was held responsible for the 1839 attack on German workers near Little Orleans.[35]

These "associations or banded confederations" were based on point of origin in Ireland and were "banded together with pledges of brotherhood, and have their secret signs and pass words."[36] As well as pursuing their factional feuds, they increasingly influenced production concerns. Through threats, vandalism and beatings, the society sought to establish workplace authority by chasing off contractors and labourers who resisted its will. Their sin usually was having taken a contract or jobs the society wished for its own men and sympathetic contractors. Action was a result of specific grievances and tactics were direct. According to Bender, "the moment any one of the affiliated feels aggrieved, he lays his case before the meeting, who forthwith decree the measure and mode of punishment." Offenders would first be warned to change their conduct or to leave the area. In November 1836, a notice posted on the office door of Lee Montgomery, contractor at the Paw Paw tunnel, warned:

we give ye a civil notice Concerning your Manager Mr. James Reynolds that you will discharge him out of your employment so that it will save us Some trouble for coming here a distance . . . any Laboring man that will work under the said James Reynolds let him mind the consequence hereafter. Any carter that works his carts under the said Reynolds let him mind it also for I give them all a fair notice that I will come with stronger forces the next time and when they will not be aware of it . . . if Reynolds leaves the tunnel in 6 or 8 days time after this notice [there] will be no more trouble.

Reynolds's crime was that he had testified against Irish workers who rioted on the Baltimore & Ohio Railroad in 1834. In July 1838, notices again were posted at the tunnel demanding that two bosses leave the line. "These notices," wrote Fisk, "are not idle threats."[37]

As warned, noncompliance with demands led to violence. Contractor

---

35 Purcell to Ingle, 23 Jan. 1834, C&O/LR; George Bender to Washington, 17 Nov. 1836, ibid.; Report of Charles B. Fisk, Chief Engineer, in reply to the Enquiries of the Commission of Ways and Means of the House of Delegates of Maryland, 5 Feb. 1838, ibid.; George W. Haller and G. W. Reid to Col. C. M. Thurston, 24 Aug. 1839, Pitchlynn Papers, Gilcrease Museum.
36 *Hagerstown Herald of Freedom*, 25 Sept. 1839.
37 A copy of this notice is enclosed in George Bender to Washington, 17 Nov. 1836, C&O/LR; Fisk, 3 July 1838, ibid.

William Brown was notified by a placard that he and his men must quit the work. When he refused, he complained that "about twenty men wantonly came and burnt down my office and stable which I had built for the purpose of prosecuting the Work Immediately and also destroying my tools and grain that I had purchased for my horses with threats that it would be renewed if I would procede any Further." The chastened Brown asked that his contract be declared abandoned so he could leave the line. Another contractor, John Daily, neglecting a like notice, had his carts and tools thrown into the river and was compelled to quit under a threat of death. A builder named Tracy also was told to quit the line. Ignoring the warning, he was first beaten, then one night an attempt was made to set afire the shanty in which he and a priest were conversing. The two, perhaps by the grace of God, managed to escape.[38]

Nor were labourers who questioned the local society's authority spared. Those working sections reserved for members of the dominant faction, and employees of disliked contractors, would be told to leave the line. "The penalty of a non-compliance by the labourers with these notices," George Bender wrote, "is usually a midnight beating, which in many cases causes death." The employees of contractors Brown and Tracy, receiving such notices and knowing the penalty, fled the canal. Halting work in this way opened jobs for favored labourers, and the societies' reach ensured that victims would not speak out. "Not one individual of the large body of Irish labourers along the line of Canal dare testify against another of their number in a court of Justice," complained Chief Engineer Fisk, whose stewardship of construction would be frustrated repeatedly by the societies. "A murder may be committed. A hundred of them may witness it. And yet not one person can be found who knows anything about it."[39]

These terrorist tactics must be seen for what they were: mad scrambles for job security nurtured by a climate of impending unemployment on a canal that was one of the first to experience the funding problems that would eventually bring the industry to its knees. Workers realized that control of the labour force was their most potent weapon in dealing with contractors and the canal company. By culling out unwanted workers, canallers sought to create an artificial labour shortage, drive up wages and impose their conditions on the line, a fact not lost on the company. "This state of things alone I know has been very instrumental in keeping up the high prices of labor upon our canal," opined Fisk. "Its effects are felt in several ways. It keeps down the supply of labor below the demand. It gives us an inferior class of workmen – and afraid to give them directions contrary to their will, – the contractor is sometimes to all intents and

38 George Bender to Washington, 17 Nov. 1836, C&O/LR; Peter Ritter to Ingle, 23 May 1836, ibid.
39 George Bender to Washington, 17 Nov. 1836, C&O/LR; Fisk, 5 Feb. 1838, ibid.

purposes under their control."[40] The underlying motive for navvies' direct action could not be clearer. While wages on the C&O were no higher than on competing canals, and, at least until 1838, natural labour shortages were equally responsible for their levels, it is clear that labour organization did play a role in keeping them at predepression figures throughout the 1830s. Only when the bottom fell out of the industry was the secret societies' grasp loosened from the work site.

Prodded by rising costs, in part resulting from labour's actions, some contractors sought to evade the societies' grip on the canal by using non-Irish labourers. These initiatives were dealt with summarily. Unexpected, in the middle of night or out of the misty dawn, Irish workers would descend on "Dutch" (German) hands, beating, pillaging and driving them from the line. In April 1836, for example, a workforce of German and "country borns" was attacked and dispersed by Irish hands. And it was a vicious assault on German workers in August 1839 that sparked the ultimate crackdown on the secret societies.[41]

While attacks on non-Irish workers were fuelled by ethnic animosities, the combustible material they fed on was concern over a continued income. As Carey argued in 1833, canallers crawled along the razor edge of subsistence, dependent on regular employment and prompt payment of wages to make ends meet. Families, on the line or in nearby cities, had to be fed and clothed. Money had to be set aside for the inevitable lost days and stretches of unemployment. In this light, it is not surprising that labour's most ambitious initiatives involved income issues.

In the late 1830s, while workers in the cities' developing industries were defeated and disorganized, labourers on the C&O (as on other canals) achieved a level of sustained militancy. Several times, they protested nonpayment of wages. Brushing aside the company's claims that contractors, as employers, were responsible, the men seized sections of the canal, halted construction and threatened to destroy their handiwork if the C&O did not make good their back pay. Such threats to property could not be tolerated. The company repeatedly called in the military to suppress disturbances and purged the line of militants with a blacklist, but these attempts to cow labourers into submissiveness failed. Eventually, following another disturbance among the hands, worker communities were levelled and labour leaders imprisoned. Plagued for a number of years by recalcitrant workers, the company would strike to reassert its authority.

The C&O labour record sounds like a litany of violent unrest. Several months after the January 1834 riot near Williamsburg, rival factions of

---

40 Fisk, 5 Feb. 1838, ibid.
41 References to "Dutch" workers almost certainly meant Germans, the word being a corruption of *Deutsch*. G. M. and R. W. Watson, [15] Feb. 1837, ibid.; M. Guth to Chas. B. Fisk, 13 Aug. 1839, Pitchlynn Papers, Gilcrease Museum.

Irish labourers were again at each other's throats near Point of Rocks, coupled this time with an attack on German workers. Seemingly also sparked by job concerns, the disturbance resulted in one to three fatalities and was put down by the militia. In early February 1835, labourers struck for higher wages and operations were interrupted for fifteen days, until a troop of horse and a company of riflemen drove them back to work. Eleven months later Corkonians warred with Longford men at Clear Spring. Two shanties were burned and several of the combatants severely wounded. Irish navvies again struck in the spring of 1836. Dutch and native workers were driven from their jobs, and work was interrupted before the discontented men left the line and an uneasy peace was restored. During this turnout, several contractors kept construction going by using "scab" labour, and their sections were the target of secret society attacks later in 1836. One of the offending contractors, Lee Montgomery, became a key figure in the ensuing conflict.[42]

Montgomery had previously built a tunnel 729 feet long on Pennsylvania's Union Canal. At the time of the turnout, he had just been chosen to oversee the mountain tunnel at Paw Paw, the most daunting section on the canal, requiring a cut through 3,118 feet of solid rock. Manpower, hand tools and gunpowder were to move this mountain, and years of blasting lay ahead with men at times working night and day. As each foot slowly receded, however, so did Montgomery's fortunes.[43] One man could not be expected to bear such a project's costs, and Montgomery was chronically short of capital. In the end, his men suffered. Wages were frequently late and work periodically ground to a halt. It was not surprising that most labour disputes centred on the tunnel, as the situation there epitomized labour relations in canal construction.

In the spring of 1837, Montgomery imported forty miners from England, both for their skill and to keep the Irish from his section. Already stigmatized as an employer of scabs, Montgomery struck a raw nerve among the Irish with his importation of English workers. His need of unskilled labourers forced him to hire Irish in the end, however, and almost immediately they began scaring off the English, so that only two remained by June the following year.[44] In the interim the tunnel had become a powder keg of labour unrest. Irish navvies mixed uneasily with the English, and there was increasing job competition from men thrown out of work on the suspended

42 *Niles' Register*, v. 46, p. 291 (21 June 1834), v. 47, p. 429 (21 Feb. 1835), v. 49, p. 337 (16 Jan. 1836); Purcell, 5 Feb. 1835, C&O/LR; C&O/PRO, 9, 25 Feb. 1835 (D 234, 256–57); George Bender to Ingle, 8 May 1836; C&O/LR; Sanderlin, *Great National Project* (see Ch. 1, n. 69 above), 119–20.
43 Hahn, "The Paw Paw Tunnel" (see Ch. 5, n. 26 above), 25. The Board accepted Montgomery's bid before they had adopted a plan and specification for the tunnel, which undoubtedly contributed to his continuously running over budget. Ingle to George Bender, 16 March 1836 (C 255–56), C&O/LS.
44 H. M. Dungan to Fisk, 13 May [1837], C&O/LR; Fisk to George Bender, 15 May 1837, ibid.; Fisk, 23 June 1838, ibid.; *Ninth Annual Report of the President and Directors of the Chesapeake and Ohio Canal Company* (Washington, 1837), 8.

transportation projects of other states. Finally, Montgomery's chronic money problems reached a crisis point in the winter of 1837–38.[45] The fuse was set, the charge ready to blow.

The year 1838 came in with a bang. On New Year's Day, four hundred tunnellers, unpaid for a month, flocked to Oldtown, twelve miles upriver, looking to ring out the old and ring in the new in fitting fashion. They ransacked several buildings before the militia rode in from Cumberland and incarcerated ten ringleaders. Chief Engineer Fisk hoped jailing their leaders would break the societies, and the prisoners' release without prosecution, he felt, only undermined the civil authorities and fomented further disorder.[46] In reality, continued nonpayment of wages guaranteed persistent unrest.

As late as March, the company had not paid January's estimate to the contractors, and February's was past due as well. "The distress among the Contractors and labourers is alarming," reported George Bender.[47] The situation at the tunnel was worse still. Wages were two months in arrears and violence again threatened. Montgomery, in no position to pay the men and fearing for his safety, retreated to Washington where he remained in late March. The hands were excited by his continued absence and by reports that another contractor had absconded one night on the western stage (leaving $5,000 in debts). They were not willing to await the mere possibility of payment, and "threats were held out by the men that they would destroy certain parts of their work" if they did not get their just dues. On 12 February they surrounded the office at the tunnel and threatened to wreck the completed works. An observer cautioned that "if Mr. M[ontgomery] appears again at his work without the pecuniary means necessary to satisify the just claims of his workmen for *labour done*, there is reason to believe that his life itself would not be safe from these exasperated men." Disorder persisted for two to three days until the men were pacified by a company agent who promised Montgomery would soon have the money. In fact, Montgomery was unable to pay his men until mid-April, when the company advanced him $25,000 and raised his prices.[48] Nonetheless, things cooled down at the tunnel. Meanwhile, things were heating up downriver at Prather's Neck, near Clear Spring.

Contractors David Lyles and Daniel Cahoon had been experiencing financial

45 *Ninth Annual Report of the Chesapeake and Ohio Canal Company* (Washington, 1837), 10; *Tenth Annual Report of the President and Directors of the Chesapeake and Ohio Canal Company* (Washington, 1838), 6; Ingle to Anson Bangs, 20 Dec. 1837 (D 242), C&O/LS; Ingle to Fisk, 21 Dec. 1837 (D 244), ibid.; Ingle to George Bender, 5 Dec. 1837 (D 236), ibid.
46 Fisk, 5 Feb., 23 June 1838, C&O/LR; Ellwood Morris to Fisk, 14 Feb. 1838, ibid.; Will H. Lowdermilk, *History of Cumberland (Maryland)* (orig. ed. 1878; Baltimore: Regional Publishing Co., 1971), 342.
47 George Bender to Washington, 4 March 1838, C&O/LR; Bender to Ingle, 5 Feb. 1838, ibid.; James McCulloh to Washington, 12 Feb. 1838, ibid.; Fisk to John G. Stone, 13 Feb. 1838, ibid.; William Gunton to Ingle, 12 March 1838, ibid.; Fisk to Morris, 15 Feb., 26 March 1838, ibid.
48 Morris to Fisk, 13, 14 Feb., 1 March 1838, C&O/LR; Fisk to Morris, 15 Feb., 26 March 1838, ibid.; Fisk to Washington, 15 Feb. 1838, ibid.; Washington to Ingle, 19 Feb. 1838, ibid.; Morris,

problems for some time. By 30 April, they were deep in debt for labour and supplies: Lyles over $27,000 and Cahoon $20,000. The former fled to Washington and the company declared his sections abandoned.[49] The workers who had already suffered through two months without pay earlier in the year were again caught in the middle. Idle for weeks, in debt to local farmers and merchants, many actually starving, the men were not willing to compromise. With Lyles gone from the line, they focused their anger on the company. They rejected the company's offer of 25¢ on the dollar for the money owed them by Lyles, "saying they must have all or none," and arguing that they had earned the money and it was the company's responsibility to see they were paid. "We have put this work together well," they warned, "We can take it down again."[50] In this way, the labourers cut through the niceties of contractual responsibility and blamed the company for their lost wages, for their hunger and want.

The C&O was defenseless and knew it. "It is vain to disguise it," lamented Bender. "We are in the laborers power; in one night they could destroy more masonry than would pay them in full twice over. Pay them in full, or pay not at all. Give them even 90 Cents in the dollars & the same feeling of being injured will remain, with less to restrain them from proceeding to extremities." He warned that "if they cannot feed their families, 'they *will* feed their revenge.'" Fisk was more concerned with the practicalities of preserving order, and made arrangements for troops to be called out in case of trouble. "But what shall be done? – here are 180 men – some of them half starved. All of them have been idle for three weeks talking over their grievances. Suppose a troop of horse [was] now on the ground – what could they do?" His answer to this rhetorical question did not offer much hope. "They must continue there until every man has left the ground and gone off . . . otherwise we should be as badly off the moment the force left as before – for it is the work of but a few minutes to do great damage."[51] In fact, Fisk was angling for his dream solution: a permanent military force on the line. The company, more concerned with the protection of their investment than the workers' rightful claims, shared this wish. Nonetheless it dallied, trying to force Lyles and Cahoon to some sort of settlement, and offering only promises or partial repayment to the workers.

21 Feb. 1838, ibid.; Morris to B. S. Pigman, 18 Feb. 1838, ibid.; Ingle to George Bender, 19 April 1838 (D 297), C&O/LS.
49 David Lyles, 20 Feb., 18 Sept. 1837, 6 Jan. 1838, C&O/LR; Fisk to Bender, 24 Feb. 1838, ibid.; Bender, 25 April 1838, ibid.; Release of Claims of David Lyles, 30 April 1838, ibid.; Release of Daniel Cahoon, 30 April 1838, ibid.; Ingle to W. Schley, 9 May 1838, ibid.; Ingle to Bender, 20, 30 April, 9 May 1838 (D 299–301, 315, 325–26), C&O/LS; C&O/PRO, 12, 16 April, 1, 2 May 1838 (E 389–91, 398–99, 401–03).
50 Fisk, 9 May 1838, C&O/LR (quotation); Schley to Ingle, 30 April, 7 May 1838, ibid.; Ingle to Schley, 9 May 1838 (D 323–24), C&O/LS; Ingle to Bender, 9 May 1838 (D 324–25), ibid.; Ingle to Fisk, 9, 11 May 1838 (D 325–26, 329–30), ibid.
51 Bender to Washington, 9 May 1838, C&O/LR; Fisk, 9 May 1838, ibid.

Unswayed, the men struck, seizing 140 casks of gunpowder from Lyles's stores and threatening to blow the locks up if they did not get their money. The engineer at the Neck asked General O. H. Williams, commander of the state militia, to muster the troops, but he reported that the citizen soldiers "positively refused to turn out" because they had not been reimbursed for their expenses the last time they rescued the company from disgruntled workers. In this, they could sympathize with the navvies. Some even went so far as to declare that if they turned out, they would "fight for the Irish." The troops, eventually lured out by assurances that their expenses would be met, marched to the canal and seized the gunpowder without incident. The militia officer reported that "the labourers on the Canal threaten no injury, but appear to be determined to keep possession of the works and to suffer no labour to be done thereon untill the matter is compromised between them and the company." A tense quiet ensued. Despite the fact that "they and their families [were] in a suffering and deplorable condition," the men were willing to be patient, believing that the company would make the contractors pay what they owed.[52]

Local citizens, also caught up in the C&O's web of debt, felt "excitement and prejudice against the Company" and sympathized with the labourers. Merchants extended credit to contractors working sections at prices below costs, and farmers fed hungry labourers and their families because they believed "the Company had withheld from the Contractors their just claims for services rendered, and that the labourers had, in consequence thereof, been deprived of the means of support, and that many families were in an actual state of starvation."[53] Eventually, Lyles and Cahoon reached an agreement with the company, out of which their men were paid.[54]

The frustrated company could not rest easy, however, as trouble was again brewing at the tunnel. Montgomery once more was experiencing money problems, his men were in an uproar and whatever discipline that existed had vanished. "The laboring men & miners have obtained, or very nearly so, the mastery," asserted Fisk. "There is unquestionably a regular conspiracy among the men to have the work carried on to their own liking. They permit no boss to remain, who endeavours to get full work out of them." And any who opposed their will were open to attack. "A boss who

52 Washington to O. H. Williams, 12 May 1838 (D 332), C&O/LS; William Price to Washington, 11 May 1838, C&O/LR; Williams to Washington, 16 (quotation), 17, 18, 24 May, 7 June 1838, ibid.; William H. Fitzhugh to Williams, 16 May 1838 (quotation), ibid.; T. Fillebrown to Ingle, 17, 19 May 1838, ibid.; J. Gore to George Bender, 16 May 1838, ibid.; Fisk to Ingle, 19 May 1838, ibid.
53 Williams to Washington, 16 May 1838 (quotation), C&O/LR; Fillebrown to Ingle, 19 May 1838, ibid.; Washington to Williams, 18 May 1838 (D 339–40), C&O/LS.
54 Fisk to Ingle, 19 May 1838, C&O/LR; Schley, Memoranda of terms of agreement, 24 May 1838, ibid.; Schley, 9 June 1838, ibid.; Fisk to Williams, 13 June 1838, ibid,; Ingle to Fillebrown, 23 May 1838 (D 344), C&O/LS. It is not exactly clear what the workers got out of this settlement, but one offer to Lyles and Cahoon, at least initially rejected, stipulated the hands would received 75% of their wages. Washington to Williams, 19 May 1838 (D 341–42), C&O/LS.

had been but a few days upon the work, & who had been sent for expressly by the contractor on account of his fitness for the situation, was lately beaten by a gang of 20 or 30," the chief engineer recounted. "These fellows broke a leg and an arm merely because he was faithful to the interest of his employer and would not permit the men to trifle away their time." This was not an isolated case, as other bosses were regularly being threatened and abused. The failure to prosecute the January rioters at Oldtown had set a bad example, Fisk argued. "They fear no punishment. They dread none, and never will untill they are punished to the outmost rigor of the law when they are detected in crimes." This loss of authority on the part of the contractor drove up costs inevitably passed on to the company; for example, expenses had been twice what they usually were during May at the Paw Paw section. "As the work is now going on at the tunnel," Fisk maintained, "there is a complete waste of money – it is robbery – and I am satisfied that the tunnel cannot be carried through to completion at a reasonable cost without what will be equivalent to a military force being stationed near it."[55] Fisk did not get his wish this time but soon would.

The C&O acted on its own in lieu of a permanent military presence by drawing up a blacklist. The company president determined to make an "example" of the labourers, so that they would see "that they cannot practice impositions or commit disorders with impunity." Work at the tunnel was to be suspended and workers were to be dismissed; money was provided to Montgomery to pay them off. The whole line would benefit from the substitution of "more orderly and submissive labourers" for those now at the tunnel, and on 1 August a list containing the names of 127 prohibited workers was circulated among contractors.[56] The blacklist quite clearly was meant to extirpate combination among the workers. It succeeded in temporarily restoring peace, but proscription did not magically cause labour grievances to disappear.

Money-hungry builders could no longer get provisions on credit, as their inability to pay was notorious; meanwhile, their labourers were not being provided for or paid. It was said that "the men . . . are becoming unruly & negligent of their work, and the contractors are unable to discharge them for want of funds."[57] Montgomery, having no money for back wages, was

55 Fisk, 23 June 1838, C&O/LR.
56 Washington to Fisk, 28 June 1838 (quotation) (D 365–66), C&O/LS; C&O/PRO, 28 June, 18 July 1838 (E 450–51, 463, 466–67); Fisk to Montgomery, 29 June 1838, p. 41, Letters Sent by the Chief Engineer, series 209, NA/RG79; Fisk, 3 July 1838, C&O/LR; Notice from Chief Engineer's Office, signed Charles B. Fisk, 1 Aug. 1838, ibid. Included in the blacklist were four "bos miners," thirteen miners and two blacksmiths, indicating that skilled workers played a role in labour organization along the canal.
57 Martin Phelan to Washington, 1 Jan. 1839, C&O/LR; M. C. Sprigg to Fisk, 29 Nov. 1838, ibid.; Sprigg to Ingle, 23, 28 (quotation) April 1839, ibid.; T. Cosley, 25 Jan. 1839, ibid.; L. Montgomery, 12 Feb. 1839, ibid.; James Taylor, 22 Feb., 11 March 1839, ibid.

unable to get rid of his hands.[58] At this point, the company held $30,000 in retained percentage on Montgomery's work and was two months in arrears, upwards of $20,000, on payment of his estimates, but this did neither him nor his workers any good. In May 1839, he had to lay off most of his men because he did not have the means to buy essential gunpowder. Fisk reported that the idle miners and labourers joined with other workers and "have been marching up & down the line, three or four hundred in number with arms, threatening & using violence when opposed by those peaceably disposed." The company prevented trouble from escalating only by issuing state-guaranteed bonds and using these as security on a loan to pay off the two monthly estimates past due.[59]

This was only a temporary solution, and contractors were soon again desperate for cash. Prospects were gloomy for all concerned. Public works in other states had been shut down, throwing thousands of labourers out of employment. This had a temporary beneficial effect for company and contractors by solving labour shortages and driving down wages, but, as there was little money to pay labourers anyway, the company could not really take advantage of the favourable market. By August, the C&O was debating whether to suspend parts of the work or to cut the number of hands employed, and maintenance crews were cut to a minimum in October.[60] C&O workers desperately sought to solidify their hold on the canal with their characteristic solution of driving off competing workers.

As was often the case, problems were magnified at the tunnel. Montgomery, repeatedly in need of cash, was receiving advances from the company almost monthly but never enough to keep his men happy.[61] It was against this backdrop of general economic malaise, labour surplus and very immediate financial problems that the Irish tunnellers acted. On 11 August 1839, about a hundred armed hands left the tunnel and moved downriver to a work camp near Little Orleans. There, they "entered the Shantee's of the Contractor and Labourers," who were German, "and beat and wounded them very much." One labourer thrown into the fire died as a result of his burns, prompting the German priest, Father Guth, to confess

58 Fisk, 26 May, 3, 30 July 1838, C&O/LR; Fisk to Fillebrown, 30 July 1838, ibid.; Montgomery to Washington, 11 July, 27 Dec. 1838, 21 Jan. 1839, ibid.; Ingle to Fisk, 9 Aug. 1838, ibid.

59 Montgomery to Washington, 23 April 1839, C&O/LR; Fisk, 4 May 1839, ibid.; Sprigg, 20 May 1839, ibid.; Ingle to Thomas Phenix, 9 May 1839 (E 215), C&O/LS; Ingle to Sprigg, 18 May 1839 (E 221), ibid.; C&O/PRO, 15, 22 May 1839.

60 *Tenth Annual Report of the Chesapeake and Ohio Canal Company* (Washington, 1838), 6; Montgomery, 26 June 1839, C&O/LR; Fisk, 16 Aug. 1839, ibid.; George Johnson to F. Thomas, 2 July, 12 Aug., 21 Sept. 1839, ibid.; D. Dougherty to Thomas, 3 July 1839, ibid.; William Lockwood to Thomas, 23 July 1839, ibid.; Sprigg to Ingle, 16 Aug. 1839, ibid.; Thomas Perry, 1 Sept. 1839, ibid.; Ingle to Fisk, 28 Aug. 1839 (E 331), C&O/LS; Ingle to John Y. Young, 5 Oct. 1839 (E 369), ibid.

61 C&O/PRO, 15, 29, 31 May, 3 July, 7, 28 Aug. (F 53, 62, 67–68, 83, 92, 96–97); Fisk, 16 Aug. 1839, C&O/LR.

of the Irish, "were I superstitious I would realy believe they are incarnate Devils." The tunnellers then reportedly marched up the river, broke into farmhouses and shanties and threatened anyone in their way. Local magistrates called out the militia and it descended on the troubled area.[62]

This rapid response did not entirely silence the canallers, however. Militia officers reported that "the cry of murder is heard almost every night, but no Contractor, or even any of the Labourers, hearing the same, dare put his foot out of the door to render the least assistance; for should any do so, their lives would be in imminent danger." As late as the end of September, a Hagerstown newspaper reported that "the line of the Canal from Oldtown to the South end of the Tunnel, has been, for some time past, the scene of the most savage and barbarous outrages." A secret society was believed to be behind the disturbances. The officers "learned that there is a well organized society among the *Fardowns* or *Longford* men, and that they are well disciplined in the use of their arms; and from their movements, appear to have their officers to command." The society also was said to have a war treasury "to give bail for any of their party, who may be taken." As a result, it was virtually impossible to get incrimating evidence, as "no Contractor can appear against them, without abandoning his work; nor dare a Contractor even discharge one of the men, without incurring the displeasure of all his comrades." The *Herald of Freedom* insisted: "They are banded together with pledges of brotherhood, and have their secret signs or pass words." And pity those that should cross them, as "at a moment's warning, a leader will march, perhaps with 100 men, and in the most lawless manner, attack any of the other party, or any inoffending citizen against whom any prejudice exists."[63]

The degree of organization among canallers may have been exaggerated, but the extent and duration of this particular outbreak, lasting almost six weeks and bringing construction to a standstill, was a true measure of worker dissatisfaction with conditions on the C&O. Striking out at German labourers was both an acting out of ethnic hostility and an attempt to secure more jobs for members of their own faction. The use of terrorist tactics also cowed contractors into submission, forcing on them a code of labour relations that served the interest of workers. In short, the Irish on the C&O had achieved a certain amount of workplace control. It was a situation that the company could no longer tolerate if it wished to stay in business.

Chief Engineer Fisk used the occasion of the August attack to attempt

62 John R. Brook and Jacob Reel[?] to Williams, 15 Aug. 1839, Pitchlynn Papers, Gilcrease Museum; M. Guth to Fisk, 13 Aug. 1839, ibid.; Haller and Reid to Thurston, 24 Aug. 1839, ibid. Also *Washington National Intelligencer*, 24 Aug. 1839; *Hagerstown Herald of Freedom*, 25 Sept. 1839; *Niles' Register*, v. 57, pp. 37–38 (14 Sept. 1839).
63 Haller and Reid to Thurston, 24 Aug. 1839, Pitchlynn Papers, Gilcrease Museum; *Hagerstown Herald of Freedom*, 25 Sept. 1839.

once and for all to root out the pernicious influence wielded by canallers. At the first outbreak of violence, the militia had descended and for the next five days was engaged in sweeping the line, rather indiscriminately, of rioters and weapons. Working from a list provided by Father Guth, they arrested about thirty alleged ringleaders, shooting about ten resisting men in the process, one fatally. At Fisk's direction, the troops also destroyed workers' shanties and levelled grog shops, the ultimate source of disorder in company eyes. Thirty to fifty buildings in all were torn down, many reportedly belonging to innocent individuals.[64] This destruction of property sparked a public outcry, and a successful lawsuit was launched by those workers' whose property was destroyed.[65]

Fisk had always been frustrated by an unwillingness to drag rebellious canallers through to the end of the legal process. In the past, prisoners had been released from jail after the line had been quieted, soft treatment which he believed fostered conflict and effectively yielded authority on the canal to the secret societies. He was not going to make the same mistake this time. The jailed labourers were to be prosecuted to the full extent of the law. Assistant engineers were instructed to gather evidence against the leaders who had been jailed. Fisk placed a labour spy, James Finney, among the workers to ferret out information that could be used against the secret societies, perhaps the first instance of a practice that was to become a common tool of employers. On the strength of Finney's testimony and Guth's list of rioters, fourteen labourers were convicted on charges ranging from riot, robbery and arson to assault with intent to kill, and were sentenced to the state penitentiary for from five to eighteen years. Nine, convicted on lesser charges, were punished by fine and imprisonment, while four were acquitted. Finney eventually received $100 for his service to the company.[66]

Even this did not satisy Fisk. Following up a petition made to the company by a number of contractors, he proposed that a system of police be

---

64 *Washington National Intelligencer*, 31 Aug., 3, 5, 9 Sept. 1839; *Baltimore Sun*, 4 Sept. 1839; *Niles' Register*, v. 57, pp. 37–38 (14 Sept. 1839); M. Guth to Fisk, 13 Aug. 1839, Pitchlynn Papers, Gilcrease Museum; William Grason to Williams, 18, 24 Aug. 1839, ibid.; Williams to Thurston, 20, 24, 27 Aug. 1839, ibid.; Thurston to Williams, 24, 25 Aug. 1839, ibid.; Haller and Reid to Thurston, 24 Aug. 1839, ibid.

65 The owners of the destroyed property, claiming that they had not been involved in the riots and were law-abiding citizens, appealed to the County, which brought suit against Fisk and two militia officers, Col. Thurston and Col. Hollingsworth. The court decided that they had exceeded their authority, and rendered a judgement of $2,737 against them. The defendants appealed to the company and the state for relief but were refused. C&O/PRO, 9 Nov. 1839 (F 118); Ingle to Fisk, 25 May 1840 (F 141), C&O/LS; Ingle to Thurston, 25 May 1840 (F 142), ibid.; Williams, *History of Washington County* (see n. 3 above), 233; Baird, "Violence Along the Chesapeake and Ohio Canal" (see Introduction, n. 11 above), 131–32.

66 Fisk to Charles Randolph, 3 Sept. 1839, C&O/LR; Fisk, 31 Oct. 1839, ibid.; *Baltimore Sun*, 4 Sept. 1839; *Hagerstown Herald of Freedom*, 25 Sept., 30 Oct. 1839; *Niles' Register*, v. 57, p. 68 (28 Sept. 1839); Baird, "Violence Along the Chesapeake and Ohio Canal" (see Introduction, n. 11 above), 129–31. For the information on Finney, see C&O/PRO, 6 Nov. 1841 (F 405).

established along the line.[67] Only in this way, he argued, could order be preserved. In truth, Fisk was asking for a permanent coercive arm for the company, a unit designed to swoop down on workers at the first sign of trouble. Secret societies would be rendered impotent by the presence of a standing army and, at last, contractors and company could operate without hindrance. A police force was the only solution, as the governor had at the height of the insurrection ruled out stationing a permanent militia troop on the canal. Not only would order be restored but the presence of such a force would, according to Fisk, "have the effect of reducing the wages paid for labor, (and which have been extravagantly and unreasonably High.) – fully twenty per cent below what they would otherwise be."[68]

Fisk did not get his police – this would only be achieved on Canadian canals in the next decade – but in many respects he did get his wish. The swift and savage repression of the August disturbance and the harsh prosecution of labour leaders – in effect the irresistible wedding of capital and state – temporarily destroyed organization among the Irish and undermined what power they had acquired. As a result, wages fell from $1.25 to 87.5¢ a day in the aftermath.[69] The threat of labour militancy was everpresent, however. This fact was brought home in 1840 when the governor pardoned those labourers imprisoned for the August 1839 riot. Within days, there were reports that some of these men had returned to "their old haunts." A contractor complained that one had visited his section, "threatening him with violence and destruction of property."[70] Fisk must have shuddered at the thought of renewed strife, but he had nothing to fear as the depression was overtaking the industry.

Turning the screw on workers did not solve the company's financial problems. Contractors still clamored for money the C&O did not have. Severe financial problems forced it to cut back on construction and the number of labourers employed. Scrip was issued in September 1839 in an effort to keep work going, but the company was almost $3 million in debt and the future looked bleak. Work faltered, contracts were declared abandoned, and the labour force dwindled. Some contractors were "compelled to turn their cattle at large, as the only means of a precarious subsistence." Unemployed men straggled off to find work elsewhere. In 1841, there were

67 C&O/PRO, 14 Oct. 1839 (F 113); Fisk, 31 Oct., 7 Nov. 1839, C&O/LR.
68 Grason to Williams, 24 Aug. 1839, Pitchlynn Papers, Gilcrease Museum; Col. C. M. Thurston to Williams, 24 Aug. 1839, ibid.; Williams to Thurston, 27 Aug. 1839, ibid.; Fisk, 7 Nov. 1839, C&O/LR.
69 Baird, "Violence Along the Chesapeake and Ohio Canal" (see Introduction, n. 11 above), 132; *Thirteenth Annual Report of the President and Directors of the Chesapeake and Ohio Canal Company* (Washington, 1841), 9. Of course, this drop was also influenced by the depression and greater availability of labour, but these market forces could only have an unhindered effect after the removal of labour control of production.
70 Proceedings of Stockholders of the Chesapeake and Ohio Canal, 21 July 1840 (B 370–73), NA/RG79.

only six or seven hundred men on the line when construction finally came to a standstill (with a game Montgomery employing a hundred of them).[71] Periodically, work was renewed, only to peter out. The C&O finally reached Cumberland, Maryland, far short of its envisioned Ohio River terminus, in 1850.[72]

The organization canallers had built up on the C&O thus was broken down by economic rhythms more than by the "union-busting" techniques of the company. But, as Fisk warned, only a permanent military force stationed on the line could have ensured rapid completion of the work. The chief engineer clearly grasped the essence of secret societies. They were labour organizations, admittedly limited in scope and parochial in vision, but geared to issues born of productive relationships and formed in the workplace. The only way to eliminate labour's evil influence and to restore the company's authority was to coerce workers into submission. This lesson was learned and put to good use on Canadian canals in the 1840s.

Promoters of the Chesapeake & Ohio Canal dreamed of breaching the Appalachians and drawing the trade of the Ohio Valley down the Potomac, at the same time opening up America's hinterland to the civilizing influence of the East. This great public work was thrust on the shoulders of labourers, largely Irish. They slogged in the mud realizing other people's dreams, and too often did not receive the pay they had coming. The C&O never made it beyond Maryland, and the navvies who held up construction and inflated costs in the 1830s were partly responsible.

As unskilled immigrant workers engaged in casual employment, canallers' experience of class conflict differed from that of most industrial workers. They were dependent on public works with more water in their stocks than in their canals, projects characterized by volatile labour demands. Their grievances were driven by claims to subsistence. Without an artisanal tradition to provide a basis of resistance, canal labourers relied on their shared ethnic heritage to impart a sense of community. Irish workers

71 Jno. Dougherty, 15 Oct. 1839, C&O/LR; William Lockwood, 17 Oct. 1839, ibid.; Philip Gormley, 23 Oct. 1839, ibid.; Sprigg, 14 Nov. 1839, ibid.; Enos Childs to Thomas, 25 Sept., 26 Nov. 1839, ibid.; Fisk, 28 Dec. 1839, 21 Jan. 1840, ibid.; C&O/PRO, 28 Aug., 4 Sept., 14 Oct., 9 Nov., 28 Dec. 1839 (F 95–97, 112–13, 119–20, 137–38); *Thirteenth Annual Report of the Chesapeake and Ohio Canal* (Washington, 1841), 9–13, 18 (quotation); *Fourteenth Annual Report of the President and Directors of the Chesapeake and Ohio Canal Company* (Washington, 1842), 3–4.

72 *Thirteenth Annual Report of the Chesapeake and Ohio Canal* (Washington, 1841), 9–13, 18; *Fourteenth Annual Report of the Chesapeake and Ohio Canal* (Washington, 1842), 3–4; *Eighteenth Annual Report of the President and Directors of the Chesapeake and Ohio Canal Company* (Frederick, Md., 1846), 25; *Nineteenth Annual Report of the President and Directors of the Chesapeake and Ohio Canal Company* (Frederick, Md., 1847), 3–4; *Twentieth Annual Report of the President and Directors of the Chesapeake and Ohio Canal Company* (Frederick, Md., 1848), 9; *Twenty-First Annual Report of the President and Directors of the Chesapeake and Ohio Canal Company* (Frederick, Md., 1849), 6; *Twenty-Second Annual Report of the President and Directors of the Chesapeake and Ohio Canal Company* (Frederick, Md., 1850), 4–7; Williams, *History of Washington County* (see n. 3 above), 216; Sanderlin, *Great National Project* (see Ch. 1, n. 69 above), 158.

perpetuated the ritualized internecine fighting common in Ireland, but, as in the old country, tribal clashes masked class conflict. Workplace issues, involving the nonpayment of wages, regular employment and control of the labour market, led to worker organization. The Irish secret society, born of exploitation in the homeland, acted as a model. From the crude materials at hand, brawn, brotherhood and the threat of violence, navvies for several years were able to assert some control over their lives. Inevitably, the labourers would be ground down into the mud by dint of military and judicial might. Canallers' fierce resistance to wage labour's inherent exploitation, their wedding of ethnic forms to class struggle, the divisions within their ranks, and the state's ultimate repression of militancy would fuse on public works during the next decade when a worsening of conditions within the industry made the situation even more inflammatory than it had been on the C&O and elsewhere during the 1830s.

CHAPTER 8

"This new order of things": the 1840s–1850s

So all you young labouring heroes get ready and come away,
And sail to the sweet land of freedom where no poor rates or taxes to pay
It's there that the dollars are plenty, employment without any fail,
You'll have beef and mutton for dinner, instead of your coarse Indian meal.[1]

Writing in 1843 at the height of labour unrest on Canada's canals, Charles Atherton, the superintending engineer of the Lachine Canal, attributed the violence to "the delusive expectations which Emigrants have been led to form in leaving their native Land." Rather than moving onto the soil as farm labour, "yielding the natural remuneration of *food*, with *moderate* wages in cash," they opted for work that offered "temporary high wages payable in Coin. Hence their misery, for the highest rate of wages to be earned at a temporary Public Work, is but poor compensation for a wandering life. Poverty & discontent are the natural consequences of such an error." While misleading about the amount of opportunity available, Atherton was nonetheless clear on life in canal construction. "Public Works are demoralizing at best, & should . . . be carried on as far as possible by the local population, & be regarded as the mere *helping hand*, not the *dependence*, of the Emigrant." A more sympathetic Lewis Drummond, Member for Portneuf, agreed that immigrant labourers were poor and dependent. "They were to have found continued employment, and been enabled to acquire means to purchase property of their own," he chastised Canada's Legislative Assembly in 1845. "They expected to meet with good treatment and what treatment had they met with? – With treatment worse than African slaves, with treatment against which no human being could bear up." To some canallers, slavery provided a fitting analogy for their condition. In the midst of a strike in 1847, Illinois & Michigan workers petitioned a canal trustee ("an independent American, who should abhor

---

1 From "A New Song on the Irishmen Now Going to America," in *Irish Emigrant Ballads and Songs*, ed. Wright (see Ch. 2, n. 2 above), 534.

oppression in Any form") to address their complaints, "So as not to have white Citizens Drove Even worse than Common Slave Negroes."[2]

Despite their different emphases, Atherton, Drummond and the I&M workers all condemned conditions on public works. Massive unemployment, shrinking income, a rootless workforce, poverty, vice and crime, ethnic rioting, strikes, and the repeated need to resort to military intervention to keep the lid on this boiling kettle – all this made it clear that something was wrong. Problems that began emerging in the 1830s reached their apex in the mid-1840s. Though conditions would brighten later, the bloom was definitely off canal building. As the industry began to wind down, class lines became more sharply drawn and conflict became commonplace. Though these changes were largely played out in Canada, they were by no means exclusively Canadian phenomena but symptoms of maturing capitalism as seen from within one industry.[3]

The rationalization of production and the gestation of a free labour system had been ongoing from the beginning of the Canal Era but were accelerated by the depression, which had created the necessary conditions for the complete transformation of the industry: the general abandonment of construction in the United States and the resulting labour surplus. There was a dramatic deterioration of conditions for wage workers, who lived in a world of vicious job competition, falling wages, increased unemployment and heightened privation. Gone was the paternalistic relationship between builder and hands, the provision of food and shelter, the shared jigger and the promise of work. Now the canaller was a truly "free" labourer, working when he could strictly for wages, buying his housing and provisions on the market, regularly confronted with unemployment. The situation had worsened by the early 1840s to the point that labourers were more dependent on public works, and the promised mobility of free labour – from job to job and up the skill ladder – was growing more illusory. If not slaves, they were all but bonded to harsh conditions of exploitation. This decline was measured by the monopolization of jobs by Irish workers, the "white niggers" of early industrial development, a process begun in the 1820s and by now virtually complete. Canaller had become worker in the worst sense

2 Charles Atherton to Major General Sir James Hope, 29 March 1843, Lachine Riots (see Ch. 3, n. 53 above); Drummond abstracted in *Debates of the Legislative Assembly of United Canada*, ed. Elizabeth Gibbs (Montreal: Press de I'Ecole des Hautes Etudes Commerciales, 1973), v. 4, pt. 2, 1460; The Petition of the undersigned Labourers To Honourable Col. Oakley, Resident Trustee on the part of the state of Ill. for the Ill. & Michigan Canal, 12 July 1847, Swift Papers, Chicago Historical Society. The petition was signed by sixty-one labourers.

3 Grace Palladino found a very similar pattern of experience in the Pennsylvania mining industry. Economic inequality grew from the 1830s, as wages declined, provision costs rose, more work was expected from miners, labour surplus became the norm, and the truck system emerged. By 1860, miners were highly exploited and socially excluded, and class conflict was clearly evident. Palladino, *Another Civil War: Labor, Capital, and the State in the Anthracite Regions of Pennsylvania 1840–68* (Urbana: University of Illinois Press, 1990), 38, 44–47.

of the word. It was a status that with greater frequency they united to resist.

The industry

Most of the construction in the 1840s took place in Canada. Lines in the States had been pushed into extinction, hibernation or retrenchment by financial problems associated with the depression. They would revive later in the decade, though on a reduced scale. The industry in Canada experienced the same financial problems, but had been insulated from the worst effects as work had already been tailing off when hard times set in. Still, the depression meant canal construction as a whole shrank.

While the economics shaping the industry were supranational, the Canadian setting had an important impact on the industry in these years. An imperially controlled colonial government, the Province of Canada was more willing to direct public works from the centre. With the support of London, it was able to reopen construction during the depression. This contrasted with the U.S. federal government, which let the states go their own way and suffer the consequences of their financial dealings. Canadian political culture also was more conservative than that of the United States. This meant a greater willingness to intervene on canals, either to succour the workers when they were suffering or, more often, to beat them down militarily when they were disorderly. By comparison, U.S. governments rarely helped out canallers, and state militias were used less often and with less sense of purpose. These national differences were only a matter of degree, but the problems within the industry were magnified on Canadian canals because construction was pushed through the depression. The Canadian experience thus gives a clearer picture of how the industry was transforming. Public works were the biggest arena in which capital and the state joined ranks at this time, and Canadian centralism solidified the union. This wedding made for a firm but rarely positive response to the problems experienced on canals during the 1840s–50s. Out of a situation marked by the deteriorating conditions of workers and the growing desire of the state to police the industry would emerge early examples of the repressive tactics of the corporate state that would dominate labour conflict later in the nineteenth century.

A new order arose in the canal construction industry during the depression. By the time survivors began to reemerge in the mid-1840s, responsible finance was the watchword. Canals took pains to be more fully involved in construction, ensuring that work was done to specification, on time and within budget. Gone was the laissez-faire atmosphere that had given contractors a relatively free hand. Greater scrutiny of operations was needed because public works continued to experience financial problems throughout the 1840s, in part a debt hangover from earlier indiscretions but also a result of their tarnished reputations as investment opportunities. A number of U.S. states that defaulted on their canal loans had their canal commissions replaced by boards of trustees composed of watchdog representatives of creditors to ensure frugality. In Canada, a Board of Works, created in 1841, consolidated power from local commissioners who had unsatisfactorily directed construction in the past.[4] Increased management supervision and the professionalization of contracting were two prevailing trends within the industry's drive to become more efficient.

Essential to this managerial activism was the engineer, always an important link in the chain of production but now having added duties. The engineer was not only a quality-control expert but was expected to be directly involved in labour discipline. By keeping an eye on contractors to make certain that they were paying the men regularly and fairly and that they were not providing alcohol or running a store, engineers sought to head off labour unrest and ensure unhindered production. When trouble developed, they mediated or, as a last resort, called in the troops. The engineer was now more clearly a middle-management figure in a growing operational bureaucracy with technical, administrative and disciplinary functions. To workers he offered a place of appeal against their employers, but it was a source of dubious justice as his interests were specifically those of capital. Management specialization had the effect of attenuating the connection between those who worked and those for whom they ultimately worked, making the industry less responsive to personal interests and more attuned to the economic stimuli of the market.

Contracting was also "rationalized" in these years. Now striving to be fiscally responsible, canals placed a greater premium on known respectable contractors rather than local farmers and lawyers with time on their hands or fly-by-night builders. As contracts were still awarded by competition and larger firms tended to be more efficient, or at least had enough capital to withstand short-term downturns, they tended to get the more desirable jobs. The "unprofessional" were shut out or relegated to the margins, often as subcontractors, living off the scrap jobs and defaulting when things went wrong. In effect, the petty builder was going the way of the indentured worker.

In the past a contractor was more a master builder who shared the work and living experiences of his men, and often a common ethnic background. With only thirty to a hundred employees, he most likely knew them all by name. By providing food and shelter he participated in an exchange that,

---

4 Shaw, *Canals for a Nation* (see Ch. 1, n. 12 above), 140, 145; Doug Owram, "'Management by Enthusiasm': The First Board of Works of the Province of Canada, 1841–1846," *Ontario History*, v. 70 (Sept. 1978), 171.

while never equal, was reciprocal and personal, and into which questions of custom and character entered as well as dollars and cents. This exploitation bore a familiar face and was shrouded in the shared sweat of labour and rough-and-tumble shanty life. But by the 1840s, the contractor was commonly a professional builder-businessman living off the canal or at least at a distance from the squalid shanties. He had probably followed the trade for quite a few years and had moved from project to project.[5] Instead of tens, contractors now were more likely to employ hundreds, like John Whitlaw with 500–800 hands on the Chambly Canal and Scott & Shaw who had 1,200–1,500 on the Lachine.[6] On an even grander scale, there were a few huge firms, often with international interests and a number of projects dispersed at great distances from headquarters.

Some bigger contractors let out sections of their work to subcontractors, a practice that became much more common. With bids cut to the bone already, they took out their profits before passing work along, and subcontractors had to scrape for their living. Such problems led canal officials to frown on subcontracting, but it remained common even though prohibited by some lines. Subcontractors were in much the same position with regard to their employees as builders of old, but were squeezed even more by the economics of construction and did not have the wherewithal or inclination to maintain a facade of paternalism as most builders had in the past. As with contractors, their relationship with their hands was now purely commercial.

Both contractors and subcontractors sought to further distance themselves from the workplace by delegating authority. The actual direction of construction often was left to hired overseers and foremen who supervised gangs of labourers, a management tactic pioneered by early canal companies but later rendered superfluous with the shift to contracting. Overseers either directed specific processes within production such as masonry, quarrying and carpentry, or they superintended entire sections. In this latter capacity they assumed the role of contractor with many of its associated duties and worries (excluding capital costs), while still remaining employees. Authority would be further delegated to foremen or gangsmen who had direct control of the workers. Use of foremen (as in later factories) was an attempt to assert greater control over the labour process, while relieving owners-employers of direct supervision. As the contractor withdrew further from the point of production something was needed to fill the vacuum. Most foremen probably were promoted workers, the appointment rewarding

5 For example, by the time George Barnett was working on the Illinois & Michigan in the mid-1840s, he had been a contractor for over twenty years in Canada, Pennsylvania and Ohio; John Black had been in the business for sixteen years in Pennsylvania, building canals, railroads and dams before ending up on the Beauharnois. *Report of the Majority of the Board of Trustees of the Illinois and Michigan Canal* (Washington, 1847), xxxvii, 9, Evidence of George Barnett in Appendix Q; Deposition of John Black (No. 7), "Beauharnois Report" (see Introduction, n. 3 above).

6 Deposition of John Whitlaw (No. 27), "Beauharnois Report" (see Introduction, n. 3 above); Scott & Shaw to Hope, 31 March 1843, Lachine Riots (see Ch. 3, n. 53 above).

skill or loyalty.[7] These individuals kept an eye on work, made sure men were not slacking and policed the shanties after hours. In effect, they took the place of the small builder, a fact reflected in the ratio of foremen to workers, which was about the same as earlier had existed between contractors and hands.[8] Their most important function was the right to hire and fire. Favoured hands worked regularly at the better jobs, and those out of favour or not known were used when needed and abandoned when not. As with earlier contractors, there were good and bad foremen. Some used their powers to develop a leadership position among the men, catering to their needs, likes and dislikes, drinking with them, and even sharing hostility to contractors. There were some indications that such "worker" foremen were involved as leaders in factions and secret societies, again as builders had been before them. Others were company men, driving labourers at work, hiring and firing for petty reasons, or practicing plain brutality. Not surprisingly, such foremen were a source of canallers' anger.[9]

A complete reordering of the canal construction industry was occurring as a result of the changing capital and labour markets. Management was growing, becoming more bureaucratic and taking a keener interest in the actual process of construction. The engineer assumed an enlarged role as operations executive protecting interests of management. Contractors, caught between the grindstones of management and competitive forces, became bigger business concerns – partnerships instead of individuals and companies rather than partnerships – and intensified management strategies by subcontracting or hiring overseers and foremen. Where before there had been builder and men, there now could be contractor, subcontractor, superintendent, overseer, foreman and worker, a much more complicated labour relationship with a vast distance between top and bottom. Contractors also sought to cut costs by lessening the wage bill, a policy made possible by labour surplus. The builder no longer had to provide for all of his workers' needs or to hire by the month as a hedge against labour shortages and the need for competent men. He now could pick and choose hands when he wanted for as long as he wanted, and let them look to their own needs. The jettisoning of subsistence responsibilities by contractors facilitated increasingly impersonal relations of production.

7 That senior workers likely staffed this post appears to be suggested by the ethnic makeup of foremen on the Lachine Canal in 1843, where there were twenty-nine Irishmen, seven Scots, six *Canadiens*, and five Englishmen, more or less reflecting the workforce composition. List of the Foremen employed by the Contractor on the Lachine Canal, 25 Feb. 1843, Lachine Riots (see Ch. 3, n. 53 above).

8 For example, on a section of the Beauharnois there was a foreman for every thirty-five to forty hands, while there was an average of one for every twenty-five workers on the Lachine in 1844. Deposition of Patrick D. Cummin (No. 21), "Beauharnois Report" (see Introduction, n. 3 above); Return of the Number of Mechanics, Labourers and Horses employed on the Lachine Canal, Aug. 31, 1844, Lachine Riots (see Ch. 3, n. 53 above).

9 Depositions of Patrick D. Cummin (No. 21), David D. Barry (No. 26), "Beauharnois Report" (see Introduction, n. 3 above); Wetherall to Killaly, 24 Feb., 1 April 1844, Lachine Riots (see Ch. 3, n. 53 above).

The St. Mary's Canal, built in the mid-1850s, exemplified the industry's growing scale and impersonality. The project was small in dimension – by passing the rapids in the St. Mary's River, which obstructed commerce between Lake Superior and the lower Great Lakes – but fraught with difficulty and ripe with economic promise. The St. Mary's really had more in common with future canal projects, being for large, lake-going ships rather than narrow boats, and its construction punctuated the transformation of the industry. This prized job was won by a company headed by Erastus Corning, owner of one of the largest American hardware concerns, who was just beginning to construct a railroad empire from his New York base.[10] The state of Michigan promised the company \$750,000 in land (granted to it by the federal government) in return for building the work, but Corning would not get title to the property until the job was done. Thus all expenses had to be drawn from capital reserves, and the finished canal would pass into the state's hands. Only a large, diversified corporation could participate in what amounted to massive speculation.

The St. Mary's was but another cog in Corning's money-making machine, and in place of direct supervision he appointed a superintendent to oversee his domain, which comprised (at its peak) 1,600 men, 100 horses, 25 cattle, 4 large cranes, 25 sail vessels, 4 chartered steamers and 6 barges, as well as overseers of excavation, stone quarrying, dredging and freighting, pier building, supply, carpentering and joining, lockgates, masonry, and so on.[11] All this was for a canal just one mile in length: quite a change from the days of shovels, barrows and a gang of men. A description of the works in operation on the canal suggests the new, factorylike scale of production.

The men upon it are as thick as bees, there being fourteen hundred in all, and the work is going on bravely. Everything seems to be like clock work. It is quite a little spectacle to see the contrivances they have for lifting and moving the ponderous masses, which form the face stones of the locks, the cranes and the pullies, and the little bits of railroads high up in the air, upon which the stone are moved to their places, after they are raised to the requisite height.[12]

In effect, a modern, multileveled bureaucratic organization was created, which shared many features with the railroad industry and required a hierarchy of managers to keep working. The distance between contractor and canaller had considerably widened, physically, economically and socially.

The net result of these developments was an alteration of the old order where petty builder lived and worked with his hands, partaking of rough

---

10 Corning was also an iron manufacturer, banker and land speculator, and had bought the Michigan Central Railroad in 1846. Neu, "The Building of the Sault Canal" (see Ch. 5, n. 68 above), 26–27; Dickinson, *To Build a Canal* (see Ch. 2, n. 14 above), Ch. 4.
11 *Lake Superior Journal*, 31 May 1855.
12 Ibid., 16 Sept. 1854.

shanty life. Within this arrangement class lines had been sublimated by shared experience and plastered over by paternalism. In the new order the wage relationship was laid bare as a commercial exchange. There was little pretense of commonality. Instead barriers were erected between worker and employer. They lived in different places, perhaps rarely met, were more likely to be of different ethnic backgrounds, and shared neither food nor the ubiquitous bottle. These diverging paths of experience merely marked the increasingly clear class lines, as the obfuscating layers of custom were pulled away to reveal starkly opposed interests. No longer was the contractor a fellow worker, but now a potential if not present enemy. As one observer noted in the wake of a particularly bitter strike on the Lachine Canal in 1843, the Irish labourers

look on a Contractor as they view the "middle man" of their own Country, as a grasping, money making person, who has made a good bargain with the Board of Works for labour to be performed; and they see, or imagine they see, an attempt to improve that bargain at their expense by giving them too low a rate of pay, or by compelling them to receive their wages in Store pay.[13]

The contractor's attitude altered as well, with workers being seen more as factors of production than individuals with personalities, needs and concerns, a new reality clearly revealed by two incidents on the St. Mary's. In the autumn of 1853, when the company withdrew its hands from the quarry on Drummond Island, it inadvertently left three men behind. One died while the other two survived on a sparse diet of acorns. That same winter, a party of workers was sent over the ice to an island with the understanding that they would be provisioned by steamship when the pack melted. They too were forgotten and had to live off the land for several weeks.[14] Castaways forgotten by all and "grasping, money making" middle men were the two poles of this new world. It was a magnetic opposition that energized class conflict in this period.

Free labour

The most important factor in the transformation of canal work was labour supply. Shortages persisted into the late 1830s, which meant comparatively good conditions for workers, but as the depression forced the closing or cutting back of construction and immigration increased, surplus labour became the norm. Even though projects were begun in Canada in the early 1840s, it was not enough to make up the difference: 7–10,000 jobs as opposed to about 30–35,000 five years earlier. Clearly many left the profession, but, with the situation the same in other industries, many desperately tried to hold on. There was a slight resurgence in demand later

13 Memorandum of Charles Wetherall, 3 April 1843, Lachine Riots (see Ch. 3, n. 53 above).
14 *Lake Superior Journal*, 1 July 1855.

in the decade as U.S. projects began reopening, and even a brief period of labour shortage occurred on Canadian canals early in the 1850s, but glut was the common reality in the declining years of the industry.[15]

When canal construction reopened in British North America in 1842, workers flooded across the border, often with families in tow, collecting as pools of surplus labour near public works. They were joined by increasing numbers of immigrants, who tended to be worse off than before and had moved onto public works fresh from the boat.[16] Canada's canals could not absorb the numbers of labourers that flowed onto its work sites. The result was high unemployment and low wages. A correspondent for the *New York Commercial Advertiser* visiting the Welland Canal in 1843 unwittingly grasped the dynamics of labour relations in this period. "A more propitious time, it is believed, will never occur for such an undertaking – Labor is cheap, and enough hands are ready to take hold." But he also noted worker anger at the situation. "True, there is some little trouble to keep the laborers in a state of quietude for, while I was on the spot they made a demand of 'another shilling' to their daily pay, but it was resisted with firmness." With a note of admiration, he detailed the final prop to a pliant if not content workforce, something of which U.S. canal officials could only dream. "There is a large civil force on the line, which is first called on to quell any outbreak, and beside these there is a military force of two hundred men ready at a moment's notice."[17] Labour surplus, low wages, worker unrest and state repression: the situation on the Welland encapsulated the industry experience at this time.

The *St. Catharines Journal* reported in the summer of 1842 that "for several weeks past, hordes of Irish laborers from the state of New-York – where all public works have been suspended – have been pouring into this village and its vicinity, together with a large number of newly-arrived emigrants, in search of employment upon the contemplated improvements of the Welland Canal." Only one in ten could hope to find work as a result. That October, it was reported that the number employed at Broad Creek never exceeded 340 but that there were 900 men and 400 women encamped there. And the following April, the end of construction meant imminent unemployment for the 3,000 then at the Creek. This prospect worried the engineer, who saw that the majority of the workforce was too destitute to

15 Bleasdale, "Unskilled Labourers on the Public Works of Canada" (see Introduction, n. 11 above), 84–85, 102–03.

16 The extent of in-migration from the United States was attested to by John Ford, a labourer on the Beauharnois, who previously had worked two years on the Erie Canal and knew about two hundred who had done the same. Deposition of John Ford (No. 2), "Beauharnois Report" (see Introduction, n. 3 above). Of five Irish workers on the Beauharnois who identified their time of arrival in Canada, three had come within the last year and a half, one three years before, and one had been in the country seven years. Depositions of Martin Donnelly (No. 3), Thomas Reynolds (No. 4), Mathew Coogan (No. 5), Francis Dowd (No. 6), William Dowling (No. 8), ibid.

17 *Niles' Register*, v. 65, p. 131 (28 Oct. 1843).

leave and the rest unwilling, as there was no work elsewhere. In July 1843, 3,000 on the Welland were without jobs and in want; by the following January 10,000 men, women and children hunkered down along the line, with only 3,000 employed on a part-time basis.[18]

The situation was the same in Quebec. On the opening of the Lachine Canal improvement in January 1843, nearly 2,000 men descended on the line "all pleading poverty, & in most cases absolute destitution as their urgent claim for work." Contractors Scott and Shaw complained that "from the entire want of Work in the United States, as well as Canada, and the general depression of all kinds of business, men kept pouring into Lachine, until they were at least double the number we could employ on the Work, which does not afford space for over 1600 men." By March, it was reported that more than one thousand men were constantly seeking employment without success, and that up to five times as many labourers could be had if required. As a result, the men and their families were in dire straits. "Privations and suffering will every day be augmented that these poor men remain unemployed," predicted a local justice of the peace. Little had changed a year later, when 1,450 men, women and children lived on the Lachine, but only 150 hands were employed. "The great difficulty," reported the canal police magistrate, "will be how to get rid of the men who are not only without the means of living but without the wherewithal to move having contracted debts with the Storekeepers in this Place."[19]

As can be seen from these few examples, job security had declined on canals. In the past canallers most commonly were employed by the month, giving some security to workers. In the 1840s, day labour had become the norm, hands being hired when needed and dispensed with when not. Finding work for only a half-day or even a quarter-day was not unusual either. "I think on an average," hazarded Thomas Reynolds, a navvy on the Beauharnois, "healthy labourers who lose no chances of day's work, can get employment in two days out of three in Canal work during the year." William Dowling, a worker on the same canal, agreed that twenty days a month was the norm, but also argued that it was not unusual for hands to have only three to four days' work in a fortnight. These figures, of course, were for those lucky enough to get fairly regular employment. Martin Donnelly, another Beauharnois labourer, averaged just eleven days per month in 1842–43, making subsistence difficult. As Donnelly noted, "We only receive payment for the days during which we have been engaged in

18 *St. Catharines Journal*, 7 July, 11 Aug. 1842; Samuel Power to Thomas Begley, 17 July 1843, 1 Oct. 1842, 14 Feb., 20 March, 8 April 1843, Welland Canal Letterbook, PAC/RG43; Thorburn to Daly, 10 Jan. 1844, Welland Riots (see Ch. 6, n. 67 above).
19 Atherton to Hope, 29 March 1843, Lachine Riots (see Ch. 3, n. 53 above); Scott & Shaw to Maj. Gen. Sir. James Hope, 31 March 1843, ibid.; Copy of letter sent to *Montreal Gazette* from Henry Mason, 23 March 1843, ibid.; William Evans to H. H. Killaly, 16 March 1843, ibid.; Wetherall to Daly, 7 Feb. 1844, ibid.

labour." And whereas in the past the unemployed might move on to find work, prevailing unemployment made the prospect less likely, and navvies were reluctant to leave the promise of part-time work for the dubious hope of finding something more regular elsewhere.[20] Canallers were caught in the conundrum of the developing capitalist labour market: freed to sell their labour where they would, at times of economic downturn they found few buyers who wanted all of their product and were tied to the few places where it could only be hawked cheaply.

Contractors also exploited the labour surplus to lengthen the workday. As the decade opened, a twelve-hour day (6 a.m. to 6 p.m.) with breaks prevailed on Canadian canals, but was soon under assault. When supervision of construction on the Beauharnois shifted from the Board of Works to contractors in 1843, the day was extended by two hours (5 a.m. to 7 p.m.). This stretching of the day was an important issue in the general strike that gripped the line in June. Similarly, hands on the Illinois & Michigan Canal in 1847, forced to work fifteen and a quarter hours, struck in protest. And on the St. Mary's Canal in 1853, canallers struck for a ten-hour day as opposed to the prevailing eleven and a half hours they worked (with only a brief lunch break).[21]

Just as labour surplus naturally bred unemployment, underemployment and an intensification of work for those with jobs, it also led to declining wages and the complete ending of customary benefits. All prior points of contact between employer and employed were whittled down to a strictly monetary basis, the "dead hand of the past" cast off and the market's "invisible hand" quite palpably laid on. By 1840, monthly wages on the Illinois & Michigan Canal, which had stood at $26–40 in 1836 and $20 three years later, were down to $14. Labourers' wages on Canada's Cornwall Canal had fluctuated from 3s. 4d. to 4s. (roughly 67–80¢) a day in the mid-1830s, while workers on the Chambly Canal were paid from 2s. 9d. to 3s. 6d. (55–63¢) in 1840, from 2s. 6d. to 2s. 9d. the next year, and a flat rate of 2s. 6d. (50¢) in 1842. Although wages fluctuated throughout the 1840s, 2s. 6d. remained the average for day labour on Canadian canals.[22]

20 Depositions of Thomas Reynolds (No. 4), William Dowling (No. 8), Martin Donnelly (No. 3), "Beauharnois Report" (see Introduction, n. 3 above).
21 Depositions of John Whitlaw (No. 27), Martin Donnelly (No. 3), Thomas Reynolds (No. 4), John Black (No. 7), ibid.; The Petition of the undersigned Labourers To Honourable Col. Oakley, 12 July 1847, Swift Papers, Chicago Historical Society; Dickinson, *To Build a Canal* (see Ch. 2, n. 14 above), 63.
22 Robert Dale Owen to Alexander Osbourne, 19 April 1840, Robert Dale Owen Papers, Indiana Division, Indiana State Library; Fleming, *Canal at Chicago* (see Ch. 6, n. 57 above), 106–07; Borgeson, "Irish Canal Laborers" (see Ch. 3, n. 31 above), 42–44; Ellis, "Labourers, Contractors and Townspeople" (see Ch. 4, n. 5 above), Table 7; Scott and Shaw to Hope, 31 March 1843, Lachine Riots (see Ch. 3, n. 53 above); Joseph McDonald to Begley, 21 March 1843, ibid.; Wetherall to Killaly, 1 April 1844, ibid.; Depositions of Martin Donnelly (No. 3), Thomas Reynolds (No. 4), John Black (No. 7), John Whitlaw (No. 27), "Beauharnois Report" (see Introduction, n. 3 above). By comparison, Edith Abbott found that unskilled-labour wages in the United States fluctuated between

Thus, in these years pay generally fell to two-thirds of what it had been in the mid-1830s. Even at these depressed rates, wages compared favourably to manual work in general and were usually above local farm labour and day labour in the cities. But a number of factors conspired to make canallers' wages seem more advantageous than they actually were.[23]

The reality of declining income was exacerbated by the severing of a subsistence relationship between contractors and canallers. In the past, custom and the need to maintain a steady workforce compelled builders to provide room and board for their hands. But the paternalistic arguments for subsistence provision soon lost their persuasiveness when supply was no longer a worry. These protections were stripped away in the early 1840s and the labour relationship converted to a market basis, the contractor, if involved at all, acting only as a vendor of these services.

Some contractors still housed their hands, especially in wilderness settings like the St. Mary's. More often, builders charged rent if they provided housing. The going rate on the Beauharnois in 1843 was 5s.–7s. 6d. ($1–1.50) per month.[24] Some labourers boarded with foremen, as did John Ford on the Beauharnois, who paid 6s. a week for food, lodging, washing and mending.[25] Others with capital built their own shanty on land let from the contractor at a ground rent, 2s. 6d.–5s. ($.50–1.00) a month for a plot twelve feet square in 1843. They could also buy boards from their employer at £2 per 1,000 feet, the average quantity required for such a building. The finished shanty usually housed fifteen to twenty hands, each of whom would be charged a boarding fee by the labourer-landlord of 7s. 6d.–8s. per week (about three to four days' wages).[26] The contractor was now land speculator, slumlord and even lumber merchant as well as builder, and the caller was now a consumer of products as well as a commodity.

Builders also acted to end food subsidies once worker glut superseded dearth. Navvies were thrust onto their own resources and food became an expense that came out of their cash wages. Like lost housing, this amounted

79¢ and 95¢ during the years 1840–53. Abbott cited in Taylor, *Transportation Revolution* (see Introduction, n. 12 above), 295.

23 In March 1843, the contractors Scott & Shaw complained they were paying both ordinary and skilled workers twice what they received in Quebec City. Scott & Shaw to Hope, 31 March 1843, Lachine Riots (see Ch. 3, n. 53 above). As the "Beauharnois Report" made clear, however, these workers were employed on a much more regular basis in a city where provisions were cheaper and their family was more likely to find employment, making their wages comparable to or better than canallers'.

24 Depositions of Patrick D. Cummin (No. 21), Francis Dowd (No. 6), "Beauharnois Report" (see Introduction, n. 3 above).

25 Depositions of John Ford (No. 2), John Whitlaw (No. 27), Patrick D. Cummin (No. 21), David Barry (No. 26), ibid.

26 Depositions of John Ford (No. 2), of Mathew Coogan (No. 5), Francis Dowd (No. 6), John Black (No. 7), William Dowling (No. 8), Patrick D. Cummin (No. 21), John Whitlaw (No. 27), G. N. Brown (No. 18), ibid.

to a fundamental drop in real earnings. Contractors at times filled the subsistence gap by acting as storekeeper in the system of "truck pay," in which workers bought on credit at a store owned by their employer or his licensed merchants. Paid but once a month, canallers were often dependent on the contractor's shop for goods, as it was the only one near or willing to sell on credit. In some cases, as on Henry Mason's sections of the Lachine, hands would be issued pay tickets redeemable at the store.[27] Contractors sometimes argued that they made essential items available in isolated spots, nominally at cost, but workers believed they paid inflated prices for goods that used to be freely provided. Charles Wetherall, a police magistrate on canals and a member of the Beauharnois Riot Commission, maintained that contractors opened stores ostensibly in the interests of their workers, "but in reality, it is known to be a source of good profit, on which all the Contractors calculate". Having taken contracts at perhaps a low price, they sought to make money not in the business of construction but from providing for those who did the digging.[28] Some workers also claimed that the stores sold expensive goods they would not normally purchase. According to Thomas Reynolds, truck stores did not stock items "most suited to the means and habits of the laborers, such as oatmeal, eggs, potatoes, milk, fresh meat, &c.," but expensive goods like "bread, butter, tea, coffee, &c. . . . I have known many labourers who were obliged to eat bread three times a day, because they had no means of purchasing potatoes."[29] With even fair prices too high for a canaller's wage, it was not surprising that truck selling became a major irritant in labour relations.

The obvious problems caused by truck led the Board of Works to try to police its operation. At Broad Creek on the Welland Canal, contractors had been reported charging exorbitant prices at a company store, leading the engineer to include a clause in the next contracts giving the board power to regulate prices at contractor stores and close them if necessary. Truck resurfaced at Broad Creek in 1846, but the board was willing to leave it alone as long as goods were sold at fair prices and the men were paid in cash upon request. In 1843, the issue of truck payment contributed to a drawn-out strike on the Lachine Canal, with workers complaining of overcharging. This led to the outlawing of the system on the canal, and when contractors on one section reintroduced it the board moved in quickly. On the recommendation of the committee investigating the 1843 strike, store pay was prohibited on the Beauharnois. Yet such were its profits that truck kept reappearing. Wetherall argued that the only solution

27 Scott & Shaw, for Henry Mason, contractor, to Bethune and Kittson, 7 Jan. 1843, copy enclosed in Norman Bethune to Maj. MacDonald, 31 March 1843, Canal Papers, PAC/RG8.
28 Memorandum of Chas. Wetherall, 3 April 1843, Lachine Riots (see Ch. 3, n. 53 above).
29 Depositions of Thomas Reynolds (No. 4), Martin Donnelly (No. 3), Mathew Coogan (No. 5), "Beauharnois Report" (see Introduction, n. 3 above).

was for labourers to receive their pay in cash and to be free to spend it where they would.[30] Even where truck was not a problem or had been stamped out, the fact that canallers now had to purchase their sustenance rather than having it provided meant a significant erosion of income.

The cumulative effect of all these changes – high unemployment, lower wages, longer hours, and loss of subsistence rights – was a significant narrowing of opportunity for canallers. Even in the best of times life had been a struggle for those dependent on public works, as Mathew Carey made clear a decade before, but the situation grew grimmer in the early 1840s. All things considered, navvies at this time were earning about a third what they had in previous years; the contractor's provision of food and shelter had amounted to 40 to 50 percent of prior income, and wages had shrunk about a third. And for every person who found steady work, there was a Francis Dowd, who earned but 6s. 1d. for labouring three days on the Beauharnois from late April till the end of May 1843, and worked only six days in June at a nominal wage of 3s., which hunger forced him to take in the form of bread.[31] While economic conditions fluctuated during the twilight years of canal building, most canallers experienced want as a matter of course.

A look at the experience of Martin Donnelly attests to this fact. Donnelly arrived in Canada with his wife and three children from County Mayo, Ireland, in July 1842, and found work on tbe Beauharnois. From August to May he worked 112 days for wages that ranged from 2s. to 2s. 6d. per day. He calculated his daily expenses at 8d. for shanty rent, 1s. 3d. for food, and one-half pence for the medical premium, making a total of 1s. 11½d. With an average wage of 2s. 6d., this left but 6½d. a day for fuel, clothing and other contingencies like lost time. Yet Donnelly only worked an average of eleven days a month, so his earnings would be less than half this small amount which barely guaranteed subsistence. Moreover, Donnelly's figures were the projected expenses of a single man; the needs of those who were married grew larger with family size. Donnelly himself, having lost his wife to illness, had to pay a servant woman 10s. a month to care for his children. The only thing that allowed him to carry on was the seven and a half sovereigns he had brought with him from Ireland. "I have never lost the chance of a day's labour from sickness. . . . I belong to the Temperence Society, having been a member of it for these three years past, so that I

30 Power to Begley, 1 Oct. 1842, Welland Canal Letterbook, PAC/RG43; Power to W. P. MacDonagh, 28 May 1846, General Correspondence Sent, Welland Canal, PAC/RG43; Bleasdale, "Unskilled Labourers on the Public Works of Canada" (see Introduction, n. 11 above), 190–92; Scott & Shaw to Bethune and Kittson, 7 Jan. 1843, v. 60, Canal Papers, PAC/RG8; Statement of Peter Dunn, 23 March 1843, ibid.; Hope to D. Jackson, 3 April 1843, Lachine Riots (see Ch. 3, n. 53 above); Wetherall to Killaly, 24 Feb. 1844, ibid.; "Beauharnois Report" (see Introduction, n. 3 above); St.Catharines Journal, 24 Aug. 1843; Memorandum of Chas. Wetherall, 3 April 1843, Lachine Riots (see Ch. 3, n. 53 above).
31 Deposition of Francis Dowd (No. 6), "Beauharnois Report" (see Introduction, n. 3 above).

have never spent six-pence unnecessarily since I came to this country," testified a bewildered Donnelly, "and yet I have barely sufficient remaining out of the money I have brought here, and that I have earned here, to meet the little debts I have contracted on the Canal for the necessaries of life."[32] If Donnelly – hard-working, sober and with capital – could not get by, what about others with nothing saved or with a taste for spirits?

Free labour was a double-edged sword. In good times, it allowed workers to seek out the best bargain for their toil, but when labour surplus was the norm, it was a freedom that left them poorly paid, underemployed, often in desperate straits. An *habitant* whose farm abutted the Beauharnois captured the poverty conditions of his canaller neighbours. "The day-labourers ought to have three shillings a day, and they cannot support themselves on less. *If less is given them they cannot live honestly.* As they are paid at present, they cannot pay their lodging money, being barely able to exist, and reduced at times to eat boiled herbs."[33] Such were the "fruits" of free labour.

A new sense of distress had seeped into the lives of canallers. They and their families were often out of work and hungry, and shanty towns became settlements of the dispossessed, at least as bad as the worst urban ghettos. A litany of reports bears this out. After work had finished on a section of the Welland in 1843, 3,000 hands thrown out of work lacked the means to move on. Samuel Power, the resident engineer, reported "the labourers are on the verge of starvation, and cannot be kept quiet much longer." The following spring, the *St. Catharines Journal* warned: "There are, at this moment, many hundreds of men, women, and children, apparently in the last stages of starvation. . . . What, in the name of humanity, is to be done with the poor wretches, it is impossible to imagine." Similar conditions obtained on the Lachine after hundreds of workers descended upon the opening of construction in January 1843. "During my long residence in Canada," confided a local justice of the peace, "I do not recollect having witnessed so many poor labourers seeking employment, and who appear so much in want of the means of subsistence." The men and their families were "suffering severe privation, as regards food, clothing, and fuel." Yet, with farming and other businesses also depressed, opening another section of the canal to provide jobs was "the only means of saving hundreds of poor families from much want and suffering." All told, more than 2,000 unemployed canallers were in Montreal, over half in a state of great want. Dr. Nelson, a member of the Canadian Assembly and sometime medical attendant on the canal, described conditions on the Lachine for workers and their families in the mid-1840s. "Their wants were of the direst kind," so

---

32 Deposition of Martin Donnelly (No. 3), ibid.
33 Deposition of Joseph Bergevin (No. 50), ibid.

that he "had frequently to prescribe for them, not medicine, nor the ordinary nourishments recommended by the profession, but the commonest necessaries of life." Such disheartening conditions did not wholly evaporate as the depression lifted. During the winter of 1854–55, a settlement of unemployed German workers and their families on Canada's Junction Canal depended on the Department of Works for food to keep them going until construction opened in the spring.[34]

Weakened by hunger or hard work, canallers succumbed to exhaustion and the dangers and diseases that thrived on public works sites. The experience of workers on the Broad Creek section of the Welland in the autumn of 1842 illustrates this. Of 900 men and 400 women and children settled there (of whom only 340 hands were working at any one time), almost half the men and three-quarters of their dependents were sick. There had been more than thirty-one deaths. Whoever was to blame for these conditions, it was clear that the shanty camps along canal banks were sometimes sinks of dispair. The difference between canaller and civilian life expectations was captured by an 1854 report in the *Lake Superior Journal* that during the preceding fourteen months twenty people had died in Sault Ste. Marie, Michigan, compared to eighty-eight canallers on the nearby St. Mary's.[35] Clearly the chasm between public works and the rest of society had widened considerably.

As in the past, sick, injured or merely unemployed workers relied on whatever earnings they had saved. When this ran out, they were thrust upon what little private and public charity existed. When canallers and their families were close to starvation on the Cornwall Canal in the winter of 1837, contractors took up a subscription and the Upper Canadian Assembly voted provisions. In the early months of 1844, when only one in ten of those camped along the Lachine were employed, most were living off credit offered by local storekeepers. Public sympathy in Montreal led to the collection of £155, which was converted into potatoes, meal and other necessities for the canallers' use. More often, aid came with strings attached in the form of make-work schemes or the provision of food on credit. The Montreal municipal government offered the distressed Lachine hands work breaking stones and preparing a new market site. They could also find temporary employment on the Lachine road, but at starvation wages of only 10d.–1s. per day. And although the destitute German workers and their families on the Junction Canal were given provisions in the early 1850s,

34 Power to Begly, 17 July, 1, 6 Aug. 1843, Welland Canal Letterbook, PAC/RG43; *St. Catharines Journal*, 16 Feb. 1844; William Evans to Killaly, 16, 27 March 1843, Lachine Riots (see Ch. 3, n. 53 above); *Debates of the Legislative Assembly of United Canada*, ed. Gibbs (see n. 2 above), v. 4, pt. ll, 1844–45, 1511; List of Unemployed German Labourers to Whom Provisions Supplied on Credit, Dec. 1854–March 1855, Williamsburg Estimates (see Ch. 6, n. 12 above).
35 Power to Begly, 1 Oct. 1842, 24 Aug. 1843, Welland Canal Letterbook, PAC/RG43; *Lake Superior Journal*, 14 Oct. 1854.

the cost was to be deducted from their wages when construction reopened.[36]

Canal companies and boards of works made it clear they were not responsible for the labourers; if employed, they were the contractor's worry, and if unemployed, they were their own concern. Individual initiatives taken in worst-case scenarios were acts of philanthropy and not of legal responsibility. Despite real concern expressed for suffering workers and limited efforts taken to ameliorate their lot, it is clear that the industry profited from the factors that lay behind their poverty: labour surplus and low wages. Charity on the part of companies and contractors grew not only out of a concern for worker welfare but also from the need of the industry to head off disorder and keep up the pace of construction. The former inevitably came second to the latter, however – a lesson overly sympathetic canal officials soon learned.

When work finished on the Welland Canal feeder in 1843, 3,000 men were laid off and were soon "on the verge of starvation." Hoping to head off the inevitable disorder, the resident engineer, Samuel Power, extended construction to open up jobs. For this kindness he was censured by the Board of Works, leading him to remonstrate, "it is very difficult for me surrounded by men infuriated by hunger to persist in a course which must drive them to despair." Power got into even more trouble when he tried to force remiss subcontractors to pay their men on a daily basis and stop running company stores. For this he had his knuckles rapped by the board, which insisted he had no right to interfere between employer and employee. Outraged, Power defended himself eloquently:

When the lake fever was raging at Broad Creek to such an extent, that at one time 800 persons were ill and 4 deaths occurred daily, when the few laborers able to work generously contributed to procure medical aid and proper food for the sick, was it *unjust* to make an effort to save from the avaricious grasp of the contractors the miserable pittance, which the poor laborer had earned, and to place within his reach the food pronounced by his medical attendent necessary for his existence?[37]

Power's rhetorical question went unanswered by a board unwilling to consider the collective good in a world increasingly driven by individual profit. The engineer's paternalism was an attitude increasingly out of favour among canal bosses.

Shanty towns were becoming more like migrant work camps (not unlike those of modern seasonal agricultural labourers). The single male worker

36 Bleasdale, "Class Conflict on the Canals of Upper Canada" (see Introduction, n. 11 above), 101–05, and "Unskilled Labourers on the Public Works of Canada" (see Introduction, n. 11 above), 183–85; Ellis, "Labourers, Contractors and Townspeople" (see Ch. 4, n. 5 above), 27–28; *St. Catharines Journal*, 26 Jan. 1844; Wetherall to Daly, 7 Feb. 1844, Lachine Riots (see Ch. 3, n. 53 above); List of Unemployed German Labourers to Whom Provisions Supplied on Credit, Dec. 1854–March 1855, Williamsburg Estimates (see Ch. 6, n. 12 above).
37 Power to Begly, 17 July, 1, 6, 18, 25 Aug. 1843, Welland Canal Letterbook, PAC/RG43; Begly to Power, 21 Aug. 1843, ibid.

was joined increasingly by married men and their families, often recent immigrants, who moved from job to job, setting up residence in each new location; bunkhouses yielded to family shanties. This offered more scope for a domestic existence but was also a sign of dependence on canal work. Increasingly, married men did not have a life off public works, a place to retreat to and perhaps investigate other employment opportunities; meanwhile, women and children were drawn more fully into the canal economy. As there was a surplus of adult male labour, and because room and board was no longer provided – a service within which family members had formerly worked – it was less likely that women and children would find employment. The consequent decline in family earnings was a main complaint of strikers on the Beauharnois in 1843. At the same time, the growing Irish domination of the workforce was a measure of canaller's exclusion from society, their ethnic solidarity an indication of their weakness, manipulated to justify harsh and unjust treatment. As was so often the case in the rise of industrial capitalism, a dialectic of economic and social exploitation powered the degradation of entire groups of people. The desperate shanty camps of this era reflected canallers' growing marginality.

As a result of these negative forces, the already fragile seams of shanty culture often gave way, as embittered people turned to tramping or thieving to try to survive, and the old points of conflict – personal, racial, ethnic and regional – sparked ever more violent internecine conflict. More positively, the depths of their shared descent periodically convinced workers that they must work as one to resist the deterioration of their condition. As a result, this period was also one marked by labour organization and action. This was the one beacon of hope in an otherwise dismal landscape – yet it was a false dawn, as the industry responded with military, legal and cultural might to stem worker power.

The fruits of their labours

It was a long hot summer of 1842 in St. Catharines, Ontario, a village under siege by "hordes of Irish laborers" flooding in from New York or fresh off immigrant boats looking for work on the Welland. As a result, there was work for only "one in ten of those who are waiting for it." Destitution and hunger bred desperation in the shanty camps, and in June fighting broke out between factions over jobs, a result of "the shameful and most unnatural feud between the Corkonians, as they are styled, and the Connaught and Far Downs men." The former drove the latter from work, but the Connaughtmen marshalled forces (to the number of 250) and assaulted St. Catharines, sending their opponents "flying in all directions, through houses, yards, and over fences." Only the intervention of the militia, ably supported by the Catholic priest, Reverend Lee, prevented an escalation of hostilities between "these strange and mad belligerent factions

– brothers and countrymen, thirsting like savages for each others blood – horrible infatuation."[38] In August, differences were temporarily put aside as the workers halted all work on the line, refusing to let any labour until jobs were provided for all, and took their protest to the streets in an unusual display of mutual need. A local magistrate wrote that "they have paraded the Streets of St. Catharines repeatedly within these few days and last night about Six hundred of them did so with a Board on which was printed 'Bread or Work' and a 'red flag' hoisted with it." "The District is in a state of anarchy," it was warned.[39] An expansion of construction temporarily stilled the troubled waters, however.

The events in St. Catharines that summer demonstrated the mixed effects the transformation of canal construction had on canallers. Unemployment, job competition and shrinking earnings sharpened the edge of existence, a knife that pricked the workers' yielding flesh. It is not surprising that some seized the bloody blade and turned it on each other. Faction fights were a continuing feature in navvies' lives, powered by both harsh work conditions and regional animosities. This was one dimension of the experience of proletarianization: the creation of a workforce fragmented into particularistic groups or even a jigsaw puzzle of individuals. At the same time, the march on St. Catharines, part bread riot, part general strike, was different from the violence and protest that welled up on canals in earlier years, showing both greater despair and more radical direction. And this incident was a small part of the new wave of labour conflict that swept canals in the 1840s and more clearly etched class lines. Thus, heightening class conflict was the other dimension of proletarianization.

Faction fighting captured the ambivalent heart of the navvy experience. At the same time an expression of very real social antipathies imported from Ireland and embellished on public works, and an outgrowth of the harsh conditions canallers laboured under, this conflict was neither wholly residual Old World squabbling nor entirely embedded in class experience. The transformation of peasant into proletarian culminated in the 1840s, and the resulting unemployment, low wages and pared-down existence caused canallers to look backwards to old loyalties and past grievances, and to turn on each other in a mad scramble for the dwindling opportunities available. This was not entirely new, but both the degree and intensity of social conflict pointed to sharpening tensions. In all, there were fifty riots during this decade (forty-seven in Canada), the vast majority of which involved faction fights. This compares to thirty-two incidents in the 1830s

38 *St. Catharines Journal*, 7 July, 11 Aug. 1842.
39 Thorburn to Thomas Murdoch, 18 Aug. 1842, Welland Riots (see Ch. 6, n. 67 above); *St. Catharines Journal*, 11 Aug. 1842; Power to Begley, 12, 15 Aug. 1842, Welland Canal Letterbook, PAC/RG43. The red flag likely symbolized blood, which, according to E. P. Thompson, was linked to bread in English food protests. "The Moral Economy of the English Crowd in the Eighteenth Century," *Past and Present*, no. 50 (1971), 135.

and fourteen in the 1820s (Table 14). These were concentrated in the harsh four years between 1842 and 1845, when forty-four disturbances occurred (Table 15).

The destitution experienced by canallers in the 1840s led to more explicitly class-conscious actions as well. Fifty-seven strikes have been identified in the period under study. Whereas there were seven in the 1820s and nineteen the following decade, there were twenty-eight in the 1840s, these overwhelmingly concentrated, like the riots, in the years 1842–45 (Tables 13–15). Early strikes had tended to be small affairs, usually the result of a contractor's failure to pay wages rather than an attempt to alter the established relations of production. By the late 1830s, strikes were becoming both more common and more aggressive in their demands. As well as protesting infringements on accepted labour practices, labourers now demanded higher wages, shorter hours and improved conditions. While many strikes were still small in scale – limited to one section, often only a few days in length – there were a number of incidents that were better organized, involved more workers and lasted longer. The backlash from employers grew proportionately.

The general strike on the Beauharnois Canal in 1843 illustrates the growing stakes in labour protest. Larger than most caller protests, the strike grew out of the same negative conditions of unemployment and poverty that prompted faction fights. And in this one instance a comprehensive record was left of the strike in the form of a government report, including testimony from workers involved.

The Beauharnois incident must be placed against the backdrop of labour disputes that seized the nearby Lachine for three months earlier that year. The entire Lachine improvement project was in the hands of Montreal contractors Scott & Shaw, but the actual work was to be carried on under subcontract by Henry Mason. Much of the conflict on the line emerged from Mason's abrasive handling of his workers. As the strikers emphasized in a posted notice, "henry mason is the Cause of our turn out."[40] When work opened in January hundreds of workers and their families rushed in from the States, but only a minority found work. Those that did were getting just 2s. a day, wages barely able to support a single person. The stage was set for "an Irish Holliday," and on the 24th the "Labourers *unanimously* combined" in protest against the "Tyranny of the Contractors & their Foremen, & Truck pay." Notices were posted reminiscent of those

---

40 Scott & Shaw to Hope, 31 March 1843, Lachine Riots (see Ch. 3, n. 53 above); *Montreal Gazette*, 7 Feb. 1843; Pentland, "Lachine Strike" (see Introduction, n. 11 above), 261; the notice is found in a copy of a letter in *Montreal Gazette* from Henry Mason, contractor, 23 March 1843, Lachine Riots (see Ch. 3, n. 53 above). A fuller treatment of the Lachine events is found in Pentland, "Lachine Strike of 1843" (see Introduction, n. 11 above). See also Boily, *Les Irlandais et le Canal de Lachine*, (see Introduction, n. 11 above), 18–22.

that C&O workers used as warnings in the 1830s, but now explicit work demands accompanied violent threats.

> Any person or persons who works here in the Lachine Canal under 3 shillings and sixpence Per day may have their Coffin and Bearer and the time they have to commence in the morning is at seven oClock and quit at five oClock in the after Noon and there is no man to attempt working even when the wages is settled untill the men all agrees on it for we are not to bear such a persecution Any person or persons who attempts taking down this notice will get the same death as is foresaid[.]

A Lachine foreman, quoted in the *Montreal Gazette*, alleged a number of the strike leaders were "old Canal-men from the United States, who have done their best to foment quarrels among the new emigrants."[41] Possibly this was the work of old hands who had lived through and learned from earlier factional and labour battles.

The Lachine strikers remained firm for over a week, but the contractors, denying all charges against them, were equally united. Worker resolve weakened and the general strike dissolved into factional fighting early in February. Two companies of regular troops were dispatched to the line to support twenty canal policemen. The strike was broken and work resumed.[42] Continuing feuding did not prevent another turnout on 21 March. The strikers demanded 3s. instead of 2s. 6d. a day, the usual spring wage increase. They also protested the discharge of some hands, and drillers wanted a higher piece rate or a day wage. The next morning, "the labours to the number of 4 to 500, with Fifes & Fiddles, Marched in a body to Montreal, and there paraded the streets in *order*." And to make sure their position was known, they again posted a notice on the Lachine tollgate insisting "no Man will work under three shillings per day and Drillers in proportion besides we expects all hands will be Employed as we require Nothing else." As well as affirming their pride in being "irishmen" and "loyal Subjects," they emphasized their conviction to "surrender To No Contractors who wants to live by the Sweat of our Brow."[43] Contractors tried to get around the strike by discharging all their hands and hiring French-Canadians (or loyal Irish) in their place, but the unemployed Irish returned and chased off the French. The former were allowed to stay at work to the number of 1,000, though the strike fizzled out with none of

---

41 Charles Atherton to Begly, 25 Jan. 1843, Lachine Riots (see Ch. 3, n. 53 above); Atherton to Hope, 29 March 1843, ibid.; notice and foreman's account in *Montreal Gazette*, 7 Feb. 1843.

42 Atherton to Begly, 25, 27, 31 Jan., 3, 5, 6, 7 Feb. 1843, Lachine Riots (see Ch. 3, n. 53 above); Scott & Shaw to Hope, 31 March 1843, ibid.; Memorandum of Chas. Wetherall, 3 April 1843, ibid.; Hope to D. Jackson, 3 April 1843, ibid.; *Montreal Gazette*, 7 Feb. 1843; Boily, *Les Irlandais et le Canal de Lachine*, (see Introduction, n. 11 above), 26–28.

43 Joseph McDonald to Begly, 21 March 1843, Lachine Riots (see Ch. 3, n. 53 above); Atherton to Begly, 24 March 1843, ibid.; McDonald to Begly, 23 March 1843, ibid.; notice in copy of letter in *Montreal Gazette* from Henry Mason, contractor, 23 March 1843, ibid.

the demands won. Throughout, troops and police were stationed on the line to keep the peace.[44] This was the background for the uprising on the Beauharnois.

Work began in July 1842, overseen directly by the Board of Works, an arrangement favourable to canallers.

The hours of labour required from the workmen each day, were never made to extend beyond twelve: some say the day's labour usually began at six a.m. and closed at six p.m., while two hours of intermission were allowed for meals. The labourers were invariably paid in cash, at the rate of three shillings per day, and they usually received their wages semi-monthly.[45]

"Under this system," affirmed the commission, "the men employed were quiet and apparently content." But as construction expanded the board did not wish full responsibility for construction nor the costs that came with it. The work was transferred in January to contractors, who rolled back wages to levels believed to be below subsistence: between 2s. and 2s. 6d. per day. Moreover, pay came at the end of the month, which forced most workers to buy provisions on credit from company stores where "few, if any, of the provisions which constitute the *necessaries* of life among the labouring classes, were to be found." Hours increased so that instead of working from six in the morning until six at night, the men now toiled from "dark to dark," from five to seven in summer, and one contractor even required his hands to work from 4:30 a.m. to 7:30 p.m. "High rents were also paid to the contractors by the laborers for the small wooden huts called shanties which could afford them shelter," although builders were bound by their contracts "to provide the workmen on the Canal with suitable lodgings." On the whole, the labourer's "condition was greatly altered." Impersonal market forces now dictated at every point of contact between employer and employed – hiring, wages, hours of labour, shelter, sustenance – terrain where in the past bargains were struck according to mutual need. A revolution in labour relations was being wrought and a "new order of things" put in place, change that resulted directly from a flooding of the labour market. Canallers on the Beauharnois banded together and waged a general strike in an effort to keep their heads above water.

The first sign of trouble appeared in March when it was reported that "seeds of discord" had been brought in by "evil disposed" men, mostly Corkonians, fleeing the problems on the Lachine. "They are driving from this canal all the opposing party [Connaughtmen] pillaging and destroying

44 Atherton to Begly, 30 March, 5 April 1843, ibid.; McDonald to Killaly, 3 April 1843, ibid. Pentland hypothesized that contractors must have given in to the workers' wage demand, citing the resumption of work and quietness of the Lachine during the Beauharnois troubles in June. This seems unlikely and, as Pentland admitted, there is no supporting evidence. Pentland, "Lachine Strike of 1843" (see Introduction, n. 11 above), 266–67.
45 Unless otherwise specified all information and quotations are drawn from the "Beauharnois Report" (see Introduction, n. 3 above).

shantees causing great distress." Work was temporarily suspended and a truce arranged among leaders of both groups, each agreeing to give up its arms.[46] Concerted worker action to improve conditions then replaced factional disputes on the Beauharnois. On 1 May, a hundred labourers from the western end of the canal proceeded along the entire line in an unsuccessful attempt to mount a turnout, though they secured a promise "that a general strike should be made on the thirty-first of May, throughout every portion of the works" for higher wages and shorter hours.[47]

Beauharnois workers argued their case in a petition signed by ninety-eight canallers.

We, the undersigned Petitioners, humbly and respectfully beg leave to lay before you the grievances under which we labour, in consequence of the tyranny exercised over us by the contractors, for whom we were obliged to work, after a long and severe winter. The great majority of the men had done no work during that time: dire necessity obliged them to work for Pierce, Black and Co. When they commenced their section, their work was exceedingly severe, their hours for work being from dark to dark – the wages was only 2s. 6d. per day, which was quite insufficient to maintain our families, taking into consideration broken time and dear house rent. These wages, though trifling, were kept back to the end of each month, in order that the men should resort to their stores for provisions, and take them at whatever price they wished to charge for them, and being of a very inferior quality, particularly bread.[48]

This "melancholy situation," marked by unemployment, low wages, long hours and truck pay, united workers across factional lines and from section to section.

"On the last day of May," recounted Martin Donnelly, a sometime worker on George Crawford's section, "all the labourers down the line gave up their tools to their respective foremen, and gave notice that they would not return to work until the wages were raised to 3s." There were two to three thousand hands at this time, the majority supporting the strike. The situation remained peaceful for ten days, despite the fact that many labourers were experiencing great want, a situation compounded by the contractors. "Directly the men struck," according to Donnelly, "the stores on Crawford's section were closed, and the ordinary means of getting supplies and the necessaries of life were thus taken away from us; and I have a personal knowledge that great distress prevailed in many of the shanties during that interval."[49] Confronted with such tactics, canallers' peacefulness wilted, but they did not vent their frustraction on each other. Instead they began mass demonstrations to coerce a wage increase, damaging property and threatening contractors. Some builders buckled but most remained firm.

46 J. B. Mills to Killaly, 23, 26, 28 March, 11 April 1843, Beauharnois Riots (see Ch. 5, n. 18 above); Killaly to Capt. Brownrigg, 15 April 1843, ibid.; Laviolette to Daly, 18 April 1843, ibid.
47 Deposition of Louis Isaac Larocque (No. 23), "Beauharnois Report" (see Introduction, n. 3 above).
48 Petition of James Carnes and others (Deposition No. 63), ibid.
49 Deposition of Martin Donnelly (No. 23), ibid.

Meanwhile, British troops has been called onto the line by local magistrates J. B. Laviolette and George Crawford, the same contractor who shut his store to strikers. On 12 June, a large crowd of unarmed workers marching on Grant's Hotel on the eastern end of the canal were confronted by the troops. Laviolette ordered the canallers to disperse, then read the Riot Act. When they remained firm, Laviolette ordered the troops to disperse the crowd by force, "whereupon a volley was fired by the cavalry, as well as by the infantry and the former charged the mob with drawn swords." The shocked Irish fled in all directions, pursued by both soldiers and mounted troops. The toll was high, "some 5 or 6 men were killed directly others wounded, some were driven into the river and were drowned," although the exact number of dead is not clear. Twenty-seven prisoners were also taken. Order was restored, the strike broken.[50]

While some contractors had been forced to raise wages and cut hours during the strike, they quickly reverted to earlier levels after it was suppressed, and other sections were slow to reopen. Thus the strike compounded the sufferings of many canallers. "To such extremities have they been reduced," reported the *Montreal Courier*, "that strong bodied men have offered to work for 1s. 3d. a day, or, in fact, for any thing to give them food." As for those canallers killed by the military, their deaths were, in the verdict of the coroner's inquest, a case of "justifiable homocide." There was enough public concern and newspaper complaints, however, that the board decided to investigate the strike.[51] The Reform government was happy to comply and before the end of June an investigating body was in place. After interviewing various witnesses it produced a report quite critical of how public works construction was carried on, blaming particularly the contracting system. At the same time, it could not condone the strike and chastised magistrate Laviolette for not impressing on the workers "the illegality of all combinations of that nature and the punishment reserved for all those, who would dare to resort to such violations of the law."

The commission was clear that "the universal dissatisfaction" with wages was the main source of the unrest. The workers' complaints were justified, as "the price paid by the contractors to their labourers . . . was not only an inadequate remuneration for the services of the latter, but was insufficient

---

50 J. B. Mills to Killaly, 28 June 1843, Beauharnois Riots (see Ch. 5, n. 18 above). See also John McBean to Begly, 13 June 1843, ibid.; Mills to Begly, 8, 27, 28 June 1843, ibid.; Mills to Killaly, 28 June 1843, ibid.; *Montreal Gazette*, 14, 17, 19, 20 June 1843. This did not mean the end of worker organization on the Beauharnois. There were reports of turnouts in Aug. and Oct. 1844, as well as Sept. 1845. See Ross, Chaffey & Co. to Killaly, 22 Aug. 1844, Beauharnois Riots (see Ch. 5, n. 18 above); L. G. Brown to Wetherall, 24 Aug. 1844, ibid.; Wetherall to Daly, 27 Aug. 1844, ibid.; James O'Neill to G. Miller, 17 Sept. 1844, ibid.; Brown to Daly, 26 Aug. 1845, ibid.

51 Depositions of Andrew Elliott (No. 22), Louis Isaac Larocque (No. 23); George Crawford (No. 52), "Beauharnois Report" (see Introduction, n. 3 above); *St. Catharines Journal*, 6 July 1843; *Montreal Gazette*, 19, 20 June 1843.

to afford them the means of subsisting." The rightful discontent with pay was exacerbated by "the unreasonable length to which their daily hours of labour were extended," as well as store pay and irregularity of work. Having validated worker grievances, the report went on to evaluate the official response. It found the practice of investing a contractor with magisterial powers problematic, as it opened him "to the suspicion of wielding the powers of the law, solely for the purpose of maintaining his own personal interests."

The report ended with a number of recommendations. First, it sought to root out the source of the problem on canals, "to remove all just causes of complaint" by including in future contracts regulations enjoining contractors to pay wages fortnightly and in cash, to abstain from keeping stores, and to abide by "such rates of wages and hours of labour as may be established by the Chairman of the Board of Works at the beginning of each season." Second, to head off future outbreaks, the commissioners recommended the establishment of a magistracy and official police force on the public works, something previously done in only piecemeal fashion. This professional force would be aided by "a system of internal Police, "in which a number of leaders among the canallers would be appointed as constables to keep the peace. The policing recommendations were easy for the board to swallow, contributing as they would to public order, and even the payment scheme and prohibition of truck were acceptable, as both had caused problems in the past. Regulation of wages and hours was another matter, however, as it entailed state intervention in labour relations and might lead to the onerous responsibilities contracting had been designed to take off the board's hands. Thus, contractual regulations about prompt cash payments were implemented on Canada's public works in the next few years, although they were never fully enforced, and a canal police force was also soon put in place. But the employer–employee contract was left untouched and wholly subject to the workings of the free market. For all its interest as a historical document, the Beauharnois Report had little impact on labour relations within the industry in Canada and did virtually nothing to better the lot of canallers.

The events on the Lachine and Beauharnois, while somewhat unusual in their intensity, were not the result of some peculiarly Canadian distemper, nor were they solely the result of the depression years. The economic climate brightened in the mid-1840s and public works began to revive in the United States, but life for navvies did not revert to the conditions of the predepression period, for all its harshness a relative golden age compared to the cruel years intervening. Contractors did not suddenly throw open their arms, shanties, larders and whiskey barrels, welcoming the boys back into the family's bosom. For the most part, canallers still had to work where and when they could, skimp and buy housing, food and all other necessities out of meagre earnings. And when they could not accomplish this they were pushed to fighting each other and the system. A revolution was being wrought and there was no looking back. Events on the Illinois & Michigan Canal bear this out.

Work opened on the I&M in 1836, and went ahead despite the concurrent financial panic and suspension of payment by the State Bank of Illinois. But as depression set in, the canal found it increasingly difficult to float the bond issues that filled its coffers. It resorted to paying contractors in scrip that trickled down to workers in a terminal drip keeping them barely alive. But it was the company that gave up the ghost, or at least went into the purgatory of default, only to be resurrected by the reorganization of finances and appointment of a board of trustees, one representing the state and two the bondholders. Work resumed but not on the previous scale; fewer men were employed and wages dropped from a peak of $40 a month in 1836 to an average of $16 in 1843.[52] When construction reopened in 1845 problems immediately materialized. By November, sickness had caused a suspension of work and contractors were in such financial straits that without an advance of their estimate they would be unable to pay their men, "which would inevitably cause a rebellion, and perhaps an abandonment of the work." The situation had hardly improved by the next spring as builders were still being paid in depreciated drafts that "they have been compelled to sell . . . for any kind of trash that the merchants or brokers chose to give them." In addition, four to five months were elapsing in some cases between estimates on completed work and payment to the contractor.[53] A number consequently failed to pay their hands, which, combined with an unusually wet season, meant "hundreds of laborers were unemployed upon the line until their means of support were wholly exhausted and they left the work discouraged and disaffected." They were reportedly writing to friends elsewhere and warning them not to look for work on the I&M. All these factors contributed to a labour shortage; meanwhile, another hard winter again forced suspension of the work.[54] It was against this background of stuttering progress, with an imminent completion deadline imposed as part of the refinancing agreement, that the company decided to take over construction of the canal's key summit section from contractors in May. Management felt the work could be finished much more quickly by cutting out the contractor, hiring its own hands and establishing direct job super-

52 *Report of the Canal Commissioners of the Illinois and Michigan Canal*, Vandalia, (1838), 30; Owen to Alexander Osbourne, 19 April 1840, Owen Papers, Indiana State Library; James William Putnam, *The Illinois and Michigan Canal: A Study in Economic History* (Chicago: University of Chicago Press, 1918), ch. 2; Fleming, *Canal at Chicago* (see Ch. 6, n. 57 above), 106–07; Borgeson, "Irish Canal Laborers" (see Ch. 3, n. 31 above), 42–44.
53 Robert Stuart to David Levitt, 5 Nov. 1845, Swift Papers, Chicago Historical Society; William Gooding to Swift, 20 Feb. 1846, ibid.; Evidence of Chas. Oakley, Appendix A, n.d. [1847], p. 6, ibid.
54 Gooding to W. H. Swift, 6 July 1846, ibid.; Leavitt to Swift, 20 July 1846, ibid; Jacob Fry to Swift, 29 July 1846, ibid.; Gooding to Swift, 14 Jan. 1847, ibid.

vision. Unfortunately, the I&M did not bargain for its "discouraged and disaffected" workers.[55]

The Irish workers on the summit struck in July 1847, sending a petition to the state trustee, Charles Oakley, complaining "That since the said work has been worked by the State Superintendants, there has been abuse of the Labour and lives of men on said works." It was at this time that they pleaded to be treated as "white Citizens" as opposed to "Common Slave Negroes." Specifically, the canallers maintained "that from $\frac{1}{2}$ Past 4 in the morning until within $\frac{1}{4}$ of 8 in the Evening is too long to be withstood at hard labour and by men who have got to stand it in A hot climate in A sickly state and for month After month." The hands were also not happy with their present wages of $1 a day. They wanted regulations giving "the men time for sleep and rest $1.25 per day, or one dollar per day & board, with hours of work from 6 oClock AM. to 7 PM. saving 2 hours for Breakfast and Dinner." They pledged to refrain from work until these demands were met.[56]

In addressing their petition to Oakley the strikers were apparently taking advantage of a split in canal management. As trustee for the state, Oakley was at odds with the bondholders' representatives and supporters, particularly the chief engineer directly responsible for the work at the summit, William Gooding. Oakley listened to the workers and brought their demands to Gooding, recommending they be met or at least a compromise struck, an accommodation the latter categorically rejected. Oakley's opponents felt he was being exploited by the strikers. "A few of the scamps here are making a tool of this poor weak man, & they will blow him up ere long, so that we will not be able to get hold of even a relick of what was once *the great negociator*."[57]

The strike dragged on two to three weeks while Oakley mediated and Gooding stood resolved to hold wages down. In adopting this policy, Gooding articulated company interests clearly detached from those of the hands. "Every man who has had the charge of a work must know," maintained the chief engineer, "that to accede to the demands of the work-people for one additional penny, would prove but the entering wedge for increased demands." Oblivious to the workers' condition, Gooding was concerned with not setting a precedent. "It was the universal opinion that the slightest advance of wages upon the Summit, would have caused a

---

55 The situation on the I&M was thus the reverse of that on the Beauharnois, where the yielding of company control to contractors caused problems; still, economic pressures within the industry and the corresponding need to cut costs and speed construction were the underlying roots of worker discontent in both cases.

56 Petition of the undersigned Labourers To Honourable Col. Oakley, 12 July 1847, Swift Papers, Chicago Historical Society.

57 Chas. Oakley to Leavitt, 15 July 1847, ibid.; Stuart to Swift, 17, 23 July, 16 Aug. 1847, ibid.

general turn out for a corresponding advance on the whole line." And contractors had threatened to abandon their contracts if this happened. Furthermore, it was not in the workers' interests to grant them higher pay. "In fact, all experience proves, that when wages are too high, men are not so well contented, are more likely to strike for still higher wages, or other unreasonable cause, and save no more money." "But the most serious objection to an advance," confessed Gooding, "is, that the principle being once conceded that a combination amongst the men to obtain what the employer is not required in justice to grant, and yields upon compulsion, induces other unreasonable exactions, and finally takes from him all power of control."[58] Labour organization was wrong because it sought to assert unnatural and "unreasonable" work conditions over those set by the market, and (more importantly) because it was aimed specifically at wresting control of production from the rightful hands of contractors and canal companies. It was this framing of labour relations, clearly in the interests of the emerging capitalist class, that shaped management's response to workers in this period. In the face of this obdurate position, the I&M strike foundered. Men gradually returned to work under the same conditions, although a good number of unrepentant individuals left the line for farm labour or public works in Michigan and Indiana.[59] The lines of class conflict could not be clearer, the meaning of free labour more apparent.

One thing that the Lachine, Beauharnois and I&M strikes had in common was that they all failed. Obviously, not all turnouts went for naught. Most were very small affairs – on one section, against one contractor, lasting but a few days – and labourers were occasionally successful in achieving their demands. Such was the case for the workers who struck on the Welland in July 1843 and were back at work the next morning, their contractors having conceded their demands for 3s. 6d. a day. Such victories were often short-lived, however. In November, as was usual, Welland wages were rolled back to 2s. 6d. and more jobs were cut.[60] Too much should not be read into such successes. They were directed at immediate goals, much a part of day-to-day labour bargaining, and, when successful, were so on this small scale. Workers on other sections often did not profit from such raises, which promoted jealousy and competition rather than solidarity, and even

---

58 *Report of a Majority of the Board of Trustees of the Illinois and Michigan Canal* (Washington, 1847), xix, 8; Evidence of William Gooding, Appendix L, 4 March 1847, pp. 9–10, Swift Papers, Chicago Historical Society.
59 Gooding to Swift, 7 Sept. 1847, Swift Papers, Chicago Historical Society; Evidence of Chas. Oakely, p. 3, ibid.; Evidence of William Gooding, 4 March 1847, p. 10, ibid. Oakley eventually levelled various charges against Gooding that were investigated by the other Trustees, and, despite no solid evidence of misconduct, Oakley's greater influence cost the chief engineer the job he had held since construction opened. *Report of a Majority of the Board of Trustees of the Illinois and Michigan Canal* (Washington, 1847).
60 Power to Begley, 17 July 1843, Welland Canal Letterbook, PAC/RG43; Thorburn to Daly, 10 Jan. 1844, Welland Riots (see Ch. 6, n. 67 above).

the victorious strikers' situation could soon change, as did that of Welland canallers when winter set in. In sum, victorious strikes, while of great importance to those involved, advanced the interests of the few workers involved more than they noticeably helped the labour cause. Like faction fighting and terroristic tactics, and even glorious failures like the Lachine and Beauharnois turnouts, the whole of strike activity from the smallest and simplest to the largest and most organized was but a holding action on the rise of industrial capitalism. As long as canallers lacked the strength of an enduring union, were riven by a variety of social stresses and were pushed into competition by brute force of material need, their strike demands, not surprisingly, were simple and their success was limited. Still, navvies were learning lessons that would be put to good use elsewhere in years to come.

The guardians of "this new order"

Contractors, canal officials and governments had a united perspective on the labour disorder that erupted in the 1840s: strikes or other acts of collective violence on the part of canal labourers to better their work conditions could not be tolerated. The role of the state in suppressing labour conflict, while somewhat novel at the time, was not surprising considering how deeply involved governments were in the financing and construction of canals. A distant and relatively uninterested force in the early years, government had played an increasingly key role. Even in the case of private companies, concerns of the boardroom and statehouse were often very hard to distinguish. In the precarious economic climate of the late 1830s to early 1840s, labour conflict, by interrupting work and driving up costs, threatened to bring down the financial house of cards that was canal promotion. Like contractors and companies, then, governments had a vested interest in maintaining order.

The actual legal status of workers' right to strike was rather unclear in this period, being subject to different judicial interpretations. In practice, strikes tended to be allowed if peaceful and repressed if they threatened disorder or violence.[61] This placed unskilled and non-unionized labourers

---

61 Eric Tucker found the law particularly inconsistent on this issue in Canada, as it was not clear exactly what British codes applied. Drawing a distinction between "formal law" and a "legal zone of toleration," he argued that, while the climate of legal opinion at mid-century viewed worker combinations as illegal, social opinion allowed labourers to join together as long as they posed no threat to order. "'That Indefinite Area of Toleration': Criminal Conspiracy and Trade Unions in Ontario, 1837–77," *Labour/Le Travail*, v. 27 (Spring 1991), 15–54. Labour law in the States was subject to the laws and court rulings of individual states, which made for a variety of readings. For the New York example, see Wilentz, *Chants Democratic* (see Introduction, n. 8 above), 271–86. See also Bleasdale, "Class Conflict on the Canals of Upper Canada" (see Introduction, n. 11 above), 121–23; Morris, *Government and Labor* (see Ch. 1, n. 6 above), 137.

like canallers at a disadvantage, as they often had to rely on force to secure their workplace goals. For this reason many of the state interventions in labour disputes during this period were in cases involving common labour like that on canals.[62] Rather than constituting backward-looking ethnic squabbles, as they are usually treated, these riots and strikes helped to decide such crucial issues as the rights of workers to combine and the role of the state in industrial conflict. It was soon apparent that employers' interests outweighed those of employees.

A free labour ideology emphasizing the unfettered movement of men and money validated intervention in labour disputes on canals. Canada's Board of Works put this proposition baldly in its 1843 annual report: "the price of labour should be allowed to be regulated solely by the ordinary principles of supply and demand." And in case of a strike "the authorities of the country" should "protect, effectually, those disposed to work at the wages offered from others, who, by violence and intimidation, endeavour to prevent them." By "disturbing the *ordinary* rules which subsist *individually* between the Labourer & his Employer" (as the chief engineer of the Lachine put it), worker organization disrupted the free play of market forces, which constituted a criminal combination if force was used.[63] Charles Wetherall, a police magistrate on the Lachine, elaborated the state's conception of how the labour market should work. A specific pay rate at a fair level should be established by a contractor with his men, who should accept it or turn it down and move on. If they refused terms but remained to cause trouble or prevent others from working, ringleaders should be arrested before the "illegal combination" gained strength. This was the logical conclusion drawn from free labour ideology. Of course, this rendering ignored the reality that most workers had little choice at this time but to accept whatever wages were offered or to combine. When they chose the latter course, however, they faced the united force of private and public interest. To make this point clear after the strikes on the Lachine in the spring of 1843, Canada's Board of Works had extracts of the laws against labour combinations printed and circulated among the men on the public works.[64] This warning obviously had no effect on the Beauharnois workers.

At stake, or course, was control of the workplace. Without the right to organize and make united demands, workers would be powerless. Strikes were meant to gain power and necessarily attacked the authority of contractors and canal companies. As Gooding argued regarding the I&M strike: contractors who yielded to combination gave up "all power of control." While an exaggeration, this fear fed management's reaction to

---

62 It is revealing that Tucker twice uses canallers as exceptions to his model of "toleration." " 'That Indefinite Area of Toleration' " (see n. 61 above), 18, 28.
63 "Report of the Board of Works," *Journals of the Legislative Assembly of the Province of Canada*, 1843, Appendix Q; Atherton to Hope, 29 March 1843, Lachine Riots (see Ch. 3, n. 53 above).
64 Wetherall to Killaly, 3 April 1843, Lachine Riots (see Ch. 3, n. 53 above).

labour disputes, as was made clear by an engineer in the wake of the Beauharnois strike:

Are the Workmen to control the Work to determine the prices of labour and the hours they are to work? Are they to Dictate as to who is to be employed upon the Canal either as labourers, Gangmen, or otherwise? . . . Are the Contractors to be . . . *protected* in directing and controlling their work – in determining who is to work for them – how much they are to pay – and what hours the men must work?[65]

The state response to labour's organizational initiatives left little doubt as to the answer to these questions.

The use of the military to oppress workers was the most obvious expression of state power on canals. Troops intervened thirty-two times on canals between 1829 and 1849, and on seventeen occasions in the 1840s alone (Table 16), a frequency that was as much an indication of state willingness to use force to preserve its interests as it was of worker militancy.[66] Incidents were equally distributed between the United States and Canada, although events in the States tended to take place in the 1830s and in Canada during the following decade. The main difference lay in the type of troops used. Militia units or more informal posses usually handled this troublesome duty in the United States, with its concern for decentralization of governmental powers and traditional dislike of a standing army, although federal troops were used in at least one incident, the 1834 riot on the C&O. In British North America, where central state power was paramount and no republican tradition eroded its will to impose order, regular troops were in charge of keeping the peace, in addition to local militias and professional police forces paid by the Board of Works. The net result was the same, nonetheless: a recurring military presence within the industry that policed potentially violent labour disputes. Yet labourers rarely clashed directly with the military. The appearance of an armed force and the reading of the Riot Act generally were sufficient to cause labourers to disperse. A rifle assault and casualties, as happened during the Beauharnois strike, was a rarity. The relative lack of violence in these confrontations illustrates the military's efficiency as the ultimate weapon in settling labour disputes in favour of contractors and canal commissions. This coupling of capital and armed force narrowly restricted the success of canaller combinations.

Use of the military in a policing role was open to abuse by contractors and canal officials, however. In the 1830s–40s, increasing emphasis was placed on having local militias or detachments of regular troops within marching distance. This was particularly true in Canada. For contractors

65 J. B. Mills to Begly, 19 June 1843, Beauharnois Riots (see Ch. 5, n. 18 above).
66 Grace Palladino noted a similar pattern in the Pennsylvania coal fields, where workers were organizing by the 1840s and employers resisting their efforts with a free labour ideology, backed by the ultimate weapon of military intervention. *Another Civil War* (see n. 3 above), 9–10.

experiencing labour problems or local magistrates nervous about their constituents' property and physical well-being, this proximity proved an irresistible lure. Contractors came to view the military as a useful tool to beat down rebellious workers and as a bogeyman with which to secure an obedient labour force. In truth, the threat of military force did not inhibit worker discontent or organization, but drove them underground into secret societies, which limited their scope and tactics. This result was enough to keep contractors repeatedly requesting aid.[67]

Yet the use of troops was always problematic. Military units in themselves did not have civil authority. This power could only be vested in them by local magistrates or higher government officials, and was meant to be used only in times of insurrection. Labour unrest came increasingly to be defined in these terms, which left the door open to private exploitation of public forces. A police magistrate made clear the dangers of this practice. For contractors who were good managers, "the presence of troops is injurious having a tendency to irritate the feelings of the Irish labourers whilst to the contractor whose management is bad their presence may serve as the means of undue coertion."[68] Eventually some interested observers noted that a continued reliance on martial force to keep workers in line was not in the best interests of either public works or the military. In 1842 the Board of Works, concerned mainly with the expense, issued orders that soldiers should be used only when absolutely necessary. The British command also rebelled at the use of troops as a preventive police force on permanent duty, wanting them used only as a last resort.[69] Growing reaction to use of a standing army in civil affairs, always a thorny issue, stimulated exploration of alternatives.

One option developed by Canada's Board of Works was that of police forces on the various canals in the 1840s. Formed in response to the labour disorder on the works, these constabularies were paid by the board and operated essentially as its enforcement branch. In addition to handling common criminal activity such as assault and theft, the police were meant to protect contractors and their property, guard strikebreakers during turn-outs and in general ensure that construction continued on schedule. Thus, while professional in the sense that they were paid, canal police were far from impartial keepers of the peace.[70] Limited in number and having little

---

67 E. G. Wakefield to Killaly, 12 July 1842, Beauharnois Riots (see Ch. 5, n. 18 above); Wetherall to Daly, 27 Aug. 1844, ibid.; Power to Begly, 14 April 1843, Welland Canal Letterbook, PAC/RG43; Bleasdale, "Class Conflict on the Canals of Upper Canada" (see Introduction, n. 11 above), 126–28.
68 Wetherall to Daly, 27 Aug. 1844, Beauharnois Riots (see Ch. 5, n. 18 above).
69 [Illegible] to Thorburn, 15 July 1842, Welland Riots (see Ch. 6, n. 67 above); Thorburn to Thomas Murdoch, 18 Aug. 1842, ibid.; Hope to Jackson, 3 April 1843, Lachine Riots (see Ch. 5, n. 53 above); J. Studholme Brownrigg to Begly, 6 April 1843, Beauharnois Riots (see Ch. 5, n. 18 above).
70 A. Coffin to Killaly, 30 Oct. 1842, Beauharnois Riots (see Ch. 5, n. 18 above); E. Parent to Killaly, 18 March 1843, ibid.; Killaly to Captain Brownrigg, 15 April 1843, ibid.; Begley to Power,

authority in workers' eyes, canal police were not very successful. They could not stem the thefts and assaults that dogged public works sites and were clearly unable to halt marauding factions or incensed strikers; hence, the continuing recourse to the military. Still, the development of professional policing on canals at a time when very few cities had them was an indication of the industry's leading-edge status.

When military means were ineffective, canal companies occasionally sought to purge the source of the problem in its aftermath by striking at individual labour leaders. This could be done formally through the courts (as on the C&O in the late 1830s). Twenty-five Lachine strikers were arrested in 1843, and about the same number were jailed during the military intervention on the Beauharnois, although they were eventually released without trial.[71] The difficulty of securing witnesses acted to lessen the use of the courts in labour disputes. In place of the legal system, canals could informally try and convict labourers by blacklisting participants in riots or strikes. In the wake of the strikes on the Lachine early in 1843, a list of "30 obnoxious characters" was drawn up and circulated on Canada's canals to prevent "such disturbers of the peace" from getting work elsewhere.[72] In either case, eliminating a few troublemakers did little to lessen labour unrest. Disorder was not a function of personalities or leadership, but of genuine grievances with working and living conditions.

Coming from a government agency funded by public monies, the actions of the Board of Works in calling in the military, establishing police forces and blacklisting workers must be seen as ultimately state-directed. The role of the state was clearer in the case of the Act for the Preservation of the Peace near Public Works, passed in 1845 by the Canadian Assembly in response to the Beauharnois Commission's recommendation that a policing alternative to the military be established. The government was empowered to station mounted police on the line, twenty-two armed constables were placed on the Williamsburg canals and all firearms on the public works were to be registered.[73] The state was concerned for continuing problems of social order in the early 1840s, but also wished to protect its investment in canals, and this act was meant both to preserve the peace and expedite

6 March 1843, Welland Canal Letterbook, PAC/RG43; Charles Penner to Sir James Hope, 3 April 1843, Lachine Riots (see Ch. 5, n. 53 above); Memorandum of Wetherall, 3 April 1843, ibid.

71 Atherton to Begley, 6 Feb., 1, 4, 7 March 1843, Lachine Riots (see Ch. 5, n. 53 above); *Montreal Gazette*, 7 Feb. 1843; "Beauharnois Report" (see Introduction, n. 3 above); Depositions Nos. 59–62, ibid.

72 Charles Atherton to Begly, 30 March, 1 April 1843, Lachine Riots (see Ch. 5, n. 53 above); Foremen's reports of instigators of the late riots, 31 March 1843, ibid. Begly to Power, 10 Feb., 8 April 1843, Welland Canal Letterbook, PAC/RG43.

73 *Debates of the Legislative Assembly of United Canada*, ed. Gibbs (see n. 2 above), v. 4, Part 2, 1443ff.; Bleasdale, "Class Conflict on the Canals of Upper Canada" (see Introduction, n. 11 above), 123–25. Significantly, the main concern expressed by members of the legislature was that the civil rights of citizens would not be infringed upon, and that only canallers would be subject to the proscriptive measures contained within this legislation.

construction. As such, it signified the interpenetration of government and business interests.

As military force and the law were not wholly successful in making workers compliant, canal commissions also turned to the church, seeking to exploit labourers' beliefs by using Irish priests to keep them in line. The more stable a social environment, it was believed, the less likely workers would rampage. Increasingly, though, clerics were used as a form of moral police, paid by canal companies to rein in vice, criminality and, most importantly, collective violence. When trouble broke out between Corkonians and Connaughtmen on the Welland in 1842, Reverend Lee saved a tavern from being demolished and drove canallers back to their shanties. Father McDonagh restored peace when conflict flared again among his hungry unemployed parishioners during the winter of 1843–44. And when labourers struck on the Gallopes Canal near Williamsburg, Ontario, Reverend James Clarke promised the board that "any assistance in my power to preserve order among the labourers is at your service." He assembled the strikers and lectured them on the evils of combination; by the next day the chastened men were "perfectly peacable" and had returned to work.[74]

This lesson was not lost on those responsible for overseeing construction. Support was offered to the church and formal ties were increasingly established with priests. Canada's Board of Works provided stone for Reverend McDonagh to rebuild a Catholic church for canallers near St. Catharines.[75] The board also hired priests and paid them out of the police budget. Father McDonagh, for example, was employed in November 1842 at £200 per annum.[76] When labour problems began emerging on the Beauharnois in 1843, the board employed two Irish-speaking priests at the going rate so they could talk to the navvies in their own language. What they ended up preaching sounded very much like the gospel of capitalism, as made clear by one of these hirelings, Father John Falvey, in his testimony to the Beauharnois Commission. "Under every circumstance, however grievous it might have appeared to the workmen, I constantly recommended the strictest observance of obedience to laws and submission to their respective employers." Before the strike Falvey had established a "Committee of vigilance . . . for the purpose of maintaining temperate habits, tranquility and good order amongst the labourers on the Canal." The committee was made up of at least one of "the best conducted and most influential workmen" from each section. When word of the planned strike got out,

74 *St. Catharines Journal*, 7 July 1842; Thorburn to Daly, 10, 17, 19 Jan. 1844, Welland Riots (see Ch. 6, n. 67 above); "Notice to the Sons of Erin" from James Buchanan, 12 Jan. 1844, ibid.; Clarke to Killaly, 6 March 1845, Williamsburg Police (see Ch. 6, n. 23 above); Wetherall to Killaly, 2 March 1844, ibid.
75 McDonagh to Killaly, 4 April 1843, Welland Riots (see Ch. 6, n. 67 above); Begly to Power, 4 May 1843, Welland Canal Letterbook, PAC/RG43.
76 Begly to Power, 14 March 1843, Welland Canal Letterbook, PAC/RG43; Bleasdale, "Class Conflict on the Canals of Upper Canada" (see Introduction, n. 11 above), 125–26, n. 139.

this god squad sought to dissuade the workers from their course, as did Falvey, who toured the line sermonizing against combination. Falvey merited a payment of £254 18s. for his role in suppressing the strike.[77] The clergy thus became explicit employees of capital, and could not avoid a conflict of interest between spiritual and temporal responsibilities. Priests did stand up for their parishioners when they were treated badly. But when it came to outbreaks of factional disorder or incidents of labour organization, the church stood firmly behind employers and the state, being unable to stomach questioning of authority and order in any form.

Confronted by the nascent partnership of capital and the state, backed by the moral authority of the Roman Catholic Church, navvies were, not surprisingly, unable to win important concessions from their employers. They were occasionally successful in securing wage hikes, but the nature of the labour market and developing industrial relations in the 1840s did not allow for significant long-term gains. Canallers had become workers, which meant effectively that they had to take what was offered – a second-class status within society, dependent on their employers and the remorseless swings of the market.

The end of an era

The great age of canal construction began drawing to a close in the late 1840s. In Canada, the Cornwall Canal was completed in 1843, the Beauharnois two years later and the Lachine in 1848, the same year as the Williamsburg canals and the Trent River locks; the Welland enlargement was finished at mid-century. The abortive Chats Canal, a two-mile line on the upper Ottawa River, and Nova Scotia's revived Shubenacadie Canal, built between 1854 and 1861, were two of a dwindling number of Canadian projects in the 1850s. The main American lines that had gone into hibernation during the depression and were revived in the late 1840s soon achieved their scaled-down goals: the Illinois & Michigan was completed in 1848, the C&O two years later and the James River & Kanawha and Wabash & Erie in 1851. Improvements to the Pennsylvania system were concluded in 1857–58, and the enlargement of the Erie network dragged on into 1862. The St. Mary's, completed in 1855, was the only major canal to be initiated in the 1850s. By 1860, for all practical purposes, the industry was dead. Its next incarnation came late in the nineteenth century with the construction of ship canals having much larger engineering specifications than the narrow and shallow barge lines of earlier years.

Canallers had witnessed many changes in these twilight years. A crisis in

---

77 Killaly to Capt. Brownrigg, 15 April 1843, Beauharnois Riots (see Ch. 5, n. 18 above); Deposition of John Falvey (No. 9), John Halpin (No. 48), "Beauharnois Report" (see Introduction, n. 3 above); Statement of the Expenses attending the suppression of the Riots on the Beauharnois Canal, ibid.

labour relations occurred in canal construction from the mid-1830s to the mid-1840s. The remnants of contractor paternalism were ripped away as canallers were freed from bonds of personal dependence. This liberation was marked by a clear deterioration in living conditions, as workers competed with each other in an overstocked labour market in a declining industry. Free labour for canallers meant underemployment, declining wages and a harsher work environment. It meant living with the ubiquitous threat of poverty, hunger and homelessness. With few other options, most relied on common labour in one form or another, if not on canals, on railroads, on docks or in resource-extraction industries. The interpersonal dependence of master and hand had become the subjection of worker to market forces. The result was not unrelieved gloom for canallers. When the depression of the early 1840s lifted, employment opened up a little and wages rose. But the harsh features of free labour were here to stay. For workers such as canallers, the market's closed fist inevitably outweighed its open hand.

Conclusion

I have got a wife and her fortune was 2,000 dollars in hand,
A farm well stocked was her portion, and 200 good acres of land,
So cheer up true lads of the Shamrock, don't be fainthearted or shy,
For in America I made my fortune although a poor labouring boy.[1]

If William Fee and Francis Murray, our two absconding servants from the Potomac Company in the 1780s, had miraculously reappeared at a C&O work camp in 1850, they would have recognized many features of their canalling trade: shanty life, manual toil, everpresent disease and injury. But the scale of the work, the absence of unfree labour forms, the presence of contractors and the distant and impersonal relations between workers and the ultimate bosses, not to mention the bitter feuds both among workers and against employers, would have struck the two Rip Van Winkles as wholly new. Clearly much ground had been covered. On the other hand, if Fee and Murray had remained in canalling after their untoward flight from the Potomac, lived to a ripe and active old age, and survived the cavalry charge at Beauharnois, they would have experienced the industrial revolution. Perhaps they would have revelled in their freedom, or maybe bemoaned the need to put a house over one's head and food on the table solely from wages that were too low or irregular. Either way, there was not much that they could do about it. For all their experience, they had been made workers and workers they would remain. Whether they had slept or lived through the Canal Era, Fee and Murray could not deny the degree of change that had gone on since George Washington and his peers bought, sold and hired people to achieve their dream of making the Potomac a new Northwest Passage.

This transformation has been addressed on two levels: the rise (and fall) of what was really the first international industry in North America,

---

1 From "A New Song on the Irishmen now going to America," in *Irish Emigrant Ballads and Songs*, ed. Wright (see Ch. 2, n. 2 above), 534.

drawing in direct state participation and recruiting tens of thousands of workers; and the moulding of a modern industrial workforce wholly reliant on wages for its existence. The growth of the canal-building industry mirrored society's movement from a small, unequal, personal, traditional world to a large, unequal, impersonal, modern one. Canallers, contractors and management played a big role in the rise of industrial capitalism.

Work on canals in the 1780s was carried on under quite different conditions from those that prevailed at the end of the Canal Era. These early projects were relatively small with modest capital and manpower requirements, relying on slaves and indentured servants as well as free labourers. There were fewer wage workers, and many laboured only temporarily on such projects, returning to their farms or other occupations for the bulk of their time. Production was organized along paternalistic lines, with companies providing food and shelter for their labourers. For good or ill, canaller and boss would most likely have known each other. While the work itself changed little, this world broke down over the next half-century. In its place appeared the large-scale public works sites of the 1840s, thronged with transient immigrant workers being palpably exploited by largely unknown contractors, while canal companies and boards of works were distant and technically divorced from the labour force.

This change naturally took place within an altered productive environment. Organizational problems mushroomed as projects grew in size, necessitating huge amounts of capital and thousands of workers. Canals turned to government, particularly on the state level, to provide investment, loans and the underwriting of stock floatations. Some governments created public agencies to take the place of companies and direct public works construction on a grand scale. The state became capital in a blurring of public and private interest that shaped the entire industry and was fraught with meaning for workers. The seeds of the modern corporate state can be espied here in canal construction.

Both private companies and public agencies developed a hierarchical management structure to direct operations on the large projects, composed of a board of directors with a body of clerks to handle administration and an engineering corps to oversee construction, while independent contractors performed the actual work and absorbed much of the risk and responsibility. Only in this way could the difficult task of implementing a production process that often stretched over tens to hundreds of miles be achieved. Canals thus had anticipated the business organization of later large-scale industry, like railways, mining and steel making.

While at the top management was growing, specializing and linking with the public sector, at the bottom thousands of workers had to be found to satisfy industry needs. All sources were tapped: native-born farmers and journeymen, African-American slaves, European immigrants, French-Canadian *habitants* and even women and children. These very different groups shared one thing: their separation from the land or craftshop and thus from control of the means of production – that is, proletarianization. Many of these people were alike in another way. They were drawn from groups that for explicit reasons – race, gender, ethnicity – were socially stigmatized, and it was this mark of shame that was exploited to funnel them into the least attractive types of work. Canal digging increasingly was seen as work beyond the pale of respectability, carried on by the dregs of free labour.

For a time, navvies were insulated from the worst effect of the market by employer paternalism. Contractors, as well as being petty entrepreneurs, were master builders who maintained a stable of dependable workers so as not to be caught short, hiring their men by the month and providing room and board. Theirs was a reciprocal relationship, an exchange of regular labour in return for steady employment and sustenance, but it was never an equal one. Contractor paternalism contained within it labour's implicit subordination to capital and merely masked the developing class lines that lay beneath. Changes in the nature of production revealed this unequal relationship by removing the need to provide for workers. The changing labour market was the key in this transformation.

The paternalistic organization of production that characterized the peak years of canal construction was disrupted by the depression that began in the late 1830s, when contraction within the industry and heightened immigration created a labour surplus that remained the norm as the industry wound down. Now builders were freed from having to provide subsistence at all, and wages dropped at the same time. As a result, workers had to find their own food and shelter with less money and, more often, less work. The reciprocal bonds joining master and labourer were severed as ever bigger contracting firms supplanted the independent builder, and as thousands of unemployed workers hung around public works sites hoping for employment, however temporary. The nature of canal work had been irrevocably altered.

A truly significant alteration in the lives of canallers had occurred. Labourers were no longer treated as individuals whose character was considered a component of their labour and whose misconduct was punished by shaming, but as economic units, part of a faceless army in which individuality was submerged and resistance repressed. Canallers (again with the exception of slaves) laboured solely for their wages, and were dependent upon their employers for work. It was a marginal existence that was tolerable when jobs were plentiful, but mean and demeaning when not. Canallers had become part of a casual army performing the myriad tasks so essential to the emerging industrial economy.

Socially, canallers lived an increasingly isolated existence, set off figuratively if not always physically from the rest of society. They dwelt in shanty camps, worker communities with strong ethnic, religious and social dimensions. But these were not the vibrant and entirely healthy communities of working-class history, their internal ties being as much an expression of their marginal and subordinated position within society as of solidarity. And the surface integrity of the shanty camp masked tensions and conflict that riddled the workforce as a whole. This underside of canaller society was as much a measure of workers' response to industrialization as was the forming of fraternal societies and unions, the waging of strikes or the adoption of radical political beliefs.

A heightening of class tensions was intimately connected with this reworking of labour relations. Slowly, driven by narrowing opportunity and rendered desperate by their mean lifestyle, canallers came to identify with each other as workers when not fighting over work scraps. Conflict between employer and workers was crystallizing by the late 1830s and the strike vied with the riot as a dominant form of collective action. But escalation in labour protest was met by a resistant, innovative class of employers that brought the weight of the state to bear in the contest. The military, professional police, clergy, courts and various government agencies were arrayed against workers who, in combination, threatened the free workings of the labour market. Capitalism waxed strong during this era. Canal companies became public agencies, attracted huge investment and built wonders of engineering with thousands of workers. The scale of business life enlarged considerably, often intermingling with government power. Interests of capital increasingly came to be identified with those of the state, values that could be imposed on society by force if not willingly absorbed. The era of state-sponsored capitalism had dawned.

From its inception in the 1780s until its timely demise, the industry had achieved much. Those responsible for these advances, the workers who did the digging, have been too long neglected, as if their experiences of toiling in the trenches had been walled off by the banks of their construction. While canals can be seen as evidence of progress, it was purchased with the exertion of thousands of navvies. As well as food, shelter or a wage, their labour also bought harsh conditions, bare living, dehumanizing treatment and growing powerlessness. Wholly alienated and socially proscribed, canallers were a leading edge of an industrial lumpen proletariat, that mass of underemployed, deprived, ghetto-dwelling manual workers – the freest of free labour – necessary to industrial production. Still, they were able to resist these changes, to survive and carve out a niche in a new world order that gave them humanity and strength if not power. They had arrived as this point by a very different route from that traversed by artisans, but the two paths were now converging. Canallers were poised on the industrial future in 1860. The current of change that had flowed through canals swept them along to this precipice of Niagara proportions, offering a dizzying glimpse of what was to come only moments before the plunge.

This still leaves the question of what to make of the canaller story. Is it merely the trials and travails of an unusual and not very representative group of workers, or is there something here of wider significance for working people in general? The overt maleness and the temporary nature of the shanty camps made canalling a somewhat different labouring life, and to a certain extent it can be argued that the navvy experience with exploitation was a function of this particular system of production, which was not a product of any particular time or place but of frontier conditions and heavy manual labour. Bunkhouse culture was usually found in resource-extraction industries such as logging and mining, as well as remote railroad camps, and the experiences of the usually young male workers, characterized by hard labour and hard living, approximated those of canallers.[2] If what happened on canals was only really applicable to bushwork, then the story, however interesting, would be of limited relevance to wider labour history. But behind the shanty walls lay a deeper truth, one that cut to the heart of common labour's experience with industrial wage relations. As a casual workforce subject to frequent unemployment, high transiency and a subsistence existence, canallers suffered roughly the same fate as many other workers in the nineteenth century, particularly the unskilled and unorganized. A necessarily tentative look at post-canalling careers lends credence to this contention.

People moved through the industry with great frequency – a measure of its casual nature – particularly as construction first stumbled, then dragged to a halt in the 1840s–50s. There had always been a core dependent upon the work amidst all this turmoil, but even these true navvies were now forced to look elsewhere for support. Scarcity of evidence makes it difficult to reach any definitive conclusions about the post-canalling experience, but scattered information gives a general idea. There were enough canallers who "made it" – either onto the land or into business – to offer hope to others, but the majority appear merely to have shifted into similar manual labour or moved marginally up the occupational scale when they left the industry. Rewarding or taxing, a brief occupational sideline or more regular employment, canal construction introduced many to large-scale industrial work and the wage relationship.

Some canallers did manage to prosper: Richard Kelley set himself up as a storekeeper; Patrick Cooney established a saltworks near Syracuse; Andrew Leary O'Brien became the founder of Andrew College in Georgia; and Michael Hedekin erected the biggest hotel in Fort Wayne.[3] The experience

2 See, for example, Edmund Bradwin, *The Bunkhouse Men* (orig. ed. 1928; Toronto: University of Toronto Press, 1972); Ian Radforth, *Bushworkers and Bosses: Logging in Northern Ontario, 1900–1980* (Toronto: University of Toronto Press, 1987).

3 Bannan, *Pioneer Irish of Onondaga* (see Ch. 3, n. 3 above), 24–26, 180–81; *Journal of Andrew Leary O'Brien*, ed. Suarez (see Ch. 6, n. 39 above); Poinsatte, *Fort Wayne During the Canal Era* (see Ch. 3, n. 64 above), 72–73.

of these individuals is unusual not only in that they enjoyed a fair degree of success but in that they can be personalized. Movement onto the land was a more likely step up the social ladder for canallers. Pádraig Cúndún, for example, left Ireland in the mid-1820s to work on the Erie Canal, but soon made a down payment on a farm; by 1834 he was in full ownership of the land.[4] There was more chance of canallers transforming themselves into farmers in frontier regions where land was cheaper and labour usually in short supply, thus driving up wages and forcing canal companies to offer extra inducements. The military superintendent of Canada's Grenville Canal, situated in the thinly settled Ottawa Valley, intended to hold back property lots in a nearby village for "Workmen who are found to be industrious, and deserving, employed on these Works." Indiana's Central Canal assured prospective workers that no "section of the country holds out greater inducements to the industrious laborer than the state of Indiana." Given high wages and cheap land, "with the avails of a few months' labor, a permanent home in this flourishing and rapidly growing state" could be had.[5] The clearest evidence lies in Illinois, where workers for the Illinois & Michigan Canal during the depression were paid in scrip that could purchase canal lands. Quite a few seem to have taken advantage of the opportunity, and historians have argued that ex-canallers dotted the line from La Salle to Chicago. How many is not clear, but most lots along the canal were forty to eighty acres in size and paid for with scrip, and there were many Irish-sounding names in evidence, all of which would suggest worker involvement. Nonetheless, Catherine Tobin, the most recent student of the I&M, remains doubtful about how common the practice was.[6] The obvious factor preventing people from acquiring farms was the cost. Throughout the period land was relatively inexpensive, but still a significant grubstake was needed to set up a successful farm.[7] By the 1830s, however, canallers found it difficult to set anything aside, and most would have found it near impossible to save the stake needed to transform themselves into farmers. It is almost certain that those who managed to get a farm constituted only a minority. Many more would remain near the canals in some sort of wage-working capacity.

There is no question that canalling was a difficult line of work that

---

4   Again I would like to thank Bruce D. Boling of the University of New Mexico for this useful information.

5   DuVernet to the Earl of Dalhousie, 17 Oct. 1821, v. 39, Canal Papers, PAC/RG8; "2,000 Laborers Wanted on the Central Canal," 1 May 1837, Broadside Collection, Indiana State Library.

6   Fleming, *Canal at Chicago* (see Ch. 6, n. 57 above), 256; Borgeson, "Irish Canal Laborers" (see Ch. 3, n. 31 above), 92–96; List of Canal Lands Sold In 1841 & 1842, *Report of the Board of Commissioners of the Illinois and Michigan Canal* (Springfield, 1842), 41–63; Tobin, "Lowly Muscular Digger" (see Introduction, n. 11 above), 245–47.

7   Henretta, "Families and Farms" (see Introduction, n. 6 above), 23. Similarly, Borgeson established that 80–160 acres cost $100–200 at the height of the Canal Era, but including the costs of building materials, tools, seeds, animals and/or machinery brought the required investment up to $550. "Irish Canal Laborers" (see Ch. 3. n. 31 above), 92–96.

extracted much from its practitioners and gave a modicum in return. Many workers paid through physical deprivation, sickness, injury or death: Benjamin Mace, the transplanted New Englander, who died of a fever contracted on the Louisville Canal; David Cardey, a young Irish miner, who "blew himself up" on the Grenville Canal; Joe, a slave listed as dead one day in the time book of his master, a contractor on the James River Canal; or Michial Mullen, the Irish humpback forced to earn his living on public works, where he was partially paralyzed and then thrust on the not-too-tender mercies of the Baltimore Almshouse.[8] These individuals were no less representative in their experience than those who escaped canals unscathed and with some measure of success.

Most navvies fell between the landed and the maimed or dead, moving into other forms of wage work not too divorced from canalling. A few were able to stay on canals as maintenance workers, while others became boatmen working the vessels that plied the finished navigation systems. Some of the Irish who had moved on from the Erie to the Ohio Canal at Cleveland remained in the town as "squatters" in the marshy area around the docks where they could find casual labour until work as boatmen opened up when the canal was completed. Similar jobs opened in the vicinity of public works. The diggers of the canals of New Orleans stayed on to work as stevedores, dockers, drayers and riverboat hands. Some of those workers who dug the Rideau gravitated to Bytown, the centre of the Ottawa River lumbering industry. The Irish who pushed the Erie through Syracuse stayed on to work in the local quarries or salt industry.[9]

Mining and railroads were two industries that were obvious options to ex-canallers. Their experience with rock excavation and tunnelling assisted them in finding work in the coal fields. As a number of canals had been built specifically to penetrate the anthracite mountains of the mid-Atlantic states, and often canal and coal company were one and the same, there appears to have been a fair amount of movement between the industries from the outset. Yet a working life in mining was hardly any better than that to be found in public works construction. Grace Palladino's study of the Pennsylvania mining industry paints a picture that would be all too familiar to canallers. After 1837, declining wages, worsening conditions,

8 Herschel Hurdy to Benjamin Mace and all friends, 16 Aug. 1826, Benjamin Mace Papers, Indiana State Library; DuVernet to Col. Darling, 22 Aug. 1821, 12 June 1822, v. 40, Canal Papers, PAC/RG8; Time Chart for James River and Kanawha Canal, April 1850, Austin-Twyman Papers (see Ch. 3, n. 25 above); Case of Michial Mullen, admitted 12 June 1833, Baltimore Almshouse Medical Records, MNS.

9 Poinsatte, *Fort Wayne During the Canal Era* (see Ch. 3, n. 64 above), 228; William F. Hickey, "The Irish in Cleveland: One Perspective," in *Irish Americans and their Communities of Cleveland*, ed. Hickey and Nelson J. Callahan (Cleveland: Ethnic Heritage Studies, Cleveland State University, 1978), 54–70; Niehaus, *Irish in New Orleans* (see Ch. 3, n. 29 above), 47–49; Michael Cross, "Shiners' War: Social Violence in the Ottawa Valley in the 1830s," *Canadian Historical Review*, v. 54 (March 1973), 1–26; John Asa Beadles, "The Syracuse Irish, 1812–1928," Ph.D. diss., Syracuse University, 1974, 88–91.

production quotas, tightening work discipline and growing inequality led to labour protest matched by company and state repression.[10] The secret society tradition that arose in mining, evidenced by groups like the Molly Maguires, and the industry's continuing experience with violent industrial conflict demonstrate further connections between mining and canalling. The construction and maintenance of railroads also attracted canallers. Workers had freely shifted from the C&O to the Baltimore & Ohio Railroad in the 1830s, and, as many canal lines were absorbed by railroads from mid-century, the labour force became increasingly promiscuous. And there were reports that the same factions that shaped life on canals were active on early railroads. The lifestyles were equally hard, especially during the construction phase, as Walter Licht has shown. Despite mushrooming regulations and the growth of unions, the industry was a hotbed of worker protest.[11]

Thousands also found work in the many cities thrust up by canals. For example, half those workers who built the canal at Lockport, New York, in the 1820s were said to have made the town their permanent home. And when the Illinois & Michigan was completed many workers naturally moved into the booming town of Chicago with all the jobs it had to offer, particularly in the building trades.[12] The working-class neighbourhoods to which many ex-canallers were drawn were fragile worlds of transiency, work shortages, ethnic bigotry, substandard living and working conditions, little hope of advancement, violence, crime, disease and death. David Gerber's study of Buffalo illuminates this reality. Buffalo's Irish in the 1850s lived in overcrowded shacks amidst squalid shanty towns that clustered around the city's canal, docks and warehouses. There, they faced "seasonality, underemployment and subemployment," and were forced to travel for jobs, with public works of one kind or another being a staple. In the city, they toiled as casual day labourers, rarely with a full day's work. Chronic joblessness and low wages were the norm. This bred an environment marred by familial desertion, crime, vice, violence, and alcoholism, loomed over by the poorhouse.[13] It was a setting not all that different from canals.

Most navvies were not as lucky as the Kelleys, O'Briens and Cúndúns, or even the nameless individuals that bought farms. By the late 1830s, free canallers had been transformed into modern workers, but at the bottom of their developing class. They were paid poor wages, toiled under severe

---

10 Palladino, *Another Civil War* (see Ch. 8, n. 3 above), especially 9–10, 46–47.
11 Licht, *Working for the Railroad* (see Ch. 2, n. 26 above); Shelton A. Stromquise, *A Generation of Boomers: The Pattern of Railroad Labor Conflict in Nineteenth-Century America* (Urbana: University of Illinois Press, 1987); Bradwin, *Bunkhouse Men* (see n. 2 above).
12 Condon, *Stars in the Water* (see Ch. 3, n. 43 above), 86; Edmund B. Thorton, "Forward," *The Illinois & Michigan Canal National Heritage Corridor: A Guide to Its History and Sources*, ed. Michael P. Conzen and Kay J. Carr (Dekalb, Ill.: Northern Illinois University Press, 1988), vii.
13 Gerber, *Making of an American Pluralism* (see Ch. 6, n. 37 above), 126ff.

conditions and regularly found themselves without work. As a result, they and their families were drawn into a marginal existence along public works lines, wholly exposed to the vagaries of the market. Their dependent and deprived class status was reinforced by their proscription as members of despised social groups. The majority of canallers were free labourers and could leave the industry at will, but for a solid core of workers the combination of their economic and social exclusion either kept them in place or funneled them into similar work. On or off the canal, they served the essential function of feeding industry's whimsical need for labour. They were the miners and sappers of capitalism, sent in to lay its foundations, dispensed with when the war was won. Few made it up through the ranks or even out of the trenches, regardless of which industrial army conscripted them.

Canalling was by no means the "typical" work experience. Those who answered its call lived and laboured in an unusual setting and had less control over their lives than the average worker. But they were no less representative than the artisans that have populated labour history. In particular, canallers shared one thing with other workers: the complete expropriation of the fruits of their labour and the absence of any significant influence over the production process. This set them apart from most skilled workers, for whom class conflict in the nineteenth century was largely over who would control the shop floor. Drawing strength from their skill, craftsmen organized to resist and even roll back the tide of industrial capitalism. Without the benefit of recognized technical knowledge and periodically without a job, common labourers such as canallers were more concerned with survival. This meant searching out work, fighting to get as much of it as possible and often moving from one town to another. Misery and deprivation were always near at hand. Such workers tended to look to other members of their ethnic group for support rather than to organizations that crossed social divides. The temporariness of their working and living environments paired with the poverty of their existence made life a struggle. While skilled workers fought on the battlements with a view ahead, common labourers dug the trenches, slogging in the mud trying to keep their heads above water. Theirs was a darker, more desperate chronicle.

The many people who dug canals did so for different reasons and were affected by the work in different ways. But taken as a whole, theirs was a story of ongoing class formation that did not necessarily begin or end on canals but which the canalling life captured in its essence. The experience of canallers reminds us that we must keep one fact front and centre: the triumphant rise of industrial capitalism was able to rework the world in its image, that is, into a world of employers and employees that replaced an entirely different set of social and economic relations. And, despite limited success in achieving certain material protections, workers lost as a class.

Divided, held down by employers who were propped up and protected by the state, dependent on collective action in an era that increasingly saw this as anti-individualistic and thus subversive, the working class took shape within a world weighted against it.

Class formation was as much a destructive as a constructive process, and left the new worker more bewildered by his condition than conscious of his new-found status. In later years, when both industrial capitalism and the working class had matured, some of this confusion would evaporate, and workers and employers would repeatedly clash over the spoils of factory production. Yet a perfect symmetry of class forces never emerged, as too many countervailing allegiances pulled at workers. Class consciousness inevitably ebbed and flowed with the tide of capitalist development. There were times when workers were able to forge a singular vision, and other times when stress fractured this consciousness into a plethora of diverse views. And those at the bottom of the working class, the unskilled and unorganized, were subject to greater pressures than their better-off peers. Oppressed and divided by the forces of production and social division, they found it more difficult to achieve the epiphany of class consciousness. This does not deny their class status, only indicates different ways in which it was experienced. It is not a matter of a single consciousness, but of multiple layers of awareness and experience over a bedrock of class, people having wrestled with the world of work as men and women, Irishmen and blacks, Catholics and Protestants, as well as workers. It was a harsh world not of their making, although they were able to blunt its sharper edges, a world that broke them down into individual units that competed as much as coalesced into a bigger, better whole. In effect, it was a world that, while changing, came before their arrival and would remain after their passing. Common labourers were unequally matched in this world, a condition that left them little influence in the course of history, though they were the stuff of its making.

Appendix I: Tables 1–16

I would like to thank Susan Weinandy-Way for her help in compiling the data in this Appendix.

All figures in the tables are rounded off to the nearest whole number.

Table 1. Length of employment on the Delaware & Schuylkill Canal, May 1794—July 1795

Days worked	No. of workers	Percentage of workforce
1–10	64	42
11–30	38	25
31–60	23	15
61–100	8	5
101–200	9	6
200+	10	7
Total	152	100

Source: Workmen's Time Book, 1793—1794, Delaware and Schuylkill Navigation Canal Company Accounts, 1792—95, in The Sequestered John Nicholson Papers, Group 96, Part IV — Individual Business Accounts, 1787—1800, Microfilm Edition from Division of History, Pennsylvania Historical and Museum Commission, consulted at Hagley Museum and Library Archives, Wilmington, Del.

Table 2. Average of days worked on the Delaware & Schuylkill Canal, May 1794—July 1795

	No. of workers	Average total days worked	Average days worked per month
Workers for 30+ days	50	107	7
Workers for 200+ days	10	264	18

Note: Many workers were paid by the month without specific number of days worked indicated. In these cases, the days worked per month figure was estimated by dividing the amount earned in a month by the average daily wage. (The average daily wage was determined by dividing the wage rate for a full month's work, usually $18—20, by the normal number of required workdays per month, 26.)
Source: Workmen's Time Book, 1793—1794, Delaware and Schuylkill Navigation Canal Company Accounts, 1792—95.

Table 3. Earnings on the Delaware & Schuylkill Canal, May 1794—July 1795 (in $)

	Number	Average total earnings	Average earnings per month
Workers for 30+ days	50	77	5
Workers for 200+ days	10	169	11

Source: Workmen's Time Book, 1793—1794, Delaware and Schuylkill Navigation Canal Company Accounts, 1792—95.

Table 4. Fluctuations in workforce on the Western Division of the Illinois & Michigan Canal, 1838–39

Date	No. of workers	Percentage increase (+) or decrease (–) from previous figure
1 March 1838	350	--
1 June	595	+70
1 Sept.	960	+61
1 Dec.	445	–54
28 Feb. 1839	475	+7
31 May	886	+87
31 Aug.	824	–7
30 Nov.	676	–18

Source: Ward Burnett to William Gooding, 1 Dec. 1838, in Report of the Canal Commissioners of the Illinois and Michigan Canal (Vandalia, 1838), 52; Burnett to Gooding, 1 Dec. 1839, in Fourth Annual Report of the Canal Commissioners of the Illinois and Michigan Canal, 1839 (Springfield, 1840), 24.

Table 5. Real monthly earnings for common labourers: wages plus board (in $ unless otherwise noted)

Year (Canal)	Wages	Board	Real earnings	Board as % of real earnings
1785—86 (Potomac)	£2	£1 11s.	£3 11s.	44
1795 (Middlesex)	9	9	18	50
1797 (Middlesex)	11	9	20	45
1825 (Ohio)	5	3[a]	8	38
1829 (C&O)[b]	12	13	25	52
1829 (C&O)	10	9	19	47
1831 (C&O)	16	9	25	36
1831 (C&O)	10	7	17	41
1831 (Pennsylvania)[b]	11	11	22	50
1832 (C&O)[b]	12	8	20	40
1833 (Miami)	10	5	15	33
1835 (Miami)	12	8	20	40

[a]Calculated from difference between pay with and pay without board.
[b]Calculated from figures of daily labour cost (wages and board).

Sources: POT/PRO, 15 April 1786 (A 17), and Payroll, Oct. 15—Nov. 12, 1785, file 4, box 4, Potomac Company Papers, series 179, NA/RG79; Report of Laommi Baldwin, 17 Oct.—1 Dec. 1795, Middlesex Canal — Reports, Baldwin Papers, Baker Library, Harvard University Graduate School of Business Administration; Baldwin to James Sullivan, 7 Feb. 1797, Middlesex Reports; John Dillon, 21 July 1825, Micajah T. Williams Papers, Ohio Historical Society; H. W. Campbell to Charles Mercer, 30 Aug. 1829, C&O/LR; John Ingle to J. Powell, 8 Dec. 1829 (A 144), C&O/LS; Report of the President of the Chesapeake and Ohio Canal Company to the Legislature of Maryland (Annapolis, 1831), 7—8; Thomas Kavanagh & Co. to Charles Mercer, 8 Mar. 1831, C&O/LR; Letter from Joseph McIlvaine, 14 Feb. 1831, in Mathew Carey, Address to the Wealthy of the Land . . . (Philadelphia, 1831), 4; J. Lackland, 25 May 1832, C&O/LR; Ohio Canal Commission, Minute Books, v.1, 333—34, Canal Commission Papers, Ohio State Archives.

Table 6. Days worked on the James River Canal, 1851 and 1855

Type of labour		No. of workers	Total days worked	Average days worked in year	Average days worked per month
Slave:	1851	27	7,065	262	22
	1855	29	7,744	267	22
Free:	1851	87	1,522	18	2

Source: Time Charts for Workers on the James River and Kanawha Canal, 1848–57 (MsV. 25), and Time Book for Gwynn Dam and Lock, 1855–56, folder 164, Austin Twyman Papers, Earl Gregg Swem Library, College of William and Mary.

Table 7. Occupation and ethnicity at a C&O work camp, 1850

Occupation	Irish	German	English	Scottish	American	Total
Labourer	380	19	--	--	8	407
Blacksmith	2	1	--	--	--	3
Stonemason	--	--	--	--	1	1
Stonecutter	6	1	2	1	2	12
Cart driver	2	--	--	--	2	4
Woodman	--	1	--	--	--	1
Cook	--	2	--	--	--	2
Tailor	1	--	--	--	--	1
Shoemaker	1	--	--	--	--	1
Total	392	24	2	1	13	432

Source: 1850 U. S. Manuscript Census, Glade District, Allegany County, Md., households 629–98, 721–31.

Table 8. Percentage skilled and unskilled by ethnic group at C&O work camp, 1850

Ethnic group	Skilled	Unskilled
Irish	3	97
German	21	79
English	100[a]	--
Scottish	100[a]	--
American	42	58

[a]There were only two English workers and one Scottish worker.

Source: 1850 U. S. Manuscript Census, Glade District, Allegany County, Md., households 629–98, 721–31.

Table 9. Sex ratios at several worker settlements

Canal	Year	Males	Females	Ratio of males to females
Welland	1842	900	400	2.25
Welland	1844	1,303	666	1.96
C&O	1850	430	80	5.38
Williamsburg	1854	32	22	1.45

Sources: Broad Creek on the Welland Canal from Samuel Power to Thomas Begly, 1 Oct. 1842, Welland Canal Letterbook, v. 2097, PAC/RG43; Division of Welland between Port Dalhousie and Allansburg, Ontario, from St. Catharines Journal, 16 Feb. 1844; C&O work camp from 1850 U. S. Manuscript Census, Glade District, Allegany County, Md., households 629–98, 721–31, National Archives of the United States; List of Unemployed German Labourers to Whom Provisions Supplied on Credit, 4–5 Dec. 1854, Williamsburg Canals — Estimates, Paylists, Accounts, v. 59, file 22, PAC/RG11.

Table 10. Household types and boarders at C&O work camp, 1850

Household type	Number of households	Households without boarders	Households with 1–4 boarders	Households with 5+ boarders
Single-family	58	25	11	22
Two-family	9	1	2	6
Nonfamily	9	0	3	6
Total	76	26	16	34

Source: 1850 U. S. Manuscript Census, Glade District, Allegany County, Md., households 629–98, 721–31.

Table 11. Father McElroy's ministrations to C&O canallers, 1830–31

27 June 1830	Said mass in woods, heard confessions
28 June	Preached, heard confessions
21 July	Said mass
12 Aug.	Sick call, gave last rites to three people
21 Aug.	Preached and heard confessions
22 Aug.	Preached and heard confessions
15 Sept.	Preached and heard confessions
16 Sept.	Preached and heard confessions
24 Sept.	Sick call
23 Oct.	Preached, sick call
10 Nov.	Said mass in the open air
17 Jan. 1831	Sick call
27 Jan.	Sick call, gave last rites to two people
25 Feb.	Sick call
28 Mar.	Sick call
30 Mar.	Sick call
22 April	Preparation for a chapel
16 Aug.	Performed a marriage
13 Nov.	Preached in a shanty chapel
30 Nov.	Sick call
11 Dec.	Preached

Source: Diaries and Papers of Father John McElroy, Archives of the Woodstock Jesuit Community, microfilm copy at Maryland Hall of Records, Annapolis.

Table 12. Incidence and location of canaller riots and strikes, 1780–1860

Location	Riots	Strikes	Total
Georgia	1	--	1
Illinois	5	2	7
Indiana	3	--	3
Louisiana	2	1	3
Maryland	13	6	19
Massachusetts	2	--	2
Michigan	0	2	2
New Jersey	2	1	3
New York	7	3	10
Pennsylvania	7	6	13
Virginia	--	2	2
Canada	61	34	95
Total	103	57	160

Source: Appendix 2.

Table 13. Ethnic and gender makeup of residents at C&O work camp, 1850

Birthplace	Males	Females
Ireland	392	69
Germany	24	--
England	2	--
Scotland	1	--
Maryland	9	8
Massachusetts	1	1
Pennsylvania	3	3
Total	432	81

Source: 1850 U. S. Manuscript Census, Glade District, Allegany County, Md., households 629-98, 721-31.

Table 14. Timing of canaller riots and strikes, 1780-1860

Decade	United States		Canada		Total
	Riots	Strikes	Riots	Strikes	
1780s	2	--	--	--	2
1790s	2	--	--	--	2
1800s	1	--	--	--	1
1810s	--	--	--	--	--
1820s	8	4	6	3	21
1830s	25	14	7	5	51
1840s	3	2	47	26	78
1850s	1	3	1	--	5
Total	42	23	61	34	160

Source: Appendix 2.

Table 15. Timing of canaller riots and strikes, 1830—49

	United States		Canada		
Year	Riots	Strikes	Riots	Strikes	Total
1830	1	--	1	--	2
1831	1	1	--	--	2
1832	--	--	1	--	1
1833	1	--	--	--	1
1834	5	--	1	2	8
1835	3	1	4	1	9
1836	6	3	--	2	11
1837	3	3	--	--	6
1838	3	5	--	--	8
1839	2	1	--	--	3
1840	2	--	--	--	2
1841	--	--	--	--	--
1842	--	--	7	3	10
1843	--	--	10	8	18
1844	--	--	15	10	25
1845	--	--	12	4	16
1846	--	--	2	1	3
1847	--	1	--	--	1
1848	--	--	--	--	--
1849	1	1	1	--	3
Total	28	16	54	31	129

Source: Appendix 2.

Table 16. Incidence of military intervention in canaller disturbances, 1829—49

Year	United States	Canada
1829	1	2
1830	--	--
1831	--	--
1832	--	--
1833	--	--
1834	4	--
1835	3	--
1836	--	--
1837	--	--
1838	4	--
1839	1	--
1840	1	--
1841	--	--
1842	--	3
1843	--	7
1844	--	3
1845	--	2
1846	--	--
1847	--	--
1848	--	--
1849	--	1
Total	14	18

Source: Appendix 2.

Appendix II: Tables 17—18

Table 17. Riots, factions fights and civil unrest on canals, 1780—1860

Date	Location	Nature	Intervention	Result
1783	Myerstown, Pa., Schuylkill & Susquehanna Canal	Dispute with German residents		
Sept. 1785	Potomac Canal, Va.	General disorder		
May 1796	Western Inland Lock Navigation Canal, N.Y.	General disorder over hiring of piece workers		
1796	Potomac Canal, Va.	General disorder		
Oct. 1804	Elkton, Md., Chesapeake & Delaware Canal	Dispute with local blacks		
Oct. 1822	Lachine Canal, Ont.	Protestants vs. Catholics		
Dec. 1822	Lockport, N.Y., Erie Canal	Dispute with local citizens		
May 1824	Lachine Canal, Ont.	Protestants vs. Catholics		
July 1824	Lockport, N.Y.	Protestants vs. Catholics	Militia	
July 1825	Kingston, Ont., Rideau Canal	Attack on Orange Lodge		

287

Table 17. (cont.)

Date	Location	Nature	Intervention	Result
Oct. 1827	Hunter's Falls, Pa., Pennsylvania Canal	Destruction of contractor's property over non-payment	Arrests	
1828	Hawley, Pa.	Faction fight, and dispute with raftsmen		
1829	Savannah, Ogeechee & Altamaha Canal, Ga.	Riot		
March 1829	Waynesburg, Pa.	Dispute with locals		
May 1829	Nanticoke, Pa., North Branch Canal	Riot	Arrests	1 dead
Sept. 1829	Rideau Canal, Ont.	Dispute with locals	Militia	
Sept. 1829	Montreal, Que.	Attack on constable		
Nov. 1829	Lebanon City, Pa.	Riot		
Dec. 1829	Rideau Canal, Ont.	Protestants vs. Catholics	Militia	
Jan. 1830	Bytown, Ont., Rideau Canal	Attack on contractor's house		
Sept. 1830	Dunnstown, Pa.	Dispute with local Germans		
May 1831	Lowell, Mass.	Riot		
Dec. 1832	Alumberston, Ont., Welland Canal	Attack on house		

Table 17. (cont.)

Date	Location	Nature	Intervention	Result
Sept. 1833	New Brunswick, N.J., Delaware & Hudson Canal	Dispute with locals		Several killed
1834	St. Lawrence Canal	Protest against wage cuts		
Jan. 1834	C&O Canal	Faction fight, jobs	Militia, federal troops	5–10 dead
Feb. 1834	New Orleans, La.	Faction fight	City guards	Several killed
June 1834	Chenango Canal, N.Y.		Militia	
June 1834	C&O Canal	Faction fight, attack on German workers	Militia	1–3 dead
Nov. 1834	Fort Wayne, Ind., Wabash & Erie Canal	Dispute with locals		1 dead
March 1835	Cornwall, Ont.	Attack on Anglican church		
March 1835	Cornwall Canal	March for wage increase and shorter hours		
July 1835	Wabash & Erie	Faction fight	Militia	
July 1835	Cornwall, Ont., Long Sault Canal	Faction fight		
Aug. 1835	Hamilton, N.Y., Chenango Canal	Faction fight	Militia	
Sept. 1835	C&O Canal	General disorder		

Table 17. (cont.)

Date	Location	Nature	Intervention	Result
Nov. 1835	Cornwall, Ont.	Attack on a whorehouse		
Jan. 1836	C&O Canal	Faction fight		
March 1836	New Orleans, La.	Dispute with sailors		
April 1836	C&O Canal	Attack by Irish on German workers		
June 1836	Binghamton, N.Y.			
July 1836	Illinois & Michigan Canal	Dispute with locals		
Fall 1836	C&O Canal	General attacks on contractors and property		
March 1837	Illinois & Michigan Canal			
March 1837	Central Canal, Ind.			
May 1837	near Balt. & Wash. Railroad, Md.	Dispute over Repeal issue		
Jan. 1838	Oldtown, Md., C&O Canal	Dispute with locals	Militia, posse	arrests
March 1838	Illinois & Michigan Canal	Dispute over firing workers	Militia	10 killed
May 1838	Illinois & Michigan Canal	Faction fight	Militia	
May 1839	C&O Canal tunnel	General disorder over nonpayment		

Table 17. (cont.)

Date	Location	Nature	Intervention	Result
Aug. 1839	C&O Canal	Attack on German workers, jobs	Militia, arrests, imprisonments	1 dead
May 1840	Rowley, Mass.	Riot		
Aug. 1840	Lockport, Ill., Illinois & Michigan Canal	Attempt to burn canal office	Posse	
June 1842	Cornwall Canal	Faction fight		
June 1842	St. Catharines, Ont., Welland Canal	Riots over unemployment and hunger	British troops	
July–Aug. 1842	Welland Canal	Faction fights over jobs	Militia, British troops	
July–Aug. 1842	Drummondville, Ont., Welland Canal	Faction fights		
Aug. 1842	Cornwall Canal	Faction fight over jobs	British troops	
Sept. 1842	Dunnville, Ont., Welland Canal	Faction fight		
Dec. 1842	Broad Creek, Ont., Welland Canal	Faction fight		
Jan. 1843	Brantford, Ont., Welland Canal	Election riot		
March 1843	Beauharnois Canal	Faction fight, protest over jobs	Troops, police	Work suspended, men discharged

Table 17. (cont.)

Date	Location	Nature	Intervention	Result
June 1843	Brantford, Ont.	Attempt to free workers from jail	British troops	
July 1843	Brantford, Ont.	Attempt to chase workers from line		
Aug. 1843	Beauharnois Canal	Irish vs. French		
Nov. 1843	Welland Canal	Faction fight, dispute over wage decrease, jobs		
Dec. 1843	Stone Bridge, Ont., Welland Canal	Faction fight	Militia	
Dec. 1843	Slabtown, Ont., Welland Canal	Faction fight	Militia, arrests	
Dec. 1843	Allansburg, Ont., Welland Canal	Faction fight		
Dec. 1843	Thorold, Ont., Welland Canal	Faction fight		
Jan. 1844	Welland Canal	Faction fight	Militia, British troops	
April 1844	Montreal, Que.	Election riot	British troops	1 dead
July 1844	Welland Canal	Anti-Orange Lodge demonstration	Troops	
Aug. 1844	Beauharnois Canal	Attacks on contractors' property		

Table 17. (cont.)

Date	Location	Nature	Intervention	Result
Aug. 1844	Lachine Canal	Attacks on contractors' property		
Aug. 1844	Lachine Canal	Attack on Orange engineer		
Aug. 1844	Lachine Canal	Attack by Irish on French—Canadian workers		
Sept. 1844	Welland Canal	Faction fight		
Sept. 1844	Williamburg canals	Factional attack on storekeeper		
Sept.—Oct. 1844	Ferren's Point, Ont., Williamsburg canals	General disorder		
Sept.—Nov. 1844	Mariatown, Ont., Williamsburg canals	General disorder		
Oct. 1844	Beauharnois Canal	Attacks on contractors		
Oct. 1844	Montreal, Que.	Election riot		
Dec. 1844	Williamsburg canals	Faction fight		
Dec. 1844	Williamsburg canals	Attack on house		
Jan. 1845	Lachine Canal	Thefts and assaults		
Jan. 1845	Williamsburg canals	Protest		
Jan.—Feb. 1845	Welland Canal	General disorder	Militia	
April 1845	Montreal, Que.	Election violence		

Table 17. (cont.)

Date	Location	Nature	Intervention	Result
April 1845	Lachine Canal	Suspension of work	British troops	
April 1845	Williamsburg canals	Riot		
April 1845	Welland Canal	Dispute over back wages		
July 1845	Williamsburg canals	General disorder		
May 1845	St. Catharines, Ont.	Rescue of woman arrested for larceny		
June 1845	Stone Bridge, Ont., Welland Canal	Faction fight		
July 1845	Stone Bridge, Welland Canal	Attack on house		
Nov. 1845	Cornwall, Ont.	Faction fight		
Sept. 1846	Port Dalhousie, Ont., Welland Canal	Attack on and burning of steam dredge		
Sept. 1846	Welland Canal	Attack on American sailors for insulting a priest		
Jan. 1849	Buffalo, N.Y.	Riot with Welland workers		
July 1849	Welland Canal	Anti-Orange Lodge attack	Militia, troops	
Winter 1849–50	High Falls, N.J., Delaware & Hudson Canal	Faction fights	Arrests	

Table 17. (cont.)

Date	Location	Nature	Intervention	Result
Feb. 1852	Edwardsburg, Ont., Junction Canal	General disorder		

Total Number: 103

Table 18. Strikes on canals, 1780—1860

Date	Location	Issue	Intervention	Result
April—May 1827	Rideau Canal	Three strikes against wage cuts		
April 1827	Pennsylvania Canal			
Sept. 1827	Pennsylvania Canal			
Fall 1828	Clark's Ferry, Pa.	Nonpayment of wages		
April 1829	Clark's Ferry, Pa.	Higher wages	Militia, arrests	Failed
Dec. 1831	New Orleans, La., New Basin Canal	Truck pay, conditions		Failed
April 1834	Cornwall Canal	Wage increase		
Dec. 1834	Cornwall Canal	Wage cuts		
Feb. 1835	C&O Canal	Higher wages	Militia	Failed
April 1835	Cornwall Canal	Wage increase		
March 1836	Pennsylvania Canal			
March 1836	Cornwall Canal	Wage cuts and hours		
April 1836	C&O Canal	Higher wages		
May 1836	C&O Canal			Strikers replaced by slaves
July 1836	Cornwall Canal	Incompetent doctor		

Table 18. (cont.)

Date	Location	Issue	Intervention	Result
June 1837	Erie Feeder, near Rochester, N.Y.	Higher wages		
July 1837	Illinois & Michigan Canal			1 dead
Aug. 1837	Susquehanna Canal	Higher wages, more grog		Failed
Feb. 1838	C&O Canal	Nonpayment of wages		
May 1838	C&O Canal	Nonpayment of wages	Militia	
May 1838	James River & Kanawha Canal	Higher wages		Failed
June 1838	James River & Kanawha Canal	Higher wages		Succeeded
June 1838	C&O Canal tunnel	Pace of work	Blacklist	
1839	Bad River Canal, Mich.	Nonpayment of wages		Failed
March 1842	Welland Canal	Higher wages		
May 1842	Chambly Canal, Que.	Higher wages		
Aug. 1842	St. Catharines, Ont., Welland Canal	Unemployment and hunger		
Jan. 1843	Marshville, Canada			
Jan.–Feb. 1843	Lachine Canal	Higher wages	British troops, arrests and trials	Failed, workers fired

Table 18. (cont.)

Date	Location	Issue	Intervention	Result
March 1843	Lachine Canal	Higher wages	British troops	Failed; attacks on French strikebreakers
May 1843	Beauharnois Canal	Higher wages, shorter hours		Failed
June 1843	Beauharnois Canal	Higher wages, shorter hours	British troops	5–10 dead, failed
July 1843	Brantford, Ont.	Competition from other workers		
July 1843	Welland Canal	Higher wages		Succeeded
Sept. 1843	Welland Canal	Higher wages		
March 1844	Williamsburg, Ont., Gallopes Canal	Nonpayment, higher wages		
April 1844	Lachine Canal	Wages		
April–June 1844	Welland Canal	Four strikes for higher wages		
June 1844	Williamsburg canals	Higher wages		
Aug. 1844	Beauharnois Canal	Higher wages		
Sept. 1844	Beauharnois Canal	Work conditions		
Oct. 1844	Lachine Canal	Abusive foreman		

Table 18. (cont.)

Date	Location	Issue	Intervention	Result
March 1845	Welland Canal	Higher wages		
March 1845	Welland Canal	Higher wages		
Aug. 1845	Beauharnois Canal	Hiring of overseer		Succeeded
Nov. 1845	Williamsburg canals	Wage decrease		
July 1846	Williamsburg canals	Higher wages		
July 1847	Illinois & Michigan Canal	Higher wages, shorter hours		Failed
Jan. 1849	Buffalo, N.Y., Erie Canal	Higher wages, conditions		
Winter 1849–50	High Falls, N.J., Delaware & Hudson Canal			
March 1850	Buffalo, N.Y., Erie Canal			
Aug. 1853	St. Mary's Canal	Shorter hours or higher wages		Failed

Total Number: 57

Index

accidents, 33, 148–51
Akenson, Donald, 96 n52
alcohol, 15, 181–7; company attitudes to, 65–6, 184–6; daily ration of, 36, 182–3; effects on workers, 186–7; as part of labour exchange, 113–14, 183
Atherton, Charles, 98, 229

Baldwin, Laommi, 24, 29, 40
Baltimore & Ohio Railroad, 95, 215, 272
Beauharnois Canal, 8, 50, 138, 178, 185, 234 n8; 1843 strike on, 2–3, 11, 239, 246, 248, 250–3, 262–3; employment and earnings on, 117, 124, 238–9; living and working conditions on, 159, 189, 240
Beauharnois Commission, 191–2, 241, 252–3, 261, 262
Bender, George, 215, 216, 219, 220
blacklists, 217, 222, 261
Black River Canal, 127
Blackstone Canal, 58, 63, 137
Bleasdale, Ruth, 7 n11
boarding costs, 36, 66–7, 114
Boling, Bruce D., 1 n1, 270 n4
Brunswick Canal, 49, 87, 126–7
Buckingham, James Silk, 129, 144, 165
Buffalo, 183, 272
By, John, 97
Bytown, Ontario, 145, 271

Campbell, John, 86, 118, 137, 146, 175
Canada's Board of Works, 177, 208, 232, 239; and labour relations, 245, 253, 258, 260, 261; and ties to Roman Catholic clergy, 262–3
Canadian-American comparisons, 12–13, 231
canal industry, 4, 7–11, 54–5, 266–8; financing of, 51–4; labour recruitment within, 55–6, 101–2; organization and management of, 50–1, 53, 56–7, 232
canal work, nature of, 10, 31–2, 133–43

Cape Fear & Deep River Navigation Company, 84, 87, 88, 126, 127, 159
Cardey, David, 150–1, 271
Carey, Mathew, 90, 138, 152, 217, 242; his budget for canallers, 122–3, 169
Catawba Canal, 89
Central Canal, 270
Chambly Canal, 239
Chandler, Alfred, 51 n7
Chats Canal, 263
Chenango Canal, 70
Chesapeake & Delaware Canal, 29, 31, 35, 43, 49, 52, 137; alcohol on, 184; contractors on, 60, 62–3, 71; financial problems of, 39, 40, 45–6; labour conflict on, 39, 40, 175; living and working conditions on, 117, 146, 159, 169
Chesapeake & Ohio Canal, 49, 55, 114, 134, 263; 1850 work camp on, 168–70, 192; accidents on, 148–9, 149–50; alcohol on, 66, 113, 185–6; contractors on, 64, 65, 66, 69, 70, 71, 213, 219; financial problems of, 219, 226–7; financial problems of contractors on, 72, 73, 74, 218–21, 222–3; financing of, 52, 53, 213; groundbreaking ceremony of, 47, 212; labour conflict on, 200–2, 212, 214, 215–17, 217–18, 219–25; labour recruitment by, 55–6, 94–6; living and working conditions on, 155–6, 157, 159–60; methods of payment on, 118, 119; practice of religion on, 188, 189, 190; secret societies on, 214–17, 218, 224, 225; violence on, 164–5, 179, 193; women workers on, 84, 112; work force on, 79, 85, 134, 214
child labour, 31, 85–6
cholera, 156–8
class conflict, 198, 205, 230, 247, 268, 274
class consciousness, 203
class formation, 10, 30, 79–80, 273, 274; see also proletarianization
Clinton, De Witt, 99